p 270 !!

F.

[illegible]

p 229 ★★

p. 87
capabilities to
emigrate
aspiration to
emigrate

p. 129

destination country labor demand
p. 114

p 35
p. 41 bottom
p. 48 graph ?
p. 58

p. 144

p 134 ?
p 154
housing

How Migration Really Works

How Migration Really Works

The Facts About the Most Divisive Issue in Politics

HEIN DE HAAS

BASIC BOOKS
New York

Basic Books
Hachette Book Group
1290 Avenue of the Americas, New York, NY 10104
www.basicbooks.com

Printed in the United States of America

Originally published in 2023 by Viking UK in Great Britain
First US Edition: December 2023

Published by Basic Books, an imprint of Hachette Book Group, Inc.
The Basic Books name and logo is a registered trademark of the Hachette Book Group.

The Hachette Speakers Bureau provides a wide range of authors for speaking events. To find out more, go to hachettespeakersbureau.com or email HachetteSpeakers@hbgusa.com.

Basic books may be purchased in bulk for business, educational, or promotional use. For more information, please contact your local bookseller or the Hachette Book Group Special Markets Department at special.markets@hbgusa.com.

The publisher is not responsible for websites (or their content) that are not owned by the publisher.

Set in 12/14.75pt Bembo Book MT Pro

Typeset by Jouve (UK), Milton Keynes

Library of Congress Control Number: 2023942406

ISBNs: 9781541604315 (hardcover), 9781541604322 (ebook)

LSC-C

Printing 1, 2023

To my loving parents

Stef de Haas
Annie de Jonge

Contents

Reader's Note ix

Introduction 1

MYTHS OF MIGRATION

Myth 1 Migration is at an all-time high 15

Myth 2 Borders are beyond control 31

Myth 3 The world is facing a refugee crisis 45

Myth 4 Our societies are more diverse than ever 60

Myth 5 Development in poor countries will reduce migration 78

Myth 6 Emigration is a desperate flight from misery 93

Myth 7 We don't need migrant workers 109

IMMIGRATION: THREAT OR SOLUTION?

Myth 8 Immigrants steal jobs and drive down wages 129

Myth 9 Immigration undermines the welfare state 145

Myth 10 Immigrant integration has failed 160

Myth 11 Mass migration has produced mass segregation 180

Myth 12 Immigration sends crime rates soaring 196

Myth 13 Emigration leads to a brain drain 209

Myth 14 Immigration lifts all boats 222

Myth 15 We need immigrants to fix the problems of ageing societies 234

MIGRATION PROPAGANDA

Myth 16 Borders are closing down 249

Myth 17 Conservatives are tougher on immigration 266

Myth 18 Public opinion has turned against immigration 279

Myth 19 Smuggling is the cause of illegal migration 291

Myth 20 Trafficking is a form of modern slavery 309

Myth 21 Border restrictions reduce immigration 326

Myth 22 Climate change will lead to mass migration 343

The Road Ahead 358

Notes 373

Acknowledgements 427

Index 431

Reader's Note

A lack of clear terminology is a major source of confusion about migration. It is therefore important to clarify a number of key concepts discussed in this book. First of all, this pertains to the term 'migration'. Geographical mobility only counts as migration if it involves a *change in habitual residence* across administrative borders. Another important distinction is between *internal* – or domestic – and *international* migration, with the first implying a movement between municipalities, states or provinces within countries, and the second a change of residence across international borders. *Immigration* means people moving into a country from abroad, and *emigration* means residents moving out of a country.

If people change residence across administrative borders for a certain period of time – in most administrative systems, six to twelve months – this counts as migration *irrespective of people's main migration motive*. Based on this definition, a migrant is a person who lives in a place or country other than their place or country of birth. This book applies the category of international migrants only to the foreign-born. In debates on the subject, children and even grandchildren of migrants are commonly included in migrant populations. While this practice is debatable, to avoid unnecessary confusion I will systematically refer to second- or third-generation migrants when doing so, but the term 'migrants' is reserved for people who have actually made the move themselves.

Within the broad migrant category, important migrant types are labour migrants or migrant workers, family migrants, student migrants and business migrants, as well as forced migrants – or refugees. With regard to labour migrants, the terms 'higher-skilled' and 'lower-skilled' are problematic, because they may evoke an image of some migrants being more intelligent than others, and because, in practice, more and more jobs are in fact 'mid-skilled'. Perhaps a more useful distinction is between manual or blue-collar and white-collar workers, but for the purposes of this book I will retain the common usage of lower- and higher-skilled migration, emphasizing that this is about the jobs that migrants do, not their actual intelligence, knowledge and skills. In fact, many migrants do jobs for which they are overqualified.

The category of *forced migrants* concerns people who primarily move because they face violence or persecution in their origin countries. Although forced migrants are commonly referred to as 'refugees', an important legal distinction is that between asylum seekers and refugees. An *asylum seeker* is a person who has applied for refugee status and is still awaiting a decision on their recognition as a refugee. According to the 1951 United Nations Convention relating to the Status of Refugees, a *refugee* is a person who 'owing to a well-founded fear of persecution for reasons of race, religion, nationality, membership of a particular social group or political opinions, is outside the country of his nationality and is unable or, owing to such fear, is unwilling to avail himself of the protection of that country'. People who flee their regions of origin but who stay within their own country are usually referred to as 'internally displaced persons' (IDPs).

Another important source of confusion is between smuggling and trafficking. Although these concepts are constantly conflated in media and political discourse, they are entirely different. *Smuggling* is the use by migrants of paid or unpaid intermediaries (smugglers) to cross borders without prior authorization, either as part of a business transaction or humanitarian activism. Contrary to common perceptions, smuggling is essentially a form of service delivery that migrants (including refugees) are willing to pay for and voluntarily engage in to cross borders without being arrested. *Trafficking* is not about abduction or smuggling, but rather the severe exploitation of vulnerable workers through deceit and coercion. In fact, many cases of trafficking don't involve any migration at all, and if migrant workers are involved, severe exploitation often happens in the context of legal migration and legal employment.

Illegal migration – the unauthorized crossing of borders – is another controversial topic and a much-confused term. Legally speaking, the spontaneous arrival of asylum seekers at international borders doesn't count as illegal migration, as, according to the UN Refugee Convention, it is a fundamental right of people to cross international borders to seek protection from violence and persecution. This book therefore uses the term 'unsolicited border arrivals' to cover the arrival of both illegal migrants and asylum seekers. The distinction between *illegal entry* and *illegal stay* is essential. In fact, the biggest source of illegal stay is migrants who entered legally but who have 'overstayed' the duration of their visa or residence permit.

There is a long debate in academia, media and politics about the appropriateness of the use of terminology like 'illegal migration' and 'illegal migrants'. On one side, there is the argument that acts can be illegal, but people cannot; that nobody is illegal, and that it is therefore unacceptable to label human beings as 'illegal'. Such critique has led to the use of alternative terms, such as 'irregular', 'undocumented' and 'unauthorized'. Although these terms can be useful, besides their obfuscating nature they have their own problems – for instance, 'undocumented' migrants lack residence rights but often possess a range of documents such as drivers' licences, registration documents, insurance papers and tax files. The counterargument is that the legal status of migrants does matter to their lives and decisions as well as to governments; in fact, migrants often use these terms themselves, and so I would argue that such words should therefore not be avoided at all costs but rather used more carefully. This book will generally avoid referring to individual persons as 'illegal', but will use the phrases 'illegal migration' and 'illegal migrants' when describing migration at a group or more general level.

A final note on the use of migration statistics in this book. Unless stated otherwise, I will draw on global migrant population data from the *Trends in International Migrant Stock: The 2017 Revision* database, compiled by the Population Division of the Department of Economic and Social Affairs of the United Nations. Despite its various imperfections – such as the use of interpolation and other statistical techniques to fill in missing data – it is the best source of internationally comparative statistics that give a good insight into overall patterns and trends of global migration. The book doesn't use more recent versions of the database because many recent estimates seem to be based on extrapolations rather than actual data. For more detailed, country-level analyses of recent migration flows, I have drawn on databases compiled for the Determinants of International Migration (DEMIG) project at Oxford University's International Migration Institute (IMI).[1] For data on population, economy and education and other country-level data, this book has drawn on the World Development Indicators (WDI) database from the World Bank, unless indicated otherwise.

Introduction

We seem to be living in times of unprecedented mass migration. Images of 'caravans' of Central Americans trying to reach the Mexico–US border, Africans crammed into unseaworthy boats desperately trying to cross the Mediterranean, and illegal migrants crossing the Channel into Britain all seem to confirm fears that migration is spinning out of control. A toxic combination of poverty, inequality, violence, oppression, climate change and rampant population growth appear to be pushing growing numbers of Africans, Asians and Latin Americans to embark upon increasingly desperate journeys to reach the shores of the 'Wealthy West'.

We are told that, through making false promises about jobs and luxurious lives in the West, human traffickers and smugglers prey on the vulnerability of migrants by luring them into increasingly dangerous journeys, only for those migrants to find themselves horribly exploited in slavery-like conditions; that is, if they survive the trip at all. Fears that migration is spinning out of control have compounded doubts about the ability and willingness of immigrants to adapt to destination societies and cultures. Images of migrant communities living 'parallel lives' in segregated, impoverished and crime-infested neighbourhoods have instilled a general belief that immigrant integration has often failed. All of this has amalgamated in the notion of a 'migration crisis' that requires drastic countermeasures – such as stronger border enforcement, refugee resettlement schemes, and development aid for poor countries.

Not everybody agrees with these views. On the other side of the debate there are the politicians, economists and activists telling us that migration is not a problem but a *solution* to pressing problems such as labour shortages and population ageing. They argue that we are in desperate *need* of migrants to boost growth and innovation and to rejuvenate our societies. In this view, the diversity that immigration brings is not a threat but a good thing, as it sparks innovation and cultural renewal. They also claim that migration benefits growth in origin countries because of the huge amounts of money that migrants remit back home, and because of the vital role of expatriates in stimulating trade and boosting entrepreneurship in origin countries. They tell us that we need workers of all skill levels, and that we should open our borders in order to fill pressing labour shortages.

This book will show that the ideas on both sides represent partial, simplistic and often outright misleading views on migration, which crumble in the face of evidence. To overcome an increasingly polarized debate, this book presents evidence that challenges simplistic pro- *and* anti-migration narratives. I will tell a different story – one that contradicts the conventional ideas about migration taught in schools and universities and espoused by media, pundits, humanitarian organizations, think tanks, movies, magazines and popular books. I will do so because we are in dire need of a radically new vision of migration, which is based not on political interests or ideological views but instead looks at migration *as it is*.

This book does not present an ideological view of migration as either a problem to be solved or a solution to problems, but one that tries to understand the nature and causes of migration from a scientific point of view. By necessity, this is a holistic view that tries to understand migration as an intrinsic and therefore inseparable part of broader processes of social, cultural and economic change affecting our societies and our world, and one that benefits some people more than others, can have downsides for some, but *cannot be thought or wished away*.

This book also aims to answer the biggest unresolved questions about migration. For example, why have politicians across the West failed to curb immigration despite massive investments of taxpayer money in border enforcement? Why is illegal migration continuing despite politicians' promises to destroy the business model of smugglers? Why have governments been so ineffective in preventing the exploitation of migrant workers, despite their repeated promises to viciously crack down on such abuses? How have politicians got away with selling the same false promises or outright lies about immigration? And, most importantly, what policies can we put in place in order to deal more effectively with migration?

I wrote this book out of a deep sense of urgency. There is much academic research on migration, but so little of that has filtered through into public debate or the policies proposed by politicians and international organizations, which partly explains why policies frequently fail or even backfire. From the years of research I have undertaken and shared, the public lectures I have given, the radio and TV debates in which I have participated, and the work I have done with governments and international organizations, I have concluded that speaking 'truth to power' isn't enough to change the tone and improve the quality of debates.

In other words, just spreading 'facts' doesn't work. Politicians and other policymakers will ignore the facts they find inconvenient. For instance, typically, after I give a lecture to senior policymakers, they enthusiastically come up to me during the drinks reception and congratulate me for the 'fascinating presentation', but then immediately quip, 'We can never implement your insights, because that would be political suicide.' Hence, my aim with this book is to cut straight through to you, the general reader, and equip you with the knowledge that will enable you to more critically scrutinize claims made by politicians, pundits and experts, and see through the various forms of misinformation and propaganda that abound on this subject.

The knowledge presented in this book is partly based on three decades of primary research I have conducted on migration in various countries around the world, and through leading research projects and working with teams at the University of Oxford and the University of Amsterdam. It also summarizes insights on migration that have emerged from research literature in the burgeoning field of migration studies, including many excellent studies conducted by researchers from across the social sciences and beyond – in fields ranging from anthropology and sociology to geography, demography and economics, as well as historical, legal and psychological sciences.

In 2015, I moved back to the Netherlands after having spent ten years researching and teaching migration at the University of Oxford. I had been freshly appointed as professor of sociology at the University of Amsterdam, at the height of the Syrian refugee crisis: the large-scale arrival of about 1 million – predominantly Syrian – refugees in Europe that led to heated debates in the Netherlands and all around Europe. I was invited to one as a migration expert, alongside local politicians and activists – including a member of an action group that organized local resistance against the establishment of asylum seeker centres. The debate quickly devolved into a clash of opinions and cheap character attacks, with nobody willing to really listen to anyone else.

While the journalist leading the debate was happy with the heat, I was frustrated that all the nuance had evaporated in favour of petty bickering. It reminded me of previous, similarly challenging experiences of debating migration, but I had been struggling for a while to really understand what was wrong with these kinds of 'migration debates' and why they were so exasperating. The epiphany came when the journalist asked the audience for a show of hands: 'Who is, with Professor De Haas, pro-immigration, and who is anti-immigration?'

At that moment, the penny dropped, as it suddenly occurred to me what was wrong with all of these debates: their simplistic framing in pro- and anti-migration terms. The journalist was annoyed when I interrupted to attack his framing, but I had learned a very important lesson: the persistent casting of migration debates in pro- and anti- terms renders them unworthy of the word 'debate' as it leaves no room for nuance.

I had also increasingly started to realize that we, as researchers, should not only spread 'facts' about migration, but should also change the entire way we talk about the subject. This is because the facts of migration don't speak for themselves; they make sense only as part of a broader story about immigration and what it means to people. After all, migration is too diverse a phenomenon to fit into a simple box of 'good' or 'bad'. Such dichotomous narratives tend to create a caricature of immigrants (as victims, heroes or villains, depending on the storyline) that defies the more complex reality and often deprives them of their humanity. More generally, the entire casting of migration debates in pro/anti terms is like questioning or thinking away a fundamental part of who we are, as human beings and as societies, and who we've always been. Migration is literally of all times, and is as old as humanity. People have always moved. Discussing migration in pro/anti terms therefore precludes an understanding of the nature, causes and consequences of migration as a *normal* process.

A few analogies may help to show how naive this pro/anti framing really is. To be generally in favour of, or against, migration would be like being generally in favour of or against, say, the economy. No serious person would ask an economist whether he is in favour of or against the economy, or markets. Or a geographer whether she is in favour of or against urbanization. Or an agronomist whether he is in favour of or against agriculture. Or a biologist whether she is in favour of or against the environment. Still, this is the way the migration debates are usually conducted, particularly in the media and politics.

As we will see, such framing also makes for notoriously bad policy. Migration policies have often failed or been counterproductive because they are based on a series of false assumptions, or myths, about the nature, causes and impacts of migration. Further drawing on the analogy with economic debates, if we wonder how to regulate markets, the premise is seldom to abolish markets (and we know how such experiments ended) or to simply deny their existence. Rather, we look at how to influence them, and how to achieve these goals. This is also the way we should be discussing migration, but it is striking how the technical, non-ideological side of migration debates – which policies work, which policies fail, and which have backfired – is almost completely ignored, particularly given the large body of scientific evidence.

In fact, most current migration debates are not debates at all, in their almost exclusive focus on opinion or wishful thinking rather than fact – on what migration *ought to be*, rather than on what migration *is* in terms of its actual trends, patterns, causes and impacts, and how policies could best deal with the realities on the ground to produce desired outcomes and avoid the errors of the past. As debates have become more and more entrenched in ideological bickering between pro- and anti-immigration camps, there is barely any place for evidence. Instead, what we usually see is that anti-immigration voices often exaggerate the downsides of migration, while corporate lobbies and liberal groups tend to exaggerate the benefits of immigration, and that each side cherry-picks evidence and arguments that fit their storyline – and simply ignores everything that is inconvenient.

In truth, most people have ambivalent feelings about immigration. As we will see time and time again in this book, there is often a large gap between how people think about immigration in general and how they relate to the migrants and refugees they meet in their personal lives. People can be concerned about immigration and be in favour of stricter border enforcement, but at the same time see it as their 'love thy neighbour' duty to help individual refugees and migrants living in their community. Although immigration is not as massive and transformative on a national scale as we often think, the impacts of immigration can be quite life-altering – and sometimes disruptive – on the local scale of neighbourhoods or towns. Yet political debates, with their increasing polarization between pro- and anti-immigration views, don't reflect such ambiguities. What typically gets lost is nuance, and nuance is what we urgently need in order to take the heat out of debates about immigration and related issues such as diversity, identity and racism, which have grown increasingly toxic.

Since the end of the Cold War, Western politicians have been waging a War on Immigration.

In Europe, this started with political panic about the large-scale arrival of asylum seekers fleeing warfare in former Yugoslavia and conflicts in the Middle East and the Horn of Africa. In the 2000s this was followed by a backlash against multiculturalism, and growing concerns about segregation and a perceived lack of integration, particularly of Muslim immigrants. From 2015, large-scale arrivals of Syrian refugees and more general concerns about trans-Mediterranean boat migration took debates to fever pitch. In Britain, ever since Tony Blair raised suspicion about 'bogus' asylum seekers, politicians have been vowing to crack down on unsolicited migrant arrivals on British shores, while the seemingly unstoppable arrival of East European workers was a major factor in the 2016 Brexit vote.

In the US, Ronald Reagan's Immigration Reform and Control Act (IRCA) of 1986 provided amnesty to 2.7 million immigrants, but also fired the starting shot for increasing border enforcement to prevent illegal immigration from Mexico and Central America under the Bush and Clinton administrations. The terror attacks of 9/11 reinforced these trends, with politicians increasingly portraying immigration as a potential threat to national security. Concerns about illegal immigration prompted the Bush and Obama administrations to pour billions of dollars (three times higher than the FBI budget) into the militarization of border controls and the detention and deportation of illegal migrants. This trend culminated in Trump winning the 2016 election on an anti-immigration platform. While there hasn't been serious hope of comprehensive immigration reform since the George W. Bush presidency, the left and right have continued to brawl over immigration policy.

Western governments have invested massive resources to curb inflows of foreign workers and their families – coming from Mexico and Central America to the US, from South Asia and eastern Europe to Britain, and from Turkey and North Africa to western Europe. For decades now, politicians from across the political spectrum have repeatedly pledged to 'fix our broken immigration system', to 'take back control on immigration' and to 'crack down on smuggling and trafficking'. Others have proposed using aid to curb immigration from poor countries. However, politicians have consistently failed to deliver on these promises. In fact, the evidence shows that many of these policies have backfired, as they paradoxically produce *more* migration while stimulating illegal migration and facilitating the exploitation of migrant workers.

In the US, for instance, massive investments in border enforcement since the late 1980s by both Republican and Democratic administrations turned a largely circular flow of Mexican workers going back and forth to California and Texas into an 11-million-strong population of permanently settled families living all across the United States. At the same time, despite massive investments in border enforcement and deportations, continuing labour shortages drove new migration from Latin America and other countries underground, leading the undocumented population to soar from 3.5 million to 11 million.

Likewise, in Europe, growing border restrictions pushed Turkish and North African 'guest workers' into permanent settlement by discouraging their return and encouraging large-scale family migration over the 1980s and 1990s – while three decades of massive investment in border controls in the Mediterranean failed to stop legal and illegal immigration from North and West Africa into southern Europe. In the UK, earlier efforts to curb immigration from Commonwealth countries equally had counterproductive effects, consolidating rather than preventing the permanent settlement of rapidly growing Caribbean and South Asian populations in Britain. More recently, instead of incentivizing East European workers to return to origin countries, Brexit only seems to have strengthened the determination of Polish, Romanian and Bulgarian workers to stay permanently, with immigration to the UK paradoxically reaching an all-time high in the post-Brexit years.

In both the US and Europe (including the United Kingdom), politicians have manifestly failed to fix their 'broken immigration systems' and curb growing immigration; similarly, three decades of efforts to limit the arrival of asylum seekers and refugees have failed to produce any meaningful results. At the same time, politicians have failed to address problems of segregation and the integration of marginalized immigrant and minority groups that find themselves the subject of exploitation and racist discrimination. Nor have efforts to combat smuggling and trafficking produced any meaningful results, as illegal migration continues to exact a high toll in terms of human suffering and border deaths.

Immigration restrictions and 'pushbacks' have not deterred refugees from seeking safety across borders, while consistent backlogs and administrative failures have left asylum seekers in a debilitating legal limbo for many years, deepening trauma, perpetuating the separation of families, and restricting people from building a new life for themselves through study and work. Meanwhile, the failure of governments in the US, the UK and continental Europe to address the situation of marginalized – often undocumented – migrant workers comes with the serious risk of the formation of a new underclass.

As this book will show, politicians have not only failed to deliver on their long-standing and endlessly repeated promises, but in many ways their policies have made things *worse*. Immigration and integration policies have not only fallen short of their objectives, they have also been counterproductive, because they are not based on a scientific understanding of how migration really works. In other words, these policies are part of the problem. The central claim of this book is therefore that such policies are bound to fail because they are in fact *among the very causes* of the problems they pretend to solve.

Why then, as so many students have asked me, do we keep on recycling the same policies that have so blatantly failed in the past? There is no simple answer to that question. Partly, this is because politicians and other decision-makers have ignored scientific evidence about the trends, causes and impacts of migration. For the most part, however, this does not reflect a lack of information or innocence, but a conscious refusal to acknowledge the facts. Politicians (from left to right, from conservative to liberal), interest groups and international organizations perpetuate a series of myths as part of *deliberate* strategies to distort the truth about migration. Such propaganda is part of active efforts to sow unjustified fear and misinformation – as exposure to the truth would expose not only politicians' failure to address problems, but also their own complicity in creating and aggravating them. In that sense, politicians have got caught up in their own lies.

But this is not only about politicians indulging in immigration fearmongering and immigrant scapegoating to win the next election. It is also about interest groups like trade unions and business lobbies that exaggerate the harms – or benefits – of migration. It's about UN agencies like the International Organization for Migration (IOM) and the United Nations High Commissioner for Refugees (UNHCR) exaggerating or misrepresenting migrant and refugee numbers in an apparent bid to generate publicity and funding. It's about politicians portraying migrants and 'bogus' asylum seekers as job thieves or welfare scroungers, to distract attention away from the real causes of declining job security, wage stagnation, growing financial insecurity, and increasingly expensive education, housing and healthcare. It's about corporate lobbies portraying migrants as heroes that will ensure nations retain their competitiveness in the global race for talent. And humanitarian organizations denying the ability of migrants and refugees to think for themselves and act in their own best interests, by unilaterally depicting them as victims who needed to be 'rescued' from smugglers and traffickers. And climate activists hijacking the migration issue and fabricating myths about waves of climate refugees to help make their (otherwise justified) case for drastically cutting greenhouse-gas emissions.

Finally, debates and research about migration are also haunted by a more general bias towards the impacts of migration on Western 'receiving' or 'host' societies. This 'receiving-country bias' has led to a one-sided focus on issues such as integration, assimilation, segregation, race and identity from a destination-country perspective. However important these issues are, this has gone along with a striking lack of interest in and research on the causes and consequences of migration from the perspective of *origin* countries.

This bias is obviously very problematic. After all, how can we develop a realistic view on migration if we miss half the picture? As we will see in this book, neglecting the 'other side' of migration hampers a proper understanding of its nature and very causes. This helps to explain why politicians, interest groups, international organizations, media, school books, experts and pundits continue to get away with reproducing a whole series of pseudoscientific truths about migration without ever being corrected.

This book is organized into three sections. The first will explore trends in global migration patterns. It looks at recent changes in the scale, magnitude and direction of migration and what factors have caused such changes. It also dispels common claims and popular myths about the causes of migration, and will show which factors really explain recent changes in global migration patterns.

The second section explores the impacts of migration on both destination and origin societies. It analyses the reasons why most migrant groups have integrated rather smoothly but others have experienced marginalization and protracted segregation. It also critically scrutinizes various (exaggerated) claims and counterclaims about the negative and positive social, cultural and economic impacts of migration, to arrive at a more balanced position.

The third and final section reveals how various popular ideas championed by politicians, interest groups and international organizations are part of deliberate strategies to distort the truth about immigration. These include the considerable gap between politicians' tough talk on immigration and their much more lenient policy practices, and the intuitive but rather misleading idea that migration restrictions reduce migration. I also dismantle several popular but scientifically unfounded myths: that public opinion has turned against immigration, that smuggling is the main cause of illegal migration, that human trafficking is a form of modern slavery, and that climate change will lead to mass migration.

In all, there are twenty-two chapters, each of which tackles a long-standing myth about migration. In the first part of each chapter, I will briefly set out the myth – and the typical narratives in which it is cast – as well as its origin as it pertains to the politicians, interest groups and international organizations that create and recycle such myths. The second part – *How it really works* – dismantles the myth by drawing on data and evidence from history, anthropology, sociology, geography, demography and economics. The aim of each chapter, and the book as a whole, is to provide evidence on the real trends, causes and impacts of migration as an intrinsic part of broader social, cultural and economic change in origin and destination societies.

By providing deep insights based on cutting-edge evidence, this book goes beyond a myth-busting exercise, aiming to build, chapter by chapter, a new, holistic vision of migration as an intrinsic part of broader national and global change. The chapters have been written in such a way that they can be read separately – which is useful for readers with specific interests – but all are part of an overarching narrative. The order of chapters builds a more general argument to guide the reader to deep insights as they continue towards the conclusion. While I will eschew unnecessary academic jargon, I will not stay away from addressing the complexity of issues and the nuances that are needed to achieve a fundamental understanding of migration processes.

I wrote this book to equip readers with an understanding of how migration really works, in a way that is firmly rooted in the best data and scientific insight, with the goal of stimulating a *real* debate on migration, in which politicians no longer get away with plain propaganda or policy solutions that perhaps satisfy the desire for political showmanship – and may help them win the next election – but don't solve any real problems and instead make them *worse*. We can do so much better.

And we have reasons to be hopeful about the prospects of doing so because, as this book will also show, research reveals that most people have nuanced opinions about migration. It is simply not true that public opinion has massively turned against immigration. The political polarization in pro/anti-immigration camps is not reflected in how most people think and feel about migration. While many people have valid concerns about immigration, integration and segregation, most also understand that migration is to a certain extent inevitable, that migrant workers fulfil essential roles, and that immigrants and refugees deserve fundamental rights – and they understand the dilemmas this generates.

Above all, this book will show that there are no easy solutions to complex migration problems. However, once we do away with unnecessary panic and fear, which has already paralysed debates for too long, we create space for an informed debate about the benefits and downsides of immigration, and about how to design better and more effective policies that avoid the errors of the past and work better for *all* members of our societies.

Myths of Migration

Myth 1: Migration is at an all-time high

Migration seems to be at an all-time high and accelerating rapidly. We are told that the world has never experienced this much migration, and that this has caused a crisis. Grinding poverty, population growth, oppression, warfare and climate change have uprooted growing numbers of people. As a result, more and more poor people are flocking to cities and destinations abroad, exceeding the absorption capacity of urban areas and destination societies. Rapidly multiplying migration and refugee crises around the world reinforce fears that, unless problems are addressed urgently, the growing exodus will soon be out of control. All of this seems to confirm the idea that we live in an age of unprecedented mass migration.

This is the image of migration that we're getting when we watch television, read the newspaper or browse the internet. Governments seem to be increasingly overwhelmed by a rising tide of migrants and refugees desperately trying to cross seas and deserts to reach the borders of the Wealthy West. With immigrants appearing to form an increasing share of national populations, levels of ethnic, racial and religious diversity seem to be higher than they've ever been.

Because of globalization, it is easier than ever to travel and to connect over large distances. Since the 1990s, satellite television, the internet and smartphones have caused a revolution in global connectivity. Even in the smallest towns and villages in countries like Guatemala, Ethiopia and Afghanistan, people can now connect to the rest of the world. This has broadened the horizons of young people around the globe. The exposure to images of wealth and luxury in the West seems to have fuelled a migration fever among youngsters eager to taste life in the lands of milk and honey.

All of this has apparently fuelled increasing migration pressures. International inequalities remain huge while many developing countries are plagued by poverty, instability, corruption and violent conflict. At the same time, fast population growth adds more hungry mouths to feed each year, increasing competition for scarce resources. More recently, climate change has been added to this cocktail of human misery, leading to increasing flooding, droughts, hurricanes and wildfires. As people lose their homes, cattle and farmland, and are driven to destitution because of repeated crop failure, they seem to have no other option than to flee. They become part of the swelling masses of uprooted people in the Global South desperate to migrate to the Global North.

The idea that we live in times of unprecedented mass migration has gained credibility because of frequent claims by prestigious international organizations – such as the International Organisation for Migration (IOM) and the United Nations High Commissioner for Refugees (UNHCR) – that migrant and refugee numbers have reached yet another all-time high. In 2021, IOM claimed that 'the current mobility of people is higher than ever before in modern history and continues to increase sharply'.[1] Adopting alarmist overtones, UNHCR has claimed that we live in times of a 'global displacement crisis', with conflict, violence and climate change uprooting more and more people from their native lands, and in 2022 it stated that, with a record-high number of 100 million displaced people, a 'dramatic milestone' was reached that few would have expected a decade ago'.[2]

All of this amalgamates into the dominant idea of a 'migration crisis'. The notion that we live in times of unprecedented mass migration is the most widespread claim about migration. Although they may advocate very different solutions, politicians from left to right, climate activist and nativist groups, humanitarian NGOs and refugee organizations and media have all bought into the idea that the current era is one of a migration crisis driven by a series of global, economic, demographic and environmental crises. According to this narrative, the world is on fire – and as a result, migration is spinning out of control.

How it really works

International migration has remained low and stable

Although the idea that migration is at an all-time high has gained the status of an almost unquestionable truth, the facts tell quite a different story. Current levels of international migration are neither exceptionally high nor increasing. In fact, over the past decades, global migration

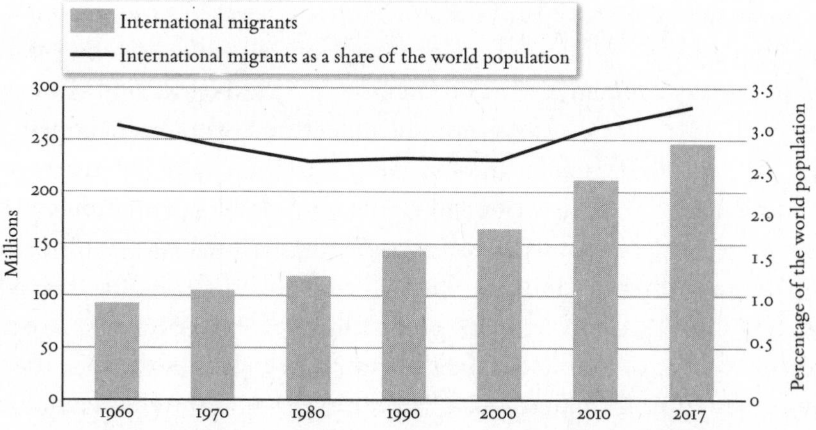

Graph 1: Total population of international migrants in the world, 1960–2017

levels have remained remarkably stable. According to most definitions, an international migrant is a person who is living in a country other than their country of birth for a period of at least six to twelve months. Using this definition, and according to data from the United Nations Population Division, in 1960 there were about 93 million international migrants in the world. This number increased to 170 million in 2000 and further increased to an estimated 247 million in 2017. At first sight, this seems like a staggering increase. However, the world population has increased at a roughly equal pace, from some 3 billion in 1960 to 6.1 billion in 2000, and 7.6 billion in 2017. So, if we express the number of international migrants as a share of the world population, we see that relative levels of migration have remained stable at around 3 per cent. In addition, past numbers are likely to be underestimates because, in previous decades, much migration went unregistered.[3]

This defies the idea that global migration is accelerating. In fact, there is evidence that global migration levels were actually higher in the late nineteenth and early twentieth centuries. This was the heyday of transatlantic migration, when tens of millions of Europeans left the 'Old World' to seek new opportunities and freedom in the 'New World' – in countries such as the United States, Canada, Argentina and Brazil, as well as Australia and New Zealand. This massive out-migration coincided with the peak of European imperialism, when many European soldiers, colonists, missionaries, administrators, entrepreneurs and workers settled in colonies in Africa and Asia.

Insatiable labour needs driven by European imperialism and industrialization also set in motion major migrations elsewhere in the world. Between 1834 and 1941, Britain, France and the Netherlands shipped between 12 million and 37 million indentured workers ('coolies') – mainly from India, China and Indonesia – to their colonial possessions in the Caribbean, East Africa and elsewhere.[4] Besides plantation workers in the Caribbean, the British recruited indentured workers for East Africa, including the Indians who helped to build the Kenya–Uganda Railway in the 1890s. As many as 1 million indentured workers were recruited in Japan to be sent to destinations like Hawaii, the US, Brazil and Peru. After the Communist Revolution of 1917 and the creation of the Soviet Union in 1922, Russian imperialism led to the large-scale emigration and settlement of ethnic Russians in Siberia and Soviet republics such as Latvia, Estonia, Ukraine, Belorussia, Moldavia and Kazakhstan, and outward movements of Russians into Siberia and non-Russian territories.[5]

In total, between 1846 and 1940 some 150 million people moved across continents – 9 per cent of the world population in 1900 – and this does not even take into account large-scale population movements within Europe. Of these transcontinental migrants, an estimated 55–8 million were Europeans moving to the Americas, 48–52 million Indians and southern Chinese migrating to European colonies in South-East Asia, East Africa and the South Pacific, and 46–51 million Russians and Chinese settling in Manchuria, Siberia, Central Asia and Japan.[6]

To put this in perspective, approximately 48 million Europeans left the continent between 1846 and 1924 alone. This was equal to about 12 per cent of the European population in 1900. In some countries the percentage was much higher. In the same period about 17 million people left the British Isles – equal to 41 per cent of Britain's population in 1900.[7] Between 1869 and 1940, about 16.4 million Italians emigrated to destinations in northern Europe and South and North America – no less than 50 per cent of the Italian population in 1900.[8]

This is a much higher rate than the emigration rates of most leading emigration countries today. For instance, the 9.5 million Mexico-born people living abroad in 2017 (including undocumented migrants) represented 7.5 per cent of the Mexican population, while the 3 million Turkey-born people living abroad represent 3.8 per cent of the Turkish population. For populous countries the percentage is even lower. The

9.5 million India-born and 5.8 million China-born people estimated to be living abroad in 2007 represented only 0.4 and 0.7 per cent of the total populations of their countries.

This picture of relatively low migration remains unaffected if we add refugees to the numbers. This is because the number of refugees is much smaller than the extensive attention that is given to 'refugee crises' in media and politics seems to suggest. Refugees represent between 7 and 12 per cent of all migrants in the world, which is equivalent to about 0.3 per cent of the world population – and refugee numbers in the mid-twentieth century were arguably much larger than current numbers (as we will see in chapter 3).

A global migration reversal

So, the level of international migration is not as high as we think. International migrants represent about 3 per cent of the world population, and that number has remained remarkably stable. To turn that number around, this means that an overwhelming share – about 97 per cent of the world population – live in their native country. This is quite striking given the huge inequalities that persist in the world.

Thus, there is no evidence that global migration is accelerating. However, that does not mean that nothing has changed. Particularly from a Western and Eurocentric perspective, there have been profound transformations in migration patterns, which have turned the global migration map entirely upside down. These transformations have little to do with numbers, but rather with changes in the dominant geographical direction of global migration since the end of the Second World War, which explains why, at least from a European or North American perspective, immigration may *appear* to be at an all-time high.

The most fundamental change has been the transformation of western Europe from the world's main source of colonists and immigrants to an important destination of migrants. Starting in the fifteenth century, Europeans ventured out to the rest of the world, occupying and populating foreign territories – particularly in the Americas, but also in Africa and Asia. This started with the 'discovery' and conquest of the Americas after Christopher Columbus set foot in the Caribbean in 1492, and the growing involvement of the Spanish, Portuguese, Dutch, French and British in establishing colonies in the Americas, as well as trading posts and colonies on the African and Asian coasts, from the sixteenth and seventeenth centuries. While Spain conquered the Philippines, the British gradually gained control over the Indian subcontinent, and the Netherlands gained dominance in Indonesia.

Particularly from the mid-nineteenth century, European colonial powers – and Britain and France in particular – colonized most of the entire territories of Africa and Asia, with a few exceptions like Ethiopia, Thailand and China. This went along with the emigration of European settlers to these new colonies, such as Britons moving to South Africa, Rhodesia (present-day Zimbabwe) and Kenya, and large numbers of French and other European *colons* settling in Algeria. Evidently, they did so without asking permission from native populations. European colonialism is arguably the biggest illegal migration in human history.

European colonialism also prompted the biggest forced migration in history, through the transatlantic slave trade, with an estimated 12 million Africans forcibly taken to the Americas.[9] The abolition of the slave trade and slavery over the course of the nineteenth century prompted the British, Dutch and French to recruit large numbers of indentured workers, mainly from the Indian subcontinent but also from Java and China, to work in Caribbean and East African colonies.

With the US gaining independence from Britain in 1776, most Latin American colonies became independent from Spain – and Brazil from Portugal – in the early nineteenth century. However, this did not stop European influxes to the Americas. Particularly from the 1850s onwards, increasing numbers of European migrants – often peasants and factory workers looking for better opportunities overseas – were attracted by economic opportunities in the United States and Canada, but also in Argentina and Brazil. This resulted in large-scale transatlantic migration. Industrialization and urbanization also drew migrant workers from China and Japan to the Americas.[10]

All of this came to an end after the Second World War. Between 1945 and 1965, most European colonies in Asia and Africa gained independence. Fast economic growth and the establishment of welfare states in western Europe meant that Europeans rapidly lost interest in emigrating to America, Australia and New Zealand. Full employment and fast-declining birth rates also meant that European countries faced growing labour shortages in various industries and mining. As a consequence, large-scale European emigration to other continents came to an end.

The result was that migration patterns reversed – with people from the rest of the world increasingly finding their way to western Europe. This often started with 'post-colonial' migrations in the form of people moving from former colonies to Europe: from the Caribbean (the West Indies), South Asia (Pakistan, India) and the Indian-heritage populations living in East Africa to Britain; from the Maghreb (Algeria, Tunisia, Morocco) and West Africa (particularly Senegal and Mali) to France; and from Indonesia and Suriname to the Netherlands.

In Germany, Austria, Switzerland, Denmark and Sweden, which did not have large overseas colonial empires – as well as in the Netherlands and Belgium – these post-colonial migrations were soon supplemented by the large-scale recruitment of guest workers from Italy, Spain, Portugal, Greece and former Yugoslavia in the 1950s and 1960s. When southern European labour resources were exhausted, governments and companies started to recruit migrant workers from Turkey and the Maghreb. Although this was initially seen as temporary migration, many migrants would settle and bring their families, laying the ground for the growth of large immigrant communities.

This 'global migration reversal' was a turnaround of international migration patterns. And the evolution of Europe from the world's main supplier of migrants into a major destination for non-European migrants also transformed migration to traditional European settler colonies in North America, Australia and New Zealand. This is because, as Europeans stopped emigrating in large numbers, migration to these countries became increasingly non-European in origin.

While Europeans had dominated immigration to the US and Canada for centuries, from the 1950s, Puerto Ricans, Mexicans, Cubans, other Latin Americans, and Asians (particularly Koreans, Vietnamese, Filipinos, Indians and Chinese) began to take their place. This went along with major changes in migration patterns in other world regions. South America ceased to be a destination for European emigrants, and patterns reversed as migration from Latin America to North America and later also to Europe grew rapidly.

Another major change in global migration patterns was the rise of non-Western migration destinations. Beginning in the 1980s, the fast-growing economies in the Arab Gulf – such as Saudi Arabia, the United Arab Emirates, Kuwait and Qatar – emerged as destinations for millions of migrant workers from the Middle East (especially Egypt) and poorer countries in Asia, such as Pakistan, India and the Philippines, and to a lesser extent also Africa. Over recent decades, Asians in particular have entered the global migration stage, with growing numbers of Chinese, Indians, Filipinos and Indonesians migrating to destinations around the world. Within East and South-East Asia, countries like Japan, South Korea, Singapore, Malaysia and Thailand have become destinations for migrants from poorer countries within and outside the continent, such as Myanmar, Nepal and Uzbekistan. In the 1990s, Russia emerged as a major destination for migrant workers from former Soviet republics like Ukraine, Kazakhstan and Uzbekistan.[11]

So, over the past half-century, patterns of international migration have gone through fundamental transformations. With the exception of traditional immigration countries such as Canada, Australia and New Zealand (where migrants represent about 20 per cent of the population), between 10 and 15 per cent of the populations of most Western countries – including the US, the UK, Germany and France – were born abroad. Such immigration levels are not exceptional from a historical point of view, however. While migration to the US has been rising over the past few decades, in 2020 immigrants formed a roughly equal share of the population (around 14 per cent) as they did a century ago.[12]

The major change is the increasingly non-European background of immigrant populations. With Europe transforming from a prime source of migrants to a major migration destination, the global migration reversal has led to increasing migration from Latin America, Asia and (to a lesser extent) Africa, to Europe, North America, Australia and New Zealand, as well as new migration destinations in the Gulf and East Asia. These changes have not so much to do with an increase in overall levels of international migration, but with a change in the dominant geographical direction of global migration flows.

This has led to the growing settlement of populations of non-European origin in Europe and North America. Without a doubt, this is a major change, and makes it perhaps understandable that many people think immigration is at an all-time high. This is particularly true when seen from the cities, neighbourhoods and towns where immigrants concentrate. However, the data clearly defies the idea that global migration is even accelerating, let alone spinning out of control. In fact, this idea reflects a Eurocentric worldview, which casts the immigration of non-Western, non-white populations as particularly problematic, but which is blind to European emigrations and immigrations of the past.

Most migrants move over short distances

Because of the preoccupation of Western politicians and media with international migration, it is easy to forget that *internal* migration – movement within countries – has always been much more important than movement across borders. This is not only because international migration is expensive, but also because people simply prefer to stay close to home. According to the best available numbers, internal migrants represent an estimated 80 per cent of all migrants in the world – or 12 per cent of the world population.[13] On that basis, we can estimate that there are roughly 1 billion internal migrants in the world.

Internal migration – also known as 'domestic migration' – is particularly significant in developing countries that are going through rapid urbanization, which triggers large-scale migration from rural areas to burgeoning metropolitan areas. This massive transfer of populations from the countryside to towns and cities is an integral – and therefore largely inevitable – part of broader processes of industrialization and modernization.

This global 'rural exodus' started in nineteenth- and early twentieth-century western Europe, North America and Japan, and was largely completed by the 1950s – more than 80 per cent of the population in industrialized countries now live in urban areas. Although the large majority of rural-to-urban migrants stay in their own country, some use cities as a staging ground to migrate overseas. A similar transition is now in full swing in middle-income countries such as China, India and Indonesia, and is just starting to gain traction in low-income countries such as Ethiopia, Afghanistan and Myanmar, where less than 30 per cent of people live in cities and towns but urbanization rates are higher than anywhere else in the world.

In many ways, the modern, industrial era has not been a story of international migration, but one of rural-to-urban migration within and across borders. Almost all of us descend from peasants. Most urbanites only have to go back one or two generations to find family members who made the major step to leave for the city in search of work, education or a different lifestyle. The switch from rural to urban lifestyle has

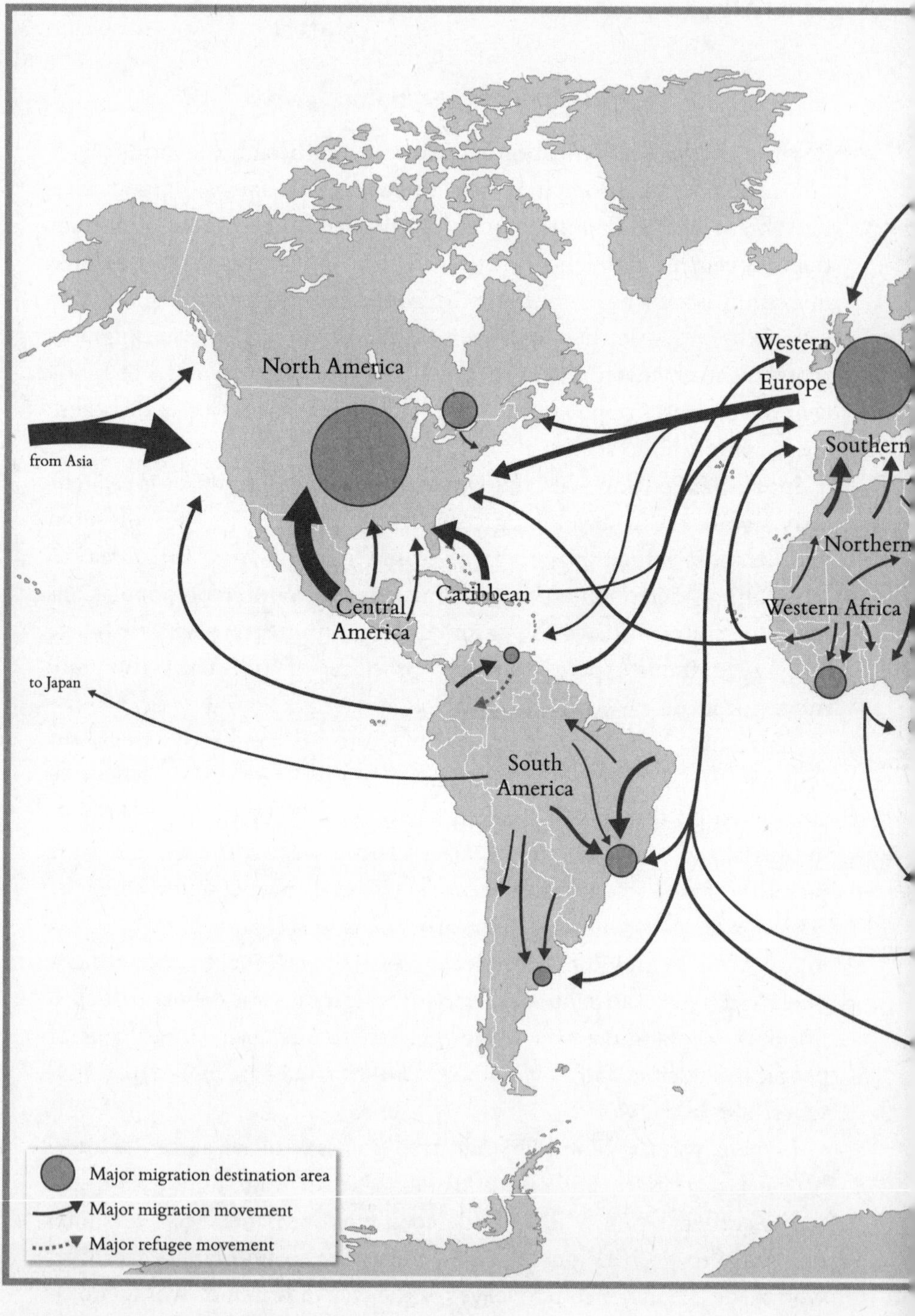

Map 1: Major long-distance migrations, 1950–2020[15]

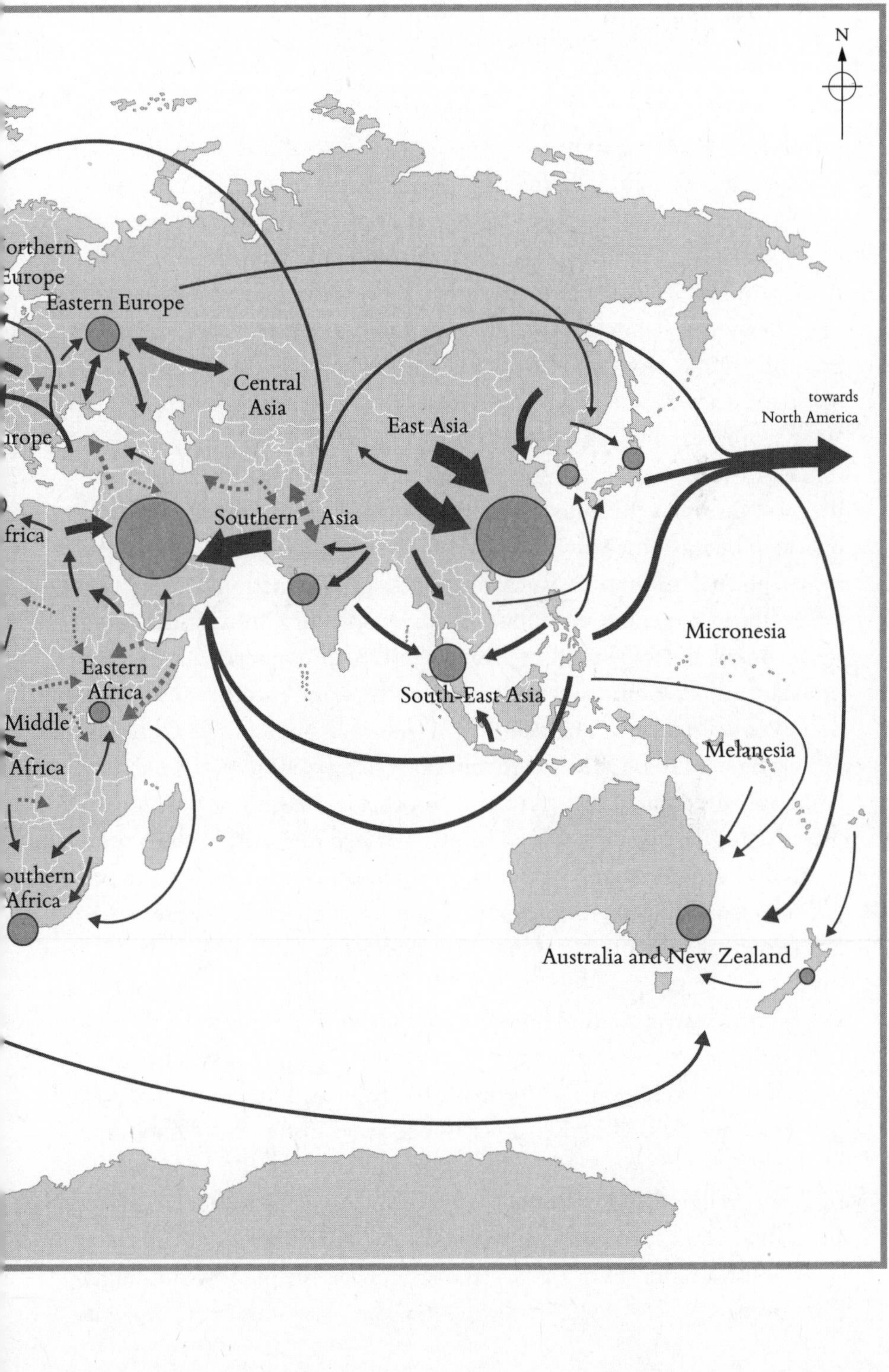

N
orthern
urope
Eastern Europe
Central
Asia
urope
East Asia
towards
North America
frica
Southern
Asia
Micronesia
Eastern
Africa
South-East Asia
Middle
Africa
Melanesia
outhern
Africa
Australia and New Zealand

been the most fundamental transformation humanity has gone through over the past one to two centuries, and that process is still ongoing in many low- and middle-income countries.

Whether this rural-to-urban migration involves a border crossing or not is often less relevant than the radical change in lifestyle, and the mixed feelings of excitement, alienation and shock this often causes. A peasant's son or daughter moving from a rural village in the state of Oaxaca in Mexico to Mexico City, or from the Tata province in southern Morocco to Casablanca, or from the Federally Administered Tribal Areas (FATA) in Pakistan to Karachi, goes through an almost equally big – or bigger – shock as if they were moving to Los Angeles, Paris or London; while most middle-class urbanites from Mexico City, Casablanca or Karachi will usually find little trouble adjusting to life in large Western metropolises.

The vast majority of young people who search for better opportunities and lifestyles thus move within countries. On average, only about one-fifth of movement within countries results in international migration. Internal migration is far higher than international migration, especially in large and populous countries such as China, India, Indonesia, Brazil and Nigeria, but also in the US and Russia. The 'floating populations' in China are testimony to the huge magnitude of these domestic migrations. The number of internal migrants in China has been estimated to be at least 270 million – compared to only 5.8 million China-born people living abroad.[14] In other words, there are as many internal migrants within China as international migrants in the world!

A good rule of thumb is: the bigger the country, the higher the proportion of migrants staying within the country, and the lower the relative number of people migrating internationally. The explanation for this is simple. In big and populous countries, most people moving out of rural villages and towns can find opportunities for work, study and a different lifestyle in large cities in their own country. Living in a small country increases the likelihood that people have to cross borders to find such opportunities. And, if people do cross borders, most go to neighbouring countries, as this is more affordable – and they are often similar in culture, language, religion and customs. Staying close to home makes it easier to adapt, find work, and visit family and friends back home.

To illustrate this, map 1 gives an overview of the main world migrations over recent history. What it shows is the extraordinary complexity of population movements, with most people moving within countries and within regions. The reality of migration strongly contrasts with the popular idea of a massive South–North exodus. For instance, the Gulf region is as important a global migration destination as western Europe, and countries like Argentina and Brazil in Latin America, Côte d'Ivoire, Gabon and South Africa in Africa, and Singapore, Malaysia and Thailand in Asia have risen as important regional migration destinations – while there are also massive population movements within large countries such as China, Nigeria and Brazil.

And, most importantly perhaps, more than four-fifths of the world's population live in their native places and areas. Despite huge geographical inequalities in economic opportunities, most people stay home. Only 3 per cent live abroad, and these percentages have remained remarkably stable for decades. In strong contrast to political rhetoric and media images, in reality migration is rarely ever about the massive uprooting of entire populations. And if such uprooting happens – perhaps through warfare or natural disasters such as floods and earthquakes – such movements tend to be rather short-distance and temporary. With most people

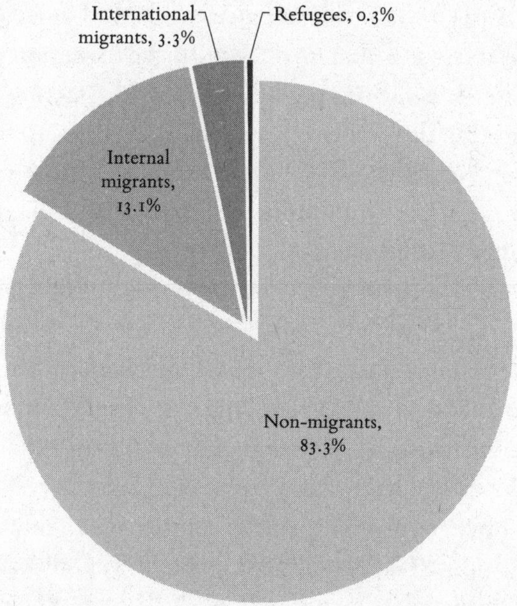

Graph 2: Migrants, refugees and non-migrants as percentages of the world population, 2020

staying close to home, long-distance migration across continents is the exception rather than the rule.

Graph 2 summarizes all of this: about 83 per cent of the world population live in their native place, 13 per cent are internal migrants, 3 per cent are international migrants, and 0.3 per cent are refugees.

A global mobility decline?

The evidence calls into question the whole idea that global migration is accelerating fast, and refutes the idea of a global migration crisis. The striking stability and non-acceleration of international migration also challenges the common idea that radical improvements in transport and communication technology have accelerated international migration. The conventional way of thinking is that cheaper transport and more accessible communication have made it easier to migrate. But we can actually turn that reasoning around: from a long-term historical perspective, technological progress has in fact enabled humankind to settle down.

For most of our history, *Homo sapiens* lived itinerantly, as we had to constantly move around in search of food as part of our hunter-gatherer and nomadic lifestyles. This meant that we lacked a permanent home, something that started to change only with the invention of agriculture in about 10,000 BCE in various parts of the world. Starting in the Middle East, Mesoamerica, the Yellow River basin and parts of Africa, this Agricultural (or Neolithic) Revolution enabled people to settle down permanently in agrarian communities and gradually abandon itinerant, nomadic or pastoralist lifestyles.

From the early nineteenth century, the Industrial Revolution triggered large-scale rural-to-urban migration, while employment in agriculture declined, mainly because of mechanization. At the same time, labour demand in industries, mines and services increased. This process started in Britain and then spread rapidly throughout the rest of Europe and North America – and from there, to the rest of the world. However, such massive rural-to-urban migration is a largely temporary phase. In rich, industrialized countries, the process of urbanization has largely been completed or 'saturated', with the overwhelming majority of the population already living in urban areas.

Seen from a long-term perspective, levels of migration may therefore go *down* in the future as part of a global mobility decline. Internal migration is already slowing down in many Western countries, including the US, UK, Germany and Japan, as the large majority of their populations already live in towns and cities.[16] In most middle-income countries in East and South-East Asia, Latin America and the Middle East, too, the majority live in urban areas (in China 63 per cent of the population, in Mexico 81 per cent, in Brazil 87 per cent) and internal migration is running out of steam. In sub-Saharan Africa as well as parts of South and Central Asia, we find the largest concentration of lower-income countries where processes of urbanization have taken off only recently. These are the only world regions where large-scale rural-to-urban migration will continue in the coming decades.

The idea that advances in transport and communication technology will automatically lead to more migration is based on sloppy assumptions about the causes of migration. The impact of technology on migration is fundamentally ambiguous. On the one hand, travel is cheaper and potential migrants can obtain information about opportunities in other places more easily. Yet more accessible transport and communication technology can also take away the need to change residency in order to access opportunities. For instance, since the mid-twentieth century, public transport, mass car ownership and the rolling-out of highway systems have allowed more and more people to commute to and from work, taking away the need for someone to relocate every time they find a new job in a different place. In countries like France, China and Japan, the building of nationwide high-speed train systems has made it possible to make daily commutes of over hundreds of miles per day.

Revolutions in communication and transport have also enabled factories, services and even agrarian production to take place in countries where labour is abundant and cheap. Many British companies have found it more economical and convenient to move call centres to India, while Americans calling customer services might be speaking to a Manila-based Filipino operator fluent in American-style English. Many US industries have moved their factories to export processing zones (*maquiladoras*) on the Mexican side of the US–Mexico border. In the same vein, Dutch rose growers have invested in huge flower farms in Kenya and Ethiopia, benefiting not only from ideal weather conditions that allow them to produce roses all year round, but also from the cheap labour.[17]

So, technology does not necessarily lead to more migration, as 'outsourcing' can actually enable capital and production to move to the location of cheap labour, rather than labour moving to production facilities in wealthy countries. This has arguably taken away a certain need for migrant workers.

The response to the Covid-19 pandemic highlighted that internet technology is enabling more and more people to work from home, particularly in the higher-skilled service sector – and it is more than possible that, in the future, even more higher-skilled service sector workers will relocate, to experience the more affordable housing and relaxed lifestyles that smaller and more remote communities can offer. However, the pandemic equally exposed the illusion that all work can be done from a distance. This particularly applies to construction, care, transport, hospitality and other service jobs that so many migrant workers do – in fact, as we will see throughout this book, persistent labour shortages in jobs that necessitate workers' physical presence are the main reason why immigration has continued over the past few decades.

All of this shows that the impact of technology on migration is uncertain. There are as many reasons to think that technology may increase migration as decrease it. While transport and information technology potentially facilitate movement and may inspire people to explore new horizons, they can also allow people to stay put. As technology facilitates 'non-migratory mobility' such as home-to-work commuting, tourism and business trips, it can also take away the need for migrating in the sense of changing residence. All of this suggests that current levels of migration are neither unprecedented nor accelerating, and future levels of migration may actually decrease as part of a global mobility decline.

Myth 2: Borders are beyond control

It seems like borders are beyond control as illegal migration is growing fast. Although levels of legal migration have remained stable, media images and political rhetoric suggest that growing numbers of migrants are crossing borders illegally in desperate attempts to reach Western countries. With smugglers and traffickers abusing people's desperation and luring them into costly and dangerous journeys across deserts and seas, Western governments seem to be failing to stop this. Politicians, pundits and media have therefore frequently sounded the alarm bell that immigration systems may collapse under ever-increasing migration pressures.

This crisis narrative is further reinforced by the common use of terms like 'mass immigration' and 'exodus' and other apocalyptic vocabulary. In 2015, British prime minister David Cameron spoke of 'a swarm of people coming across the Mediterranean'.[1] In the same year, in response to the large-scale arrivals of Syrian refugees in Europe, Dutch prime minister Mark Rutte stated that: 'As we all know from the Roman Empire, big empires go down if the borders are not well-protected.'[2] Three years later, US president Donald Trump warned that immigration 'threatens our security and our economy and provides a gateway for terrorism'.[3] In 2022, UK Home Secretary Suella Braverman referred to growing numbers of boat crossings from France across the English Channel as an 'invasion on our southern coast'.[4]

Politicians frequently portray immigration as an assault on our borders by foreigners, something that is happening *to* us – or what French politicians habitually call an *immigration subie** when they argue in favour of an *immigration choisie*, a 'chosen immigration'. This has gone along with increasingly harsh political rhetoric – such as in Britain, where successive Labour and Conservative governments have endeavoured to create a 'hostile environment' for illegal migrants.

In the United States, too, politicians and pundits have frequently

* The French verb *subir* means to 'undergo' or 'suffer' something that you cannot control.

invoked the term 'invasion', while media images and political rhetoric about 'migrant caravans' fuel fears about a massive Third World exodus often portrayed as an attack on the sovereignty and safety of the US. This is anything but a new phenomenon. Back in the 1990s, growing immigration from Mexico gave rise to a narrative that portrayed Latino immigration as a threat to American society and culture. This was part of a broader resurgence of xenophobia in the US, with media and pundits comparing immigration to an 'invasion of illegal aliens'[5] in narratives that typically conflated legal and illegal immigration.

Similar language can be heard in Europe, where media and politicians have created the perception that millions of Africans are just waiting on their chance to move to Europe. In 2011, in response to the arrival of almost 5,000 boat migrants – mainly from Tunisia – on the Italian island of Lampedusa, Italian exterior minster Franco Frattini warned of 'an exodus of Biblical proportions', while interior minister Roberto Maroni talked about 'an invasion [. . .] that would bring any country to its knees'.[6] The popular 'exodus' narrative is often paired with the equally powerful 'invasion' narrative, which portrays immigration to Europe as increasingly clandestine in character.

But it is not only Western politicians who have bought into the idea of an impending immigration invasion. Leaders of countries of origin or transit, too, have used it as a negotiation chip to exact diplomatic, military and financial support. African leaders have frequently played into deep-seated European fears of a 'Black invasion' in their efforts to secure larger aid packages, or in seeking a return for their collaboration with border controls and taking back illegal migrants and rejected asylum seekers.

In 2010, Libyan leader Muammar Gaddafi warned that Europe 'could turn into Africa' as 'there are millions of Africans who want to come in', and argued that the EU should therefore pay Libya at least $6.3 billion (£4 billion) a year to stop illegal African immigration and avoid a 'Black Europe'.[7] In 2020, the Guatemalan president Alejandro Giammattei proclaimed that 'hunger, poverty and destruction do not have years to wait . . . If we don't want to see hordes of Central Americans looking to go to countries with a better quality of life, we have to create walls of prosperity in Central America.'[8]

The fear that migration is spinning out of control has prompted many politicians to argue that we need to step up border enforcement.

Others have argued that border controls won't solve the problem unless we (also) address 'root causes' such as poverty and conflict in origin countries. However, they all share the same perception: illegal immigration is getting out of hand. The extensive attention in politics and media given to border crises has fuelled the idea that South–North migration is mainly, and increasingly, about illegal immigration.

How it really works

The vast majority of people migrate legally

It is true that, over recent decades, Western countries have experienced increasing levels of immigration. It is also true that the share of non-European immigrants in Europe and North America has increased. As we saw in the previous chapter, this is part of a global migration reversal in which Europeans stopped massively emigrating to other parts of world. However, the idea that South–North migration is increasingly, and predominantly, about illegal migration is not backed up by evidence. Contrary to popular belief, the overwhelming majority of international migrants – including those moving from the South to the North – move legally, with passports and visas in hand. The extensive media coverage of illegal migration hugely inflates the true magnitude of the phenomenon.

The best data we have to estimate illegal migration trends is the number of people apprehended at international borders. Not all of these are illegal migrants. A small but significant share of border crossers are asylum seekers, who do not officially count as illegal migrants because seeking asylum is a fundamental human right. When referring to the arrival of both illegal migrants and asylum seekers this book therefore uses the term 'unsolicited border arrivals'. Border apprehensions are not an accurate reflection of the real number of unsolicited border crossings, because other migrants move across borders without being detected – for instance by hiding in trucks, vans or cars, or walking across borders, or climbing fences, with or without the help of smugglers.

Apprehension statistics also depend on the intensity of controls. The more intense the controls, the higher the number of migrants detected – but there is also the chance that the same person is counted twice as

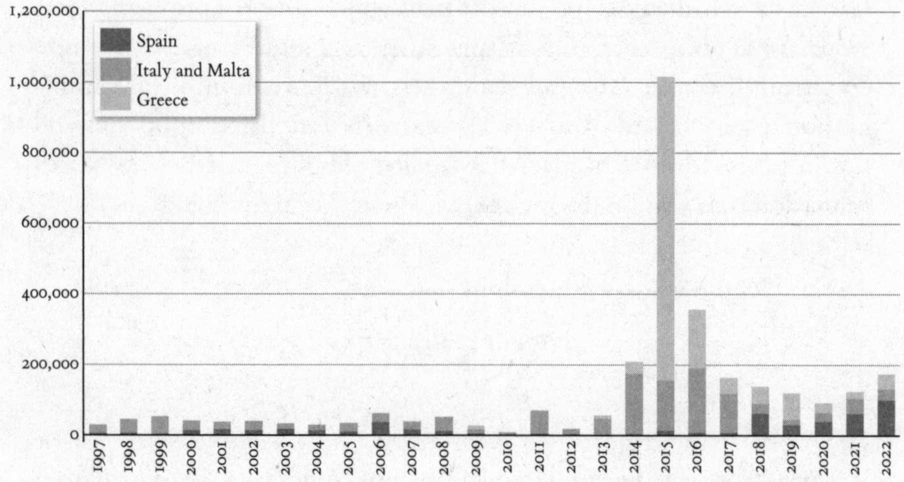

Graph 3: Registered unsolicited arrivals by boat of migrants and asylum seekers in Europe, 1997–2022[9]

deportees often try to migrate again. Such double-counting has inflated recent surges in apprehension statistics in the United States. But while apprehension statistics are anything but perfect, they are the best data we have to at least get some idea about long-term trends in illegal border crossings.

So, what does the data say? First of all, that illegal immigration seems to be a bigger problem in the US than in Europe. In the US, between 1990 and 2020 the average number of border apprehensions stood at just over 1 million per year. This is almost one-quarter – 23 per cent – of the average legal immigration to the US over the same period, which stood at 4.7 million per year – 1,024,000 permanent and 3,685,000 temporary migrants.

Compared to those numbers, illegal immigration to European countries is quite small. Graph 3 shows the number of border apprehensions of illegal migrants and asylum seekers crossing the Mediterranean. Between 1997, when systematic measurements started, and 2020, the average yearly number of registered sea border arrivals from North Africa in Italy, Spain and Malta stood at levels of around 47,300, 16,200 and 1,100 respectively. This makes a total average number of 64,600 yearly arrivals to these three countries.[10] Although these are significant numbers, this is only around 3–3.5 per cent of the (on average) 2 million non-EU migrants legally arriving in the EU every year. The number of arrivals reached a one-off peak in 2015, with almost a million asylum seekers and refugees from Syria and other countries crossing the Aegean Sea from Turkey into Greece, but the long-term pattern is relatively stable.

Of course, the real numbers are certainly higher, because much illegal migration has gone undetected, particularly in the 1990s when border enforcement was low and illegal migrants could cross borders rather easily. However, there is no doubt that illegal immigration accounts for a minority of arrivals in Europe.

Another way of estimating the magnitude of illegal migration is to look at the size of undocumented migrant populations. This is important, because the majority of undocumented migrants actually crossed the border legally, but *became* undocumented because they stayed longer than their visa or work permit allowed them. Such 'visa overstaying' – which no wall can stop – is the main source of illegal stays.

As with illegal border crossings, it's impossible to know exactly the number of undocumented migrants, but available estimates give a good idea about the relative magnitude. For Europe, the best available estimates – which date back to 2008 – tell us that there were an estimated 1.9–3.8 million undocumented migrants in the EU (including the UK), equal to 0.4–0.8 per cent of the total population and 7–13 per cent of the immigrant (foreign-born) population.[11] A review of recent studies estimated the size of the undocumented population in the UK at levels of between 674,000 and 800,000, or around 1 per cent of the British population.[12]

Compared to most of Europe, in the US illegal immigration seems a bigger problem. In 2018 there were about 10.5 million undocumented immigrants living in the US – that is, one-quarter of the total foreign-born population of 44.8 million in the same year, and 3.2 per cent of the total US population.[13]

Illegal immigration in Europe seems lower than in the US for several reasons. Geography is one factor – the Mexico–US border is easier to cross than the Mediterranean Sea. The virtual non-enforcement of laws prohibiting the employment of undocumented migrant workers in the US is another – although in Europe, too, worksite enforcement is rather low. Another explanation is that, with the fall of the Berlin Wall in 1989 and the EU enlargements in 2004 and 2007, western European countries tapped into new free-migration labour sources in eastern Europe.

However, another major factor is that European countries pursued several legalization ('amnesty') campaigns over recent decades, which meant that many undocumented migrants gained legal status, whereas the last migrant amnesty in the US dates back to 1986 because of a decades-long political stalemate on the issue.

In the longer term, illegal migration is not increasing

Most importantly, available evidence suggests that these numbers are relatively stable. This is also visible in the relative stability of the undocumented migrant population in the US – which, after a fast increase between 1990 and 2005, has been hovering at levels of around 11 million over the past two decades. While some undocumented migrants go back and some gain legal status, new illegal border-crossers and visa-overstayers are added. The main changes have been to the composition of the undocumented population, particularly through a decreasing share of Mexicans and an increasing share of Central Americans and Asians.[14]

It's clearly a myth, then, that Latin American migration to the US or African and Middle Eastern migration to Europe is mainly, or increasingly, about illegal border crossings. The myth of invasion ignores the fact that most migrants arrive without breaking any laws. For instance, based on available data we can estimate that about nine out of ten Africans migrating out of the continent cross borders legally.[15] However, these legal border passages that happen on a day-to-day basis – in airports and at land borders – are invisible, and rarely attract any media attention. Sensationalist media coverage and alarmist political rhetoric therefore exaggerate the true scale of the problem. Most importantly, there is no evidence of an increase in unsolicited border crossings. The pattern is rather an erratic one, with flows going up and down depending on labour demand in destination countries (for illegal migration) and conflict in origin countries (for refugee migration). While the media usually report on surges, they don't tend to report on the usual post-surge decline, which partly explains why we get the impression that illegal migration is increasing fast and spinning out of control.

What typically happens is that every surge in unsolicited border crossings is extrapolated into the future, creating the usual migration panic about impending migrant invasion. However, these surges are usually one-off peaks, which are always temporary. Surges are generally the result of pressing labour demand in destination countries in the absence of sufficient legal migration channels, or spikes in violence and conflict in origin countries. Surges can also be seasonal, with crossings usually increasing when weather circumstances improve during spring. As we only hear about such migration when it's rising, and hardly ever when it's plummeting, we're easily left with the skewed impression that the number of border crossings is ever-increasing and getting out of hand.

Most immigration stems from active labour recruitment

The myth of invasion disguises the fact that the vast majority of South–North migrants, including illegal immigrants, are not as unwanted as politicians often make us believe. Such rhetoric conceals that, by and large, immigration has not been something that is happening to us, or an external force threatening our society, but rather something that stems from deliberate efforts by governments and businesses to recruit migrant workers in response to job scarcities in sectors like agriculture, mining, healthcare, domestic work and hospitality.

Few Americans and Europeans realize that the presence of large Latino populations in the US, Caribbean and South Asian populations in the UK, and North and West African and Turkish populations in continental Europe all stem from active efforts to recruit workers. These countries *asked* them to come – it was an *immigration choisie*. Contrary to popular images, most migrants did not just 'show up' or 'pour in' or leave their homes out of desperation, but were workers who were actively sought in origin countries. The real migration story of the post-Second World War era is not one of massive arrivals of illegal immigrants, but of major changes in patterns of labour recruitment. Growing immigration was not a natural, spontaneous phenomenon, but was set in motion by deliberate recruitment prompted by growing labour shortages.

The increase in the number of non-European migrants to Western countries has been primarily driven by fundamental geographical shifts in the global supply of and demand for migrant labour. In Europe, initially, decolonization marked the end of European world hegemony *and* large-scale European emigration. The dismantling of the British, French, Dutch, Portuguese and Belgian colonial empires between 1945 and 1975 prompted the large-scale – both voluntary and forced – departure and repatriation of colonial administrators, soldiers, settlers, and other groups that no longer felt welcome or safe in the atmosphere of political turmoil and anti-colonial nationalism in newly independent countries. This triggered substantial migration from decolonized countries to the nations of former colonizers, such as Algerian *colons* moving to France, Indonesian mixed-race 'Indos' moving to the Netherlands, and Indian-heritage populations in Uganda and Kenya moving to Britain.

After the first phase of post-colonial migrations, labour demand soon took over as the main cause of increasing migration to western European countries. Over the course of the 1950s and 1960s, rapid economic growth fuelled increasing job shortages in industries and mines. This prompted the large-scale recruitment of migrant workers. For instance, between 1948 and 1971 Britain recruited many migrants from the Caribbean – named the 'Windrush generation' after the first ship that brought workers from Jamaica, Trinidad, Tobago and other islands – to help fill the post-war labour shortages in public services such as London Transport, British Rail and the National Health Service (NHS), while various industries, including mining, recruited workers in Pakistan and Bangladesh.[16]

French industries sent recruiters to the rural areas of their former colonies in the Maghreb, Senegal and Mali to recruit able-bodied, hard-working peasant sons to work in mining, car manufacture, and other heavy industries and jobs the native French no longer wanted to do. Between 1963 and 1982, the French government also recruited 186,000 workers from the overseas territories Réunion, Guadeloupe and Martinique to work in various government services.[17]

In the First and Second World Wars, the French and British had enlisted hundreds of thousands of colonial 'subjects' to fight on Europe's battlefields. The French army recruited Senegalese, Malian, Moroccan, Algerian and Tunisian soldiers.[18] Likewise, some 2 million Indians served in the British Indian Army, and 24,000 died in the Burma, North African and Italian campaigns. Some 30,000 Jamaicans and other Caribbean men served in the army on the battlefields, and with the Royal Air Force and Merchant Navy. This would sow the seeds for the labour migrations to Britain and France that ensued soon after the Second World War. For example, the migration of Sikhs to Southall in West

London was initiated by a former British officer in the Indian Army working for the R. Woolf Rubber Factory.[19]

Likewise, industries and mining companies in Germany, the Netherlands, Belgium, Switzerland and Sweden pressed their governments to sign guest worker agreements with governments in Italy, Spain, Portugal, Greece and former Yugoslavia from the 1950s. However, as growing prosperity in southern European countries decreased their emigration potential in the 1960s and 1970s, governments and employers tapped into new sources of migrant labour by recruiting workers from Turkey, Morocco and Tunisia.

Once migrant communities were established, new workers started arriving more spontaneously, and sometimes illegally, with migrants being informed about new jobs and helped by already-settled migrants. Although some workers arrived without permits, there were no visas, and as there were huge labour shortages, most of them could secure legal residency relatively easily.

How the United States recruited migrant workers

In Europe, and France and Britain in particular, the social, economic and cultural ties created through centuries of colonial occupation led to a reverse flow of migrant workers from former colonies through recruitment after independence. In a similar way, increasing global US hegemony from the late nineteenth century would shape twentieth-century migration patterns towards America.

The US occupation of Puerto Rico and the Philippines after the Spanish-American War of 1898 prompted the large-scale recruitment of workers. Puerto Ricans started migrating as contract workers, first to sugar-cane plantations in Hawaii – another US overseas territory before its full incorporation as a state in 1959 – and from there to the US mainland. The extension of US citizenship to Puerto Ricans in 1917 further boosted migration.[20]

Filipino migration to the US also had roots in recruitment: in 1906, the first Filipino workers were hired to work on the sugar-cane and pineapple plantations of Hawaii. From there, they migrated to the US mainland, attracted by farm jobs in California, Washington and Oregon, and the salmon canneries of Alaska, while others were employed in the Merchant Marine. As de facto colonial subjects, Filipinos could move freely to America until Congress established a Filipino immigration quota in 1934.[21] Many Filipinos served in the US Navy, which also provided a route to US citizenship. Likewise, immigration to the US from Korea began with active labour recruitment. This was set in motion after the Chinese Exclusion Act of 1882, which prohibited Chinese immigration, encouraged employers to recruit Korean workers, although Korean and Filipino immigration dropped after Congress passed the Oriental Exclusion Act of 1924.[22]

In the US, immigration from southern and eastern Europe halted after 1914 because of growing anti-immigrant sentiment – while the relatively modest Asian immigration was also being curtailed. The resulting labour shortages prompted employers to recruit Black workers in the US South. This would set in motion the 'Great Migration' of approximately 6 million African American workers fleeing racism and economic exploitation in the Southern states to work in the industries of the Northeast, Midwest and West.[23]

From 1942 onwards, however, the war effort and massive military conscription – combined with fast economic growth – again created huge job shortages in various sectors. This pushed the US government to initiate the Bracero Program, which between 1942 and 1964 recruited 4.5 million young Mexicans to work in agriculture and railway-track maintenance in twenty-four states. Although it was officially considered temporary labour, the programme effectively kicked off large-scale permanent migration from Mexico to the US. Increasing labour demand in manufacturing, agriculture and domestic work would also stimulate immigration from Puerto Rico and other Latin American countries.[24]

Most illegal migrants are wanted workers, too

In the 1970s, West European countries as well as the US stopped active recruitment, followed in the 1980s by the introduction of travel visa requirements to prevent free entry, and the stepping-up of border enforcement from the 1990s. However, this did not stop immigration, as labour demand remained high, particularly with the resumption of economic growth and growing labour shortages. The fall of the Berlin Wall, the end of communist regimes, and EU enlargement all helped to create a new migration frontier in eastern Europe. Over the 1990s and

2000s, central and eastern European countries evolved into major sources of migrant workers for western Europe. However, increasing labour demand and family reunification would continue to fuel growing migration of lower- and higher-skilled workers from outside the European Union – from traditional origin countries in North Africa and Turkey but also from countries such as Ukraine, Russia, China, Nigeria, Ghana and Senegal.

Another change was that former origin countries in southern Europe, which had supplied workers to West European and American industries for over a century, started evolving into major migration destinations themselves. Particularly in Spain and Italy, growing labour shortages in agriculture, construction, domestic and other service jobs led to increasing immigration from North and West Africa, Latin America and later also eastern Europe.

While most workers continued to arrive legally, growing border restrictions increased visa overstaying and illegal immigration – in the US principally from Mexico, and in Europe principally from Morocco, Algeria, Tunisia and Turkey. However, this illegal migration has nothing to do with an 'exodus' or 'foreign invasion', but is largely a response to labour shortages, often facilitated by informal recruitment systems and word-of-mouth referrals. In other words, most illegal migrants are wanted workers.

Despite anti-immigration rhetoric and massive investments in border enforcement, governments have largely tolerated this, just as they have turned a blind eye to the illegal deployment of undocumented workers, as they fill urgent labour shortages in sectors such as agriculture, construction, domestic work, hospitality, and child and elder care. It's not so much borders that are beyond control, but immigration systems that are partly dysfunctional or 'broken' – with a large gap between the demand for foreign workers and the number of legal immigration channels to accommodate such a demand. This is helping to drive migration underground and facilitating the widespread exploitation of migrant workers.

The main point is that most immigration remains legal. However, because the days of official recruitment by governments are largely over, this 'wanted' dimension of legal and illegal immigration has become less visible. Reflecting a general move towards economic deregulation, private recruitment agencies have increasingly taken over the role of governments in recruiting workers. But while Western governments no longer play the central role, they continue to facilitate the recruitment of migrant workers either through official immigration policies or through policies whose euphemistic names avoid the controversial M-word but in reality are designed to facilitate immigration. Good examples of these are au pair programmes that allow the entry of care and domestic workers into western Europe, international traineeships in Japan and South Korea, and holiday worker programmes run by Australia.

The myth of invasion

The arrival of refugees and migrants at borders represents a major humanitarian problem. Many migrants and refugees are injured or die during their attempts to cross borders, and suffer severe abuse and extortion by police, border guards and criminals. However, in order to find solutions to these problems it is important to understand the true nature, scale and causes of the phenomenon. And the reality has little to do with political fearmongering about increasingly uncontrollable immigration waves crashing on the shores of the Wealthy West.

First of all, there is no evidence that immigration is spinning out of control. It is true that Western societies have experienced levels of immigration and settlement that are higher than most expected a few decades ago. But this increase is mainly down to *legal* immigration, largely driven by labour demand. There is a large gap between labour demand and legal migration channels, and so a significant share of migration has been illegal, but it is not as massive as many people think.

However, the most important observation is that immigration is not something happening to us (an *immigration subie*), but largely stems from active efforts by governments and businesses to recruit migrant workers (an *immigration choisie*), even though such workers are officially framed as 'undesired'. The evidence shows that legal and illegal immigration is much more 'wanted' than belligerent political rhetoric about 'fighting illegal migration' and 'combating smuggling' seems to suggest.

The modern-day immigration of migrant workers, families and refugees – whether legal or illegal – can simply not be compared to invasions or the ventures of European colonialists who, over five centuries, invaded and occupied foreign lands by brute military force. Such

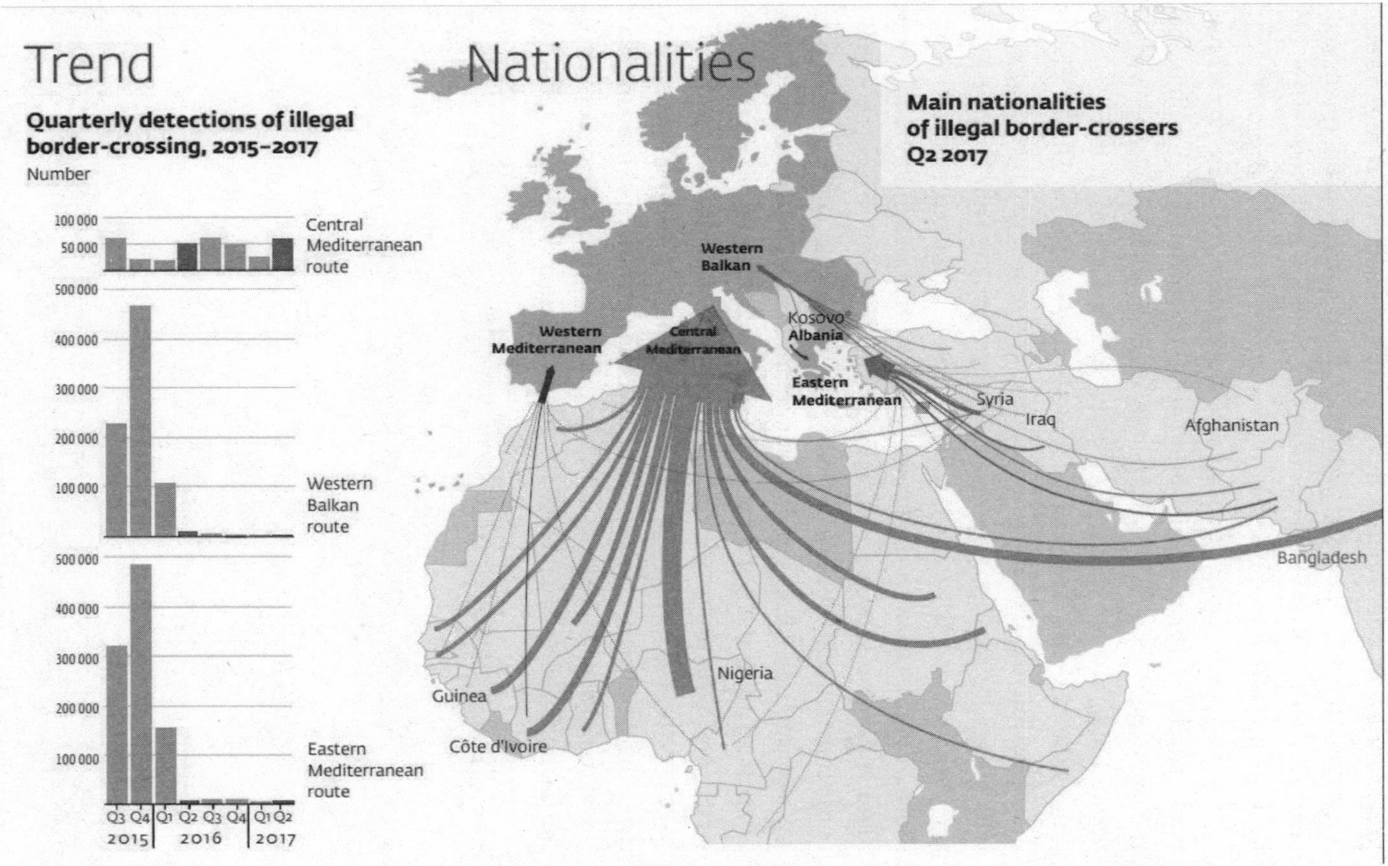

Map 2: A migration map published in 2017 by Frontex, the European border and coastguard agency, depicting illegal border crossings

comparisons expose the myth of invasion for what it really is: a form of propaganda that is deliberately designed to sow panic and fear. Governments, media and migration agencies have actively fabricated and recycled the idea that the West is besieged, not only in the way they talk about illegal migration, but also in how they – literally – depict it.

For instance, Frontex, the EU's border agency, regularly publishes maps that depict illegal immigration as a foreign invasion. Map 2 is one such map, published in 2017.[25] An array of huge arrows, coloured red in the original and all menacingly pointing to Europe, reinforces the impression that these are gigantic flows – an onslaught on Europe's borders. By depicting illegal immigration as a huge security threat, against which we have to arm ourselves, politicians tap into our deepest fears and tribal instincts while portraying themselves as strong leaders or saviours who will defend their people against foreign enemies by fighting illegal immigration, smugglers and traffickers.

Of course, both the scale and nature of illegal immigration do not in any way resemble a foreign invasion. Immigrants and refugees do not arrive with gunboats, fighter jets, or with the aim to overthrow governments. Nor is there a massive exodus of illegal migrants from the Global South to the Global North. These are myths that reinforce narratives depicting immigration as out of control, and therefore as a fundamental threat to economies, security and identity. These fears are a product of the imagination. In brief, there is no need to panic.

Myth 3: The world is facing a refugee crisis

Politicians, experts and media often claim that there is an unprecedented global 'refugee crisis'. This belief is linked to the widespread perception that growing conflict and oppression in Latin America, the Middle East and Africa are prompting more and more people to flee their homelands and seek a better future in the West. As a consequence, swelling tides of refugees seem to be increasingly overburdening asylum systems in Western countries.

In Europe, the debate about refugees reached fever pitch in 2015, when about 1 million Syrian refugees moved into Europe. Since then, a series of new border crises have occurred in other parts of the world – such as the increasing numbers of people fleeing violence and poverty in Central America, using Mexico as a transit country to move to the US, and the massive movements of refugees out of Venezuela. From March 2022, the Russian invasion of Ukraine prompted millions to flee to Poland, Slovakia, Hungary and Moldova, and from there into western Europe, seemingly adding to the rapidly multiplying number of refugee crises elsewhere in the world.

As the cycle of violence and conflict seems never-ending, the situation of refugees trying to cross borders seems increasingly desperate. The idea that we are facing a refugee crisis is sustained by claims from international organizations. In 2022, UNHCR chief Filippo Grandi claimed that 'every year of the last decade, the numbers have climbed', and warned: 'Either the international community comes together to take action to address this human tragedy, resolve conflicts and find lasting solutions, or this terrible trend will continue.'[1]

In brief, as the world seems on fire, the global refugee crisis seems to be getting out of hand. Politicians, experts and media have also been fuelling the common perception that numbers of refugees have soared rapidly in the recent past – and will only continue to increase, as a result of a toxic mix of warfare, conflict, poverty, inequality and climate change.

The refugee crisis narrative is also based on the widespread belief that more and more asylum seekers are not 'real' refugees, but are in fact economic migrants posturing as refugees. Politicians and media have repeatedly claimed that these 'bogus' asylum seekers abuse the asylum channel to avoid deportation and gain legal status. By trying to play the system, they are muddying the waters for 'real' refugees. Tapping into similar narratives, agencies like UNHCR and IOM have spread the idea that refugee flows have increasingly become 'mixed', with more and more economic migrants mingling with 'real' refugees.

This has created the impression that a soaring number of asylum applicants have put Western refugee systems under such pressure that they are on the verge of collapsing. This would leave us with no other choice than to dismantle current asylum systems. The United Nations High Commissioner for Refugees was created in 1950 to address the refugee crisis resulting from the Second World War. The modern refugee regime is based on the UN Refugee Convention that was established one year later. According to the Convention, it is a fundamental human right to cross international borders to seek protection from violence and persecution, so the idea of an 'illegal asylum seeker' is a contradiction in terms. Importantly, the Convention prohibits signatories from expelling or deporting asylum seekers to countries where they may fear danger of persecution, without first investigating whether they have made a legitimate claim for refugee status. This 'non-refoulement' principle is still the linchpin of the modern refugee system, and is quite unpopular with tough-on-immigration politicians.

UN refugee

The argument now is that this system that was designed to manage European refugee flows is no longer sustainable in an increasingly violent and unstable world. As socialist French prime minister Michel Rocard famously argued back in 1989, '*La France ne peut pas accueillir toute la misère du monde*' ('France cannot welcome all the misery of the world'). Politicians have increasingly claimed that, given the huge surge in refugee numbers, we have no choice but to curtail the right to asylum and reinforce border controls, and that these policies are a 'necessary evil' to prevent our borders being overrun and our asylum systems becoming overwhelmed. This has gone along with regular pleas to revise the UN Refugee Convention. In 2003, Tony Blair called it 'completely out of date' in terms of its ability to tackle the problems of the mass migration of people around the world.[2]

All of this reflects a growing political consensus that, in order to prevent our asylum systems from collapsing, we have no other choice than to: (1) put in place 'firm but fair' asylum policies that sift out 'real' refugees from 'bogus' asylum seekers; (2) deter 'bogus' asylum seekers by sending them back to transit states, or process their cases in 'third countries'; and (3) provide 'regional solutions', or in other words have the international community create safe havens and economic opportunities for refugees in their regions of origin so that they no longer have to come to the West.

Destination countries have increasingly tried to outsource asylum processing by seeking collaboration with third countries. In 2013, the Australian government led by Labor prime minister Kevin Rudd pioneered this 'tough line' approach by sending asylum seekers to the small Pacific islands of Manus and Nauru to be detained while awaiting the outcome of their asylum applications. Other Western countries have followed Australia's example: Greece's mass detention of asylum seekers in camps on a few islands like Lesbos (essentially turning Greece into a 'buffer state'[3]); Trump's 'Remain in Mexico' policy (forcing asylum seekers to await processing of their asylum claims in Mexico[4]); and Denmark's and Britain's attempts to send asylum seekers to Rwanda.

How it really works

Refugee numbers are relatively small and not accelerating

The idea that the West is facing an unprecedented – and increasingly untenable – refugee crisis is based on the assumptions that: (1) refugee numbers are at an all-time high; (2) the number of refugees coming to the West is increasing at a staggering pace; and (3) more and more asylum seekers are in fact economic migrants ('bogus' asylum seekers). However, the facts challenge every one of these three assumptions.

First of all, contemporary levels of refugee migration are anything but unprecedented. Refugee migration is much smaller than media coverage and political rhetoric suggest. Since the 1950s, refugee numbers have been between 0.1 and 0.35 per cent of the world population, and refugees form only a small part of the international migrant population. Between 1985 and 2021, the estimated size of the total international refugee population fluctuated between 9 and 21 million, which is roughly between 7 and 12 per cent of the total number of international migrants in the world.

Second, there is no evidence of a long-term increase in refugee migration. The pattern is rather one of fluctuation, with refugee numbers going up and down according to levels of conflict in origin countries. Refugee numbers peaked at 16 million in the early 1990s, a period of increasing conflict around the world – in former Yugoslavia, the Horn of Africa (Somalia in particular), and countries in the African Great Lakes region such as the Democratic Republic of Congo, Rwanda and Burundi. The wars in former Yugoslavia in particular led to increased refugee movement to western Europe, accompanied by growing political panic about the alleged mass movements of 'bogus' asylum seekers. After 1993, however, global refugee numbers plummeted – falling to 9 million by the early 2000s. Numbers were so low that refugee experts were increasingly out of work and insiders even started to question the *raison d'être* of UNHCR.

Numbers started going up again in 2005, partly because of protracted conflicts in Afghanistan and Iraq following the US-led invasions of 2001 and 2003. From 2011, the Arab Spring sparked a wave of pro-democracy street protests that were met by severe government repression. This sparked civil conflict in various countries, particularly

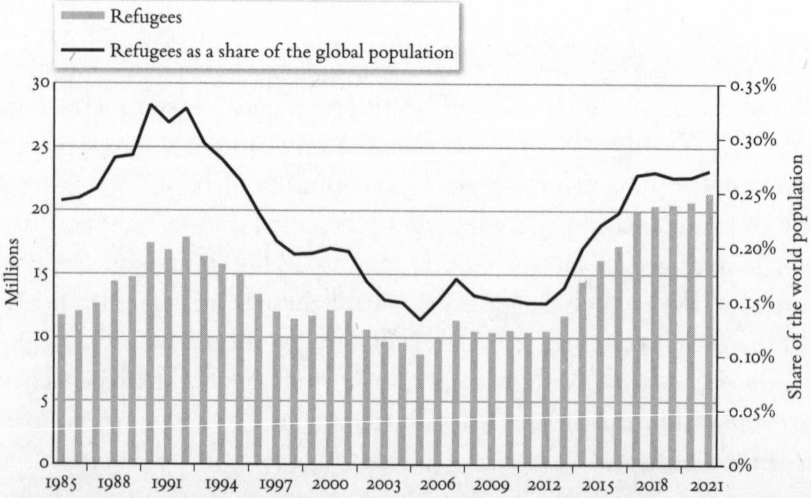

Graph 4: Total worldwide refugee numbers as a percentage of the global population, 1985–2021

Libya, Yemen and Syria. In Syria, it prompted the internal displacement of 6.2 million Syrians, while 5.6 million sought refuge in neighbouring countries. In more recent years, violent conflict and repression in South Sudan and Eritrea, the expulsion of the Rohingya Muslim minority from Myanmar, political crisis in Venezuela and the 2022 Russian invasion of Ukraine have further increased global refugee numbers.

These crises explain why the total number of international refugees had grown to 21.3 million at the end of 2021, and 26.7 million in 2022 (mainly because of the war in Ukraine).But although refugee numbers have increased, current levels are in fact similar to those in the early 1990s. As graph 4 shows, in 1992, 0.33 per cent of the world population were refugees, and this percentage was 0.25 in 2021. Looking at long-term trends, current refugee numbers are therefore not as unprecedented as they may seem at first sight.[5]

The real refugee crisis is in origin regions

The facts also defy the idea that swelling masses of refugees are on their way to the Wealthy West. In reality, the vast majority of refugees stay in neighbouring countries. According to official UNHCR data, in 2017 about 80 per cent of refugees resided in neighbouring countries and 85 per cent of all refugees had stayed in developing countries, percentages that have remained relatively stable in recent decades.[6] The main reason why most refugees generally don't travel far is because most prefer to stay close to home, in countries that are more familiar in terms of culture, religion and language. This also makes it easier to remain in touch with family and friends left behind in origin countries, and to return as soon as the situation allows. Furthermore, fleeing over large distances requires considerable resources. For those wishing to move further away, only a minority of refugees have the money, connections and papers required.

Despite politicians' talk about 'regional solutions' (the idea that refugees should be hosted by neighbouring countries to prevent massive numbers coming to the West), this has already been the reality for half a century. In 2018, Turkey hosted more than 3.6 million Syrian refugees, equivalent to about 4.4 per cent of its population of 82 million. In the same year, almost 1 million Syrian refugees lived in Lebanon, out of a total population of 6 million. By comparison, in the same year, 532,000 Syrians were living in Germany, 15,800 in France and 9,700 in the UK.[7] In the same vein, the majority of people who fled war-torn parts of Ukraine in 2022 moved either to safer regions in their own country or to neighbouring countries – principally Poland.

As most refugees stay close to home, the real refugee crisis is occurring not in the West, but in origin regions. Some of the poorest countries in the world host large numbers of refugees. While in 2018 the number of refugees born in African countries stood at 6 million, African countries hosted 5.5 million refugees in that same year, almost all of them from other African countries. About 92 per cent of African refugees remain in Africa, where the main refugee-hosting countries are Uganda, Ethiopia and Kenya – which have received large groups fleeing violent conflict in South Sudan, Somalia and the Democratic Republic of Congo. In 2021, of the 2.6 million registered Afghan refugees in the world, about 2.2 million (or 85 per cent) lived in Iran and Pakistan. And we see the same pattern in other world regions: Bangladesh hosts most refugees from Myanmar, while Colombia, Peru and Chile host most Venezuelan refugees.

Refugee numbers in Western countries only spike when there is conflict in the relative geographical vicinity, such as during the wars in former Yugoslavia in the early 1990s, the Syrian civil war and the Russian invasion of Ukraine. Numbers vary a lot across western Europe. Refugee numbers are highest in Germany, the fifth-most important refugee-hosting country in the world (after Turkey, Colombia, Pakistan and Uganda), with 1.15 million refugees in 2019 representing 1.38 per cent of the total German population. In relative terms, Scandinavian countries and the Netherlands also host large refugee populations. In many other countries, such as the UK and France, the numbers are actually rather low. In 2018, the 152,000 refugees and asylum seekers living in the UK represented 0.23 per cent of the total population.

In Canada, Australia and New Zealand, historically most refugees have arrived through official resettlement programmes, with governments inviting limited quotas of refugees to migrate permanently, after careful vetting in origin regions. They can do so partly because these countries are geographically further away from major conflict zones, hence there are far lower numbers of spontaneous arrivals of asylum seekers at the border. In Australia, for instance, despite the political upheaval around wow!

boat arrivals of asylum seekers, these numbers have never exceeded 21,000 per year – a small fraction of total legal immigration into Australia of 600, 000–800,000 per year over the 2010s.

There is no evidence of a rise in 'bogus' asylum claims

The evidence also contradicts the popular idea that the number of 'bogus' asylum seekers is rising fast and that migrant flows are becoming increasingly mixed because of growing numbers of asylum claimants posturing as refugees. Of all the available indicators, asylum rejection and acceptance rates are the best estimate we have of the relative share of legitimate asylum applicants. This is of course a highly imperfect measure, because some countries have much tougher procedures than others, and asylum rejection and acceptance rates vary across countries and over time. Yet trends in acceptance and rejection rates can still give us some general sense of the proportion of 'real' refugees among all asylum applicants.

The data reveals that in most Western countries, asylum rejection rates have remained remarkably stable over the past decades. For instance, in 2020, about 521,000 people applied for asylum in the EU, or 0.12 per cent of the total EU population of 448 million (excluding the UK). Of these applications, 40.7 per cent resulted in initial positive decisions. Of these 212,000 positive decisions, half were granted official refugee status. Another quarter received 'subsidiary protection status', which is given to asylum seekers who cannot prove that they are personally persecuted but who could face serious risk to their life or personal safety if deported. The latter category often includes people coming from war-torn countries.

Another quarter received a temporary authorization to stay for humanitarian reasons – because of illness, or because they were minors. If we include positive outcomes of appeals procedures, in total 281,000 asylum seekers were granted permission to stay in 2020. This is 9.5 per cent of the 2,955,000 people who legally migrated to the EU from non-EU countries in the same year.[8]

We see similar patterns in the UK. According to data compiled by Oxford University's Migration Observatory, in 2019 about 388,000 foreign-born people living in the UK had originally come to Britain to seek asylum. This is equivalent to 4 per cent of Britain's 9.5 million foreign-born population during that year.

In 2019, there were about five asylum applications for every 10,000 people living in the UK, or about 0.05 per cent of the total population. British refugee recognition rates are roughly comparable to those of the EU. Including appeals, around 54 per cent of original asylum applications submitted between 2016 and 2018 had received a grant of asylum-related protection by May 2020 – up from 36 per cent at initial decision.[9]

Since the 2010s, the US has seen a significant increase in the number of asylum seekers spontaneously arriving at the border, partly because of growing violence and political crises in Central America, Venezuela and Haiti. Still, refugee recognition data does not provide evidence of a massive increase in the numbers of 'bogus' asylum seekers. In the US, the asylum denial rate fluctuated between 50 and 60 per cent over the period between 2000 and 2017, although it has been increasing in recent years because of a political drive to deny asylum seekers access to the US refugee admission system.[10]

So, if we focus on the longer term, trends have been remarkably consistent across most Western countries. Roughly half of asylum applicants see their cases eventually approved. In an analysis of recognition rates for asylum applicants from sixty-five origin countries to twenty European countries from 2003 to 2017, economic historian Timothy Hatton even found a certain increasing trend. This was mainly because a growing share of asylum seekers were coming from countries with high levels of political terror and repression, such as Syria, Eritrea and Yemen. EU directives seeking to harmonize asylum policy between countries – to prevent a 'race to the bottom' – have also played a modest role in increasing recognition rates. However, there are big differences across Europe, with countries like France, Greece, Spain and Hungary having recognition rates of below 20 per cent; Denmark, Norway and Switzerland above 40 per cent; and Germany and the UK occupying more intermediate positions.[11]

If it were really true that unsolicited migrant flows had become increasingly mixed and the number of 'bogus' asylum seekers had increased, we would have expected an *increase* in rejection rates. Recognition rates have remained remarkably stable, suggesting that a large share are valid asylum claims. Such evidence defies the idea that modern refugee migration is increasingly about 'mixed flows'.

Inflating refugee numbers

The facts challenge the idea that the West is succumbing under the weight of increasing arrivals of refugees and asylum seekers. The chance of a legitimate claim to asylum not being approved is arguably higher than the chance of a 'bogus' asylum seeker slipping through the net. The number of asylum applications filed in Western countries has primarily fluctuated with levels of conflict in neighbouring regions,[12] and there is no evidence of a long-term increasing trend. This reveals a simple truth: most people flee because of conflict and oppression.

So why do we then *think* that refugee numbers are spinning out of control? Part of the answer is that ever since the fall of the Berlin Wall in 1989, political rhetoric and sensationalist media coverage have created the *impression* that refugee flows are much bigger than they really are. And organizations like UNHCR and IOM present their data in such a way as to back up these claims. For instance, UNHCR data seems to show that the total number of displaced people in the world increased from 1.8 million in 1951 to 20 million in 2005, accelerating to 62 million in 2018, and then suddenly hiked up to almost 89 million in 2021 and 100 million in 2022.[13]

I have always found such claims difficult to believe. After all, levels of warfare and political oppression were actually higher in the post-Second World War decades than in more recent years. So why would refugee numbers be higher now? To investigate the validity of such claims, my colleague Sonja Fransen and I conducted a study in which we analysed long-term trends of refugee migration around the world based on historical UNHCR data.[14] We discovered that what *appears* to be an unprecedented increase in refugee numbers is in reality a statistical artefact caused by the inclusion of populations and countries that were previously excluded from displacement statistics.

In 1951, one year after its establishment, UNHCR started registering refugee data. In that year, its database covered information for only 21 countries, and the real number of refugees was of course much higher. From then on, the number of countries and territories included in UNHCR statistics increased, to 76 in 1970, 147 in 1990, 211 in 2010 and 216 in 2018. As the number of countries included in the UNHCR database went up, so did refugee numbers. This means that official UNHCR data severely underestimates past refugee numbers, because the data for most countries is missing over the 1950–1990 period.

A second source of problems is that UNHCR has added new categories of displaced people to their databases. In particular, internally displaced persons (IDPs) – a very broad category that includes all persons forced or obliged to leave their home because of armed conflict, violence, persecution or natural or human-made disasters, without crossing borders.

Most of the huge hike in global displacement levels reported by UNHCR is explained by a sharp increase in IDP numbers, from 4.2 million in 2003 to 41.4 million in 2018. This 41.4 million was two times higher than the number of international refugees in the same year. This does not of course mean that there were no IDPs in previous years, but that they were not included in past displacement statistics. By basically comparing apples and oranges, most of what appears to be a spectacular increase in refugee numbers is the artificial result of a rather misleading presentation of data.

Refugee flows go up and down with warfare

Graph 5 shows how many people were displaced by violent conflict and oppression in the years between 1977 and 2022. It confirms that, instead of a linear upward trend, refugee movements have gone up and down alongside the outbreak of violent conflicts. In the late 1970s, the Ogaden War produced many refugees, particularly those moving from Ethiopia to Somalia. The Soviet invasion of Afghanistan produced 4.2 million refugees between 1980 and 1982 alone, and 5.8 million refugees in total until the Soviet withdrawal in 1989, the bulk of them fleeing to neighbouring Iran and Pakistan. Over the 1980s, conflicts in sub-Saharan Africa displaced refugees mainly from Ethiopia, Rwanda, Mozambique and Liberia, although globally the numbers of refugees subsided until the 1991 Gulf War displaced 1.4 million Iraqis, most of them fleeing to Iran. The same year also marked the beginning of the Yugoslav Wars, generating major refugee flows, particularly from Bosnia.

In 1994, the Rwandan genocide prompted some 2.3 million – equal to one-third of the country's population – to flee, almost exclusively to the Democratic Republic of Congo, Tanzania and Burundi. In 1999, the Kosovo war and NATO bombings in Serbia would generate the latest

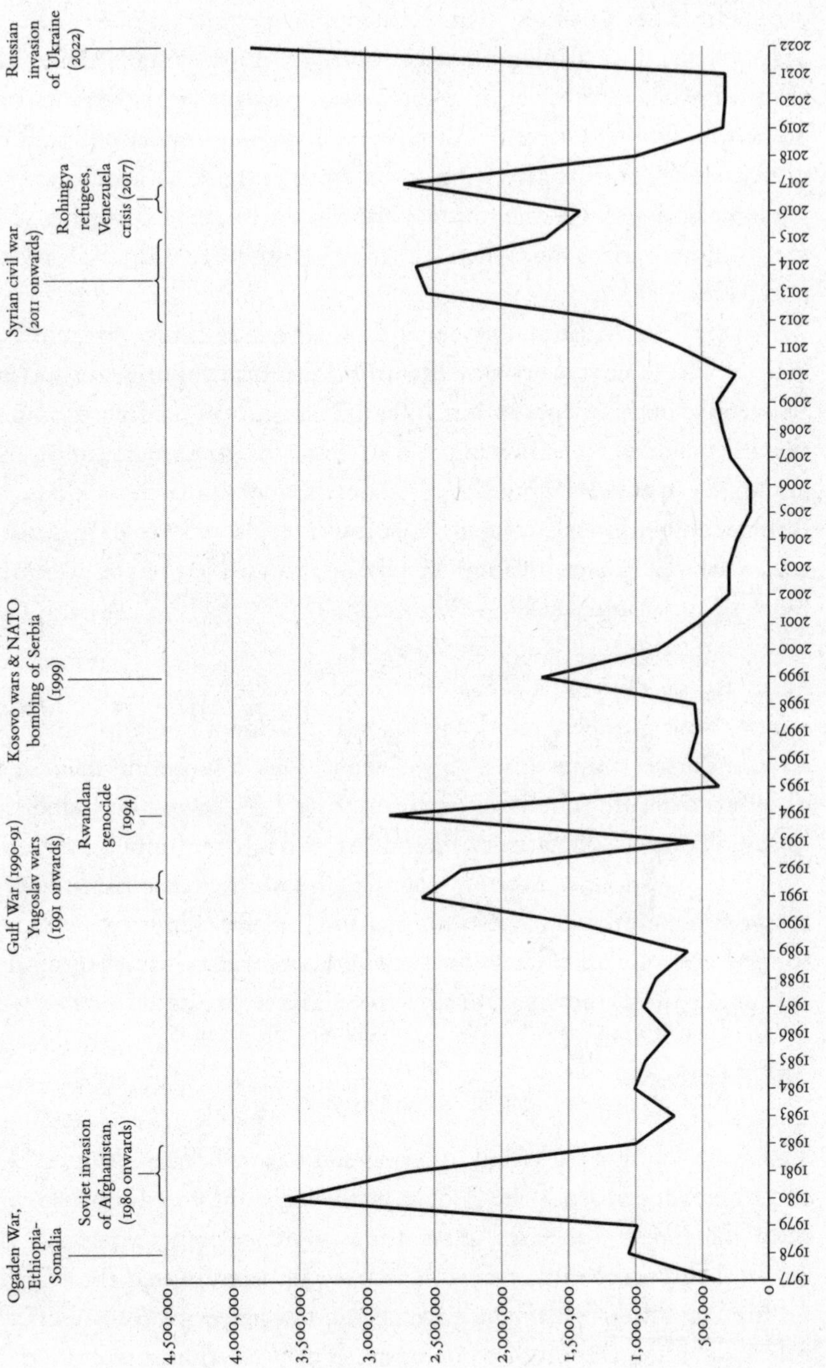

Graph 5: Global refugee displacements, 1977–2022[15]

major refugee flow in former Yugoslavia, displacing almost 1 million people from Serbia and Kosovo. The 2000–10 period was one of relative peace, with most displacement occurring in sub-Saharan Africa; this changed when protest against dictatorial regimes in the Arab world broke out in 2011. Government repression and ensuing conflict caused displacement, particularly from Syria, with extreme violence generating large-scale refugee migration. Over the entire 2012–21 period, some 8.7 million Syrians fled their country, 41 per cent of the pre-war population.

In 2017, the Myanmar government expelled almost 700,000 Rohingya. The violent repression of anti-regime protests in Venezuela and an overall climate of corruption, hyperinflation and insecurity prompted the first major refugee flow in Latin America for decades, causing 4 million to flee in 2018 and 2019 alone – mainly to Colombia, Peru and Chile. Refugee migration then stabilized at lower levels, only to peak again in 2022 with the Soviet invasion of Ukraine, which led to the westward flight of at least 2.3 million Ukrainians – principally to Poland, Germany and the Czech Republic.

Instead of showing a long-term trend, therefore, the pattern is very erratic, with numbers rapidly going up and down but not showing a clear linear trend over time. This challenges the assumption that we are experiencing a global refugee crisis. As Sonja Fransen and I concluded in our study on refugee statistics, recent surges in refugee numbers as well as asylum applications in Western countries do not reflect a 'rising tide' of refugee migration, but rather a normal and therefore temporary response to increases in conflict levels in particular countries, with refugee numbers usually going down again after the conflicts subside.

The world has become more peaceful

Thanks to satellite television, internet and smartphones, images of war and oppression reach more people, more frequently and more powerfully than ever. Increased *exposure* to violence and oppression and political rhetoric easily creates the wrong impression that the world is on fire. Sensationalist media coverage and political propaganda play a role in creating the myth of invasion, but ideas about huge floods of refugees overwhelming asylum systems are also based on overly pessimistic thinking about the state of the world.

Going further back in time, there are good reasons to believe that displacement levels in the early and mid-twentieth century were much higher than in the post-Second World War period covered by UNHCR data, simply because this was a much more violent period. For instance, between 1914 and 1918 the First World War displaced an estimated 9.5 million Europeans. In 1923, the formation of the modern Turkish nation out of the ashes of the Ottoman Empire prompted the forced migration of over 1.2 million Greeks out of Turkey, and 350,000–400,000 ethnic Turks from Greece to Turkey.[16]

In Asia, the war between China and Japan (1937–45) displaced an estimated 60–95 million people,[17] while Japanese aggression during the Second World War led to mass displacement and forced labour throughout South-East Asia, and between 3 million and 10 million deaths.[18] It is thought that the Second World War displaced approximately 60 million Europeans.[19] About 6 million European Jews and millions of ethnic Serbs, Poles and Russians were murdered by the Nazi regime. The Nazis killed 20.9 million in total, 8.3 million of whom were East Europeans.[20]

The end of the war led to large-scale population movements of Holocaust survivors, displaced persons and various ethnic groups, such as the approximately 12 million ethnic Germans expelled as part of ethnic cleansing policies in eastern Europe.[21] In total, some 55 million Europeans would have been displaced between 1939 and 1947.[22] In the direct aftermath of the war, according to some estimates, the global population of displaced people was as high as 175 million just *before* UNHCR started compiling refugee statistics.[23] This was approximately 8 per cent of the world population at the time, significantly higher than the 0.3 per cent that are refugees now.

Many refugees of the post-war decades were not included in official statistics, particularly if they were not European. Between 1947 and 1951, the withdrawal of the British from India and the inter-religious tension and violence surrounding Partition prompted the displacement of about 14 million people, many of whom crossed the border between the two new states of Pakistan and India.[24] Furthermore, the foundation of the State of Israel in 1948 led to the mass expulsion of Palestinians.

In 1962, over 1 million *colons* (descendants of French and other European settlers) and *harkis* (Algerians who served with the French Army) left after Algeria achieved independence from France.[25] Between 1945 and the early 1960s, 375,000 mixed-race 'repatriates' from the former

Dutch East Indies (now Indonesia) felt forced to move to the Netherlands.[26] In 1972, about 50,000 ethnic Indians – descendants of former contract workers and traders – fled Uganda (mainly to Kenya and Britain) on the orders of military dictator Idi Amin, who accused Ugandan Asians of being 'bloodsuckers' who were 'milking Uganda's money'.[27]

So, the idea that we face a global refugee crisis is partly based on the flawed assumptions that levels of warfare and oppression have generally increased. The evidence rather points in the opposite direction: the world has generally become more peaceful. Using data on the number of battle-related deaths as a measure for violence, Sonja Fransen and I found that there has clearly been a long-term decreasing trend in the intensity and severity of warfare.[28] Although the *number* of conflicts has not decreased, they have become much less lethal.

The refugee crisis is a political crisis

The evidence shows that UNHCR and other humanitarian organizations misrepresent refugee numbers, sustaining the idea that refugee and asylum migration has reached unprecedented heights. While these organizations may do this to attract attention and funding to pursue their important activities, it also makes them complicit in reinforcing the perception that refugee migration is getting out of hand. This perception of a 'refugee crisis' has become deeply ingrained in the collective psyche, even extending as far as school atlases: for instance, a 2015 edition of *De Grote Bosatlas*, used in many schools in the Netherlands, continued this alarmist misrepresentation by including large red arrows in their maps to depict the flows of asylum seekers.

Unfortunately, such misrepresentations undermine the case for refugee protection if people start to believe that current numbers of refugees are indeed exceeding the absorption capacity of destination societies and asylum systems. Politicians, too, have an interest in claiming that refugee numbers are unsustainably high, as this can provide justification for further stepping up border controls, illegally 'pushing back' asylum seekers and subjecting them to harsh and inhumane treatment.

Obviously, the arrival of large numbers of refugees can be challenging for populations living near border-crossing points or in towns and neighbourhoods where asylum seeker centres are located. Sudden refugee influxes can overwhelm communities and put significant pressure on local resources. But while the problems that large refugee inflows can generate on the local level should not be trivialized, there is no scientific basis for the claim that, on a national or international level, asylum systems are on the verge of collapsing because refugee numbers have reached record levels.

The data clearly defies the widespread belief that the West is besieged by a rising tide of refugees that exceeds the capacity of asylum systems. As we have seen, in the post-war decades, Western countries – and those in Europe in particular – were able to deal with much higher refugee numbers. While refugee numbers are not much higher than in the past, most refugees stay close to home, and some of the poorest countries in the world bear the heaviest burden. What is commonly called the 'refugee crisis' is therefore not so much a crisis of numbers as a political crisis, reflecting a lack of political will to host refugees and to share that responsibility with other destination states.

Myth 4: Our societies are more diverse than ever

Growing immigration has led to historically unprecedented levels of racial, cultural and religious diversity in Western societies. This is perhaps the most commonly held belief about immigration, shared by both immigration enthusiasts and immigration sceptics. It seems to make a lot of sense: after all, immigrant populations in the West have become increasingly non-European, non-white and non-Christian.

Whereas for five centuries Europeans used to move and settle in other parts of the world, these patterns reversed in the decades following the end of Second World War. As Europeans stopped venturing out overseas in large numbers, more and more Asian, Latin American, Caribbean and African migrants settled in western Europe, North America, Australia and New Zealand. This has fuelled the idea that contemporary Western societies have reached levels of diversity that are unique and unprecedented. While liberal groups celebrate diversity as a vital source of innovation and cultural renewal, conservatives see contemporary levels of diversity as a potential threat to social cohesion and the cultural integrity of destination societies.

In the US, the large-scale settlement of Mexican, Puerto Rican and other Latino migrants has raised anxieties among some white majority groups about the growing influence of the Spanish language and Latino culture. In western Europe, concerns have focused on the perceived lack of integration of certain migrant groups, primarily those from Muslim-majority countries such as Pakistan, Bangladesh, Turkey and Morocco. The 9/11 terror attacks in the US and a subsequent series of attacks by Islamist radicals in Europe reinforced concerns that 'too high' immigration is a potential threat to social cohesion, national identity and security.

As a result, politicians have come under mounting pressure to acknowledge the challenges that current levels of diversity bring, and to take people's concerns about immigration more seriously to prevent social tensions and the erosion of trust and social cohesion. Increasingly, politicians and pundits have expressed concern that diversity may be exceeding the absorption capacity of destination societies. This has gone along with worries that growing numbers of immigrants and minorities of non-Western origin are living parallel lives, undermining the lifestyles, cultures and core values of destination societies.

Pundits and commentators have regularly cast these problems as part of a broader 'clash of civilizations' between Western-secular cultures of toleration and liberalism and allegedly religious cultures of rigid conservativism or even intolerance and religious fanaticism.[1] This is often linked to the idea that the core values of the latter's societies and religions are too different from, and therefore irreconcilable with, those of host societies. These ideas have gained considerable traction at the highest political level, although usually in a more civil tone. In 2015, for instance, Theresa May said in an official speech that: 'When immigration is too high, when the pace of change is too fast, it's impossible to build a cohesive society.'[2]

Not everybody agrees with such views. Many other observers reject such ideas as racist and xenophobic, taking the opposite position and celebrating increased ethnic, racial and religious diversity as a vibrant force of cultural renewal and good. Corporate lobbies also tend to advocate immigration and diversity as important engines of innovation and economic growth. Other people are more indifferent, or take a more ambivalent position. However, despite the often diametrically opposed *opinions* about the issue, all camps seem to agree on one fundamental thing: the 'fact' that we currently live in exceptionally diverse societies.

How it really works

We come from a much more diverse past than we think

In chapter 2, we saw that about 3 per cent of the world population is composed of international migrants, and that – contrary to popular belief – this percentage has remained remarkably stable since the Second World War. For similar reasons, we have to question the widespread assumption that contemporary Western societies have reached levels of cultural and ethnic diversity that are extraordinary and without precedent.

One can be easily mesmerized by the diverse range of ethnic groups, cultures and languages that can be seen on the streets of large Western metropolises. However, if we zoom out and take a long-term and global view, we start to realize that levels of diversity – and immigration – in contemporary Western societies are perhaps not as exceptional as we think.

The idea that our societies are more diverse than ever is based on a distorted image of past societies as much more homogeneous than they really were. First, many North American and European countries have experienced past episodes of high immigration. In 1910, for instance, the 13.5 million migrants living in the US constituted 14.7 per cent of the US population, a similar percentage as today.[3] Various European countries – including Britain, France, Germany, Austria, the Netherlands and Belgium – are steeped in deep, long and controversial histories of immigration that many people have forgotten.[4]

Global migration rates have remained remarkably stable over the past century. The major change has been a reversal in the dominant direction of global migration flows, largely because Europeans have ceased colonizing and populating other continents, with more migrants moving in the opposite direction – that is, from former colonies (in the Global South) to Western countries. So, the idea of growing diversity reveals a strongly Eurocentric – and racist – bias, as it implicitly casts non-European migrants as essentially more 'diverse'.

Second, it is easy to forget that immigrant and minority groups that majority populations now consider as fully 'theirs' were seen as the unassimilable 'other' in a not-too-distant past. While groups like Muslim immigrants (particularly in western Europe) and Latino immigrants (particularly in the US) stand in the limelight of diversity discussions now, throughout modern history various other immigrants and (non-migrant) minority groups have been seen as a fundamental threat to national identity and security.

In Europe, Jewish and Romani people (the latter often derogatorily referred to as 'gypsies') have been looked upon with suspicion and hostility, and were the target of violence for centuries, whether immigrants or not. Different factions within Christianity also tended to see each other as culturally and religiously different. While Protestant minorities were repressed in Catholic-majority countries – such as the Huguenots in seventeenth-century France – Protestant-majority societies have often questioned the loyalty of Roman Catholics, whether native or immigrant.

Britain has a long history of anti-Catholicism, particularly directed against the Irish. Throughout nineteenth- and twentieth-century Britain, there was widespread hostility against large numbers of Catholic migrant workers coming in from Ireland, who were stereotyped as 'hard drinking, quick-tempered navvies'.[5] Anti-Semitism was directed against poor Jewish immigrants fleeing racism and pogroms in eastern Europe in the late nineteenth and early twentieth centuries.

There is also an old tradition in western Europe of treating East European people as inferior and a potential threat to the nation. In late nineteenth-century Germany, there was widespread anti-Polish sentiment. Max Weber, one of the founding fathers of sociology, warned in 1895 that Polish agricultural migrants of a *tieferstehende Rasse* (lower-standing race) would be displacing German farmers.[6] From the 1930s, nativist sentiments in Germany and elsewhere in Europe were increasingly directed towards Jews. Feeding on age-old anti-Semitism, this culminated in the Holocaust, the systematic persecution, enslavement and murder of around 6 million Jews – around two-thirds of the European Jewry – by the Nazi regime.[7]

In France, besides virulent anti-Semitism, southern Europeans were long considered to be culturally and racially inferior, unfit to assimilate into the French nation. In the first half of the twentieth century, France attracted large numbers of Italian, Portuguese and Spanish workers, who were generally treated with contempt and often lived in urban slums and *bidonvilles* (shanty towns).[8] The infamous French aphorism that '*L'Afrique commence aux Pyrénées*' ('Africa starts at the Pyrenees') reflects deeply ingrained feelings of superiority towards the Spanish and Portuguese, who were often considered too 'primitive' and 'backward' to be compatible with French civilization.[9] This resonated with colonial ideologies which deemed that total assimilation into French culture was the only conceivable option for colonized people as well as immigrants from 'inferior' cultures and societies. Not only in France, but across north-west Europe, racist discrimination against southern Europeans endured until the 1970s.[10]

The red, black and yellow perils

Despite attempts by the powers that be to define the essence of the United States as 'white', from its very foundations the US has in reality always been an inherently diverse society. Because they arrived with superior military power, the white invaders ('settlers') tried to implant an exclusively European society on foreign soil, to which only white, Christian (preferably Protestant) Europeans could really belong. For that reason, these settlers always fiercely opposed the idea of racial mixing.

In the Americas, the first targets of racist violence were the indigenous peoples who were, if not exterminated, then systematically expropriated and – literally – driven off their lands. Much 'Wild West' heroism revolved around popular slurs like 'the only good Indian is a dead Indian'.[11] The second targets of systematic racist violence were the approximately 12 million Africans who were violently transported across the Atlantic to be sold to work on plantations as slaves – and their descendants.

The United States of the nineteenth century was an equally – if not more – ethnically and racially diverse country as it is now. During the early days of European settlement, Native Americans were still in the majority, although the Native American population would dwindle fast from an estimated 600,000 in 1800 to 250,000 in the 1890–1900 decade.[12] Throughout the early nineteenth century, African Americans – the descendants of enslaved Africans – formed 15–18 per cent of the total US population. (This percentage has dropped to around 12.4 now,[13] mainly because of Latino and Asian immigration.)

However, this was not seen as a 'diversity problem', as African Americans and Native Americans were not legally considered full and equal US citizens until far into the twentieth century. The gradual abolition of the slave trade and slave labour over the course of the nineteenth century did not eliminate systemic racism and discrimination. In the US South, after the formal abolition of slavery in 1865, racist Jim Crow laws served to keep African Americans as sharecroppers in the plantations of the Southern states and institutionalized discrimination against Black people by introducing a de facto apartheid system. As long as African Americans were segregated and prevented from mingling and intermarrying, they could not form a threat to the American nation whose identity was seen as essentially White Anglo-Saxon Protestant (WASP).

From a white supremacist perspective, abolition created a 'need' for segregation – a system which could only be kept in place through violent oppression. Until the 1960s, public lynchings were a common phenomenon in the US South. White mobs justified these on dubious grounds and fabricated accusations – such as the rape of white women. While lynchings typically evoke images of Black men and women hanging from trees, they also often involved torture, mutilation, decapitation and desecration, while some victims were burned alive. It has been estimated that, between 1882 and 1968, 4,743 lynchings occurred in the US.[14] They served to intimidate and terrorize African Americans and to 'keep them in their place' in the interest of maintaining white supremacy.

Approximately 6 million African Americans moved to the northern industrial cities as part of the Great Migration between 1914 and 1970, in the hope of finding better economic opportunities and escaping racism in the South.[15] However, they found themselves subject to policies of segregation and 'redlining' that condemned them to live in separate neighbourhoods, essentially because white Americans did not want to have Black neighbours. Interracial marriage was outlawed in many states until the late 1960s.[16] Despite the successes of the civil rights movement, systemic racism, discrimination, and racial profiling and police violence remain major problems in the present day.

Myths about the inherent racial inferiority and less civilized cultures of Native and African Americans served to justify violence towards them and deny them a place in the new American nation, in order to create and maintain a homogeneous white nation. Because it was inconceivable that racial minority groups such as Native Americans and descendants of enslaved Africans could ever aspire to belong fully as equal members of the nation, they were relegated to live on reservations or in segregated neighbourhoods.

Although the most violent forms of racism in the US have historically been reserved for Native and African Americans, new immigrant groups have frequently been the target of hostility from majority groups, who see them as a danger threatening the American nation. From the late nineteenth century, politicians and media started to frame the growing numbers of Chinese and Japanese immigrants as a 'yellow peril'.[17] In 1882, in response to virulent anti-Chinese sentiment drummed up by labour leaders and politicians, the US adopted the Chinese Exclusion Act, prohibiting the immigration of Chinese workers and barring them from citizenship.[18] After the Pearl Harbor attacks in 1941 by the Japanese military – which drew the US into the Second World War – the US government interned about 110,000 people of Japanese descent, even though this violated the Constitution because most of them were US citizens.[19]

Cleansing the 'scum' from the melting pot

White majority groups have routinely portrayed newcomers and minorities as a potential threat to identity, national culture and even security. It may be difficult to imagine now, but Germans, Italians, Irish, Polish, Japanese, Jews and Catholics were once seen as unassimilable and even a menace to the nation in ways that are not fundamentally different from the way Muslims and Latinos have been portrayed in more recent times.

German immigrants were once seen as a threat to American identity and security. In the nineteenth century, large-scale German immigration generated nativist anti-German sentiment and widespread opposition against the growing use of the German language. By 1890, the US had more than 1,000 German-language newspapers and even a German-language school system. In 1910, the 8 million German Americans were the largest non-English-speaking group in the US.[20] This even led to mounting fears that German would take over from English as the national language.

The loyalty of German Americans to the American nation was questioned, too, particularly when the First World War reinforced anti-German sentiment. German Americans were suspected of being 'hyphenated Americans' who suspiciously held on to their own traditions instead of 'assimilating' into mainstream American culture.[21] In 1919, President Woodrow Wilson admonished that 'any man who carries a hyphen about with him, carries a dagger that he is ready to plunge into the vitals of this Republic when he gets ready'.[22] German Americans were commonly referred to as 'Huns' – a population group that allegedly invaded Europe in the Middle Ages – casting them as 'a race of Barbaric raiders'.[23]

After German minorities largely assimilated into the American mainstream by the second and third generations – leaving only some linguistic traces like 'kindergarten' and culinary traces such as the hot dog – nativist hostility shifted to Catholics as well as Jewish East Europeans. Up to the mid-twentieth century, the arrival of large groups of Catholic immigrants from Ireland, Poland and Italy provoked hostile reactions among Protestant majority groups, who either saw them as unassimilable or considered their immigration as an outright threat to the WASP identity. Sicilians and other southern Italians, for instance, were often barely considered 'white'. This partly reflected domestic racism in Italy, where northerners had long held that darker-skinned southerners – and Sicilians in particular – were an 'uncivilized' and racially inferior people, 'too obviously African to be part of Europe'.[24]

Anti-Italian sentiment was common and considered to be perfectly respectable. An editorial in the *New York Times* from 1891 called Sicilians 'the descendants of bandits and assassins' and 'a pest without mitigation'.[25] Between 1890 and 1920, about fifty public lynchings of Italians were documented. Racist slurs were common even in the highest intellectual and 'civilized' circles. In 1914, Edward Ross, a prominent US sociologist, argued that white Americans were effectively committing 'race suicide' by admitting southern Europeans and those of 'African, Saracen, and Mongolian blood'.[26] Ross also claimed that 'the mysterious decline that came upon the American people early in the twentieth century' was caused by 'the deterioration of popular intelligence by the admission of great numbers of backward immigrants'. A decade later, Edwin Grant, another sociologist, called for 'a systematic deportation' that 'eugenically cleanses America' of the 'Scum from the Melting-Pot'.[27]

This is not essentially different from the fears voiced by contemporary adherents of the 'great replacement' conspiracy theory, who also cast culturally and racially different immigrants as a threat to Western civilization. The main difference is the target: what was once applied to Irish, Polish, Italian, Jewish and Chinese people is now applied to groups such as Latinos (in the US) and Muslims (in Europe). For example, in 2006 the American political commentator Pat Buchanan – author of a book *State of Emergency: The Third World Invasion and Conquest of America* – alleged that illegal migration was part of an 'Aztlan plot' hatched by Mexican elites to reconquer lands lost in 1848, stating that 'if we do not get control of our borders and stop this greatest invasion in history, I see the dissolution of the US and the loss of the American southwest'.[28]

In 2010, the German author and former Social Democratic politician Thilo Sarrazin published a book with the telling title *Deutschland schafft sich ab* (or *Germany Abolishes Itself*), where he expressed worries that Germany was increasingly overwhelmed by influxes of migrants and asylum seekers from Muslim countries who were reluctant to integrate, often dependent on welfare and more prone to crime, violence and terrorism. Arguing that there 'is a different multiplication of population groups with different intelligence', he claimed that the average intelligence level in Germany was falling because of the mass arrival of lower-skilled migrants.[29] This is basically the same argument as was used by Edward Ross in America a century earlier.

These examples show that narratives that cast the diverse 'other' as a threat are anything but new. In many ways, concerns about diversity and the casting of immigration as a threat to mainstream culture and identity – as well as rather vague allusions to immigration exceeding the absorption capacity of destination societies – seems a covert way of expressing fears among majority groups about a perceived loss of hegemony that, a century ago, would have been expressed in more shameless racist terms. In essence, much of what is said now about new immigrant groups recycles older narratives. Take for instance the nativist allegation that Muslim immigration is part of a secret plot to Islamize the West. Such ideas are remarkably similar to the older conspiracy theories claiming that Jews are involved in a plot to achieve world hegemony through predominance in matters of money, business, culture and politics.

In a similar vein, suspicion towards Catholics in northern Europe and North America was partly fuelled by the allegation that, if push came to shove, they would be more loyal to the Pope in Rome than to the nation and its constitution. As the first Catholic US president (of Irish descent), John F. Kennedy's religious affiliation was still a major issue in the 1960 presidential election. The fact that this is barely imaginable now shows how quickly things can change. As previous outsiders become insiders, majority groups find it difficult to imagine that these groups were once considered the unassimilable 'other'. In reality, boundaries between 'them' and 'us' are constantly shifting, with the newest immigrant groups typically being framed as the 'other'. This shows the dangers of adopting idealized images of past societies as culturally and ethnically more homogeneous. We come from a much more diverse – and racist – past than we usually imagine.

Societies and cultures have become less diverse

While minorities and immigrants have often been considered a threat to the nation, there are actually good reasons to believe that societies and mainstream cultures have become more homogeneous than ever. Europe has always been home to an extremely diverse tapestry of ethnic, linguistic and religious groups which far outnumber the nation states. Local and regional identities have always been very strong, often with each area and town having their own dialect, customs and habits. Inhabitants of nineteenth-century Paris, for instance, would have felt hardly any affinity with rural Bretons flocking into town, as they did not even speak French![30]

From the sixteenth century, larger states started to form – and this process was further accelerated after the French Revolution in 1789 and during the subsequent formation and consolidation of modern European nation states over the course of the nineteenth century. Powerful symbols such as a national flag, currency, stamp and anthem, and central state institutions such as the constitution, army and bureaucracy – as well as the proclamation of a national language – instilled in people from very diverse backgrounds a feeling of common destiny, belonging and identity. Education, military conscription, expanding bureaucracy and the development of railroads all served to spread a common language and national identity. This is how people who didn't even know each other could develop a joint sense of belonging.

In his seminal book *Imagined Communities*, published in 1983, political scientist and historian Benedict Anderson aptly called nations 'imagined communities': social constructs that give people living in the same territory a sense of common purpose and destiny, even if most of them have never met.[31] International football tournaments and Olympic Games are probably the best proof that nationalism is a double-edged sword: not only a potential cause of war and destruction – and of hooliganism – but also a unifying force that can be used for good, in tearing down barriers between peoples who once saw each other as arch-enemies, and encouraging them to see a common interest and collaborate.

From a state perspective, the project of nation building has been remarkably successful. From the sixteenth century, a certain overarching British identity was forged out of successive unions between England, Wales, Scotland and (Northern) Ireland, leading to the near-universal adoption of the English language across the United Kingdom. In the early nineteenth century, few people inhabiting the eight independent states on the Italian peninsula would have believed a unified Italian state could ever exist, as regional identities were strong and interregional animosity ran very high. However, between 1848 and 1871 such a unified state was effectively created.[32] In 1871, the modern German state was created from over 300 monarchies, princedoms and other smaller states.[33]

Nation building, the expansion of state bureaucracy, rail and road networks, the propagation of an official language and national culture through schools, radio and television, as well as growing contact with people from other regions through the military draft, internal migration and the deliberate circulation of teachers and administrative personnel, meant that local and regional identities, dialects and customs gradually started to weaken. As national languages became more and more widespread, fewer and fewer people started to speak regional dialects and languages – often pushing those smaller languages to the brink of extinction.

Societies, and the world, are becoming more the same than ever

The forces of cultural and linguistic homogenization are at work everywhere, because of the influence of the state, education, media, and more recently the internet. This homogenization process has helped to forge national identities, but has also acted as a steamroller, effacing the identities, customs and languages of local groups. The nationalist drive to coalesce around a single identity has also gone along with the exclusion of – and extreme violence towards – minorities who have resisted assimilation into the national mainstream, regularly resulting in mass killings and producing major refugee flows.

Compared to western Europe, the process of homogenization around a single national identity is more recent in central and eastern Europe, where the Habsburg, Ottoman and Russian empires tolerated and accommodated extraordinary levels of cultural, ethnic and religious diversity far into the twentieth century. Much recent warfare in this region – such as the Greco-Turkish War of 1919–22, the 1990s wars in former Yugoslavia and the various conflicts between and within the republics of the former Soviet Union – was essentially driven by the nationalist desire to create a homogeneous national population and identity out of the ashes of the multicultural Ottoman and Soviet empires as well as the Yugoslav republic.

War is often instrumental in forging national identities and driving out, oppressing or killing minorities that don't fit into the new nation – while it also emboldens states to expand their power. As sociologist Charles Tilly famously put it: 'war made the state, and the state made war'.[34] In the post-Second World War decades, military oppression by colonial powers against independence movements in ethnically diverse countries like Algeria, India and Indonesia only strengthened nationalism. In the same way, Russian military aggression against Ukraine after 2014 backfired by arguably solidifying a sense of nationhood and common destiny in a rather diverse country – strengthening, not weakening, the position of Ukrainian as the national language.

However, the forces of nationalism can also lead to the expulsion of minorities. The creation of the modern Turkish state over the early twentieth century involved the mass expulsion of Greeks from Turkey, and of Turks from Greece – and, more generally, stimulated the migration of Turkish groups from Central Asia to the Turkish 'motherland' over much of the twentieth century. Similarly, following Indian independence in 1947 and the Partition between India and Pakistan, about 8 million Hindus and Sikhs fled Pakistan (which then included Bangladesh, formerly East Pakistan) for India, and about 6 million Muslims moved from India to Pakistan.[35] After the Second World War, and particularly in the 1990s, some 4.5 million ethnic German *Aussiedler* moved from the former Soviet Union and eastern Europe to Germany.[36]

As ethnic groups have increasingly huddled up in 'their' nation states – and minorities have been oppressed, killed or expelled, or have emigrated – ethnic, religious and linguistic diversity within many countries has gone down rather than up. Simultaneously, with the break-up of large multi-ethnic empires and the ensuing rise of new nation states, the internal and external forces of homogenization have rolled on. At the same time, the diminishing influence of organized religion and increased secularization have softened harsh religious divisions within Western countries.

As regional, ethnic and religious barriers collapsed, 'mainstream' national and international culture was strengthened. Starting in the 1920s, and accelerating since the 1950s, the rise of an increasingly global youth culture made it easier for young people all over the world to find common reference points around food, music, cinema, literature and other forms of artistic expression. Jazz and other African American music crossed the Atlantic to Europe, Africa and elsewhere, to amalgamate with local musical styles. Meanwhile, Italian, Chinese and Middle Eastern cuisines transformed eating worldwide. International travel and the advent of cable television and the internet further fostered the development of a national and international culture in a process also known as 'globalization', marked by a growing use of English as a de facto global *lingua franca*, and the increased convergence of middle-class taste and the spread of global youth culture.[37]

The two homogenizing forces of national unification and globalization have provoked strong regionalist pushbacks in the form of independence movements – Catalonia in Spain, Scotland within the United Kingdom – while the predominantly English resistance to the European Union's drive towards political unification was a strong motivating force behind Brexit. However, despite such pushbacks, from a long-term perspective Western societies have undeniably become culturally less diverse.

Homogenization is happening all over the world. The demise of minority languages is probably the most powerful indicator of this trend. According to UNESCO data, 230 languages went extinct between 1950 and 2010, and today a third of the world's 7,100-odd languages have fewer than 1,000 speakers. It is estimated that every two weeks a language dies with its last speaker, and 50–90 per cent of them are predicted to have disappeared by the next century.[38] Because language is the prime carrier of shared culture, imagination and identity, the significance of this development cannot be underestimated.

Diversity is no threat to social cohesion and national identity

It's clearly a myth that the current levels of cultural and ethnic diversity experienced by Western countries are unprecedented. The evidence also undermines the claim that ethnic diversity created by immigration undermines social cohesion. Throughout human history, societies around the world have successfully dealt with levels of diversity that were often much higher than that experienced by many contemporary Western societies.

Various modern states have been able to accommodate the cultural differences of some population groups, either by giving minorities special rights or by creating decentralized, federal state models that allow room for regional identities. Many Western states, including the United States, Canada, Spain, Belgium, Germany and Switzerland, have federalist, decentralized structures as well as regional governments – which allows for generally peaceful cohabitation between population groups with quite distinct regional and linguistic identities. This often goes along with national ideologies that do not see ethnic, religious, local and 'hyphenated' identities as incompatible with belonging to a nation that supersedes such identities.

In this way, many societies around the world have been able to successfully accommodate significant ethnic and religious differences. Map 3 depicts levels of cultural diversity in countries around the world. This is based on an index developed by researcher Erkan Gören of the University of Oldenberg in Germany, which combines data on ethnicity and race with a measure based on the similarity of languages spoken by major ethnic or racial groups. The map suggests that there is no obvious link between levels of diversity and the effective functioning of states. Large countries such as Indonesia and India are examples of states that have managed to instil a certain sense of national unity despite huge internal ethnic, linguistic, religious and cultural differences – and levels of diversity that are often much higher than those typical of most Western societies.

In reality, many people foster 'multiple identities', combining a feeling of belonging to one (or more) nation and strong regional or local allegiances. In the UK, for instance, the idea of 'Britishness' provides an overarching sense of belonging that partly supersedes regional and ethnic identities – and many immigrants find they are able to subscribe to

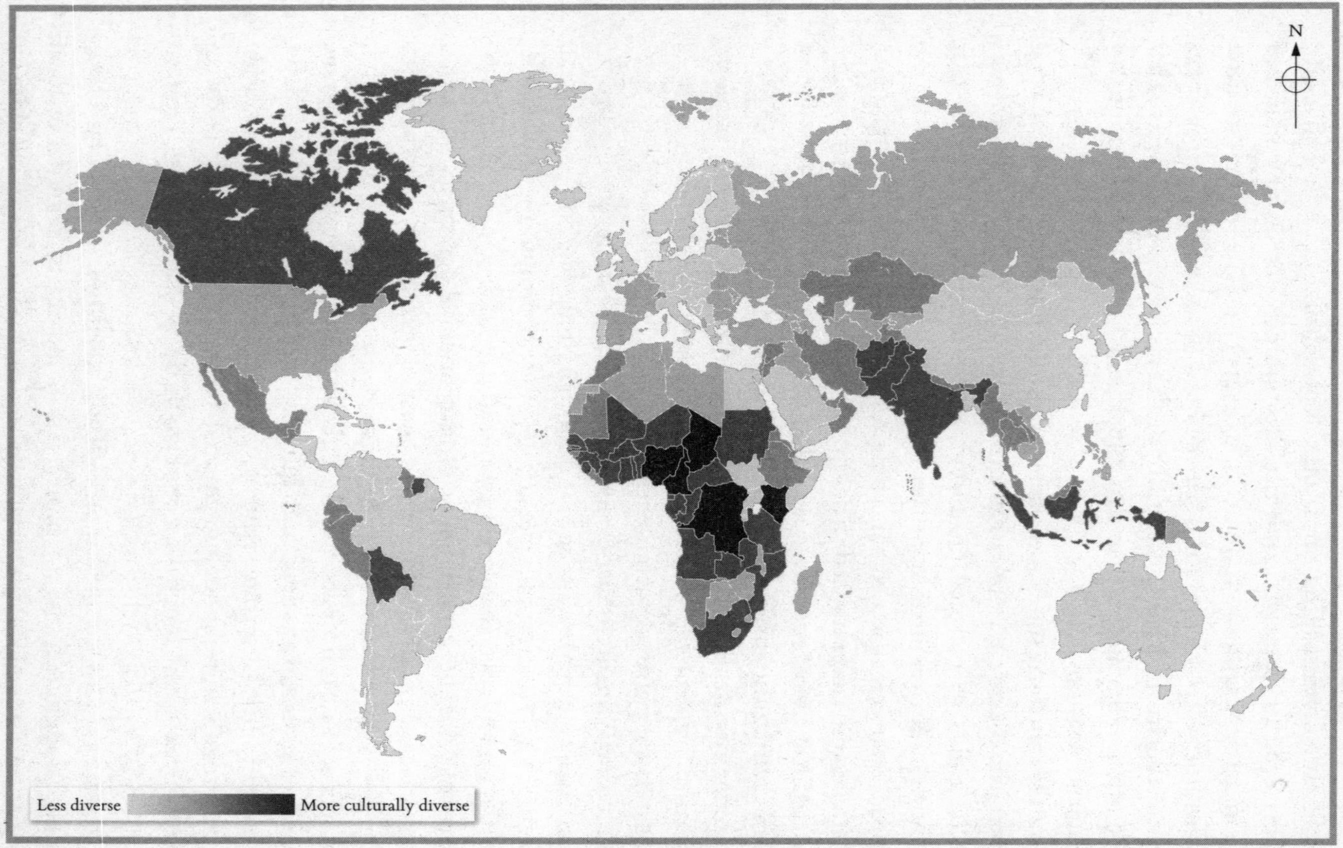

Map 3: Cultural diversity around the world[39]

it more easily than the idea of being English, Welsh or Scottish. The same applies when it comes to local identities, often passionately expressed in strong inter-ethnic support for football teams. The daughter of Pakistani immigrants in Liverpool can feel Liverpudlian, British and Pakistani, all at the same time.

It's true of course that experiments in nation building can lead to bitter conflict, particularly when politicians fan the flames of xenophobia, regional leaders fuel nativist tension, and regimes oppress regional or ethnic minorities. The experiences of Jews in Nazi Germany, Tutsis in Rwanda and Bosnians in former Yugoslavia provide stark warnings that even groups that were once part of the mainstream can be 'othered' if politicians are effective in framing them as the enemy of the nation.

But there is no *inherent* contradiction or trade-off between levels of cultural and ethnic diversity on the one hand and social cohesion and peaceful cohabitation on the other. It should therefore not come as a surprise that studies have failed to find a clear link between levels of immigration/ethnic diversity and social cohesion/trust. Some Western societies have experienced a substantial decline in social trust over recent decades. Trends have been most negative in the United States. In his book *Bowling Alone*, Harvard sociologist Robert Putnam showed that while in the 1960s about 55 per cent of adult Americans agreed that 'most people can be trusted', by 2000 this percentage had sunk to around 35 per cent.[40] As Putnam meticulously documented, this has gone along with an overall decline of social interaction and civic engagement. In Europe, trends have been more varied. Trust in other persons as well as in political institutions has been rising in Scandinavian, Baltic and north-west European countries such as Germany, the Netherlands and Belgium, but has been falling in Mediterranean countries, the UK, Ireland and several post-communist countries in eastern Europe.[41]

However, empirical studies have failed to find a systemic link between social trust, social cohesion, and immigration and ethnic diversity.[42] In reality, social trust is mainly explained by factors unrelated to immigration and diversity, such as inequality, income, employment and trust in government. For instance, analyses of the US General Social Survey (2006–14) revealed that declining social trust is mainly explained by unemployment, low income and a decreasing confidence in political institutions.[43] As Putnam argued, economic inequality in particular seems detrimental for trust, social cohesion and people's involvement in community life.[44] In their book *The Spirit Level*, British epidemiologists Richard Wilkinson and Kate Pickett confirmed this by showing that levels of trust between people are lower in Western countries (and, within the US, states) where income difference is larger.[45]

In fact, many societies combine high or increasing levels of immigration and diversity with consistently high or even increasing levels of social trust. In economically more egalitarian societies, and where cultural minorities are recognized, immigration can actually even have a positive effect on trust.[46] Immigration and diversity as such are not the problem therefore – it really depends on how governments and societies deal with the issue. Some of the most diverse societies in the world belong to the most prosperous and democratic countries, while some of the ethnically most homogeneous societies in the world – such as North Korea – can be extremely oppressive. In brief, as economists Alberto Alesina and Eliana La Ferrara argue, 'similar levels of ethnic diversity are associated with very different degrees of conflict and interethnic cooperation'.[47]

Canada, Australia, New Zealand and – at least until the 1970s – the United States are all high-immigration societies with fairly high levels of social trust. This is because their political leaders and institutions have fostered a plural form of national identity centred around some idea of *e pluribus unum* (one from many). However, politicians also have the power to sow division and hatred by accusing particular minority groups of plotting to undermine the nation. And when politicians encourage the monster of racism and conspiracy thinking to rear its head in this way, even well-integrated and successful groups whose sense of belonging and loyalty to the nation was never questioned previously, whose ethnic or religious identity did not necessarily play a big role in their daily lives, and whose families may be ethnically or racially mixed, can be set apart and redefined as enemies of the nation and become the target of systematic exclusion and violence or even genocide. Diversity as such does not undermine social cohesion, but hate speech by political leaders can.

The facts highlight that we, as nations, have in many respects become less diverse. The idea that our societies are more diverse than ever ignores not only past diversity but also the fact that 'mainstream' cultures have become increasingly homogeneous as part of the consolidation of national cultures and the growing spread of international norms, values and forms of cultural expression. Ironically, as the Dutch sociologist Jan Willem Duyvendak has argued, political concerns about supposedly growing diversity may in fact reflect the increasing homogenization of national cultures rather than a fundamental change in the way migrants behave and identify.[48] The more homogeneous national cultures become, the more hostile they seem to be towards groups that are seen as not fitting into this national identity. Societies around the world have successfully dealt with much higher levels of diversity than contemporary Western societies. The real danger is not diversity itself, but ideologies that set groups apart as fundamentally different.

Myth 5: Development in poor countries will reduce migration

Confronted with the manifest inability of border controls to curb legal or illegal immigration, politicians, experts and aid agencies have often argued that the only way to do so is to tackle the 'root causes' by reducing poverty and promoting economic development in origin countries. This is not a new idea. The concept of using development aid and trade as tools to diminish migration pressures has been popular for decades, particularly in progressive circles.

In the US in 1993, one of the arguments the Clinton administration used to gain congressional support for the North American Free Trade Agreement (NAFTA) was that trade liberalization would generate economic growth and therefore reduce migration from Mexico.[1] Politicians and development agencies have frequently promoted aid as a 'smart' way to prevent unwanted migration. In 1995, Poul Nyrup Rasmussen, then prime minister of Denmark, invoked the spectre of mass immigration to increase foreign aid, arguing that 'if you don't help the third world . . . then you will have these poor people in our society'.[2] In 2005, in response to a surge in boat crossings from Libya into southern Italy,[3] the president of the European Commission, José Manuel Barroso, claimed that 'the problem of immigration, the dramatic consequences of which we are witnessing, can only be addressed effectively through an ambitious and coordinated development cooperation to fight its root causes'.[4]

A decade later, in response to the drownings of migrants and asylum seekers in the Mediterranean, the European Union set up the Emergency Trust Fund to prevent illegal migration from Africa. During the launch in 2015, EU president Jean-Claude Juncker pledged to work together with African countries 'in addressing the root causes of illegal migration and promoting economic and equal opportunities, security and development'.[5] Governments of origin countries have adopted similar narratives, portraying migration as a problem that can only be solved through development. Responding to border crises, African leaders have repeatedly called upon European countries to launch a Marshall Plan for Africa. In 2016, Senegalese president Macky Sall argued that African countries must work together to reduce emigration through promoting development, and that Europe should help Africa in these efforts to prevent illegal migration, through development cooperation.[6]

Similar narratives can be heard in the Americas: when confronted with a surge in border crossings in 2021, the Biden administration vowed to address the root causes of migration from Central America to the US by providing aid to Central American countries and rooting out corruption. As part of its official 'Root Causes of Migration' policy, the administration pledged to focus on a 'coordinated, place-based approach to improve the underlying causes that push Central Americans to migrate', such as 'corruption, violence, trafficking, and poverty', further exacerbated by the Covid-19 pandemic and extreme weather conditions.[7]

Thus migration prevention has become a central argument for bringing down trade barriers and disbursing larger aid packages. Politicians, aid agencies and humanitarian organizations have enthusiastically jumped on the 'development instead of migration' bandwagon. And the underlying logic certainly sounds simple, sympathetic and powerful: we need to help poor people to stay at home so that they no longer need to embark upon dangerous journeys to the Global North.

How it really works

Migration increases as poor countries get richer

Because of its humanitarian ring, the 'development instead of migration' argument sounds much better than tough-on-immigration narratives. That also explains its popularity, particularly in left-wing circles, as it connects migration to the injustices of poverty and inequality. At first sight, the argument seems to make a lot of sense: development is the only long-term solution in fighting the root causes of migration. It seems a smart way of solving migration problems – as poor people in the Global South will no longer feel tempted to embark upon desperate and dangerous journeys to the West, or be driven into the hands of smugglers, traffickers and exploitative employers.

Although this may all *sound* very nice – and leaving aside the controversial questions about the overall credibility of such programmes[8] and whether relatively small amounts of 'aid' can make any difference in the first place* – the whole idea that aid and development will reduce migration from poor countries is very unrealistic, because it is based on entirely wrong assumptions on the causes of migration. The whole argument lacks any scientific basis, as it is based on a flawed understanding of the causes of migration. In fact, we have to turn the entire argument around, because the evidence shows the exact opposite picture: economic development in poor countries leads to more, not less, migration! The paradox is that emigration is generally *higher* in countries and regions that have already achieved a certain level of economic development, urbanization and modernization.

I made these observations for the first time when I was in Morocco in 1993 and 1994 to do research on migration from oases south of the Atlas Mountains to cities in northern Morocco and Europe.[9] My fieldwork there forced me to question the popular assumption that poverty and underdevelopment are the root causes of migration. I noted that the highest levels of international emigration to European countries like France, the Netherlands, Belgium and Spain were in the relatively wealthy, connected and centrally located oases, while migration from comparatively poorer and more isolated oases was mainly short-distance or directed at large Moroccan cities such as Marrakech, Casablanca and Agadir.

My fieldwork in the south Moroccan Todgha valley between 1998 and 2000 and in more recent years revealed a perhaps even more intriguing puzzle: since the 1960s, the Todgha valley has known intensive migration to Moroccan cities as well as to Europe. The flow of remittances emigrants sent back has made local inhabitants and the entire region more economically prosperous. However, despite decreasing poverty and significant improvements in income and general living

* For instance, the total €5 billion pledged for the EU Emergency Trust Fund for Africa is equal to a mere 0.25 per cent of the EU's annual gross domestic product (GDP) of €2 trillion in 2017. These are symbolic amounts compared to the EU's support for its own economy. In 2021 alone, the EU spent €55.7 billion on its Common Agricultural Policy (CAP) – 94 per cent through direct subsidies to European farmers. In addition, only a fraction of the aid money pledged has actually been provided. By 2022, donor countries had actually paid only €623 million to the EU Emergency Trust Fund for Africa, 12 per cent of the promised amount.

farmers emigrate to urban areas and Canada - Spain

conditions, out-migration from the Todgha valley to big cities in Morocco and particularly Europe actually *increased* in intensity. While emigration to traditional destinations such as France and the Netherlands continued, more and more people also started to migrate to Spain, Italy and in recent years Portugal and Canada.[10]

Later, I observed the same paradox in Morocco as a whole. Over the past decades, Morocco has made significant progress in terms of income growth, poverty reduction, literacy and education levels and infrastructure development. Between 1982 and 2014 the adult literacy rate went up from 30 to 76 per cent. The rural population with access to electricity shot up from 13.9 per cent in 1992 to 100 per cent in 2017, while yearly population growth slowed from 2.7 per cent in 1982 to 1.1 per cent in 2019.

However, to my surprise, after compiling migration data from various sources, I found out that, despite the suspension of free movement to southern Europe since the early 1990s, Moroccan emigration had increased to record levels – from 30,000–40,000 per year in the mid-1990s to almost 150,000 in 2008. After a slump in emigration because of the 2007–2008 global financial crisis and soaring unemployment in southern Europe, economic recovery prompted emigration to bounce back after 2014 to 144,000 in 2019. Between 2000 and 2019 an estimated 2.3 million Moroccans entered European and other Western countries – 8

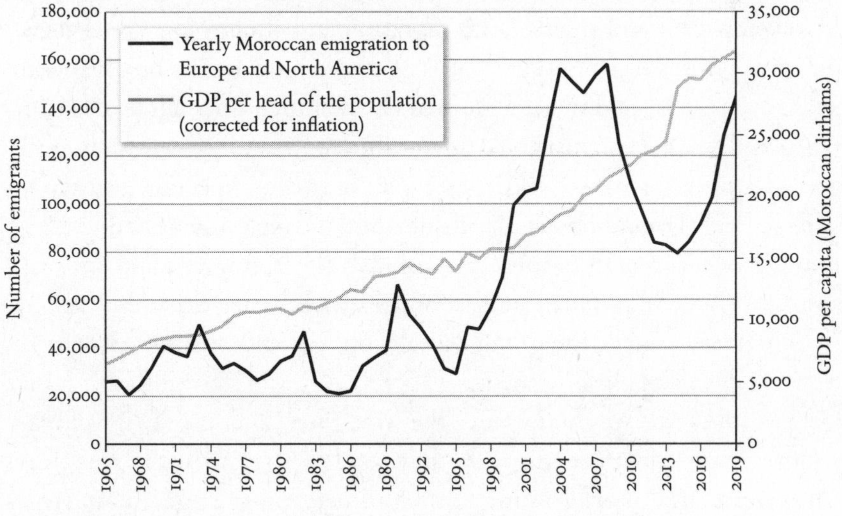

Graph 6: Income levels in and emigration from Morocco, 1965–2019

mid income nations are most prominent
emmigration countries
couldbe that emigration
costs
$?

per cent of its population in 2000.[11] As graph 6 illustrates, Moroccan emigration soared while income per capita increased steadily.

These observations did not fit at all within conventional migration theories rooted in neoclassical economics, which see migration as the outgrowth of income differences and other development disequilibria, and would have predicted decreasing migration as a consequence of improved living conditions and decreasing poverty. In fact, we have seen the same result in other prominent emigration countries. Even a cursory look at real-world migration patterns forces us to question the entire assumption that poverty is a major cause of South–North migration. If poverty really causes migration, how do we explain the fact that emigration rates from the poorest countries in the world – such as in sub-Saharan Africa – to Western countries are actually very low?[12] Or that the world's most prominent emigration countries, such as Mexico, Turkey, Morocco, India and the Philippines, are typically middle-income countries?

Development leads to more – not less – migration

The insights I gained during my fieldwork in Morocco urged me to investigate this issue on a more global level. In 2010, the University of Sussex and the World Bank released a new data set with the first-ever estimates on immigrant and emigrant populations for the entire world. This enabled me to conduct the first global test of the relationship between levels of development and trends in immigration and emigration.[13] I used two different indicators to measure levels of development. The first was GDP per capita; the second was the Human Development Index (HDI), a composite index used by the World Bank which is based on education levels, gross national income (GNI) per capita and life expectancy. Graph 7 depicts the relation between levels of human development and levels of immigration and emigration – measured as the immigrant and emigrant shares of the total population of countries within each category.

On the one hand, the graph reveals a linear and positive association between levels of development and levels of immigration that is rather intuitive. As we might expect, the wealthier and more 'developed' countries are, the more migrants they tend to attract. In the wealthiest countries of the world, immigrants represent on average about 15 per cent of the population. This corroborates the idea that rising levels of

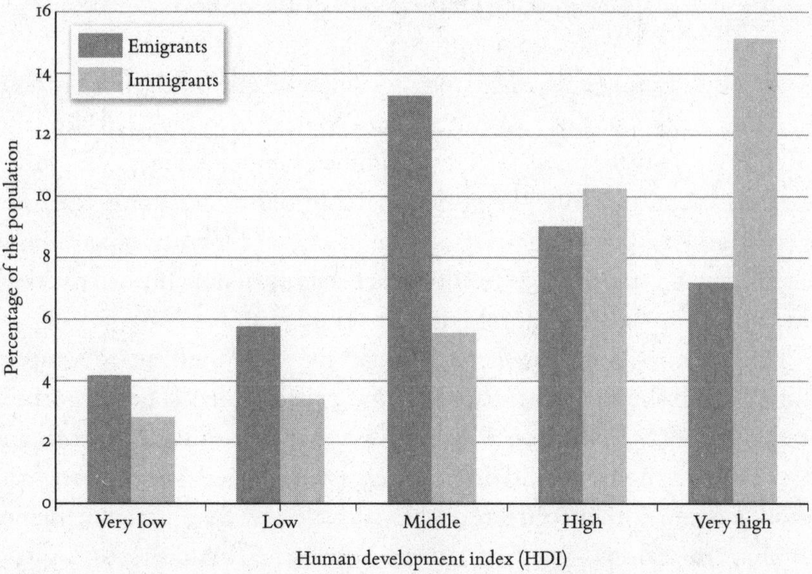

Graph 7: The relationship between levels of human development and the size of immigrant and emigrant populations[14]

immigration are the almost inevitable by-product of long-term growth and prosperity, particularly if this generates labour shortages that typically attract migrant workers.

However, the real surprise is in the non-linear relation between levels of human development and levels of emigration. The graph indicates that emigration goes up when poor countries become richer, and only goes down when countries move from middle- to high-income status. Emigration peaks at mid-development levels, at an average of about 13 per cent of the population living abroad. The analysis I conducted using per capita income – as measured by GDP – instead of HDI data yielded similar results.

To verify this, I ran regression analyses, which control for the effects of other factors that may influence migration levels, such as political freedoms, population growth and country size. These analyses revealed a similar non-linear relation between development and emigration. The findings of my original study, which used 2000 census data, have been confirmed by various follow-up studies using older and newer data and various statistical techniques to track emigration patterns of countries over time.[15]

Migration is an intrinsic part of development

My findings resonated with historical studies of European emigration in the nineteenth and early twentieth centuries, which revealed the same paradox of development initially leading to more emigration. In the research literature, this phenomenon of initially increasing and then decreasing levels of emigration is known as the 'mobility transition' or the 'migration transition' – resulting in the typical non-linear, inverted-U relationship between development and migration.

The phenomenon was first described by the American geographer Wilbur Zelinsky in a revolutionary 1971 article called 'The Hypothesis of the Mobility Transition'.[16] He argued that all forms of internal and international mobility initially *accelerate* when societies transition from rural-agrarian into urban-industrial societies and go through demographic transitions. The Scottish geographer Ronald Skeldon tested Zelinsky's ideas through his research in Latin America and Asia. His findings confirmed that the volume and geographical scope of internal and international emigration increases with levels of economic development, urbanization, and transport and communication links.[17]

In his landmark book *Migration and Development*, published in 1997, Skeldon argued for the need for a new paradigm on migration – to see it not as the antithesis of development but as a constituent, and therefore in many ways inevitable, part of development. 'Migration *is* development', as Skeldon succinctly wrote, summarizing his entire argument in the very last sentence of his book. Reading *Migration and Development* was a revelation during my fieldwork in Morocco, as it connected so well with the paradoxes I had been observing.

In 1998, the economic historians Timothy Hatton and Jeffrey Williamson identified similar patterns in their book *The Age of Mass Migration*, a detailed analysis of the large-scale migrations from Europe to the Americas and Australasia between 1850 and 1913.[18] In the mid-nineteenth century, most immigrants in the United States came from Britain and other North Sea countries, which were the most advanced and industrialized countries in Europe at the time. Emigration from poorer, more rural countries in southern and eastern Europe, which were lagging behind in industrial development and urbanization, took off later and only reached a peak in the early twentieth century.

Recent and historical evidence thus undermines the entire idea that in poor countries growth will reduce migration. In fact, the opposite seems to be true: it will lead to *more* migration.

Development increases capabilities and aspirations

So, how can we explain the paradox that emigration increases as poor countries get richer? This observation forces us to fundamentally change the way we tend to think about migration, moving away from intuitive-sounding but erroneous ideas of migration as a more or less linear function of poverty and inequality. Such models – also known as 'push-pull' models, which unfortunately still dominate migration curricula at schools and universities – naively assume that migration decreases as people get richer and inequality between places of origin and destination lessens. To summarize the evidence: the relation is fundamentally *non-linear*, with emigration initially going up if countries transition from lower- to middle-income societies, and only going down when they reach the top tiers of the global income hierarchy.

To understand this paradox, we need an alternative theory that can give us a realistic understanding of the developmental causes of migration from an origin-country perspective. Instead of viewing migration as the outgrowth of poverty, underdevelopment or inequality, or 'push' and 'pull' factors, in my work I have argued that we can achieve a better understanding of the causes of migration if we see migration as the function of people's aspirations and capabilities to migrate.[19] This 'capabilities-aspirations' model is depicted in graph 8.

This model provides a micro-level theory to explain the macro-level paradox of development-driven increases in emigration. The core argument of the model is that economic growth, improved education and greater media exposure in poor countries initially leads to more emigration because it simultaneously increases people's (1) capabilities and (2) aspirations to migrate.[20] Migration requires considerable resources, certainly when people move over long distances and want to cross international borders. People need money to pay for tickets, passports, visas, food and lodging, as well as fees to be paid to recruiters and other middlemen. As it usually takes time to migrate, settle and find work at the destination, families in origin countries also need to be able to forgo the income from the labour of migrated family members for several months, or even longer.[21]

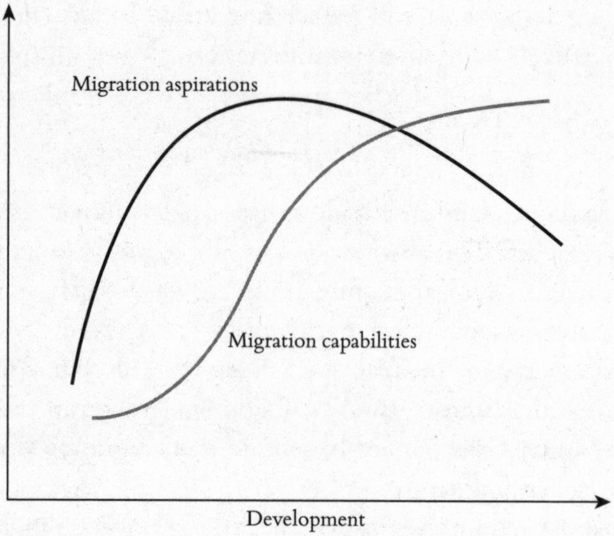

Graph 8: The capabilities-aspirations model

International migration to Western countries is particularly expensive in terms of travel and the costs of obtaining passports and visas, and slightly better-off people can more easily afford these costs than the poorest can. Besides rising incomes, improving education also increases people's migration capabilities because people with skills and diplomas find it easier to get jobs abroad and secure visas. Even illegal migration is not an option for the poorest of the poor who lack connections with family abroad, as it is expensive to pay smugglers, bribe border agents, and find lodging and work at the destination. This is why the poorest people often either cannot move or only move over short distances, such as to the next village or town. And extreme poverty can deprive people of the ability to move at all.

As low-income societies get richer and poverty decreases, more people are able to bear the financial costs and risks associated with migrating abroad. The richer and more educated people get, the more likely they are to move over increasingly large distances. This is why the geographical scope of emigration typically increases with development. When poor economies start to grow and more and more people go to school, as is currently the case in many parts of sub-Saharan Africa, South Asia and Central America, most international migration is still mainly directed at middle-income countries within the region. However, as countries reach middle-income status, more people can assume the costs of moving to more lucrative destinations in the Global North, while rising levels of education equip more people with the qualifications and diplomas needed to secure jobs and visas abroad.

Besides increasing migration *capabilities*, up to a certain point development also tends to increase people's *aspirations* to migrate. To understand this, we have to think beyond narrow understandings of development as economic growth, considering it instead to be a much broader process of social transformation and cultural change.[22] Once people go to school, listen to the radio, watch television, surf the internet, obtain smartphones, are exposed to advertising, see foreign visitors and tourists and start to travel themselves, this leads to a broadening of their mental horizons. Exposure to education, media and different lifestyles almost inevitably leads to profound changes in people's aspirations, typically making them want to move away from rural lifestyles and towards urban areas, but increasingly also abroad. In addition, improved education and knowledge of the world 'out there' often cause a certain disaffection with traditional, rural lifestyles among younger generations, who imagine a different future than tilling the land or herding the flocks.

In the south-Moroccan Todgha valley, for instance, improved education and increased media exposure have rapidly transformed the material and social aspirations of younger generations. Although local living conditions have improved significantly in recent decades, people's life aspirations have increased even faster, leading to increasing migration aspirations. The regular summer-holiday return of migrant 'role models' and their relative wealth has also contributed to changes in social aspirations among people living in the valley. International migration in particular has become so strongly associated with success that many youngsters have become almost obsessed with leaving. This has gone hand in hand with more Todghawis having the financial resources, skills and knowledge needed to migrate. So, growing aspirations and improved capabilities have inspired and enabled increasing numbers of people to leave the valley despite – or paradoxically *because of* – significant improvements in local living standards, income and education.

Development inevitably drives people out of rural areas

The capabilities-aspirations model shows the need to adopt a totally different vision of migration: not a conventional one that sees migration as the outgrowth of some sort of problem (such as poverty, population growth or environmental problems), but one that considers it an intrinsic part of broader development processes. The best example is perhaps the relation between urbanization and migration, as we really cannot imagine one without the other. Urbanization has been part and parcel of profound processes of economic change and social transformation leading to a progressive relocation of economic activities and people from rural to urban areas, with rural-to-urban migration as the inevitable by-product of that process.

This fundamental transformation has been observed in peasant societies all over the world, with young, better-educated people typically aspiring to move out of rural areas to explore new opportunities and lifestyles. It explains the failure of development interventions that were partly motivated to reduce rural out-migration, such as the building of schools, roads and agricultural development projects. Such interventions can even backfire by unintentionally accelerating the 'rural exodus'.[23]

Study after study has found that education in particular has a strong effect in increasing young people's aspirations to migrate.[24] Ironically, building schools seems the best recipe to spur rural out-migration in the longer term, because after having attended school for several years, local youth can no longer imagine living as peasants, and they increasingly wish to move to urban areas within their own countries or abroad. The desire to get an education is often a strong motive to migrate – which starts at a young age if primary or secondary schools are absent in small villages and towns. Once young people finish secondary school, they are more likely to migrate to another place to pursue higher education. And once they graduate, there is a good chance they will have to move again to find a job that matches their aspirations and qualifications.

Migrating also requires a certain mindset. In 1970, the prescient Nigerian geographer Akin Mabogunje observed that, in Africa, migration is not only a 'means to an end' – to get a job, earn more money or earn a degree – but also reflects a (largely irreversible) change in ideas about the 'good life'.[25] If young people living in rural areas get access to education and information through newspapers, radio, television and the internet, this often leads to a change in tastes and preferences, away from traditional agrarian and rural lifestyles. This typically instils a desire to live the 'modern life' – imagined to be in urban areas.

Obviously, this is anything but a specific 'Third World' phenomenon: many who come from a small town (like me) will know what this feels like. For small children, such places are often great to grow up in, but beyond a certain point, what once seemed like paradise can start to appear rather boring, and many young people will feel the pull of the big city.

For many, the lure of urban life has proved to be irresistible. As more and more people become educated and as societies transform to industrial and service-based economies, it is inevitable that more and more people will move to urban areas. I have often heard development experts – for instance, from the UN's Food and Agriculture Organization (FAO) – and government officials argue that we should promote agricultural development by helping peasants and small farmers to modernize and increase production, so that people can build a life back home and don't need to migrate.

However, if successful, attempts to promote rural development are more likely to speed up the rural exodus: they will lead to more, instead of less, rural out-migration, for the very reason that the mechanization of agriculture typically means that there are fewer jobs for farm workers. The more modernized and productive agriculture becomes, the more tractors and other machinery are used, and the fewer hands are needed on the farm. The share of people working in agriculture therefore goes down with development.

In high-income countries, less than 5 per cent of people work in agriculture, as opposed to over 90 per cent in pre-industrial societies. As agriculture modernizes and provides fewer jobs, the simultaneous growth of urban employment in industrial and service sectors motivates young people to leave rural areas. In the same vein, bringing infrastructure such as roads and electricity to 'backward' rural places can paradoxically accelerate out-migration, as it brings down transport costs and increases exposure to the outside world. For all these reasons, it has proved impossible to stop rural-to-urban migration *and* international migration, as they are an intrinsic part of development.

So, economic growth, education and a structural shift of labour out of agriculture and towards the urban sector all lead to increasing migration from rural places to urban areas. Most people move within their own county – about 80 per cent of all migrants in the world are internal migrants. But as societies get even richer, and move into the middle-income category, more people can afford to move abroad, either straight from the countryside or by using migration to the city as a stepping stone for migrating overseas. Initially, international out-migration from lower-income countries tends to be short-distance, as most migrants lack the resources to move to faraway overseas destinations, which is generally only something the affluent can afford. For this reason, most emigrants from low-income countries go to middle-income countries within their own region, such as Zimbabweans moving to South Africa, Nepalese to India, and Haitians to the Dominican Republic. However, as countries get richer, more and more people will have the money, diplomas and knowledge needed to migrate to faraway destinations.

The migration paradox

The evidence shows that the belief that development of origin countries is the most effective way to address the root causes of migration is based on wrong assumptions about what the root causes of migration actually are. In fact, the complete opposite is true: development in low-income countries leads to more, instead of less, emigration.

As poverty decreases, and incomes and education increase, emigration rises because it simultaneously increases people's aspirations and capabilities to migrate. Societies that are in the middle of the transition from agrarian-rural to industrial-urban economies produce the highest volumes of rural-to-urban migration as well as international emigration. Only once a society moves from middle- to higher-income status does rural-to-urban migration tend to slow down. Once a country has achieved higher-income status, aspirations to move abroad decrease because more people can realize their life aspirations by staying at home.

Beyond a certain tipping point of economic development, emigration levels start to decrease while the country begins to attract workers from poorer countries. This generally happens when countries move into the 'upper-middle-income' category. For a while, such countries experience significant emigration and immigration at the same time. In 2020, the economist Michael Clemens showed that, on average, the rise in emigration starts to slow down when a country crosses a wealth threshold of per capita GDP income levels of $5,000 (corrected for purchasing power parity), and reverses after roughly $10,000 – GDP levels that high-emigration countries like Morocco, the Philippines and Guatemala are nearing.[26]

Beyond this peak emigration point, the 'migration transition' gradually transforms countries of net emigration to countries of net immigration. As economies grow further, general levels of immigration start to exceed the levels of declining emigration. Spain, Italy, Ireland, Finland, South Korea, Taiwan and Thailand all went through such a transition over recent decades. Mexico and Turkey – major sources of foreign labour for the US and EU, respectively – also seem beyond this peak emigration point. They are experiencing falling emigration while increasingly attracting migrants from poorer countries south and east of their borders.

However, for the sixty-odd countries in the world with lower income levels, any improvements in income and education are likely to increase people's capabilities and aspirations to migrate for decades to come. In Asia and the Middle East this applies to countries such as Yemen, Afghanistan, Tajikistan, Bangladesh, Cambodia, Nepal, Myanmar and Papua New Guinea. In the Western hemisphere, development is likely to increase the emigration potential of the poorest countries in Central America and the Andes region, as well as Haiti. And it particularly applies to most of sub-Saharan Africa – currently the poorest region in the world – which still has significant emigration potential.

Of course, this does not mean that governments should not stimulate economic growth, education and infrastructure – although it is good to question the credibility and appropriateness of the colonial-sounding pretensions that rich countries can and should bring 'development' to poor countries. And, of course, rapid growth, trust in government and social security can have some moderating effect on emigration levels. However, governments should be under no illusion that the migration transition can somehow be a shortcut. In order to dash any naive hopes that politicians and experts continue to harbour when it comes to this issue, it is important to stress that the migration transition is a *long-term* process linked to fundamental social and economic transformations that usually take several generations to materialize.

Thus the evidence turns on its head the entire idea that development can be a 'cure' for migration. Development in low-income countries inevitably leads to more, instead of less, emigration, because higher incomes, better education and improved infrastructure simultaneously increase people's *capabilities* and *aspirations* to migrate. This migration paradox reveals the need to radically change the conventional ways of thinking about migration that have dominated debates, reporting and teaching for too long. In particular, it shows the need to see migration as an integral, inseparable – and therefore largely inevitable – part of the processes of economic development, urbanization and modernization.

This perspective also allows us to look into the future. In many ways, the second half of the twentieth century has been the age of Asian emigration, in which Asia massively entered the global migration stage, with growing numbers of migrants from countries such as China, India, South Korea and the Philippines migrating to an increasingly wide array of destination countries around the globe. The coming half-century is likely to become the age of African migration, with migration from poor countries in sub-Saharan Africa increasing – not despite but paradoxically *because of* development.

Myth 6: Emigration is a desperate flight from misery

Each year, millions of migrants are lured into expensive and perilous journeys based on smugglers' and recruiters' false promises about opportunities in the Wealthy West. Yet instead of landing in El Dorado, they find themselves tricked into marginalized positions on the bottom rungs of the labour market, toiling away in dirty, dangerous and degrading jobs – if they survive the trip at all.

This idea – that much South–North migration is a 'desperate flight from misery' driven by unrealistic mirages of wealth and luxury in the West – has increasingly dominated popular perceptions about migration spread by politicians and media. Based on the conviction that it would therefore be better for would-be migrants to stay at home, Western governments have invested large sums of money in information campaigns to discourage migration, often with the help of UN agencies like the International Organization for Migration (IOM). This usually takes the form of ads on television and online to inform young people in poor countries in Africa, Asia and Latin America about the costs and risks of migrating to the West. Sometimes these ads feature celebrities.

Invariably, the central message is the following: 'Don't believe the lies told by smugglers about the wonders of life in the Wealthy West! It is dangerous to migrate! Those who went before you regret their decision. Don't leave your family behind in despair. It's better to stay in your own country and build a future there.' Such campaigns resonate with the images and stories we often see and hear in the media about migrants who suffer severe exploitation by working as 'modern slaves' in sectors such as agriculture, construction, restaurants, meatpacking, hospitality, sweatshops, domestic work or prostitution. To prevent this, would-be migrants should be informed about the grim realities of migrating.

The ads used by these information campaigns are usually centred around stories about the experiences of former migrants who went through horrible experiences, but then saw the light and decided to build a future in their own countries, often with the help of return programmes funded by destination countries. Such programmes allow them to follow some form of training and education before or after returning, to prepare them for their new lives back home.

Between 2015 and 2019 the EU and member states launched over 130 migration awareness campaigns, with estimated costs of around €45 million.[1] As part of its immigration prevention policy, in 2021 the Biden administration launched a programme to influence migrant decision-making in Central America through campaigns disseminating information about the dangers of travel to the US. In Mexico and Central America, the US State Department has funded IOM to run *Piénsalo 2 Veces* (Think Twice), a campaign aiming to provide migration information to migrants and provide alternatives to migration through development activities.[2]

The dominant image is that these workers' dreams have been shattered, as they find themselves tricked and trapped in marginalized positions at the bottom rungs of the labour market, living in squalid, cramped and unhygienic apartments they have to share with other migrants. Things seem particularly bad for illegal migrants. Living under the constant fear of being arrested and deported, they are vulnerable to abuse by employers, and often make barely enough money to pay for lodging and food, let alone to send money home. The need to pay off debts, and the shame of returning empty-handed, leaves them no choice but to endure years of suffering and exploitation. If only they had known . . .

How it really works

Migration is an investment in a better future

The message seems clear: 'There is nothing there, don't believe the lies told to you, it's better to stay at home.' However, when migrants see such ads, they usually respond with scorn. When I ask, as part of my fieldwork, young, eager-to-migrate Moroccan men and women about such information campaigns, they typically smirk and say: 'If life is really that bad in Europe, why would they ask for visas and build those fences?' Their words speak to a simple reality, which is that, for the vast majority of migrants, leaving is still a much better option than staying at home – despite the costs, risks and suffering that migration may entail. Even if they do unattractive jobs, are exploited and stay illegally, the pay and future prospects are much better than if they were doing similar jobs back home – or worse, not working at all.

Migration prevention campaigns are biased towards the worst-case scenarios of the 's/he was scammed, lost everything, was forced to work like a slave, and then died or got deported' genre. They are generally based on fictionalized stories using animations and actors. Horrible things do indeed happen to many migrants, but the point is that these stories are not representative of the experiences of most migrants. And most migrants know this fact. As international organizations and humanitarian NGOs tend to pull out – and sometimes fabricate – the most 'gory' stories about migrants' suffering and abuse, we lose sight of the bigger picture.[3] Crucially, such representations fail to answer the question: if things are really that bad, why do people keep on migrating? In fact, there are several reasons why we need to question narratives that unilaterally portray vulnerable migrant workers as victims.

The idea that information awareness campaigns can prevent migration is based on the assumption that much South–North migration – particularly when it's illegal – is essentially a non-rational act of desperation, and potential migrants therefore need to be told, 'Stay home, it's in your own best interests!'

We often only hear the stories of poverty and violence that allegedly push people to migrate. This is linked to the common portrayal of South–North migration as a desperate flight from poverty, hunger and violence, which resonates with Western prejudices about 'poor countries' as pools of poverty, tyranny and violence, where droughts and floods have driven the poor and desperate off their land to live miserable lives in unsanitary urban slums, making them increasingly desperate to move abroad. This is often based on the media's tendency towards reporting that casts entire countries or even continents – particularly Africa – as humanitarian disaster zones.

Such characterizations tap into crude stereotypes of 'Third World misery' that, although usually couched in humanitarian rhetoric, in their underlying assumptions of what drives people to migrate are not essentially different from the ideas behind the 'shithole country' rhetoric espoused by Donald Trump and other politicians.[4] More fundamentally, the portrayal of migration as a desperate flight from misery ignores the crucial fact that migration, even if it is illegal, generally allows people to earn much more money than they could ever have earned at home. From that perspective it is a rational decision to migrate. But this is the story we generally don't hear.

The media and organizations involved in migration prevention campaigns thus create a biased, one-sided representation of migration. This usually reduces migrants to passive victims of various crooks, such as smugglers, traffickers, recruiters and employers. The reality of most migration is rather different from the usual 'desperate' stereotype.

First, as we saw in the previous chapter, the poorest and most vulnerable people – those who have most reason to despair – generally don't have the resources to migrate, and certainly not over long distances and to faraway countries. This is why most international migrants are neither from the poorest countries nor from the poorest sections of origin-country populations. If you are a street vendor or cleaner in Manila, Mexico City or Casablanca, your chances of migrating abroad are virtually zero.

Second, as numerous field studies by researchers who have actually talked to migrants have shown, for most people the decision to migrate is a conscious and deliberate one that is generally a far cry from the desperation stereotype endlessly recycled by media reporting and political rhetoric. In strong contrast to the image of 'desperate departures', migration is generally a deliberate investment in a better future. By and large, research has shown that migrating abroad is an undertaking that needs careful planning, requires a lot of resources and is therefore rarely ever a decision that is taken light-heartedly.

Migration is a rational decision

Particularly in low-income countries, migration is not so much an individual but typically a collective decision, with families investing in the migration of one or two household members. As a large body of research has shown, the migration of a few household members to cities has an important insurance function for rural families, as it provides them with a potential extra source of backup income. This makes them less vulnerable than they would be if they only depended on uncertain agrarian income, where one bad harvest can send a family into absolute poverty. By earning extra money from the urban sector, families no longer put all their eggs in one basket – what economists refer to as 'risk spreading'.[5] Going abroad usually comes with even bigger gains.

Stay-at-home campaigns deny the reality that, for most migrants, migration is a life-changing opportunity to improve their lives beyond anything they could have achieved back home. As much as migration to the New World represented a hope for an unimaginably better future for millions of Europeans until the mid-twentieth century, the same is true today for numerous people living in Latin America, Africa and South and South-East Asia.

Other than much better salaries, strong motivations for people to move are better career opportunities and better prospects for their children. Migration is generally not about gaining 'quick bucks' or a reckless act by desperate 'fortune seekers' (who basically don't know what they're doing) gambling away the family savings, but rather an investment in the long-term well-being of families. Migration is a real chance to obtain a stable source of family income, decent housing, the ability to seek treatment for an illness, money to start a business and the opportunity for children to study. Instead of an act of desperation, migration is generally a rational decision people take in the best interests of themselves and their family.

For instance, in Mexico the average wages for farm workers in 2019 were 3,400 pesos or $196 a month[6] – while in California the pay rate for migrant farm workers was around $15 per hour or about $2,500 per month.[7] In Morocco in 2022, the typical salary of an unskilled worker was around €8 per day, while even undocumented migrants employed as agricultural workers in southern Spain could earn at least €5–6 per hour or €40–50 per day. Meanwhile, salaries for manual workers in France and the Netherlands are at least €10 per hour, or €80 per day, so *ten times* higher than in Morocco.

Even undocumented workers generally see a long-term benefit in migration, and that's why they are willing to endure exploitation and difficult circumstances, as they are in it for the long haul. I have seen this in my fieldwork in southern Morocco. In the 1990s and 2000s, many young Moroccans migrated illegally to Spain, attracted by jobs in the booming agricultural and construction sectors. Although they were *clandestinos*, their work still provided them with a much higher salary than they would have earned back home, and many eventually received residency papers because of several regularization campaigns, which then allowed them to bring in their families.

This is why, contrary to the assumptions of migration information campaigns, most undocumented workers don't regret their journey. A survey among foreign-born Latinos living in the US showed that the vast majority (78 per cent) of those without a green card, many of whom are likely to be undocumented, would migrate to the US if they could do it again – only slightly lower than the 87 per cent among green card holders and naturalized US citizens.[8]

Migration is the most effective form of development aid

Remittances are the best proof that most migrants have very good reasons for leaving their homes. Each year, migrants all over the world send back huge amounts of money. The money remitted by migrants has become a vital lifeline for millions of families and communities in origin countries. Over recent decades, the total volume of remittances sent back by migrants to developing countries has soared to unprecedented levels. According to official data compiled by the World Bank, in 1990 migrants sent back the equivalent of $29 billion to lower- and middle-income countries. This amount had more than doubled to $74 billion in 2000, after which it quadrupled to $302 billion in 2010 and reached $502 billion in 2020.

To put this in perspective, in 2020 remittances sent to developing countries were almost 2.6 times higher than the $193 billion in official development assistance (ODA), and 94 per cent of the $536 billion in foreign direct investment (FDI). Particularly in middle-income countries, which tend to have the highest emigration rates, remittances have dwarfed ODA to near obliteration. In 2020, Mexico, the Philippines and India received $43 billion, $35 billion and $83 billion in migrant remittances – compared to $1 billion, $1.5 billion and $1.8 billion in official development assistance. On average, over the 2010s remittances flowing to middle-income countries exceeded aid ten times over.In lower-income countries, too, remittances have grown in volume, and on average are equal to 60–70 per cent of development aid. [9]

Official data on remittances only captures money sent back home through banks or money operators such as Western Union and MoneyGram, however, so the real importance of remittances is even higher

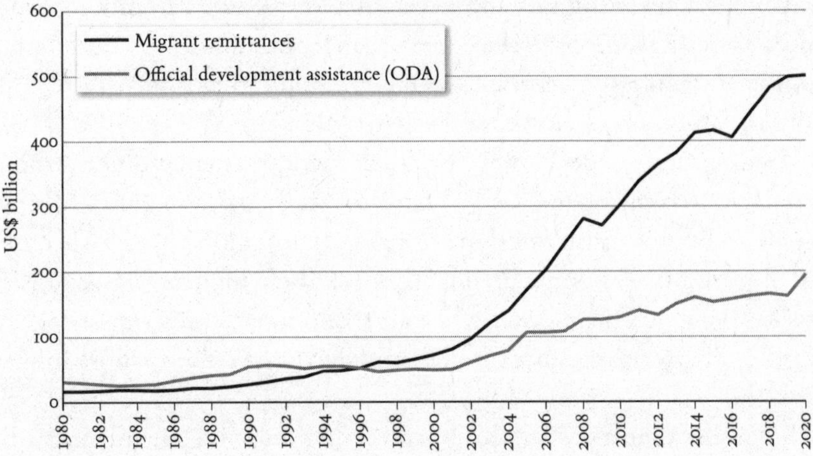

Graph 9: Migrant remittances and development assistance aid (to lower- and middle-income countries), 1980–2020

than we might infer from these measures. Partly because of the hefty fees charged by money transfer agencies, many migrants send their money through informal operators or bring money in cash or as goods on visits back home. According to some estimates, such unrecorded remittances through informal channels are likely to add at least 50 per cent to recorded flows.[10]

Many remittances are also sent in kind. Over Christmas, millions of Filipino migrants around the world sent 'balikbayan' boxes home to their families, filled with foodstuffs and valuable items. *Balikbayan* means 'return to the country', and for Filipinos this is a powerful practical and symbolic way to maintain connections with family. During their summer holiday trips home, Turkish and Moroccan workers in Europe typically load up their cars and vans with items like clothes, car parts, fridges, washing machines, television sets, satellite receivers, computers and mobile phones, as gifts and merchandise – and may return with prized assets such as olive oil and dates, and products like clothes and furniture.

Remittances are arguably the most effective form of bottom-up development aid in the world. Not only are they more than double the official development assistance, they also flow directly from migrants to their families – that is, to those who need them. No money ends up in the pockets of corrupt politicians or is siphoned off by state bureaucrats and expensive consultants and development experts.[11] Remittances are an essential lifeline for rural and urban communities in developing countries, helping to increase the income and living standards of millions of families back home.

As an insurance mechanism for families, remittances provide an additional source of income and a vital financial buffer in times of crop failure, economic crisis or other setbacks. Remittances have also become an important economic lifeline because they tend to be 'countercyclical' – which means that when an economic crisis or earthquake or another disaster strikes back home, migrants start sending more money back.[12]

So, rather than a desperate departure, migration is generally part of a long-term strategy to improve the living standards of entire families. Migrants are willing to endure years of hard work and loneliness because of the real hope of a better future. In the first years after migrating, remittances are typically used to meet immediate needs, such as food, clothing, medical care and the construction of a house back home. Migrants may also invest their hard-earned money in small-scale commercial enterprises, such as grocery stores, cafés, restaurants, guesthouses, small taxi companies or other transport businesses. For many migrant workers the long-term goal is to provide their children with a better education, either in their origin country or at their destination.

Hitting the migration jackpot

In the regions and places where many people have migrated abroad, the impacts of migration and remittances are often transformative. Depending on where workers were originally recruited, migrants often come from very particular areas in origin countries, and have settled in specific cities and even neighbourhoods in destination countries. For instance, several states in western and central Mexico such as Jalisco, Michoacán and Zacatecas have traditionally been the heartland for Mexican emigration to the US, although other sending regions have emerged more recently. Many Moroccans in Europe come from the Rif Mountains, the Sous valley and a limited number of southern oases. Many Pakistanis in Britain come from Mirpur, many Bangladeshis are from Sylhet, and a large part of the Indian-heritage population in Britain can trace their origins back to Bihar, Uttar Pradesh and Tamil Nadu.[13]

In origin regions, emigration has acquired such a central place in the daily lives of people that researchers speak of a 'culture of migration', in which most families have people living abroad, and where emigration is widely considered as the main avenue to a better future. Mirpur, in the north of Pakistan, was once one of the poorest areas of the country, but thanks to large-scale migration to Britain the region has now become wealthy in terms of living standards for ordinary people. This migration started in the 1960s when the British government recruited workers for the factories of the Midlands and the north of England. Many had been evicted from their villages because of the construction of a huge hydroelectric dam in the nearby Jhelum river. Their migration to Britain marked a radical change in fortune as far as ordinary Mirpuris were concerned. As Roger Ballard, an anthropologist who did extensive research on Mirpuri migration, put it: 'Mirpuris have hit the jackpot.'[14]

Mirpur's connection with Britain has transformed the region. This is visible in the huge villas that migrants have constructed. Many British Pakistanis, including the second generation, have invested in businesses back home. In Mirpur – also known as 'Little Britain' – such investments include real estate, shops and bakeries. There are direct flights to and from Britain, and hundreds of thousands of people from the UK visit Mirpur every year. Western-style streets and businesses have even been created to cater to them.[15] In Mirpur it is possible to get all the comforts from Britain, and it is even possible to pay in pounds. Mirpur's radio station has a phone-in programme that has listeners and callers in Mirpur and in Britain. There is so much communication and travel between Mirpur and places like Birmingham and Bradford that they sometimes feel like one community, despite the huge geographical distance.[16]

From oasis to paradise

Inhabitants of the Todgha valley in southern Morocco have equally hit the migration jackpot. I visited the valley for the first time in 1994, and between 1998 and 2000 I lived there to conduct research. I have been going back there almost every year ever since for shorter visits and new research, enabling me to follow long-term change.

Years of intense migration to France, the Netherlands and more recently Spain have totally transformed what used to be a predominantly agrarian region and a modest hub in the trans-Saharan caravan trade into a bustling regional economic centre. This migration started in the 1960s when French and Dutch mines and factories sent recruiters to the region, while almost the entire Jewish population of the Todgha emigrated to Israel. Labour migration to Europe was followed by large-scale family reunification in the 1970s and 1980s.

From the 1990s, increasing numbers of oasis dwellers moved to Spain in search of new work opportunities, such as in Spain's booming greenhouse sector. Most did so illegally, either by paying fishermen to bring them to the other side of the Strait of Gibraltar, or by entering on tourist visas but staying after their visas expired. Most of these overstayers managed to obtain residence papers during several regularization campaigns in Spain in the 2000s. After a temporary dip in emigration after the 2007–2008 global financial crisis, emigration from the Todgha resumed as labour demand in Europe rebounded over the 2010s – particularly in Spain and Italy, but more recently also in Portugal (and, outside Europe and for the higher-skilled, Canada).

Nowadays, no less than 40 per cent of all families living in the Todgha valley have members living in Europe. My surveys have shown that remittance-receiving families' incomes are at least double the incomes of other families, and often many times more. Investments by migrants in new houses and small enterprises have fuelled a construction boom and the rapid growth of Tinghir – the bustling urban centre of the Todgha valley – where new employment opportunities are now attracting internal migrants from more remote villages in the surrounding mountains.[17]

In many areas of rural Morocco, access to migration opportunities has become a make-or-break factor in defining people's life prospects. In regions of southern Morocco, migration has been an important avenue for upward mobility for the Haratin, a low-status ethnic group mainly consisting of Black sharecroppers and smallholders. Instead of traditional divisions between Black and white, sharecroppers and landowners, former slaves and free people, peasants and nomads, in the Moroccan deep south the main social divide now runs between migration 'haves' and 'have-nots'. Across the country, emigration is not only a way to earn more money but also means access to healthcare and social security, as well as education and career opportunities for children.

In the eyes of local people, emigrants are extraordinarily wealthy, and seem to almost come from a different world. The cars they drive, the clothes they wear and the gifts they bring home all speak of their relative wealth, and are a testimony to the fact that emigration is the most secure avenue towards a better future. This has become a phenomenon all over the Moroccan countryside. Each year during the summer holidays, about 3 million Moroccan migrants – almost one-tenth of the total population of Morocco – drive their cars and vans from all across Europe to southern Spain, take the ferry and then drive to their home towns further south. In large swathes of the Moroccan countryside, the summer holiday season has taken the place of the harvest season of the past, when most weddings and other feasts happen, because that's when the migrants are back.

In rural Morocco, this holiday season is exciting for eager-to-migrate young men and women. Migrants' children and grandchildren, the second and third generations, are the centre of attention – not only because of their nice cars, clothes and gadgets, but also because marrying a migrant means a secure ticket to Europe. Similar stories can be told about countless rural areas in other emigration countries such as Mexico, Guatemala, the Philippines and Tunisia. In such countries, emigration cultures often acquire a truly national dimension, not because migration is some kind of mirage, or illusion, but because migration really does offer the most realistic and secure prospect of a better future for many non-elite groups.

Better to be indebted than stay at home

Because migration is expensive, many migrants borrow money or take on debts with recruiters and employers in order to migrate. Most migrant workers pay back their debts through salary deductions or other arrangements. However, it's a huge misunderstanding that paying back debts means that migrants are by definition essentially forced labourers or trafficking victims. For instance, media images and political narratives portray many, or most, women working as domestic workers in Gulf countries as 'modern slaves', having their passports taken away, being locked up in houses and subjected to severe abuse and even rape. Such things do happen, but these experiences are not representative of the overall experience of migrant workers. To portray them as such denies migrants' agency. Although many migrant workers must often work several months or years to pay back the costs of the journey to family members, recruiters or smugglers, international migration is *generally* an investment that eventually pays off.

I learned a lot about this from Dovelyn Rannveig Mendoza, a migration policy analyst currently at the University of Cambridge who has done two decades of extensive research on the recruitment of migrant workers in Asia, the Pacific, the Gulf and in Europe. Through her countless interviews with migrant workers, recruiters and government officials, Mendoza found out that debt repayment is a very common part of contractual arrangements between migrants and recruitment agencies, in which migration debt is for instance being repaid through salary deductions during the first months of employment. In the case of illegal migration, debt repayment can be part of arrangements with smugglers.[18]

Although indebtedness in such labour situations is clearly far from what many would consider a fair deal, the fact that migrants pay back debts to recruiters, smugglers or employers does not automatically make them victims. Each year, millions of migrants around the world borrow money to move abroad. This is a largely *voluntary* affair. Nobody forces them to do so. As Mendoza argues, the truth is that without taking on debts, many relatively poor people would still be stuck at home, unable to amass the financial resources needed for migrating.[19] Taking on debts is the way millions of poor people can create a better future for themselves by migrating to the West, the Gulf and other wealthy countries – mostly legally, sometimes illegally. Migrant workers are keen to pay off their debts to set themselves free and earn more money to send home. It would therefore make no sense to unilaterally cast these migrant workers as victims, since they would not consider themselves as such. Having made a huge investment of time, effort and money, they would do anything to avoid going home empty-handed, and have a strong interest in staying and paying off their debts.

For sure, the need to pay back such debts makes migrants vulnerable to various forms of exploitation and abuse. Recruitment agencies often overcharge migrant workers at the origin and destination or fail to deliver on their promises in terms of salary, deductions and working conditions. Mendoza's research also shows that 'contract substitution' – forcing migrants to sign new contracts at the destination with radically different and generally inferior conditions than the contract signed at the origin – is common. In practice, this means lower wages than legally allowed or previously agreed, a worse job and reduced or forgone benefits.[20]

Migrants whose work permits are tied to one employer are particularly vulnerable to abuse. This is common in the *kafala* system in Gulf countries like Saudi Arabia, the United Arab Emirates and Qatar – workers are typically bound to one sponsor (the *kafala*), which doesn't allow migrant workers to switch employers. In Western countries, too, many foreign workers in sectors like domestic work, care and hospitality migrate on temporary contracts that are tied to one employer, making them vulnerable to exploitation. Mendoza has therefore argued that, in this sense, Western countries run their own *kafala* systems.[21]

In the vast majority of cases, such abuses have to do with labour exploitation. Mendoza's research shows that most abuse cases reported by Filipino and Sri Lankan domestic workers in Jordan are not about violence or sexual assault – which dominate popular perceptions about these workers – but about non-payment or underpayment of salary, and living and working conditions.[22] In the West, too, many employers exploit the temporary or undocumented status of migrant workers by making them work long hours for low pay in bad and sometimes dangerous conditions.[23]

However, the fact that many migrant workers around the world are exploited does not mean that they don't see a benefit in doing this work and would not have migrated if they had known. Of course, while the evidence shows that most people have good reason for migrating, some migrants are inevitably disappointed. Life abroad is not always what they imagined it to be, but still, only a minority of migrants end up regretting having left, as the alternative – staying at home – would have been much worse. That's why migrants keep on coming back. For instance, data from the Philippine government shows that almost two-thirds of migrant workers going abroad are 'rehires' – that is, people who have worked abroad before.[24]

South–South migration is the main road out of poverty

It is not only migration to the West that can be a game changer. Unless people are lucky enough to be directly recruited from the countryside – as was the case for the Mirpuris from Pakistan, North African and

Turkish guest workers in western Europe, and Mexican guest workers recruited through the 1942–64 Bracero programme – migration to Western countries is out of reach for most ordinary people because it is too expensive. Because of border restrictions and visa rules, migrating to Western countries is a costly affair that is usually accessible only to people with enough money or with family members already living abroad who can provide migration assistance. In the Philippines, for example, it is not a coincidence that overseas migration has traditionally come from regions with the lowest poverty rates, such as the National Capital Region, Central Luzon and Southern Tagalog.[25]

A recent study by Mendoza shows that Nepalese workers wanting to go to the EU have to pay approximately €7,000 to recruitment agencies. Considering the wage levels in Nepal, this is the equivalent of four annual salaries for low-wage workers, and a full year of average salary levels. This is a huge sum of money. Using GDP per capita levels in Nepal as a benchmark, it would be the equivalent of a West European citizen paying some €150,000 in recruitment fees. Mendoza found that migrants were willing to pay such amounts because they see their migration as a long-term investment, with the goal of gaining permanent residence in the EU for themselves and their families.[26]

Given the huge financial hurdles, migration to the city or easier-to-access non-Western destinations can therefore be an attractive second-best option for those who cannot afford this. Beside Gulf countries, Singapore, Malaysia, Thailand and Taiwan have emerged as attractive destinations for migrant workers from poorer Asian countries such as Indonesia, the Philippines, India, Myanmar and Laos. Thai migrant workers in Hong Kong earn four to five times more than they would earn at home – explaining why they are willing to pay substantial fees to recruitment agents equalling more than six months of salary for someone on a two-year domestic worker's contract.[27]

Within Africa, relatively wealthy countries like South Africa, Nigeria and Côte d'Ivoire and oil economies such as Libya and Gabon have emerged as important regional migration destinations. For many non-elite groups in Asia and increasingly also Africa, the oil-rich Gulf countries of Saudi Arabia, the United Arab Emirates, Kuwait and Qatar, and other Middle Eastern countries such as Jordan, Lebanon and Israel, have become significant migration destinations. Compared to Western countries, it is generally easier and cheaper to move to the Middle East. Although Gulf countries don't give many rights to migrants, and expect them to return home, the flip side is that it is relatively easy to obtain work visas.[28]

This is the story that the Western media typically miss, as they almost exclusively focus on when things go wrong and migrants are horribly abused and exploited. In Ethiopia, for instance, fieldwork by the sociologist Kerilyn Schewel revealed that increasing numbers of young women from villages around the town of Ziway in the central lowlands of the Rift Valley have discovered migration to the Middle East as a fast-track to a better future.

The main alternative is to work in the greenhouses of a Dutch-owned flower farm exporting millions of roses to European markets daily. In 2016, work in the greenhouses would have earned them $35–42 per month – barely enough to cover their living expenses, as 85 per cent was spent on food and housing alone. This is why many are keen to migrate to Beirut, Dubai, Riyadh or other destinations in the Middle East. Domestic workers in Beirut earn on average $150 per month, while living expenses are covered. Instead of toiling away on local farms for wages that barely cover the costs of living, two- or three-year contracts to do domestic work for families in Saudi Arabia, other Gulf countries or Lebanon give them a unique opportunity to, as they put it, 'change their life'.[29]

To facilitate their migration, most families invest the equivalent of $280–560 (2016 prices) to pay the upfront costs of the passport, health checks and transportation to and from Addis Ababa. The agency covers the rest, including flight and visa applications, as well as charging its own fee, which it deducts from the worker's first few months' salary. Working abroad for a few years allows many young women to save enough money to return, build a house in town and open a small business, such as a roadside coffee stand, restaurant or corner store. Although to an outsider such businesses may not look very spectacular, for the women involved they represent an empowering experience that has literally changed their lives. The money they save also enables them to leave their native villages and settle in towns, and their independent economic status gives them more choice of marriage partners, while they still contribute to their family's income.[30]

Migrants can think for themselves

First impressions can be deceptive. The way politicians and the media portray migration from poor countries is often driven by stereotypes about 'Third World' poverty and misery. The evidence challenges the stereotype that migration from developing countries is generally based on irrational mirages about life abroad. Although many migrants endure considerable hardship, are often exploited, and some are disappointed, for most leaving is still a much better option than staying at home. The money migrants send home is a vital source of income. Remittances enable huge improvements in housing, health, education and living standards, while the prospect of family reunification creates unique opportunities for migrants' children. It is therefore an illusion that information campaigns will dissuade people from migrating.

The whole idea that migrants are massively tricked into migrating based on false promises by smugglers and traffickers derives from Western stereotypes of poor non-white people as being ignorant, naive and somehow less rational, and who should therefore be informed by Western countries and aid agencies that it is in their own best interests to stay at home. This not only reveals a condescending 'we know what is good for you' attitude, but it also ignores that fact that, for many non-elite groups, migrating abroad is the most secure avenue towards a better future – for which they are willing to take significant costs and risks. Migrants actively seek to migrate because they see a clear benefit in doing so. In other words, migrants can – and do – think for themselves.

Myth 7: We don't need migrant workers

'What we want to do is bear down on migration, particularly of unskilled workers who have no job to come to.' These were the words of British prime minister Boris Johnson in a TV interview in December 2019, ahead of Britain's formal exit from the EU on 1 February 2020, and a few days before the general election, which he would win by a landslide. In the interview, Johnson guaranteed voters that the UK would use the border sovereignty regained through Brexit to clamp down on lower-skilled immigration from the EU while introducing an Australian-style points-based system to attract highly skilled workers.[1]

Johnson's remarks resonate with a general consensus in Western countries that lower-skilled migrants are no longer needed. This is different from the post-war decades, when Western countries massively recruited migrant workers to work in industry, mining and agriculture.

However, those times of urgent need for migrant workers seem over once and for all. In our post-industrial economies, the number of factory and farm jobs has been shrinking because of mechanization and automation as well as 'outsourcing' – the relocation of labour-intensive industries to low-wage countries. Most of the manual jobs that attracted foreign workers in the post-war decades have disappeared rapidly since the 1970s, as machines replaced hands, and manual jobs were shipped abroad. Industrial decline went along with a strong growth of service sector jobs in research, engineering, medicine and management, needing more advanced levels of education and training.

As factories and mines shut down in the 1970s and 1980s, workers were massively laid off. This led to mass unemployment in industrial regions across the Western world, such as the US Rust Belt states, the British Midlands and all across the industrial heartlands of north-west Europe. Although this affected both native and foreign-born workers, migrant workers were hit particularly hard, as they were often the first to get fired. Protracted unemployment, welfare dependency and government neglect contributed to problems of segregation and integration among some lower-skilled migrant communities – experiences that few would like to see repeated.

The overall consensus now is that governments should attract higher-skilled workers – such as managers, engineers, lawyers, accountants and doctors – through points systems, special immigration schemes and tax exemptions, as part of a 'global race for talent' or 'battle for brains' to serve the 'knowledge economy' of the twenty-first century.

All of this has reinforced the belief that in our post-industrial economies there seems to be less and less room for lower-skilled workers perceived as having poor economic prospects. Given the huge inequalities between poor and rich countries, there simply appear to be way too many young people in developing countries eager to migrate – at best, they seem to be condemned to a marginal existence in the informal economy of destination countries. Instead of recruiting migrant workers, it seems to make more sense to reserve for local workers the limited amount of blue-collar jobs that are still available. This has led to a broad consensus that the immigration of lower-skilled migrant workers should therefore be prevented, or only allowed on a temporary basis.

How it really works

Labour demand is the main driver of migration

The idea that, without stringent border restrictions, Western countries would surely be flooded with lower-skilled migrants is based on the popular assumption that economic inequality between countries is the main driver of migration. This is also how economists tend to view international migration: as a more or less linear function of income or wage gaps between countries. The higher economic inequality and wage gaps are, the more people in origin countries will be tempted to migrate. Following this logic, reducing international inequality by stimulating economic development in origin countries is the key to reducing migration pressures. However, since it takes decades to significantly reduce such inequalities, we seem to have no choice other than to tightly control borders, since there are simply too many eager-to-migrate people 'out there' for whom there will be no jobs available.

Although it may all *sound* very logical, this is not how migration works. Contrary to what many economists believe, economic gaps do not automatically 'lead' to migration. In reality, people are not pushed and pulled around the world by abstract economic forces. Real-world migration patterns are anything but a simple function of economic inequalities. If inequality really drives migration, why is there so little migration between the poorest and the richest countries? Why do most migrant workers come from middle-income rather than the low-income countries? And why do so few people from the poorest countries migrate in the first place?

We already have answers to some of these questions. As we saw in chapter 5, poverty actually prevents people from moving over long distances, because migrating is expensive. This partly explains the paradox that emigration generally increases when poor countries get richer and wage gaps with destination countries become smaller. In fact, most migrants move between regions and countries – such as between the US and Canada, Germany and the Netherlands, or Australia and New Zealand – in the absence of any significant wage gap at all. This is because *labour demand*, not inequality or poverty, is the main driver of international migration.

Many people migrate not primarily because of wage gains, but because they have particular skills, qualifications and professional aspirations that fit jobs that can only be found elsewhere. Such skills-matching to jobs partly explains why rich countries continue to have significant levels of immigration *and* emigration. For instance, in 2020, about 3.9 million German-born people lived outside Germany, equivalent to over one-third of the 10.3 million foreign-born people living in Germany. In the same year, an estimated 4.7 million British-born lived abroad, half the number of the 9.5 million foreign-born living in Britain; while the 3.3 million Italian-born living abroad represented over half of the 6.3 million foreign-born living in Italy.[2]

A useful rule of thumb from economic geography is that the more skilled and specialized people become, the larger the geographical scope of labour markets, and the higher the chance that people have to move to find jobs that match their needs and aspirations. Farm workers, cashiers or plumbers are likely to find jobs where they live. Engineers, surgeons or university professors often have to move – first to be educated and then, upon graduation, to find jobs that fit their skills, aspirations and career plans. I therefore tell my students that higher education is potentially signing couples up for trouble, because the more specialized partners become, the more difficult it will be to find dream jobs for both in the same place.

The elephant in the room (of migration debates)

As we saw in the previous chapter, the stereotypical image of desperate migrants being irrationally attracted by mirages of the land of milk and honey is a myth that is not representative of the experiences of most migrants. International migration involves a considerable investment of money, time and effort, and can come at high emotional and social costs.[3] Long-distance migration often requires families to borrow money, take on debt or sell land and other assets, requiring careful planning. The image of would-be migrant workers massively 'pouring in' in the false hope of finding jobs that don't exist is therefore misleading.

To understand this, it is important to distinguish what *motivates* people to migrate at the micro level from the *structural causes* of migration at the macro level. While the prospect of earning a (much) higher wage abroad can obviously be a strong motivation to migrate, in reality most people only move if they know there will be *concrete* opportunities for work, study or other forms of personal advancement. The truth is that most would-be migrants don't like to gamble away their savings or take on migration debts without knowing about real opportunities and prospects in destination countries. They will only go if they know they can earn money abroad.

As counterintuitive as it may sound, inequality in itself does therefore not lead to migration. In 2012, I published a study that I conducted with the economist Mathias Czaika, my former colleague at Oxford University, on the impact of global income inequality on migration.[4] To our surprise, we did not find a significant effect of the position of countries in the global income hierarchy on levels of emigration. When we estimated the impact of income inequality between pairs of countries on migration, we did find some effect, although it was much smaller than we had expected. We therefore concluded that it is unrealistic to expect that lower international inequality will lead to a huge decline in international migration. More generally: economic inequality is neither a necessary nor a sufficient condition for substantial international migration to occur.[5]

To understand this, it can be useful to turn the question 'Why do people migrate?' around. Why are *only* about 3 per cent of the world population international migrants? Why does 97 per cent of the world population choose not to migrate, and stay in their country of birth despite the persistence of huge economic inequality? Apart from the fact that for many poor people international migration is out of reach because it's too expensive, another important factor is 'home preference': the simple fact that most people prefer to stay close to family and friends, and the communities and societies they are strongly attached to.

People are not spontaneously uprooted by international inequalities. Migrants generally don't sit at the kitchen table making statistical analyses of GDP per capita statistics and average wage differentials across countries. They look at concrete jobs they can get and concrete wages they can earn doing those jobs. While wage gaps can motivate people to migrate, most would stay home if there were no jobs to go to. Without concrete labour opportunities, migrant workers would stop coming. This highlights the central role of labour demand in driving migration.

All of this shows the shocking extent to which political rhetoric, media portrayals and 'root causes' narratives peddled by humanitarian NGOs and international organizations have come to dominate our perception and cloud our understanding of the forces driving international migration. The assertion that poverty and global inequality lead to migration systematically conceals and ignores the most important root cause of all, the *sine qua non* of large-scale migrations: persistent labour demand.

To a certain extent, this also applies to humanitarian migration. When in January 2023 I visited the US–Mexico border in El Paso and Ciudad Juárez with Alejandro Olayo-Méndez, assistant professor at the Boston College School of Social Work, migrants and asylum seekers from Central America and Venezuela and internally displaced people (IDPs) from Mexico would tell us stories about gang violence, extortion and a general lack of prospects back home, but when asked why they were going to the US, they would also mention job opportunities and the desire to start a new life by working hard and sending money back to their families. Without the huge surge in US labour demand, border crossings would probably not have reached anywhere near the same levels, in spite of the violence experienced in countries and regions of origin.[6]

In many ways, the crucial role of labour demand in driving migration is the elephant in the room in migration debates. For instance, in 2022 and 2023, when millions of migrants and asylum seekers tried to cross the Mexico–US border, it was quite revealing that politicians, journalists and experts failed to make the connection with historical labour shortages in the US, and record low unemployment caused by the post-pandemic economic revival. Migrants, often undocumented, typically filled the resulting labour shortages.

Immigration – it's the economy, stupid!

Although illegal migration attracts the most attention, it's important to emphasize that the vast majority of migrants move *legally*, and that this legal migration is predominantly driven by destination-country labour demand. It's a myth that most migrants just show up at the border without having any idea what to do. This may be true for some young adventurers – there are always exceptions – but most people will only move when they have a concrete job offer, because they were recruited, or because family or friends living abroad told them about vacancies and other opportunities.

Contrary to what politicians tell us, most migrants *do* have jobs to come to. And, contrary to another popular belief, the biggest demand is not for higher-skilled workers but rather lower- and mid-skilled migrant workers. Only a minority of immigrants fulfil the 'expat' stereotype of engineers, doctors and managers. While immigrants are still over-represented in manual jobs in fields such as agriculture, factory work, domestic work, food processing, cleaning and landscaping, an increasing number of migrant workers do mid-skilled jobs as plumbers, carpenters, builders, chefs, nurses and other caregivers. These might not officially count as 'higher-skilled' positions – which are usually defined as jobs needing a higher education diploma – but they still require significant skills.

Destination-country labour demand is the main driver of international migration. Perhaps the best proof of this is the close link between business cycles and immigration levels. To illustrate this, graph 10 depicts the correlation between economic growth and migration levels for Germany. The dotted line shows annual economic growth as measured by gross domestic product. To smooth out strong inter-annual

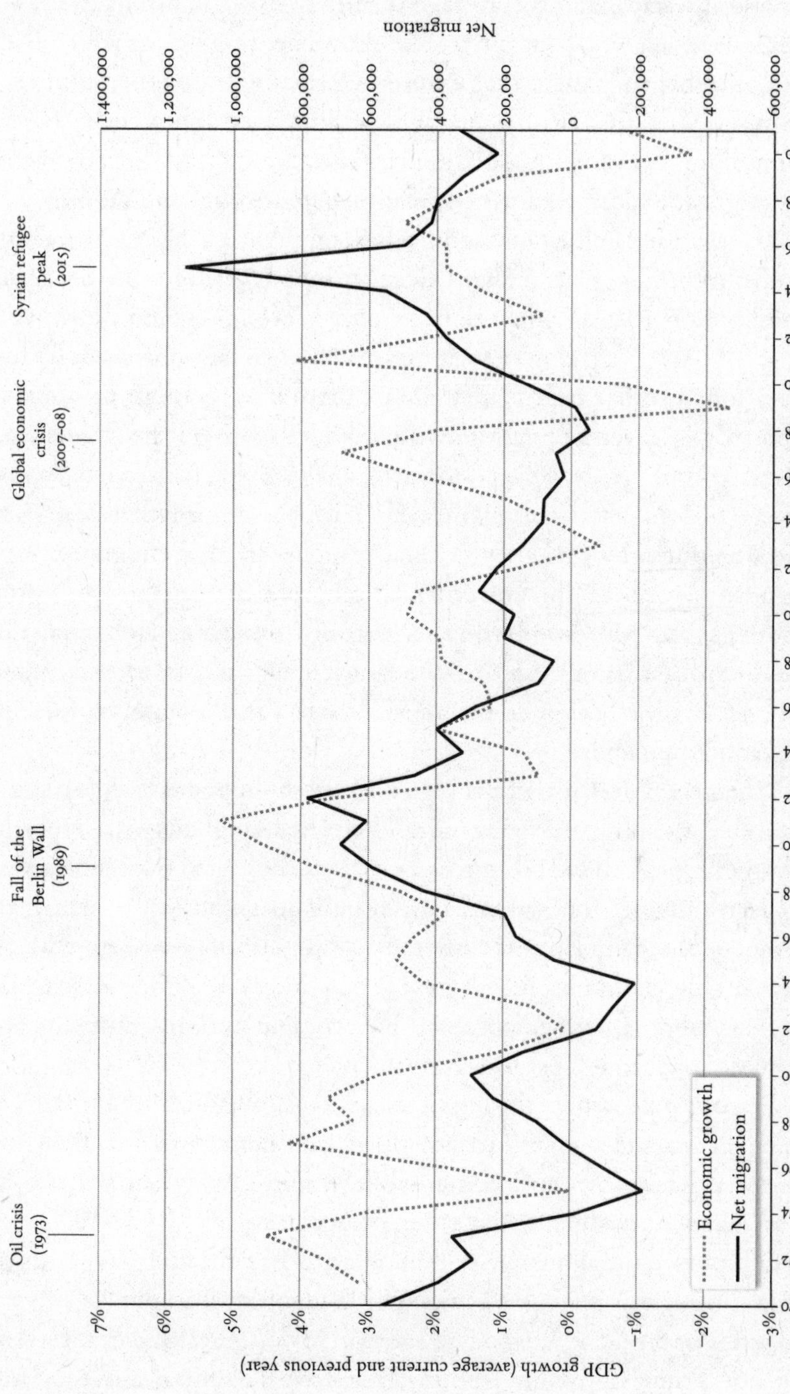

Graph 10: Economic growth and net migration in Germany, 1970–2021[7]

variation, I calculated the average of GDP growth in the current and previous years. The continuous line shows net migration, which is the total number of people that entered Germany minus the number of people that left Germany during the same year. Thus, negative net migration means a net population loss through migration, and positive net migration indicates a net population gain through migration.

The picture is clear and consistent: immigration follows economic trends, generally with a slight delay of about six months to a year. Immigration goes up when the economy is booming, and down when the economy is tanking. Obviously, such correlation does not prove causation, as other factors may in fact drive immigration. In addition, there may be reverse causation, with immigration leading to higher economic growth. However, econometric analyses that controlled for such effects confirm that variations in levels of economic growth have a strong effect on immigration levels.[8] This also applies to illegal migration – for instance, there is a rather neat correlation between unauthorized border crossings from Morocco across the Strait of Gibraltar and job opportunities in Spain. Likewise, in 2008 the global financial crisis caused a major decrease in illegal migration from Mexico to the US because of declining labour demand.[9]

When economic growth is high and unemployment low, job shortages increase. This makes it more likely that migrants will apply for jobs, get hired and qualify for work visas if they need one. In this way, modern immigration systems have a built-in flexibility in which the numbers of legally admitted migrants automatically fluctuate with the state of the economy. Job shortages also motivate employers to seek workers abroad, either through government-run recruitment programmes or through private recruitment.

The opposite applies during times of recession. With labour demand going down and unemployment rising, migrants who lose their jobs are more likely to return home, while would-be migrant workers are more likely to postpone their emigration plans.

Of course, not all people migrate for work. For family migrants the main motive is to join loved ones. For students, it is to pursue a degree abroad. For refugees, it is to find safety. However, even migrations that are not primarily about labour often have an important economic dimension. Much family migration is an indirect consequence or by-product of labour migration, with spouses and children following workers. If they have the resources and connections, refugees, too, are more likely to move to countries where they can find opportunities for work or do business, or are likely to adjust the timing of their migration to economic circumstances. Dynamic economies also tend to attract international students, as they offer the possibility of working while studying and provide employment opportunities after graduation.

Of course, such evidence shows that politicians are much less in command of immigration than they like to pretend. It should also take away any illusions that immigration is a phenomenon that can be micromanaged. Although politicians love to portray themselves as sitting firmly in the driver's seat, in practice immigration is not something than can be turned on and off like a tap. Immigration is a partly autonomous process that largely follows economic trends in destination countries. If economies are booming and labour demand is high, it's difficult to stop people from coming – whether legally or illegally. When the economy is tanking, fewer people will come. Of course, politicians will be keen to take credit and ascribe any change to their policies, but the next time immigration goes down, remember that rising unemployment is a more likely cause of the plummet.

An increasing demand for migrant labour

Besides business-cycle-driven fluctuations, over the past decades there has been a *structural* long-term increase of labour migration to Western countries, driven by a chronic demand for foreign workers. Defying the political mantra that we 'don't need migrant workers', the number of legal migrant workers arriving in many Western countries has shown a consistently increasing trend.

For instance, graph 11 shows that, since the early 1990s, Britain has transformed from a net emigration country to a net immigration country. Unlike most western European countries, the UK remained a net emigration country until the 1980s, reflecting its imperial heritage (with strong traditions of emigration to the US, Canada, Australia and New Zealand), weak economic performance and high unemployment. As a consequence of economic recovery and growing skills shortages, UK immigration has demonstrated a consistently increasing trend – with migrants coming from eastern Europe, but also from outside Europe, and annual legal in-flows roughly tripling from around 200,000 in the

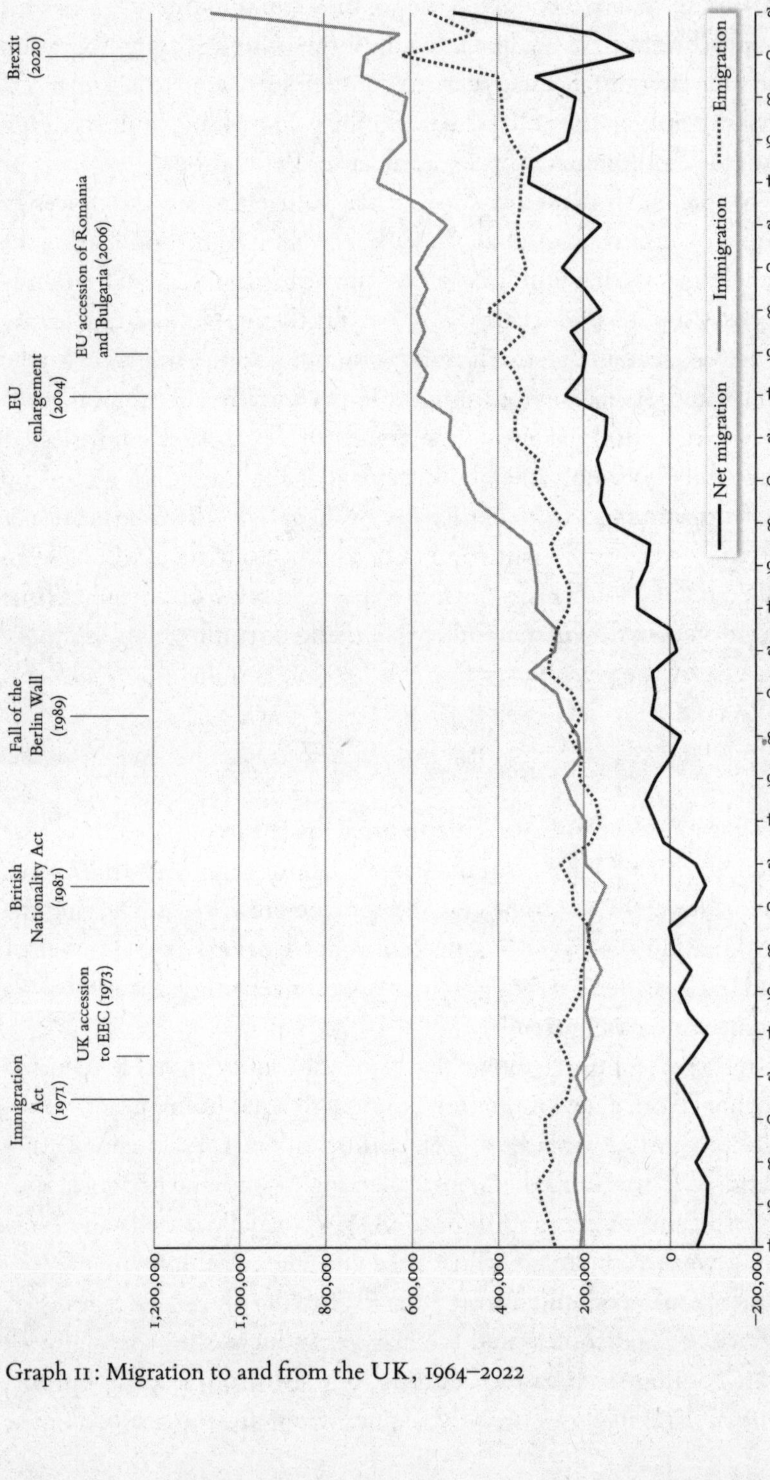

Immigration Act (1971)
UK accession to EEC (1973)
British Nationality Act (1981)
Fall of the Berlin Wall (1989)
EU enlargement (2004)
EU accession of Romania and Bulgaria (2006)
Brexit (2020)
1,200,000
1,000,000
800,000
600,000
400,000
200,000
0
−200,000
1964
1966
1968
1970
1972
1974
1976
1978
1980
1982
1984
1986
1988
1990
1992
1994
1996
1998
2000
2002
2004
2006
2008
2010
2012
2014
2016
2018
2020
2022
Net migration
Immigration
Emigration

Graph 11: Migration to and from the UK, 1964–2022

late 1980s to around 600,000 in the 2000s and 2010s. In the UK, it's widely believed that rising migration was caused by the eastward enlargement of the European Union in 2004 and prime minister Tony Blair's decision to open borders for workers from Poland, Lithuania and other EU member countries in eastern Europe. However, that's largely a myth, as immigration to the UK had already shown a structurally increasing trend since the 1990s, mainly caused by increasing labour demand.

We see similar trends in the US and the EU. Particularly since the 2000s, the US has seen a structural increase in the number of temporary migrants admitted at all skill levels, including seasonal Mexican and other Latin American workers on H1B skilled worker and H2-category seasonal worker visas, investors and traders, and academics and students. Between 1998 and 2019, numbers of (nominally) temporary legal admissions rose from around 2 million to 6.5 million. Over the same period, the number of border apprehensions (a proxy for illegal migration) averaged around 1 million per year. And the number of permanent admissions (green cards) – which mainly concerns family reunification – remained stable at much lower levels of around 1 million per year. This highlights the structural growth of labour immigration.

Likewise, registered migration from countries outside the European Union to the EU has seen a structurally increasing trend: from around 1 million legal immigrants per year in the late 1980s to around 2 million over the 2000s and 2010s – much higher than the estimated annual average of 65,000 unsolicited border arrivals (asylum seekers and illegal migrants combined) over recent years. Besides family migrants, international students and asylum seekers, an increasing component of these inflows are workers – with the number of non-EU workers legally admitted to EU countries tripling from 375,000 in 2010 to 1.2 million in 2019.[10]

Why labour migration has continued

An important question is why lower-skilled immigration has not only continued but even *increased*, despite industrial decline. The simple answer is that there has been a continued demand for migrant workers because of real skills shortages. In more recent decades, such labour needs have increased rather than decreased. What has changed are the types of workers that are most in demand. Many jobs in industry, mining or agriculture that used to attract migrant workers up until the 1970s have been either automated or shipped overseas to low-wage workers in lower-income countries. Examples of such outsourcing include the relocation of the garment and footwear industry to China, Taiwan, Thailand and Malaysia (which themselves attract migrants from poorer countries such as Myanmar, Laos and Cambodia[11]); the relocation of the US car industry to Mexico; the relocation of British and American call centres to India and the Philippines; and the global relocation of the accounting and software industries.

But not all jobs can be replaced by machines and computers or moved abroad. This particularly applies to lower-skilled personal services that require the actual physical presence of workers. Immigrants are still over-represented in agricultural and industrial jobs that are difficult to automate – such as fruit and vegetable picking, construction, and meat and fish processing – but there has been an overall shift towards the service sector. Demand for migrant labour has boomed in domestic work, healthcare, cleaning, hospitality, landscaping, gardening, washing, ironing, hairdressing and manicuring. Migrant workers play an increasingly vital role in making sure that our meat and vegetables are processed, packed, stored, shelved, sold, cooked, served and delivered. The taxi, transport and delivery sectors also depend increasingly on migrant labour.

Migrants typically do jobs that native workers are no longer able or willing to do. These low-status roles are also known as '3D' (dirty, dangerous and demeaning) jobs and the supply of local workers able and willing to do them has decreased. This is because of three interrelated changes that have transformed Western societies and economies: (1) increasing education, (2) women's emancipation and (3) rapidly plummeting birth rates.

As children and young adults have gone to school for longer, and more of them go on to pursue higher education degrees, the domestic supply of lower-skilled workers has plummeted.

Women's emancipation is the second reason for the drop in the domestic supply of lower-skilled workers. Before the feminist revolution of the 1960s, married women were expected to do domestic chores and take care of the children. Although they were often allowed to work during adolescence and young adulthood, upon marriage they were usually expected to stay home – if they could afford it. In practice, working-class women would take on informal jobs in agriculture, homecrafts and domestic work for wealthier families to supplement family income – but the full-time employment of married women was generally frowned upon.

Since the 1960s, this has completely changed through the massive entry of women into the formal labour market and dramatic improvements in their education levels – in most Western countries, women have increasingly outperformed men in terms of enrolment in and completion of higher education.[12] Whereas 29 per cent of women in the US were doing paid work in 1950, the share had nearly doubled to 57 per cent in 2016. Similar increases can be seen in other Western countries.[13] As more women have aimed for jobs that match their level of education, local supplies of women wanting jobs as harvest workers, nannies, domestic workers and cleaning ladies have rapidly dried up.

Last but not least, women's emancipation, their increased formal labour market participation and the increasing length and cost of children's education have also contributed to a dramatic drop in birth rates since the 1950s. This has further exacerbated the shortage of local workers willing and able to do manual work or hard physical labour. In the future, an ageing population is likely to further increase demand for workers in health and elder care.

The new servants

So, the combined effects of increased education, women's emancipation and falling birth rates have reduced the supply of local workers and increased demand for migrant workers in the service sector, who are increasingly women themselves. As Western families progressively moved away from the classic breadwinner model – with men working outside the house and women staying at home – the modern norm became that both partners worked. As a consequence, women have become less available to do the domestic chores such as cleaning, cooking, laundry and child rearing that were traditionally seen as 'female'. This helped to fuel the growing migration of female domestic and care workers.

Female migrant workers from countries such as the Philippines, Indonesia, Brazil, Colombia and Ecuador have played an increasingly important role in informal arrangements for domestic work, childcare and elder care around the world.[14] Women's emancipation and the rise of the dual-income family prompted more couples to start outsourcing such activities, causing the demand for cleaners, domestic workers and childminders to soar. And as middle-class families started to eat out more often, instead of cooking their own food, the restaurant and food delivery sector boomed, too. The rising incomes of dual-income households also meant families could spend more money on weekends and holidays, further boosting labour demand in the leisure and hospitality industries.

The shift from industrial to service jobs in the formal and informal sectors has increased the demand for female migrant workers. Besides formal or informal work for private businesses, migrant workers play an increasingly crucial role in informal childcare (nannies) and elder care, particularly in countries such as the US, the UK, Spain, Italy and Germany, which lack extensive government-subsidized care facilities.

In 2013, the Italian sociologist Maurizio Ambrosini estimated that, in Italy alone, 1.5 million migrants were working in private households, and one Italian household out of ten employed a *badante* – a migrant domestic worker – to care for children or the elderly. In 2010, between 150,000 and 200,000 migrants were estimated to be working as caregivers for the elderly in Germany, and the numbers only seem to have increased since. With the government turning a blind eye to their often-illegal employment status, German sociologists Helma Lutz and Ewa Palenga-Möllenbeck called the situation an 'open secret'.[15]

The demand for female domestic and care workers has been soaring not only in the West, but also in the Middle East, East and South-East Asia, and among increasingly large groups of well-to-do families in middle-income countries pretty much all around the world.

The recruitment of officially 'unwanted' workers

Contradicting their own anti-immigration rhetoric, politicians often give in to employers' lobbying by allowing more migrant workers in or by tolerating the employment of undocumented migrants. The fact that this immigration is more desired than it seems is further highlighted by the central role that the recruitment of officially 'unwanted' foreign workers has continued to play in facilitating migration and the tapping of new labour sources.

Compared to the post-Second World War decades, when major migrations – from Mexico to the US, from Mediterranean countries to western Europe, and from the Caribbean and South Asia to the UK – were put in motion through concerted efforts to recruit workers, governments have become less directly involved and therefore also less visible in the recruitment process. This is part of a more general shift towards economic liberalization and deregulation, as well as the rise of 'flexible work', giving increased leeway to private sector operators to recruit and hire local workers *and* migrant workers alike.

Nowadays, staffing firms such as Randstad, Manpower and Adecco are involved in the recruitment of foreign workers. In the Netherlands alone, there were no fewer than 4,830 official employment agencies in 2021, helping to recruit East European workers for the Dutch horticulture, warehousing and distribution sectors. In 2022, the US had around 25,000 registered staffing and recruitment agencies, and the UK had 20,096 employment placement agencies.[16] While private agencies are doing most of the actual recruitment, governments cater to employers' needs by allowing legal labour migration and turning a blind eye towards the illegal deployment of migrant workers. Although we usually don't read about this in the newspapers, all Western countries continue to operate temporary and seasonal worker schemes and programmes facilitating the recruitment of foreign workers for specific sectors.

Most of this recruitment happens below the radar, out of sight of the public. For instance, in 2014 the Dutch government and associations of Asian restaurant owners signed the *Convenant Aziatische Horeca* (Agreement on Asian Catering). This agreement enabled the legal immigration of Asian cooks whose visas depended on that specific employer and job, creating conditions for severe labour exploitation.[17]

Because migration is a politically sensitive issue, such programmes usually don't even feature the M-word. 'Au pair' and 'trainee' are well-known euphemisms for migrant workers. The au pair programmes run by many Western governments recruit private domestic and care workers, who often end up staying longer than their initial visas allow and whose presence is widely tolerated as everybody knows their labour fulfils essential economic and social functions. Even South Korea and Japan, which have long resisted the idea of admitting foreign workers, have succumbed to pressures to allow in workers from countries like Vietnam, Indonesia and Nepal. The trainee or intern programmes run by these East Asian countries are in reality a way of recruiting industrial and service sector workers.

Lower-skilled migrant workers do essential jobs

Migrant workers grease the wheels of rich economies. They are not always very visible, but they are all around us. In the major cities of Western countries, cleaning and other domestic work for private households has been increasingly dominated by legal (as well as illegal), mainly female migrant workers. The same goes for the cleaning and maintenance of office buildings and universities. I often tell my students that they should, for a change, get themselves out of bed really early and come to the university at 7 a.m., so that they can see who is making sure the corridors, classrooms, lecture theatres and restaurants are clean before they start their day.

The same goes for essential behind-the-scenes work in agriculture, food processing, meatpacking, warehousing, transport, hotels, restaurants, construction, maintenance, landscaping and gardening. Sometimes it is about more visible jobs, in the taxi, delivery, beauty and hospitality sectors. Many sex workers are migrants, too.

'Migrant jobs' are often physically demanding, requiring excellent physical health, endurance and a strong motivation to work under the most difficult circumstances. On both sides of the Atlantic, migrant workers are over-represented as personal caregivers, drivers, transport and storage labourers, and slaughterhouse, meatpacking and other food-processing workers.[18] Migrant workers have the skills, determination and motivation to do such jobs. They are often keen to do the '3D' jobs that native workers find too degrading because this allows them to earn a salary that is much higher than they could ever have earned back home. They often care less about the low social status of such jobs because the money they remit allows them to improve the living conditions of their families and send their children to school.

The Covid-19 pandemic revealed the full extent to which many typical 'migrant jobs' have become 'essential' jobs that our economies rely on. The irony is that the migrant workers that politicians portray as 'unwanted' often do work that is equally or perhaps even more essential than the higher-skilled workers cast by politicians as the 'desired' migrants. While many white-collar workers could work from home during the pandemic, manual and care workers actually had to show up to get the work done. And these same workers ran the highest risks of contracting coronavirus because their jobs required them to be within close physical distance to others.

An inconvenient truth

The reality of migration contradicts political narratives claiming that 'we don't need lower-skilled workers'. There is a real and consistent demand for lower-skilled migrant labour. In fact, the demand exists at all skill levels. Migrant workers are not as 'unwanted' as politicians claim. And they are generally not pouring in via desperate and irrational attempts to reach the Wealthy West. In reality, immigration is primarily driven by labour demand.

Employers and agencies actively recruit foreign workers, as migrants fill crucial job shortages in vital sectors. It's one of the best-kept open secrets in Western societies, happening under our very noses, but most politicians are afraid to admit it. Immigration restrictions that deny the central role of labour demand in driving migration will not stop immigration; in fact they typically prompt migrant workers to overstay their visas or cross borders illegally.

Politicians find it hard to admit the fundamental truth, as it goes against their main talking point that workers have no jobs to come to. That's a lie, and they know it. The truth is that our wealthy, ageing and highly educated societies have developed a built-in structural demand for migrant workers that is impossible to eliminate as long as economies keep growing. From that perspective, the most effective way to bring down immigration is to wreck the economy.

Immigration: Threat or Solution?

Myth 8: Immigrants steal jobs and drive down wages

Over the past half-century, immigration has gone up; meanwhile, it has become increasingly difficult to find stable jobs, and real wages for many workers have stagnated or even gone down.

It's easy – and for politicians very tempting – to connect both trends and suggest a causal relationship. That because migrants are willing to work hard for lower pay and longer hours, immigration puts downward pressure on wages and increases job insecurity. This creates unfair competition for local workers, who are crowded out of stable, well-paid jobs, forcing them to accept substandard labour conditions.

This is an argument that seems to make a lot of sense. Between 1980 and 2020, Western economies experienced a major rise in productivity, mainly because of technological innovation and increasing levels of education and specialization. However, most workers have barely benefited from this growth, or have even lost out. In many countries, the real wages of middle- and particularly lower-income workers in terms of actual purchasing power have stagnated as nominal wage increases have been neutralized or outpaced by the rising costs of living.[1] At the same time, job insecurity has gone up, with more and more workers hopping between temporary low-paid jobs or working in quasi-independent jobs in a rapidly expanding 'gig economy'.

In the US, for instance, labour productivity (the value of the output of goods and services per hour worked) grew by a whopping 75 per cent between 1973 and 2017. Yet over the same period, the median real (inflation-adjusted) wages of average workers only grew by 10 per cent.[2] In fact, the bottom 80 per cent of workers barely reaped any benefits from growing productivity and wealth, while the lowest-income earners saw their real wages decline. At the same time, the real wages of the top 1 per cent of earners rose 160 per cent, while the top 0.1 per cent enjoyed a 345 per cent income growth.[3]

Across the Atlantic, too, income inequality has been increasing, although not to the same extent as in the US. However, since the

2007–2008 global financial crisis, and particularly in liberalized economies such as the UK, we have seen a stagnation or even decline of real median wages.[4] So, almost all of the benefits of economic growth have gone to higher-income earners. As the French economist Thomas Piketty extensively documented in his book *Capital in the Twenty-First Century*, this has gone along with a growth of the share of capital as a source of income as opposed to labour, and an increasing concentration of wealth among the top 10 and particularly 1 per cent pretty much across the West.[5]

Over the same period, Western countries have experienced sustained immigration. This makes it tempting to make a causal connection between increasing competition from migrant workers on the one hand and growing inequality, growing job insecurity and wage stagnation on the other.

This has traditionally been a left-wing issue. As Senator Bernie Sanders, often seen as the leader of the progressive movement in the US, argued in 2007: 'If poverty is increasing and if wages are going down, I don't know why we need millions of people to be coming into this country as guest workers who will work for lower wages than American workers and drive wages down even lower than they are right now . . . on one hand, you have large multinationals trying to shut down plants in America, move to China, and on the other hand, you have the service industry bringing in low-wage workers from abroad. The result is the same: the middle class gets shrunken, and wages go down.'[6]

Len McCluskey, former general secretary of Unite the Union – the second-largest trade union in the UK – voiced a similar sentiment in 2016 when he claimed that: 'The elite's use of immigration to this country is not motivated by a love of diversity or a devotion to multiculturalism. It is instead all part of the flexible labour market model, ensuring a plentiful supply of cheap labour here for those jobs that can't be exported elsewhere.'[7]

Unions have always looked with suspicion at the recruitment of migrant workers, as they often see it as a corporate divide-and-rule plot to break the power of unions by importing cheap labour. However, since the 1990s unions and left-wing parties have become more ambiguous about immigration, partly because they have started to recognize that migrants form an increasing share of the working classes and are therefore their new constituencies.

As unions and left-wing parties abandoned their ardent opposition to labour immigration, conservative and far-right politicians took over this classic left-wing anti-immigration argument. They did so in an apparent bid to appeal to disgruntled native workers who felt that the left-wing politicians who had traditionally represented their interests had grown out of touch with their day-to-day concerns. Right-wing populist politicians filled this vacuum by blaming immigration – as well as progressive and liberal politicians who had supposedly encouraged 'mass immigration' – for declining job security and wage stagnation. In this way, a working-class issue was turned into a nationalistic one.

How it really works

Immigrants don't steal jobs, they fill vacancies

It is true that lower-income earners have barely benefited from economic growth over the past forty years, and they have seen job security and labour standards eroding while the rich only get richer. However, immigration has barely anything to do with this. The idea that immigration is a major cause of unemployment and wage stagnation is not grounded in any evidence, because what seems a causal connection is in fact a spurious correlation.

First of all, although there is indeed a correlation between levels of immigration and levels of unemployment, this correlation is *negative*. This means that immigration goes up during times of high growth and low unemployment, and goes down when unemployment goes up. If migrants take away jobs, we would rather have expected a positive correlation.

Second, the claim that migrants steal jobs from native workers is turning the main causality of the relationship upside down: immigration is mainly a *reaction* to labour shortages rather than the cause of unemployment and wage stagnation. This is also visible in the time lag between business cycles and immigration levels. Immigration trails economic growth and unemployment, usually by six to twelve months. This is because it takes a while before labour shortages translate into increased immigration, as it takes time for news about jobs to travel, and to recruit and register migrant workers. As we saw in the previous chapter, immigrants don't steal jobs, they fill vacancies. Immigration is primarily a response to labour shortages caused by a dwindling supply of local workers willing and able to do various manual jobs in agriculture, construction, cleaning, domestic work and various other services. This is the main reason why immigration surges in Western economies precisely during periods when unemployment goes *down*.

These facts alone cast doubt on the assertion that immigration is a major cause of wage stagnation and unemployment. This does obviously not mean that there cannot be some degree of 'reverse causality', with immigration having an impact on wages and employment in its own right. After all, according to standard 'neoclassical' economic theory, wages reflect supply and demand for labour. Since immigration increases the supply of labour, it therefore seems plausible to believe that the large-scale influx of lower-skilled workers should put at least some downward pressure on wages, and that as migrant workers take up vacancies, this will increase unemployment among native workers to some degree.

A Cuban exodus to Miami: The Mariel boatlift

What does the evidence show about the wage and employment effects of immigration? Under normal circumstances, these effects are hard to reliably isolate and measure – mainly because immigration is itself largely a response to labour demand. It is therefore notoriously difficult – and it is hard to disentangle cause and effect.[8] In some exceptional cases, however, immigration is not so much a reaction to labour demand, but rather the result of external factors. The best evidence is provided by studies that look at the effects of what economists call 'exogenous' (external) shocks to the supply of labour. Sudden, large-scale refugee influxes seem to best fit the bill. Because these are caused by political crises, not by economic factors such as labour demand, labour supply shocks caused by refugee immigration can be largely considered to be exogenous. This has prompted economists to use refugee crises as 'quasi-natural experiments' to study the labour market effects of immigration.

The best-studied case of such an external immigration shock is the 'Mariel boatlift'. In April 1980, after decades of trying to prevent people from leaving, the Castro regime announced that all Cubans wishing to go to the US were free to board boats at the port of Mariel, west of Havana. Cuban exiles already living in the US rushed to hire boats in Miami and Key West to ferry refugees across the ninety-mile stretch of water separating Mariel from Miami. Fidel Castro's goal was to test how far America's hospitality towards refugees really went – Cuban border guards even helped them to pack boat after boat. This mass influx overwhelmed the United States Coast Guard and embarrassed President Jimmy Carter. In October 1980, the US government negotiated an agreement with the Cuban government to end this migration. By then, around 125,000 Cubans had made the sea crossing to Florida in 1,700 boats. The vast majority of 'Marielitos' settled in and around Miami.[9]

As a result of the Mariel boatlift, the labour force in Miami suddenly shot up by about 7 per cent. As most Marielitos had low levels of education, this caused a 20 per cent surge in the lower-skilled workforce. In a research article published in 1990, David Card, a labour economist and 2021 Nobel laureate, used the Mariel boatlift as a case study to measure how the wages of native workers responded to a sudden increase in labour supply. As this labour supply shock was entirely caused by political factors, any wage or employment effects could therefore be largely or even solely ascribed to immigration. Card found that the Mariel influx had virtually no effect on the wages or unemployment rates of lower-skilled workers, not even among Cubans who had migrated earlier.[10] This challenged economic orthodoxy – according to which the labour supply shock should have decreased wages.

Card's findings were contested by economist George Borjas, who in an article published in 2017 argued that an accurate measurement of the wage impacts of immigration should focus on the specific sectors in which migrants compete for jobs with local workers. His analysis indicated that the Mariel boatlift caused a 10–30 per cent drop in average wages for the least-skilled Miamians.[11] Borjas's claims were in turn contested by economists Michael Clemens and Jennifer Hunt, who argued that these wage drops reflected a change in the way workforce survey data was collected.[12] Another recent study on the Mariel boatlift – using different methods yet again – also did not find evidence for large negative wage effects.[13]

Amid such methodological controversy, it is easy to overlook the common denominator of virtually all these studies: the labour market impacts of even large immigration shocks are quantitively small and often insignificant. Other studies on the labour market effects of other 'immigration shocks' have drawn similar conclusions. The mass arrival of over 1 million *colons* (descendants of French and other European settlers) and *harkis* (Algerians who served in the French army) after Algerian independence in 1962 had a negligible effect on labour market outcomes in France.[14] Likewise, the huge inflow of close to 1 million Russian immigrants to Israel after 1989, which increased the Israeli population by 12 per cent in the first half of the 1990s, had almost no adverse effects on the wages and employment of native workers.[15] The huge labour supply shock generated by the fall of the Berlin Wall – leading to the migration of 2.8 million people from East to West Germany over a period of fifteen years – had a (largely temporary) negative effect on employment, while the wage effects were zero.[16]

Research into the economic effects of the large-scale arrival of Syrian refugees in Turkey shows similar outcomes. Between the outbreak of the Syrian civil war in March 2011 and 2021, about 6.6 million Syrians sought refuge in other countries. The largest number – approximately 3.6 million in 2021 – live in Turkey, making up roughly 4.4 per cent of that country's population of 82 million. One study estimated the economic effects of immigration by comparing south-eastern regions (bordering Syria) hosting high and low refugee numbers.[17] It found that while the impact on wages was negligible, large-scale refugee arrivals had led to small increases in unemployment among native informal-sector workers but had increased employment among formal-sector workers.[18] With these positive and negative effects largely cancelling each other out, this yielded an average negative effect on employment of just 1.8 percentage points. Considering the massive scale of Syrian immigration – with refugees representing over 10 per cent of the populations in some regions – these effects are quite small.

The labour market effects of immigration are negligible

If anything, the accumulated evidence confirms that, even in the case of extremely high immigration shocks, the wage and employment effects are minimal. It is therefore not surprising that studies on the economic impact of normal, smaller-scale immigration have generally found that the effects are also very small. There are several ways to measure the impact of immigration on wages. One common method is to estimate the effect of fluctuations in immigration on average wages and incomes. More sophisticated methods estimate the effect of immigration on wages across different income and skill groups or regions. The results of such estimates vary depending on methods and data used – and on countries, migrant groups and periods covered. Some studies have found a slightly positive effect, others a slightly negative one, while many others have failed to find any significant effect at all.[19]

In 2017, the US National Academy of Sciences (NAS) published a major report involving many prominent migration researchers that summarized a large body of evidence on the economic consequences of immigration to the US.[20] The report showed that immigration has virtually no effect on employment, although there is evidence that lower-skilled migration can reduce the number of hours worked by teens as well as prior immigrants, as they tend to work in the same sectors as incoming migrants. The immigration of higher-skilled workers has positive effects on the incomes of native workers across virtually all income levels, while the expansion of the labour force because of immigration reduces the costs of several goods and services, such as childcare, food preparation, construction, and house cleaning and repair.

With regard to the impacts of immigration on wages, the most important conclusion of the NAS study was that these were very small. As far as negative effects were found, these were also small and mostly affected prior immigrants – and, to some extent, native-born high-school dropouts, again because they often do similar jobs to migrants. So, ironically, immigrants seem to have the most reason to worry about the arrival of more migrant workers. For instance, Somali refugees are apparently displacing Latino workers in US meatpacking plants in states such as Nebraska, Iowa, Kansas and Minnesota.[21]

Available research on Europe yields largely similar results. Studies led by Christian Dustmann, an economics professor at University College London, suggest that the average wage effects of recent immigration to the UK have been positive, although the impact differs across income groups.[22] As in the US, if any negative effects are found, they are concentrated among the lowest-income earners, and migrant workers in particular. One study led by Dustmann found that immigration depressed wages among the lowest-income earners but led to slight wage increases among higher-income earners.[23] But, again, the most important insight is that the size of any wage effects – whether positive or negative – is actually very small. The study estimated that each 1 per cent increase in the immigrant population (as a share of the native working-age population) led to a 0.5 per cent decrease in wages among the bottom 10 per cent of income earners, a 0.6 per cent increase in wages among median incomes and a 0.4 per cent increase in wages among the top 10 per cent of earners. In concrete terms, that means that immigration over the 1995–2005 period held wages back by £0.007 (0.7 pence) per hour for the bottom 10 per cent contributed about £0.015 (1.5 pence) to wage growth for median wages, and slightly more than £0.02 (2 pence) for the top 10 per cent. The same analysis estimated that a 1 per cent increase in the size of the foreign-born population would lead to an increase of 0.1–0.3 per cent in *average* wages. On that basis, immigration contributed between 1.2 and 3.5 per cent to annual real wage growth over the entire 1997–2005 period.

So, the main conclusion we can draw based on the accumulated evidence is that the wage effects of immigration – whether positive or negative – are very small, to the point of being negligible. This should give reason for scepticism about any grand claims of the economic benefits – or harms – of immigration.

How immigration can create more jobs

The evidence is clear: immigrants generally don't steal jobs from local workers, and immigration has not played any major role in wage stagnation. How is this possible? Why would wages not go down and unemployment go up if immigration increases the supply of workers and labour? It sounds counterintuitive to those familiar with the economic laws of demand and supply. It defies standard economic theory – according to which, increased competition for jobs should depress wages and increase unemployment amongst native workers.

The problem is that the theory is based on two misguided assumptions: (1) migrants compete for the same jobs as native workers; and (2) the demand for labour is fixed and independent of immigration. To address the first of these: because immigration is generally a response to skills shortages in particular sectors, immigrants usually don't compete with local workers for the same jobs. To understand this, it is important to realize that labour markets are anything but homogeneous – instead, they are strongly *segmented* across myriad sectors, skill levels and job types.

As migrant workers tend to be concentrated in particular sectors, immigration mainly affects employment and wages of workers doing the same jobs. The immigration of, say, farm workers, domestic workers and restaurant workers is unlikely to directly affect the wages and employment of local teachers, accountants and government employees.

In fact, immigration can increase the wages of all workers as long as their skills are complementary, and migrant workers can help native workers to become more productive. Migrant workers washing dishes, cooking food, waiting tables or delivering food increase the capacity of restaurants to serve more customers, thereby increasing jobs for senior management and income for the owners. This also allows customers to eat out, or have food delivered for affordable prices, thereby freeing up more time to spend on their own work and be more productive. Meanwhile, the sufficient supply of support staff like janitors, cleaners and various office workers enables (migrant and non-migrant) higher-skilled workers to concentrate on the work they're best at instead of doing manual tasks themselves. In this way, all workers can derive mutual benefits from immigration.

The second flawed assumption is that there is a fixed number of jobs in an economy. This is what economists call the the 'lump of labour fallacy'. In reality, economies and labour markets *expand* as populations increase, either because of natural growth (if birth rates exceed death rates) or because of immigration, or both. Immigration increases the total size of the economy in terms of productivity, as well as the total number of jobs.

Immigrants are not only employees receiving wages, but also consumers who spend their salaries on goods and services, boosting profits and the expansion of the businesses delivering those goods and services. This encourages these businesses to hire more workers who earn wages. In turn, these additional workers will spend part of their wages on other goods and services, further boosting the profits of businesses and leading them to expand and create even more jobs. This virtuous cycle in which expenditure and consumption of goods and services creates more jobs is what economists call the 'multiplier effect'. Because of this, immigrants increase the total size of the economic pie, and therefore also the total number of jobs.

Immigration tends to increase the total size of the economy and the labour force at roughly the same pace as the increase in the number of jobs. This mechanism explains the remarkable capacity of national economies to absorb large inflows of migrants without any major lasting effects on wages and unemployment. But while immigration expands the total size of economies in terms of GDP, the effect on *per capita* income and average wages is negligible. The economic pie gets bigger as populations grow, but, on average, the slices remain about the same size.

Immigrants are exceptional people

Immigration also tends to boost profits and encourage innovation, entrepreneurship and investment, which further boosts economic growth. As Ian Goldin, Geoffrey Cameron and Meera Balarajan showed in their 2011 book *Exceptional People*, throughout history, migrants have often fuelled the engine of human progress.[24] Immigrants not only fill urgent job shortages in vital economic sectors, they also bring new ideas and knowledge that boost innovation and productivity.

Entire nations, particularly in the Americas and New Zealand and Australia, were built upon the drive and determination of settlers who left everything behind to start a new life. However, we should not forget that this also led to the violent oppression and genocide of native populations as well as the slave trade. In modern times, too, immigrants and refugees have played a central role in scientific and economic innovation. When the Nazis started persecuting Jews after Hitler rose to power in 1933, this led to a sizeable exodus of German Jewish and Austrian German intellectuals and scientists, who boosted intellectual life, research and innovation in Britain and particularly the United States. Albert Einstein fled Nazi Germany and settled in the US. Sigmund Freud, the founder of modern psychoanalysis, escaped to Britain. The philosopher Hannah Arendt fled Nazi Germany via France and Portugal, and settled in the US – where she rose to global prominence.

The Allied victory over Nazi Germany and the subsequent rise of the US as a superpower was further facilitated by the contribution of refugee scientists to warfare technology. Jewish exiles revolutionized US science and technology; after 1933, the number of patents increased by 31 per cent in fields common to Jewish scientists. The innovative impact of this immigration rippled for generations, as these scientists attracted more researchers and scientists from abroad, who trained other newcomers, often immigrants themselves.[25]

In a more cynical turn of events, immigration's contribution to America's rise as a superpower also involved former Nazi engineers and scientists recruited by the US. Wernher von Braun, once a leading Nazi scientist who developed the world's first ballistic missile – the V-2 rocket – for Adolf Hitler, played a key role in the development of NASA's space programme in the 1950s and 1960s, alongside other former Nazi scientists as well as a large number of American Jewish scientists.[26] What was perhaps a 'brain drain' for Europe was hugely beneficial for America's rise as a global hegemon.

In the post-war decades, the United States emerged as the prime destination for scientists, researchers and engineers from countries all over the world. The brainpower and innovation of these talented immigrants fuelled economic growth and America's economic, political, cultural, academic and military power. As immigrants often belong to the more talented and ambitious groups in origin societies, they also disproportionately contribute to innovation, research and development. Immigrants continue to be over-represented among Nobel laureates and patent holders in the US.[27]

The positive contribution of immigration to the success, innovation and profitability of the business sector is undisputed. Migrants are often entrepreneurs themselves, who invest and employ other workers. Immigrant entrepreneurs are frequently active in the most dynamic sectors, such as IT – where talent is most scarce and innovation reaps the highest rewards. Many leading businesses were founded, owned or led by immigrants.

Immigrants have often played a leading role in innovation and growth – in science, technology and business. In the same vein, British universities and the UK's financial services industry greatly benefited from EU membership, as free movement boosted their ability to attract talent from other European countries. In the UK, immigrants have been found to be 50 per cent more likely to be entrepreneurial than people who were born and bred in Britain.[28] The diversity that immigration brings can be highly beneficial for business, as culturally diverse teams tend to be more creative and able to discuss ideas from different angles – stimulating innovation and leading to superior business and marketing strategies.[29]

Native workers are unfit for migrant jobs

Even in cases of large-scale refugee influxes, the resulting extraordinarily large expansion of the labour force has had surprisingly small long-term effects on wages and employment. This shows that labour markets have a much larger ability to absorb immigration than economists previously assumed. Still, for many the question remains: why does immigration even continue when there is significant unemployment? Shouldn't governments force employers to put unemployed local workers to work rather than importing foreign workers? This idea is the basis for political claims like 'American jobs for American workers'.

However, this is not how labour markets work in practice. First, as mentioned above, they are not homogeneous but strongly segmented. This means that job markets are highly specialized in terms of the skills and motivations needed for each job. Farm workers compete for different jobs than cashiers or cooks, and it is difficult to transfer skills from one sector to another. Depending on the sector-specific supply and demand for labour, we can therefore have labour shortages and zero unemployment in one sector and high unemployment in another sector. Because of increasing education, an ageing population and the increased labour participation of women, the domestic supply of lower-skilled workers has decreased dramatically, while demand for all sorts of lower-skilled jobs has increased.

Second, the extent to which local lower-skilled workers who are unemployed can be retrained and motivated to do other jobs is limited; and the impacts of such programmes should therefore not be exaggerated. Many unemployed people are too old, too ill or too unmotivated to do the types of jobs that migrants do – which typically involve hard physical labour and working long shifts at irregular hours. Such jobs require excellent health and high self-motivation. The truth is that the supply of local workers able and willing to do backbreaking work in the fields, factories, restaurants and hotels has shrunk dramatically – as new, better-educated generations aim for higher-earning, higher-status jobs, and would rather not work than do jobs they find degrading or that they think may tarnish their CVs.

As the MIT economist Michael Piore showed in his seminal book *Birds of Passage: Migrant Labor and Industrial Societies*, published in 1979, labour migration was the unavoidable consequence of the intrinsic need of industrialized societies for workers who were willing to work hard for low wages under insecure and difficult conditions.[30] Piore emphasized that the growing reliance on migrant workers cannot only be explained by the increasing education of the domestic workforce, women's emancipation and declining birth rates, which have decreased supplies of native workers. Motivational factors play an important role, too. Native workers simply don't want do bottom-level jobs, particularly when they get branded as 'migrant jobs'. Piore argued that the demand for migrant workers has become a 'chronic' feature of industrialized economies, as migrants are a convenient source of flexible and 'malleable' labour. In particular, the low social status of such jobs explains why many people would rather not work and will often rather forgo income than do such jobs.

Nevertheless, despite their low status, these are crucial jobs for which demand persists even during economic crisis, for instance in childcare and elder care. The huge gap between politicians' endlessly recycled 'we don't need foreign workers' mantra and the migration realities on the ground can be found in all industrialized countries. Persistent labour shortages in the agricultural sector are a case in point. The biggest agriculture sectors of the Western world – such as US horticulture (particularly in California), the Westland greenhouse sector in the Netherlands, and the agri-food sector in southern Spain and Italy – all heavily rely on the constant supply of migrant workers.

Why British workers refused to 'pick for Britain'

Above all else, labour shortages are real. There are simply not enough local workers who are willing and able to do such jobs. This is proved by the failure of policies that actually tried to put the idea of 'own workers first' into practice. Responding to calls to preserve American (or British, French, German . . .) jobs for American (or British, French, German . . .) workers, governments have tried to run schemes that put the native unemployed – instead of immigrants – to work. Yet such attempts to bus in the unemployed have invariably failed, because it proved impossible to find enough local workers who were willing to do those jobs – and the few native workers who did show up did not come back the next day because they found the work too hard, for too little pay. Native workers simply don't want to do certain jobs anymore.

In 2013 the UK government announced it would abolish the Seasonal Agricultural Workers Scheme (SAWS) that had existed since 1945. The official goal was to help unemployed UK-resident workers into horticultural work. Farmers' organizations found the idea 'laughable', arguing that there were simply not enough workers willing to do the job. One employer argued that the low supply of local workers was 'the effect of a gradual transition to a service-based economy in the UK' and that 'due to lifestyle changes . . . many Britons are not cut out for the hard graft of farm work'.[31] Such statements are backed up by the fact that nine in ten seasonal agricultural workers in Britain are EU immigrants.[32]

Growers' organizations argued that the policy change did not solve the problem – pressing labour shortages – and that the government's main motivation was to play to the crowd after disappointing election results. In the end, the suspension of SAWS did not change the sector's structural reliance on foreign farm workers. As a result, and with Brexit in sight (which cut off the free movement of East European workers to and from Britain), SAWS was resurrected in 2019 – albeit under the different name 'Seasonal Workers Pilot' – with the government expanding the yearly quota for East European, and particularly Ukrainian, workers.[33]

The Covid-19 pandemic highlighted the structural reliance of various economic sectors on migrant workers. In the spring of 2020, European borders were closed because of the lockdown. However, farmers still needed workers to prevent strawberries, tomatoes and lettuces from rotting in the fields. This prompted several European governments to launch campaigns to recruit local workers. However, these campaigns failed to produce any noticeable results. As a consequence, the British, German, Dutch and other governments allowed farmers to recruit tens of thousands of foreign workers – bussing or flying them in even in the midst of the pandemic.

The 'Pick for Britain' campaign exemplifies these failed European attempts to replace migrant workers with local workers. In May 2020, the UK government launched a campaign to encourage people to sign up for farm jobs to meet labour demand created by the suspension of seasonal inflows of East European workers because of the lockdown. The campaign, which strongly appealed to national pride and the duty to 'do your part' for Britain, included a video in which Prince Charles called upon Britons to show up at the farm to pick and pack fruits and vegetables in the national interest. However, only a few local workers showed up, prompting the government to scrap the programme and fly in East European workers instead.[34]

The UK's reliance on migrant labour became clear again in the autumn of 2021, with shortages of essential workers like lorry drivers resulting from Brexit's restriction of free inflows of East European workers. As vacancies were no longer filled, this caused a major 'supply chain crisis', which led to problems such as empty supermarket shelves and petrol shortages. This again prompted the government to recruit foreign workers. In fact, visas granted to seasonal workers rose from 2,493 in 2019 to 34,532 in 2022.[35] Though Brexit successfully curtailed free inflows of workers, it clearly did not eliminate labour shortages.

Governments, not immigrants, are to blame for the low-wage economy

So, sweeping statements about immigrants taking jobs or sending wages spiralling down have no basis in evidence. This doesn't mean that immigration can under no circumstances have any negative effects on wages or employment of lower-skilled workers. However, the overall impact of immigration on average wages and employment is minimal. Labour markets have a much larger ability to absorb and adapt to large immigrant influxes than politicians often claim. The evidence shows that immigrants and refugees tend to assimilate into local labour markets with remarkable speed – at least, if they are allowed to work.

Indeed, the most important insight from the accumulated evidence is that the effect of immigration on wages and unemployment – whether positive, neutral or negative – is very *small*. As David Card has argued, 'the economic arguments are second order . . . They are almost irrelevant.'[36] This should take the heat out of debates, as it is the tendency of both pro- and anti-immigration camps to hugely overstate the economic case for, or against, immigration. Immigration is less of a factor than we often think, and immigration policies should be decided on grounds other than economic considerations alone.

While our societies are wealthier than ever, inequality has grown, wages have stagnated or even declined, and new generations are growing up with more economic anxiety than their parents about issues like student debt and the ability to find a stable job and affordable housing. Job security has decreased, and more and more young people are relegated to temporary, precarious jobs in the gig economy. However, the real causes of these problems are not immigration, but deliberate policy choices that deregulated labour markets, decreased job security, weakened trade unions, eroded workers' rights, depressed wages and increased income inequality. This has made lower-income earners and new generations economically worse off, while the middle classes have felt increasingly insecure about their ability to maintain living standards in the future.

It has therefore become tempting for politicians to blame immigration for these problems in an attempt to distract attention away from the fact that politicians, not immigrants, are to blame for the low-wage economy.

Myth 9: Immigration undermines the welfare state

Large-scale immigration is incompatible with the welfare state. This is what we're told by politicians and experts – and the argument seems to make a lot of sense. After all, uncontrolled immigration is putting growing pressure on public healthcare and education systems while leading to increasing shortages of affordable housing. As lower-skilled migrants and refugees have above-average unemployment and welfare-dependency rates, they are also a net burden to the taxpayer.

Politicians and media have frequently portrayed immigrants and asylum seekers as 'welfare scroungers' or 'welfare tourists', blaming immigration for overcrowded classrooms, soaring house prices, substandard healthcare and ever-longer waiting lists for social housing. This has reinforced public perceptions of immigrants and minorities as 'queue jumpers' and 'line cutters' who get preferential access to public provisions – such as welfare payments, public healthcare and social housing – while native workers cough up the costs by paying taxes.[1]

However, this is not only an issue for populist politicians and the tabloid press. In fact, many opinion makers and economists have expressed concern that migrants are disproportionately attracted to countries with generous welfare provisions. Because of this 'welfare magnet' effect, immigration would undermine the viability of social security and welfare systems. After all, since the 1980s, across Western countries, the quality of public education and access to healthcare has come under pressure, while real-estate prices have soared and affordable housing is difficult to obtain even for the middle classes. Younger generations can barely afford a mortgage, and are often confronted with expensive rent and crippling student debt. Over the same period, immigration has increased, seemingly putting even more pressure on welfare, healthcare, education and social housing.

The view that we therefore need to curb lower-skilled immigration to preserve adequate social security, healthcare and housing for native populations has been popular on the political left and right. In 2007, UK Home Secretary John Reid, a prominent Labour politician, launched a clampdown on 'foreigners [who] come to this country illegitimately and steal our benefits'.[2] In 2015, Conservative prime minister David Cameron called for a 'wide-scale change to the rules on welfare and benefits' for EU immigrants coming to Britain.[3] The perception that immigrants are a burden to the welfare state, and the National Health Service (NHS) in particular, played an important role in the 2016 Brexit vote.

In continental Europe, too, the idea that immigration is a potential threat to the welfare state is prevalent across the political spectrum. In 2010, Horst Seehofer, a prominent Christian Democratic politician, warned that Germany should, under no circumstances, 'become the social welfare office for the whole world' by letting in too many migrant workers.[4] In the US, concerns about the welfare impacts of migrants have centred around the issue of illegal immigration, as they would make use of public services such as education without paying taxes. Or, as Donald Trump argued, 'illegal immigrants are lower skilled workers with less education' who 'draw much more out from the system than they can ever possibly pay back'.[5]

This reflects a broad political consensus that the unfettered immigration of lower-skilled workers, refugees and their families potentially drives welfare systems to bankruptcy. The conclusion seems clear: we need to curb lower-skilled immigration to preserve the welfare state and secure adequate social security, healthcare and housing for native workers.

How it really works

The fiscal impact of immigration is negligible

Do immigrants make disproportionate use of welfare and public services? Are they therefore an increasing fiscal burden on native taxpayers? Although many people believe this, in truth there is no evidence that immigrants are a significant drain on government finance or that immigration is a significant threat to the viability of welfare systems.

To investigate this issue, economists have tried to measure the net fiscal impact of immigration. This is the difference between the taxes and other contributions migrants make to public finances and the costs of the social benefits and public services they receive in a given year. There are two main ways for measuring this. The *static approach* compares the contributions of migrants with the services and benefits received for a specific year. The *dynamic approach* estimates the net value of contributions and costs over the lifetime of migrants and, in some cases, their children. Although the dynamic approach seems superior, the outcomes of statistical estimates remain strongly dependent on assumptions about various factors – such as future labour participation, return migration and tax rates.[6]

Some studies have found that the overall fiscal impact of immigration is positive, where others find negative effects. It often depends on *how* we look at the data, and whether we're considering short- or long-term impacts – and whether the children of immigrants are included in the estimates. This can create a temptation for think tanks and advocacy groups to analyse data in such ways that it supports their (pro- or anti-immigration) political agendas. The fiscal impact also differs depending on whether we are looking at the national, regional or local level. In the US, for instance, most fiscal *benefits* of migration go to the federal government while most costs, particularly for schooling, are paid at state and local levels.[7]

However, what easily gets lost in the methodological controversies about this issue is that the *size* of the fiscal impacts, whether positive or negative, is actually very small. In an extensive review of studies from the US, the UK and continental Europe published in 2008, the Cambridge economist Robert Rowthorn concluded that the net fiscal contribution of immigration normally lies within the range of ±1 per cent of a country's GDP.[8] Four studies that estimated the government surplus from *all* immigrants residing in the US found the annual net fiscal contribution of immigration to be −$16 billion, −$40 billion, $27 billion and $23.5 billion.[9] This may sound like a lot, but these effects are equivalent to only −0.2 per cent, −0.6 per cent, +0.4 per cent and +0.35 per cent of the total GDP of the US.

For the UK, one study estimated the net fiscal contribution of immigration to be positive but effectively 'close to zero' at £0.4 billion, which is equal to 0.04 per cent of total GDP – whereas later studies found more mixed, but generally small, effects.[10] As Robert Rowthorn put it: 'These figures may seem large in absolute terms, but they are small in relation to the economy as a whole.' He therefore concluded that the desirability of large-scale immigration should 'be decided on other grounds' than fiscal considerations.[11]

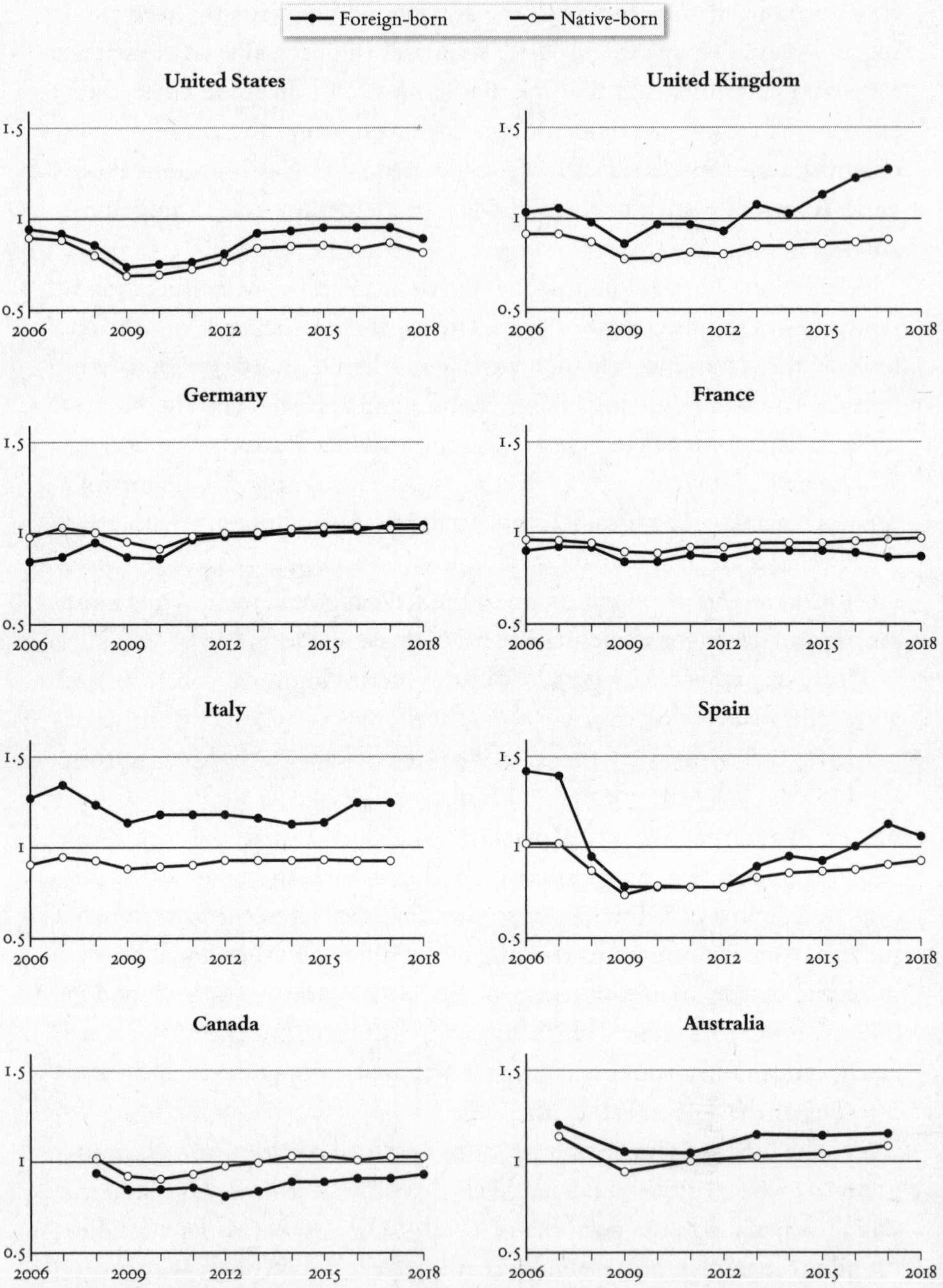

Graph 12: Total fiscal ratio (fiscal contributions divided by fiscal costs) of foreign- versus native-born people in major Western countries, 2006–2018[12]

Recent comparative studies have confirmed such findings. In 2021, the economist Ana Damas de Matos conducted an analysis for the OECD comparing the fiscal impact of immigration in twenty-five Western countries between 2006 and 2018. In line with Rowthorn, she concluded that the fiscal impact of immigration remains small, at levels ranging from −1 per cent to +1 per cent of GDP.[13]

Graph 12 depicts the net fiscal contribution of immigrants for some of the major countries of her study. In the UK, Spain, Italy (and also Ireland, Greece and Portugal), the fiscal impact of immigration was positive, and higher than that of native-born residents. In the US, Germany and France (and also the Netherlands, Austria and Denmark), no major differences between immigrants and native-born were found. In some other countries, like Canada (and Sweden and Belgium), the fiscal balance for immigrants was more negative compared to native-born. However, differences between the two groups were really small, generally between 0.1 and 0.2 percentage points.[14] In line with Rowthorn, Damas de Matos argued that such evidence 'calls into question the relevance of the fiscal lens to assess the effectiveness of migration policies'.[15]

Fiscal impacts change as migrants settle and integrate

Fiscal impacts change over immigrants' lifetimes, typically following a U-shaped pattern – first positive, then negative, and then positive again as migrants get older. Recent immigrants tend to be net contributors to public finance, as they are generally young, employed, healthy and have no children. However, as migrants settle, marry, have children and become older, they may become a net cost to public finances, as they increasingly use public services like schools and healthcare. Fiscal impacts tend to turn positive again once immigrants' children finish schooling and enter the labour market. However, when migrants grow into old age, their labour participation decreases and they are more likely to use health and elder-care facilities.

This U-shaped pattern, where fiscal costs change through the life cycle, is not a particular feature of migrants, however, as it also applies to native workers. Contrary to the idea that immigrants are 'welfare scroungers', the major long-term fiscal cost of immigration is not welfare, unemployment or healthcare, but the education of children.[16] And such investments generally pay themselves back once young people start working and paying taxes. This is one of the main reasons why states fund public education: to train the next generation of productive workers.

All modern democracies have progressive taxation systems based on the solidarity principle that high-income earners pay a larger share of their income in taxes than low-income earners. From that perspective, it is no surprise that lower-skilled immigrants generally contribute less to welfare systems compared to higher-skilled immigrants on average, because this applies to lower-income earners *in general*. And a one-sided focus on the *fiscal* contribution of migration can also be misleading, as it ignores the significant contribution of migrant workers to profits, economic productivity and hence incomes of affluent groups.

The fiscal impacts of immigration strongly depend on skill levels, labour participation and the family cycle of particular immigrant groups. Because recent immigrants have generally higher skill levels than immigrants a generation ago, the fiscal impact of recent immigration is often more positive. One study by economists Christian Dustmann and Tommaso Frattini looking at the fiscal impact of migration to the UK found that for immigrants arriving since 2000, fiscal impacts were positive for both lower- and higher-skilled workers, with immigrants from East and Central European countries paying more in taxes than taking out in benefits and services.[17]

Things almost always improve as new generations grow up. As lower skilled immigrants and their offshoots climb the educational and economic ladder, the average fiscal contribution of immigration improves as new generations come of age.[18] A major study on the US estimated that, for the 2011–13 period, the net cost to state and local budgets of first-generation adult migrants (including their dependent children) is, on average, about $1,600 each. In contrast, second-generation adults create a net positive fiscal impact of about $1,700. By the third generation, the economic performance of descendants of immigrants is indistinguishable from other residents – and this applies equally to people of Asian, Latino and European ancestry.[19]

The myth of the welfare magnet

The hypothesis of a 'welfare magnet' – the idea that generous welfare states attract disproportionate numbers of lower-skilled migrants, as originally proposed by the American economist George Borjas[20] — has been the subject of intense controversy among economists. There is no room in this book to fully review this debate, but the bottom line is that there is no convincing evidence for the existence of a significant welfare-magnet effect. Studies on migration *within* the US found mixed and generally weak evidence for the idea that welfare-induced interstate migration is a widespread phenomenon.[21] Likewise, studies that tested this hypothesis for international migration found mixed results, with some studies finding an effect of welfare generosity on levels of immigration and others not. However, the overall effect is generally very small in any case – far too small to sustain the hypothesis that immigration undermines the fiscal sustainability of welfare provisions. Therefore, fears around immigrant abuse of welfare systems are generally 'unfounded or at least exaggerated'.[22]

These findings may seem counterintuitive, as welfare has come under pressure at the same time as immigration has gone up. However, as so often with migration, what appears to be a causal link is in fact a spurious correlation. The welfare magnet hypothesis is based on the assumptions that (1) many people migrate to live off benefits, (2) access to welfare is instantaneous and (3) immigration is free. All three assumptions are problematic.

First, there is overwhelming evidence that the vast majority of people migrate to work, study or join family members, not to live off welfare. Latino workers in the US, South Asian, Caribbean and EU workers in the UK, and Mediterranean workers in north-west Europe migrated for work. Unemployment and welfare dependency became a problem after the closure of factories and mines in the 1970s and 1980s – exactly the sectors in which most migrants worked. But this reflected the more general problem of mass unemployment that Western countries were struggling with in that age of industrial decline, which hit migrant and minority workers even harder than it did the white working classes.

The nature of welfare regimes is, at best, only a minor factor in affecting migrants' choices. There will always be cases of migrants and asylum seekers trying to game the system, but they are not representative of the whole. In general, immigrants don't come for a life on benefits; they come for jobs, as shown by the strong correlation between labour demand and immigration. And if welfare really were such a big factor in determining migration decisions, how to explain that the greatest migration magnet in the world – the United States – is also the country with the weakest welfare system in the West?

Second, migrants' access to welfare provisions is generally not instantaneous. The image of immigrants claiming benefits upon arrival is misleading, as migrants can generally not yet claim the full package of social benefits, with refugees the only major exception to this rule. In practice, foreign workers have to earn their way into these systems by paying taxes and premiums for several years. Access to unemployment and welfare benefits is generally dependent on the years people have worked and lived in a country. In this way, governments have generated pathways into welfare entitlements, permanent residency and citizenship.

Even in cases where we have totally free migration, there is no evidence that it has been a significant threat to the welfare state. The Schengen agreements, the Maastricht Treaty and EU enlargement over the 2000s – creating the biggest free-migration zone in the world, comprising some 500 million EU citizens – is the closest we can come to a real experiment to see what happens if migration restrictions fall away in a region where countries have very different levels of living standards and welfare provisions. Some feared that free EU migration would create a 'race to the bottom', not only in terms of wages and labour standards, but because southern and eastern Europeans would flock to the honeypots of the generous north-west European welfare states.

And what happened in practice? Not much at all. The fear that free EU migration would create a race to the bottom turned out to be unfounded. There is no evidence that intra-EU migrants flocked to the most generous European welfare states in disproportionate numbers. Most went to countries where demand for foreign workers was high, such as Poles moving to Germany and the UK, and Romanians to Italy and Spain. And, most importantly, they migrated to work, not to live on benefits. This explains why the fiscal impacts of recent migrations from and to the European Union have generally been positive, reflecting migrants' young ages, high employment rates and tendency to return to origin countries during economic recessions. All of this defies the idea that immigration is a threat to the welfare state.

Illegal migrants are the biggest boon to welfare systems

Almost all studies find that, on average, higher-skilled immigration has a more positive impact on public finance compared to lower-skilled immigration. This can hardly be surprising as it is also true for the general population. As argued above, all modern welfare states are based the redistribution of resources from the rich to the poor. Because higher-skilled immigrants have higher average earnings, they also tend to pay more taxes, and rely less on welfare provisions.

However, that does not mean that lower-skilled migration drains welfare systems. Compared to higher-skilled immigration, the net fiscal impact of lower-skilled immigration is generally less positive, but not necessarily negative. In the US, the UK and southern Europe, the net fiscal impact of lower-skilled immigration tends still to be positive. The fiscal impact of immigration is more positive in countries where there is greater tolerance for migrants to work illegally and thus pay taxes without having access to benefits. This is the case with tourists and visitors taking up work, foreign students working more hours than they are allowed to, and migrant workers taking up extra jobs.

In fact, the irony is that the most vilified migrant category of all – illegal migrants – tend to be the biggest net contributors to states. Millions of undocumented migrants in the US pay taxes but do not receive social security benefits. Many undocumented migrants work using borrowed social security numbers and other people's ID cards. The Internal Revenue Service (IRS) allows undocumented migrants without a social security number to file taxes, meaning they pay federal income taxes and payroll taxes – as well as local and state taxes. A study from 2016 estimated that undocumented migrants in the US pay $11.7 billion in state and local taxes every year, equal to 8 per cent of their total income.[23] Yet their undocumented status precludes them from benefiting from federal public services and social benefits, except for emergency Medicaid and child tax credits (if they have US-born children). If they get laid off, neither their employer nor the government will bear the financial cost of their unemployment. Illegal workers therefore often represent the lowest burden to the taxpayer. If illegal immigration becomes protracted, fiscal costs go up, particularly because of the costs of children's education, although such costs are more than offset by the boost of immigration to the economy.[24]

The fiscal contribution of migration tends to be particularly high in countries where labour enforcement is largely symbolic and undocumented migrant workers find it easier to do formal jobs (and, thus, pay taxes) by borrowing IDs of family and friends, such as is the case in the US, but also in southern Europe.[25] In north-west Europe, on the contrary, government regulations have made it increasingly difficult for illegal migrants to do formal jobs, relegating them to the shadow economy, which also means that governments miss out on labour tax income.

Austerity, not immigration, has caused the social housing crisis

One of the most common grievances against immigration is that it has caused the social housing crisis. Refugees are a particular target of such accusations, because in some countries they get priority access to social housing. As waiting lists get longer and longer, and rents keep on increasing, politicians have often blamed the 'mass' arrival of refugees and other migrants for the growing lack of affordable housing. In reality, the uptake of social housing by migrants and refugees is often exaggerated. In Britain, UK-born and foreign-born residents have similar levels of participation in social housing – 16 per cent and 17 per cent, respectively.[26] However, with waiting lists still getting longer, the question remains what the role of immigration actually is.

The root cause of the growing lack of affordable housing across the West is not immigration, but a sharp decline in the stock of social and rent-protected housing units because of changes in housing policies. This is perfectly illustrated by the situation in the Netherlands, where the share of social housing declined from 44 per cent in 1992 to 31 per cent in 2012.[27] In his book *Uitgewoond* (*Worn Out*), the Dutch urban geographer Cody Hochstenbach shows how the Dutch housing crisis is the result of years of government policies focused on homeownership, which deliberately privatized social housing, slashed subsidies to social housing corporations, and dismantled tenant protection and rent controls. As a result, house prices soared, private rents skyrocketed, the Netherlands has 100,000 homeless people, and homeowners are now ninety times wealthier than renters on average.[28]

Hochstenbach's research highlights that austerity-driven housing policies, not immigration, have caused the social housing crisis. For instance, between 2013 and 2020 the total housing stock in the Netherlands increased by 5.9 per cent; if Dutch social housing had grown at the same pace this would have resulted in 245,000 additional social housing units. However, instead of increasing, the stock of rent-protected social housing units *shrank* by 115,000 over this period – a decline of 5.3 per cent.

The rapid decline of Dutch social housing stock is the result of the sale, demolition, liberalization and privatization of social housing, alongside a massive slowdown in the construction of new social houses and the defunding of social housing corporations. In the early 1980s, Dutch social housing corporations built an average of 60,000–70,000 new homes per year. Hochstenbach's research shows that between 2009 and 2013, this pace had slowed to an annual average of about 27,000 social homes, and further decreased to 15,000 per year over the 2014–19 period. If corporations had continued building at the 'old' rate of the 2009–13 period, this would have resulted in 82,000 additional homes over the 2014–19 period.[29]

Equally, the number of new or vacated social houses available for new tenants has been steadily declining while demand has gone up. In 2015, 224,000 social houses became vacant as opposed to 163,000 in 2020, a decrease of 27 per cent in five years. Approximately 15,000 social housing units were allocated to refugees every year, 9 per cent of all newly vacated homes. So, the percentage of refugees taking up social houses has been increasing, but that reflects the rapid shrinkage of the social housing stock rather than refugees crowding out Dutch-born tenants.[30]

Developments in the UK have been even more dramatic. From 1980 the Thatcher government encouraged tenants to buy council houses at heavily subsidized rates as part of the Right to Buy initiative, in an attempt to create a 'homeowning democracy'. This policy, which was continued by the Blair government, was supplemented by 'buy to let' policies which encouraged multiple homeownership and contributed to a massive hike in house prices. At the same time, the government slashed subsidies for the building of new social housing. In the post-Second World War decades, between 169,000 and 245,000 council houses were built annually. By 1979, the year of Thatcher's election, this had already dropped to 86,000. In subsequent years this number continued its nose-dive, coming to a virtual standstill under Blair, and reached an all-time low in 2004, when only 130 council houses were built.[31] All of this massively reduced the total social housing stock from 6.5 million units in 1979 to roughly 2 million units in 2017, and the proportion of homes that are social housing has fallen from 31 per cent to 17 per cent.[32]

While the large-scale sale of public housing was a boon for tenants who could become homeowners at bargain prices, it also exacerbated affordable-housing shortages and contributed to soaring rents paid by tenants to private landlords. This in turn increased public expenditure on housing benefits, with taxpayers effectively subsidizing landlords benefiting from the housing boom.[33] The selling-off of social housing and the slump in new housing construction – combined with high real-estate prices – put non-homeowners in a difficult position.[34] In 2000 the average English home cost four times the average salary; in 2021 this had risen to eight times. As younger generations were priced out of owning a home and denied social housing, they had no option other than to pay rent increases in the private market, leading to overcrowding and increasing homelessness. High rents have made it incredibly difficult to save enough for the deposit needed to secure a mortgage, creating a vicious cycle in which affordable housing has become a distant mirage for a millennial cohort of would-be homebuyers who cannot afford it.[35]

In the US, where social housing has always been a much more marginal affair, trends have been similar. When Congress passed the Fair Housing Act of 1968, it planned to produce 2.6 million housing units a year, including 600,000 for low-income families.[36] In his first year in office (1981–2), President Ronald Reagan halved the federal budget for public housing and reduced housing subsidies for the poor. This caused a rise in public housing shortages, from 300,000 housing units in 1970 to 3.3 million in 1985, and a steep increase in the numbers of homeless people – often Vietnam veterans, unemployed workers and children.[37]

Although subsequent administrations tried to address some of these problems, funding for low-income housing was never restored to anywhere near previous levels. As of late 2020, the US had an estimated housing-supply deficit of 3.8 million units, largely because of the loss of public housing and privately owned subsidized housing. With millennials being at their peak first-time homebuying age, this has sent housing and rental prices skyrocketing, making housing less and less affordable – particularly for low-income but increasingly also middle-income households.[38]

We see similar developments in other countries. In Berlin, for instance, which has high levels of public housing compared to the German national average, 30 per cent of housing was public housing in 1990, whereas in 2007 that number had halved to 15 per cent as a result of privatization policies.[39]

Despite large differences in housing policies across countries, the overall trend is the same: the total volume of affordable houses has decreased while demand has gone up, as housing markets were liberalized while social housing was defunded and privatized. This made housing less and less affordable for lower-income earners – both non-migrant and migrant – particularly in gentrifying neighbourhoods. Although immigration has surely put *additional* pressure on housing markets, it would clearly be misleading to portray immigration as a major cause of these problems. In fact, migrant workers themselves are among the groups most likely to suffer, as they often don't have access to social housing or government assistance, and find themselves relegated to living together in crowded apartments and paying exorbitant rents to private landlords.

Migrant workers shore up the welfare state

While high levels of unemployment and welfare dependency among some immigrant and refugee groups are a valid reason for concern, it is a logical fallacy to conclude from that that immigration is therefore an existential threat to the welfare state. While some groups of lower-skilled migrant workers and refugees have comparatively high levels of welfare dependency, other groups are net contributors to welfare states – and, on balance, the fiscal impact of immigration is simply too small to support any such sweeping claims. So, in a striking parallel with the debate on the impacts of immigration on wages and unemployment, the main conclusion is that the fiscal impacts of immigration are negligible and almost irrelevant.

The impact of immigration on the fiscal balance is minuscule compared to the overall size of fiscal deficits. We should therefore view immigration neither as a major source of fiscal deficit nor as a potential solution to solve such deficits.[40] It is true that, in many countries, access to welfare provisions and high-quality public healthcare, education and affordable housing has become more difficult. However, this is mainly the result not of immigration, but of political decisions to roll back the welfare state and defund or privatize public services such as education, healthcare and social housing. Queues became longer mainly because subsidies were cut. Austerity, not immigration, has undermined welfare provisions.

What gets entirely lost in these debates is that migrant workers fulfil an essential function in upholding affordable welfare provisions – not just indirectly through the taxes they pay, but also more directly through the work they do. Across the Western world, migrants have played increasingly important roles in providing essential services. Immigrants have increasingly buttressed care systems that suffer from a chronic lack of supply of locally trained staff. The NHS in the UK would already have collapsed were it not for the immigration of foreign doctors and nurses.

In 2022, 33 per cent of all doctors working for the NHS were foreign-born, up from 26 per cent in 2012. In the same year, 24 per cent of all NHS nurses were immigrants, up from 14 per cent in 2012. In London and other big cities, these percentages are much higher. The proportion of new healthcare workers recruited from abroad has been growing fast. Between 2017 and 2022, the share of newly hired NHS nurses with non-UK nationalities rose from 20 to 45 per cent, the vast majority of them from outside the EU. Half of all foreign-born NHS nurses are from either India or the Philippines, and two-thirds of foreign-born doctors are either Indian or Pakistani, while the number of health professionals from African countries such as Nigeria, Ghana and Egypt is increasing fast. About 29 per cent of general practitioners (GPs) in England earned their degree abroad. Of this share, 54 per cent qualified in Asia, 28 per cent in Africa and 18 per cent in the EU.[41]

The same applies to child and elder care. As we saw in chapter 7, particularly in countries where government-subsidized care facilities are largely absent, middle-class and elite families are increasingly dependent on migrant caregivers. Without (mostly female) caregivers from countries such as the Philippines, Colombia and Brazil, as well as eastern Europe, there would be nobody to take care of many Italian, Spanish and German seniors. More and more well-to-do families in the West, the Gulf, as well as East and South-East Asia depend on nannies and domestic workers to perform essential household and caretaking tasks.

As local supplies of these workers have largely dried up, it is largely thanks to immigrants that such care is still provided at affordable prices – and that family members of those in need of care are free to actually work and earn money. The importance of immigration in upholding care systems is unlikely to diminish in the future. The number of elderly people in need of care is increasing because of ageing, and as women have massively entered the higher-skilled labour force, this is likely to sustain or even increase the demand for migrant care workers.

So, there is no evidence that immigration undermines the viability of the welfare state. There is even reason to reverse the whole argument: instead of a threat to welfare states, the immigration of foreign workers is vital for upholding healthcare systems and providing care for children and the elderly, particularly in strongly liberalized economies like the UK and the US and weak welfare states like Spain and Italy. Contrary to what politicians tell us, instead of being a burden to the taxpayer, in reality migrant workers increasingly shore up the welfare state.

Myth 10: Immigrant integration has failed

Large-scale immigration and settlement of non-European immigrants in Europe, Britain and North America has coincided with increasing concerns about their perceived lack of integration. The perception is often that large sections of immigrant and minority populations have become trapped in situations of protracted unemployment, welfare dependency and segregation. Because of these problems, the second generation has found it difficult to escape disadvantage through study and work. In this way, disadvantage would be passed down through the generations. Particularly in Europe, a new political consensus has arisen that 'multicultural' policies – which encourage migrant groups to maintain their cultures – have prevented their integration.

Voicing these concerns, Chancellor Angela Merkel gave a speech in 2010 in which she declared: 'We are a country that brought guest workers to Germany from the early 1960s. And now they live with us. We have been kidding ourselves for a while. We said: "They won't stay. Eventually they will be gone." That's not the reality. And, of course, the approach to say: "Now let's do Multikulti here, live side by side and be happy about each other" – that approach has failed. Utterly failed!'[1] In the wake of Merkel's speech, other European leaders, including David Cameron and Nicolas Sarkozy, hastened to publicly declare that multiculturalism had 'failed'.[2]

The belief that immigrant integration has failed – or, at least, has severely lagged behind – has become an article of faith that has increasingly dominated public debates about immigration. This resonates with the fact that most people's concerns with immigration are not so much about economic impacts, but about social and cultural consequences. More and more, cultural difference has become the linchpin to explain differences in the perceived failure – or success – of the integration of immigrant groups.[3] This is linked to the idea that the cultures of recent immigrants are very different from – or incompatible with – Western secular values and democratic societies. In addition, governments' attempts to encourage integration are seen to be continuously thwarted by the 'chain migration' of lower-skilled family members from origin countries. In brief, current levels of immigration seem to exceed the absorption capacity of destination societies and exacerbate racial tensions while 'too much diversity' puts social cohesion under pressure.

In western Europe, Muslim immigrants and their descendants are often portrayed as a group that finds it particularly difficult to integrate, because the norms and values of conservative Islam are fundamentally incompatible with mainstream secular or 'Judeo-Christian' Western values. Perceived problems of educational underperformance, unemployment and crime among Afro-Caribbean immigrants in Europe, who are particularly numerous in Britain and the Netherlands, are also often cast in cultural terms.

In the US, older concerns that German, Irish, Italian, Polish, Jewish, Chinese and Japanese immigrants would imperil the American nation have given way to fears of the large-scale arrival and settlement of Mexicans and other Latin American immigrants. Echoing such fears, in 2004, the political scientist Samuel P. Huntington warned that 'the persistent inflow of Hispanic immigrants threatens to divide the United States into two peoples, two cultures, and two languages', adding that unlike past immigrant groups, Mexicans and other Latinos 'have not assimilated into mainstream US culture . . . rejecting the Anglo-Protestant values that built the American dream' and that 'the United States ignores this challenge at its peril'.[4] Among some white majority groups, Latino immigration has typically evoked concerns about social problems like drugs, crime and sexual harassment that migrants might bring, and about the growing use of the Spanish language in public spaces. Since 9/11, Muslim immigrants have also been looked upon with increasing suspicion in the US.

While working-class migrants of non-European ancestry have been singled out as difficult-to-integrate 'problem groups' on both sides of the Atlantic, other immigrants – and particularly those with ancestry from Asian countries such as China, South Korea and India – are often portrayed as 'model immigrants', supposedly because their cultures value thriftiness, education and hard work. On the other hand, anti-Asian racism has never entirely disappeared, and the Covid-19 pandemic saw a resurgence of racism against Chinese and other Asian immigrants.

However, even among observers who reject racist narratives and are more positive towards immigration, the apparent accumulation of problems such as unemployment, poverty and high-school dropout rates among marginalized working-class migrant communities has led to growing worries about the possible formation of new ethnic underclasses. Growing concerns about the problematic integration of immigrants has provoked a political backlash against multiculturalism and a renewed emphasis on the responsibility of migrants to adapt to host societies, learn the language and assimilate into mainstream culture.

How it really works

In the longer run, immigrant integration is a remarkable success

Has integration failed? And do the cultures or religions of certain groups stand in the way of their success? The short answer is no. It is easy to get mired in the problems of integration, discrimination and adaptation that many migrant groups encounter in the first decades after settlement. However, when we look at the longer term, these problems are generally transient, as the evidence shows that the vast majority of immigrants – including those from disadvantaged or entirely different cultural backgrounds – have been remarkably successful in 'pulling themselves up by their own bootstraps' within one or two generations through education and hard work. When looking at the performance of immigrants' children and grandchildren in terms of language, education, employment and income, progress has been impressive.[5] And this success has almost exclusively been the result of migrants' own efforts to overcome disadvantage and discrimination. There is also no evidence that incompatible cultural differences would generally stand in the way of the integration of so-called non-Western immigrants.

Language and education

The pattern of success is clearest if we look at language skills and education. As migrants' children grow up, they almost automatically adopt the language and local dialect and accent. The migrants themselves – the 'first generation' – often still use the native language at home and in their communities. They may struggle to learn a new language, particularly if they barely went to school in their origin countries. However, almost without exception, the second generation becomes fully fluent in the destination-country language, although they may still be partly or wholly bilingual. By the third generation, knowledge of the origin-country language is often rudimentary at best. For instance, research from the US shows that language integration is happening as rapidly as or faster than it did for the earlier waves of mainly European immigrants in the early twentieth century. In other words, Latino and Asian children in the US now often learn English faster than German or Italian kids did a century ago.[6]

The children of lower-skilled migrants achieve much higher levels of education than their parents, although it can take two or three generations before they have fully caught up with majority populations. Among Mexican American men in the US, there is an increase in average education levels from around 9.5 years in the first to 12.7 in the second generation, approaching the average of 13.9 years for non-migrant white Americans.[7] In Europe, too, the children of former Turkish and Moroccan guest workers in countries such as Germany, France, the Netherlands and Belgium have much higher education levels compared to their parents, as they move closer to the educational levels of white groups of non-immigrant origin. Although a significant gap remains, this provides evidence for a remarkable intergenerational catch-up in education.[8]

Lower-skilled migrant workers who were recruited to work in factories, mines, farms and domestic jobs in the post-Second World War decades often faced a huge disadvantage. Recruiters often deliberately selected workers with limited education, as they preferred hard workers who wouldn't complain or join trade unions. Given the fact that many first-generation migrant workers were illiterate or semi-literate, the progress by the second generation is all the more remarkable.

There remain substantial differences in academic performance across different origin groups. However, this largely reflects class rather than cultural differences. For example, the children of Chinese and Indian immigrants in the US and the UK, and of Iranian refugees in the Netherlands, tend to do particularly well at school. In fact, they often outperform native-born white children. However, this mainly reflects the high education levels of their parents. While much has been written about particular cultures or religions supposedly assigning high importance to education, studies have generally failed to find an independent ethnic or cultural effect on performance at school. In the UK, children of Black African immigrants have been found to outperform white children *and* children of Indian and other South Asian heritage, again reflecting the generally higher education of their parents.[9] Such evidence defies the idea that there is a specific Muslim, Latino or other 'cultural' factor in explaining the below-average school performances of some migrant-origin groups. Once studies control for factors like the education and income of parents, they have generally failed to find a consistent, significant relationship between cultural, religious or national background and education outcomes, other than what can be attributed to disadvantage and discrimination. Class seems to trump all other explanations.[10]

For instance, in the UK, second-generation minorities of Indian heritage outperform those of Pakistani and Bangladeshi origin as well as white British children. This is not because they are Indian, or Hindu, or Sikh, but because of their class background. A substantial number of the Indian-heritage populations in Britain originate from middle-class communities of entrepreneurs and professionals in Kenya, Tanzania, Uganda, Mauritius, and other parts of the former British Empire. They are often descendants of indentured workers and other migrants from Gujarat and the Punjab who came to these British colonies in the nineteenth century, and prospered as an administrative and entrepreneurial middle class between the local Africans and the British ruling class.

In the 1960s, many were expelled from Uganda as part of Idi Amin's anti-Asian racist campaign, and came as refugees to Britain.[11] They had a significant class advantage compared to the lower-skilled workers who were recruited from regions such as Mirpur in Pakistan or Sylhet in Bangladesh to work in British factories and mines. Meanwhile Turkish, Moroccan, Algerian and Tunisian migrant workers in Europe, and Mexican and other Latino migrants in the US, were often from a rural background and had had little schooling on arrival.

It can hardly be surprising that the children of, say, Indian and Chinese engineers have on average higher exam scores than the children of Mexican or Moroccan farm workers. For the same reason, children of higher-skilled Egyptian, Ghanaian or Nigerian migrants in the UK tend to outperform white British kids. Lower-skilled migrants simply have a longer way to go – although for these groups, too, progress has been impressive. If anything, recent evidence from Britain suggests that, by the third generation, children of Bangladeshi and Pakistani origin have started to reach education levels similar to those of white British children, providing further evidence of remarkable intergenerational educational progress.[12]

With regard to Muslims, Islam is as diverse as any other major world religion, and most Muslims put high value on education for boys *and* girls. In fact, among the second and third generations in Europe, Muslim girls often outperform boys at secondary school and in higher education.[13] This reflects a general trend in the Western world, with girls increasingly outperforming boys at school, but among conservative communities in particular, schooling is also a socially acceptable way for girls to gain more independence. For that reason, education often has a strong emancipatory function for girls living in conservative, patriarchal migrant communities.

Discrimination in job hiring is real

While progress in terms of language and schooling has been generally impressive, access to stable jobs and professional careers has proved to be more difficult. While there is strong intergenerational improvement in jobs and income, migrants and their children still suffer significant disadvantages. Prejudice and discrimination often stand in the way of securing apprenticeships or invitations for job interviews. This is a common cause of frustration, and sometimes disillusion, anger and alienation, particularly among the second generation.

Racist discrimination remains a huge obstacle towards labour market integration. One study by Swiss sociologists Eva Zschirnt and Didier Ruedin reviewed forty-three scientific studies conducted between 1990 and 2015 among twenty migrant-origin groups in eighteen Western countries. They found that discrimination in hiring decisions was still widespread in both North America and Europe. On average, equally qualified minority candidates needed to write around 50 per cent more application letters to be invited for a job interview compared to white majority groups. Discrimination was highest among applicants of Arab or Middle Eastern origin – who had to write twice as many letters – followed by applicants of South Asian and Chinese origin.[14]

A major international research project led by Dutch sociologist Bram Lancee analysed the job application experiences of members of fifty-three different migrant-origin groups in the US, the UK, Germany, Spain, the Netherlands and Norway. Lancee and his colleagues sent out 19,181 fictitious applications to online vacancies. They used random differences in the application packages about country of origin, language abilities, religion and (in countries where it is common to include photographs in applications) physical appearance, to assess how often employers would react and express interest in their application. The study found robust evidence of discrimination – on average, immigrant-origin groups had to send 40 per cent more applications compared to majority populations to receive a callback.[15]

The more 'different' immigrant-origin groups were in terms of social and cultural background, the more they were discriminated against. This particularly applied to applicants from African or Middle Eastern origin, with Muslims facing the most discrimination. Yet Lancee and his colleagues found large differences across countries: similar groups were not treated the same in different places. For instance, Moroccan- and Turkish-origin minorities faced higher discrimination levels in the Netherlands, Norway and the UK than they did in Germany and Spain.[16] The same study found that Latinos faced substantial discrimination in the US labour market, while discrimination against Latin Americans in Spain was rather low. Possible explanations are that, in Spain, Latin American immigrants are seen as linguistically, religiously and culturally closer. However, Latin American men and women were treated quite differently in both countries. In the US, Latino men experienced intense discrimination practices, but Latino women didn't. This is presumably linked to the enduring stigmatization of Latino men in the US. In Spain, the patterns were opposite, with Latino women being the main target of discrimination, while Latino men experienced little prejudice.[17]

Lancee and his colleagues therefore concluded that national variations in stereotypes and prejudice, rather than cultural or religious traits of migrant groups themselves, mainly explain differences in discrimination. They also found differences in the general level of discrimination across countries, with Germany and particularly Spain having relatively low levels of job market discrimination. In line with this, another analysis of job hiring discrimination in nine countries in Europe and North America identified substantial differences in discrimination levels on the national level: it found that France had the highest discrimination rates, followed by Sweden, with white applicants receiving nearly twice as many callbacks as non-whites with similar qualifications. In Britain, the US, Canada, Belgium, the Netherlands, Norway and Germany, discrimination rates were lower, with white applicants receiving about a quarter more calls.[18]

Migrants pull themselves up by their own bootstraps

Despite solid evidence of prejudice and discrimination towards particular migrant and minority groups, the overall long-term picture is still one of remarkable success. The evidence of studies and reports that have been written about immigrant integration defy doom-and-gloom narratives and show that, although it takes time, even the most disadvantaged migrant groups are able to succeed through hard work, entrepreneurship and community solidarity.

A major review of research evidence on immigrant integration by the US National Academy of Sciences (NAS) showed that the longer immigrant groups stay in America, the more economically integrated they become – regardless of whether they came from Mexico, Central America, Asia or from other countries.[19] While recently arrived migrants generally earn less than native-born workers of similar skill levels, wages grow significantly with length of residency, although immigrants do not fully catch up with the native-born. Compared to their lower-skilled immigrant parents who mainly did manual jobs, second- and third-generation immigrants are generally able to access higher-level jobs. This pattern of upward intergenerational mobility is particularly steep for women.[20]

A study on immigrant integration in America by the Center for American Progress shows that recent immigrants to America have largely followed in the footsteps of European immigrants of the past.[21] On the whole, this also applies to groups seen as most at risk of 'failure', such as Latinos. Only 9.3 per cent of Latinos who recently arrived in the US owned homes in 1990, but that number had surged to 58 per cent by 2008; the rate of citizenship grew at a similarly fast rate, from below 10 per cent in 1990 to 56 per cent by 2008. Second-generation Latinos are more likely than their immigrant parents to have undergraduate degrees (21 per cent), higher-paying occupations (32 per cent), live in households above the poverty line (92 per cent), and own homes (71 per cent).

Despite this pattern of overall success, the relatively high incidence of poverty among a significant number of Latino groups may provide evidence of a pattern of what American sociologists have called 'segmented assimilation', marked by overall success but also the protracted exclusion and marginalization of a discriminated-against minority. This is also visible in higher school drop-out rates among second- and third-generation Mexican Americans.[22]

On the other side of the Atlantic, too, studies on immigrant integration from across western Europe show a pattern of long-term progress and remarkable intergenerational social mobility. The second generation have consistently higher employment and income levels compared to their parents. In the UK, for instance, migrant groups of Irish, Indian or Chinese background have employment situations as good as or better than white British groups.[23] Other groups are worse off in terms of jobs and incomes, with a descending hierarchy of Black Caribbean, Pakistani and Bangladeshi,[24] but the long-term pattern is unmistakably one of strong intergenerational success.

According to an analysis by the UK Office for National Statistics from 2019, the size of the ethnicity pay gap for those aged 30+ years is larger than for those aged 16–29 years. In fact, many immigrant-origin groups have not just caught up to but have surpassed the average earnings of white British groups. Median hourly pay among Black African, Indian and Arab-origin groups aged 16–29 is 13, 15 and 23 per cent more than among white Brits. Even disadvantaged migrant groups have caught up with remarkable speed. While Pakistani and Bangladeshi groups aged 30+ earn 16 and 23 per cent less than the median hourly pay for white Brits of the same age, Pakistanis and Bangladeshis aged 16–29 earn about the same median wages as white Brits of a similar age.[25]

Likewise, in western Europe, the children and grandchildren of migrant workers who arrived in the 1960s and early 1970s from Turkey, Morocco, Algeria and Tunisia – and in France, from Senegal and Mali – have made huge progress in terms of income, work and housing despite the considerable disadvantage their parents faced as they were hit particularly hard by mass unemployment during the crisis years of the 1970s and 1980s.[26] However, as in the US, there is evidence for concentrated problems of economic exclusion and protracted poverty and segregation among a relatively small but significant minority of groups that may have experienced 'downward assimilation' (see chapter 11).

The evidence also suggests that, generally, the labour market integration of immigrant groups seems to progress more slowly in north-western European countries as compared to the UK and North America,[27] which is presumably related to their more flexible and open labour markets. This is visible in the high gap in unemployment levels between foreign- and native-born in countries such as Sweden, Norway, Austria, Belgium, the Netherlands, Denmark and Germany.[28] However, problems should not blind us to the fact that, in general, by the second generation even the most disadvantaged groups have dramatically improved their labour market position in line with their much higher educational levels.[29]

So while the struggles of first-generation migrant workers and refugees frequently give rise to concerns about their supposed 'unassimilability', the picture has usually changed fundamentally by the second and third generations. This general pattern of long-term integration is also visible in signs of socio-cultural integration, such as increased mixed marriages and the rapid adoption of destination-country norms about family size and the number of children (see chapter 15). In all EU (and other OECD) countries, over 80 per cent of immigrants report feeling close or very close to their host country.[30]

Another integration indicator is the names that parents give to their children. In France, for instance, only 23 per cent of the grandchildren of immigrants from Morocco, Algeria and Tunisia have typically 'Muslim' first names – as against 90 per cent for the first generation. While the most popular names among first-generation immigrants are Mohamed, Ahmed for men and Fatima and Fatiha for women, by the third generation this has changed to the culturally more ambiguous names Yanis and Nicolas for boys and Sarah and Inès for girls.[31]

Access to work and entrepreneurship is key to success

Assimilation and integration are processes that 'happen' largely independently of whatever official integration ideologies governments adhere to. Traditional immigration countries like the US, Canada, Australia and New Zealand have never had much of an official integration policy. They have always adopted a more laissez-faire approach, where immigrants are expected to climb the ladder through education and work. Until the 1970s, West European countries never had official integration policies either, and despite this, past migrants to European countries (such as the Irish in Britain, Polish in Germany, Italians in France and Dutch Indonesians in the Netherlands) – have also fared remarkably well, despite the initial hostility and prejudice they encountered.

So, past and present experiences give reason for considerable optimism about the long-term prospects of integration, as it is something that migrants largely do on their own account, through their own willpower and their own determination to work hard to build a better life for themselves and their children. As we will see in the next chapter, it only seems to go wrong when systematic discrimination, intergenerational disadvantage and government neglect of problems excludes minorities (whether migrant or native-born) from education, jobs and opportunities, and condemns them to go to segregated schools and live in segregated areas that become poverty traps.

Sceptically, one might therefore ask whether official integration policies matter that much at all. Given the many bookshelves that academics and pundits have filled about such policies, and the heated debates – particularly in Europe – around integration and the supposed failure of multiculturalism, it is stunning how few studies have attempted to actually measure the effectiveness of integration policies, and those that have done so using appropriate methodologies found that the effects were generally really small.[32]

Much more than official ideologies, what really seem to matter are bread-and-butter issues such as migrants' access to education, work and housing. Targeted employment, anti-discrimination and education policies can have positive effects,[33] particularly for unemployed migrants with low levels of education or refugees with traumatic experiences, provided that governments offer facilities and resources that enable migrants and refugees to learn the language and get an education.[34]

In many ways, the best integration policy is to make sure migrants can get jobs or can easily start a business, as work remains the single most important avenue towards emancipation, language acquisition and integration. Access to schooling and work is determined by general policies that have little to do with specific integration policies. For instance, Germany's effective system that combines vocational education with apprenticeships seems a factor in explaining why Turkish Germans have higher employment rates than Turkish Dutch.[35]

With regard to economic integration, laissez-faire approaches seem to work remarkably well, as long as governments try to combat racism and remove obstacles so that migrants can participate through work and entrepreneurship. This partly explains why immigrants tend to fare so well in 'Anglo-Saxon' countries such as the US and the UK, as their labour markets tend to be more open and their legislation gives more room for entrepreneurship. In the 1990s and 2000s, a number of Somali refugees who were unemployed and living on benefits in the Netherlands moved to the UK because it was easier to start small enterprises like grocery shops.[36] The Dutch government learned their lesson and relaxed the requirements for starting a business in the 1990s, and since then, the number of Turkish and Moroccan grocers, butchers, bakers, kebab joints and sandwich shops has mushroomed.[37]

The worst policies seem to be those that discourage or prohibit migrants and refugees from working. Nothing seems more detrimental for the well-being *and* economic contribution of migrants and refugees than to force them to remain in legal limbo zones for years because of administrative backlogs and appeals procedures. This leaves them unable to work, increasing trauma and isolation and often pushing them into welfare dependency.

In her research, the Iranian-Dutch sociologist Halleh Ghorashi, professor at the VU University in Amsterdam, has compared the situation of Iranian refugee women in the Netherlands and the United States. She found that the restrictive refugee policies and dominant political discourse in the Netherlands, which treats refugees like temporary sojourners, discourages initiative and pushes them into welfare dependency, reinforcing the prevalent image of refugees as a 'problem group' in Dutch society. By comparison, Iranian refugee women living in the US felt accepted as permanent residents and fared better in terms of work, well-being and overall spirit.[38]

Citizenship is the best integration policy

The evidence shows that official 'integration policies' don't make that much difference. Yet there seems one major exception to this rule: citizenship policies. The Dutch political scientist Maarten Vink has done extensive research on the impact of citizenship rules on integration. His evidence is unequivocal: the sooner immigrants and refugees get access to permanent residency and full citizenship, the safer they feel about their ability to stay, the more motivated they are to invest in a better future. The more migrants identify with their new nation, the better integration outcomes are.[39] Vink's analyses show that access to citizenship is beneficial for the economic integration of immigrants, as it leads to increased labour market access and higher earnings.

One of the studies led by Vink followed the employment and income of 74,500 migrants living in the Netherlands between 1999 and 2011. It found that naturalization gives a major boost in earnings, particularly among migrants who were unemployed or born in low-income countries. Interestingly, the biggest average rise in earnings occurred in the years *leading up* to naturalization. This shows that the mere prospect of gaining access to citizenship motivates migrants to invest in their education and skills.[40] If migrants feel certain that they can stay – and that they will not be deported one day – it gives them the reassurance to invest in their new life in their new home country.

The offering of clear pathways to citizenship is the most concrete gesture through which governments can show that they are genuinely willing to accept migrants and refugees as full and equal members of destination societies. It is by far the best governments can do in terms of encouraging integration.[41] In other words, as long as governments allow migrants to work, protect their rights and provide pathways to permanent residence and citizenship, migrants do most of the integration on their own. All of this resonates with a central insight emerging from a century of research on immigrant integration: to a considerable degree, migration and integration are *autonomous social processes* that will happen anyway, largely irrespective of political rhetoric or of what politicians do (or don't do).

However, this evidence also highlights the dangers of letting migrants wait for too long with an undocumented status or in other legal limbo zones. This is why the inability of the political establishment to provide pathways to legal status for large undocumented migrant populations (in the US and elsewhere) comes with the huge risk of the formation of a structurally disadvantaged underclass.

'Apartheid lite'

What to make, then, of all the 'fuss' about integration and multiculturalism? In western Europe, politicians have been preoccupied with integration policies for decades – particularly in the UK, Germany, the

Netherlands, Belgium and Scandinavia. This issue has been the source of heated debate ever since the 1980s, pitting those in favour of multicultural policies that encourage minorities to foster their own identity and culture, against those stressing the need and responsibility of immigrants to 'fit in' and adapt.

The point is that this has always been primarily an ideological debate[42] – more about 'us' than about 'them', and about what to make of the ways immigration challenges how societies see and define themselves. Immigration has always been an emotional topic, because it is in many ways the most concrete manifestation of the ways in which societies and the world are changing. Immigrants are the literal embodiment of that change – and if it happens quickly, it almost inevitably creates resistance among some native-born groups, at least initially. This is because immigration seems to challenge not only established ways of living, but also the identity of destination societies.

As we saw in chapter 4, this also applies to nations that have immigration in their DNA, such as the US, Canada, Australia and New Zealand, as their nationhood was initially imagined to be (1) white, (2) Protestant, (3) north-west European and preferably (4) English-speaking. Therefore, the immigration of Catholic, Jewish, Latino and Caribbean groups was seen as a challenge and a threat to the nation. Native Americans in the United States, First Nations in Canada, Aboriginal people in Australia and Māori in New Zealand have lived much longer in these lands, but were for a long time not recognized as full citizens or full members of the nation – and they may, in fact, resist inclusion in the nation as defined by their invaders.

Although having lived in America longer than most white immigrants, African Americans only achieved full and equal citizenship rights in 1963, and their centuries-old struggle for emancipation generated violent reactions among those who had always imagined the 'true' American to be white. And the same still applies to the Roma in Europe and numerous other racial, cultural and linguistic minorities around the world, who seek recognition of their identity as part of – or distinct from – the nation, as opposed to total assimilation into the dominant culture of the 'mainstream'.

So, integration is not about immigration per se, but about the genuine acceptance of the 'other' as full members of the nation. Racist ideologies have always served to deny non-majority groups that equal status and to give a moral justification to that denial. From this perspective, multiculturalism can perhaps best be seen as a (perhaps well-intended, but rather misplaced) attempt to deny the new reality of having become a de facto immigration country, effectively denying immigrants recognition as full and equal members of the nation by degrading them to 'minority' status.

Multiculturalism – in brief, the ideology or belief that it was a good thing if migrant groups maintain their language, religion and culture – was particularly adhered to by European governments who kept on denying that reality of permanent settlement for too long, in the false hope that migrants would one day go back to their origin countries, and they therefore failed to address the real problems of long-term unemployment, isolation and segregation that were becoming an increasingly pressing reality in the 1980s and 1990s. Overall, the tendency was to look the other way, and then to wake up one day and realize that immigrants were 'there to stay'.

In this respect, it is quite telling that leading politicians of countries like Germany and the Netherlands kept on recycling the 'we are not an immigration country' mantra far into the 1980s, in plain denial of realities on the ground, and that it took Germany until 1991 to reform its citizenship law to make it easier for non-ethnic Germans to become German. This also reflects the social reality that many north-west Europeans still have difficulty fully accepting the idea that a non-white person can be 'truly' German, Austrian, Dutch, Belgian, Swiss, Swedish, Danish, French or English. A typical, and quite disheartening, experience for non-white minorities in European countries, even if they were born there and speak the national language fluently, is to get asked: 'But tell me, where are you *really* from?'

What few people know in this context is that many of the policies typically known as 'multicultural' have their roots in government efforts to prepare guest workers as well as their children for an eventual return to their homeland. The idea was that, to prevent their assimilation and settlement, maintenance of their own identity, culture, language and religion should be encouraged. For instance, the subsidizing of own-language and own-culture classes for children of Turkish and Moroccan immigrants was initially geared to prevent their full integration, and hence to prepare them for their return to their 'home countries'. For similar reasons, governments subsidized cultural and religious organizations that had a strong origin-country focus. Such provisions continued well into the 1990s and 2000s, by which time it had already become abundantly clear that migration was permanent.

As my first research job after graduating, in 1997 I worked for a think tank in Maastricht, the Netherlands, where I was involved in an EU-subsidized network which connected civil servants working on integration policies at local authorities across western Europe. While I was organizing meetings and writing background reports with typically 'multicultural' titles like 'The Role of Self-Organisations of Migrants and Ethnic Minorities in the Local Authority',[43] it struck me that all participants involved, except for one Pakistan-born civil servant from Birmingham in the UK, were of non-migrant, white backgrounds, and that the whole tone of debate – and the type of research I had to do – set groups apart rather than considering them as (current or future) full members of European nations. One of the reports I wrote was about the *consultative* (instead of full) political participation of migrants and minorities in local authorities.[44] However good the intentions undoubtedly were, and with all the politically correct lip-service paid to the principles of tolerance, equality and anti-racism, only now do I fully realize how misguided this was. Migrants were still, in essence, being treated like temporary sojourners.

So, the irony is that the policies later sold as 'good for integration' were actually designed to prevent just that! This also puts the term 'tolerance' in a different, more negative light, as an expression of a rather patronizing attitude that sets groups apart. For instance, the Dutch have often prided themselves on their historical tolerance towards 'minorities'. But the attitude can also be read as: 'We accept your presence, you can go your own way as long as you don't bother us, but you will never be one of us.' From that perspective, multiculturalism is a form of repressive tolerance, or 'apartheid lite'.

In practice, the multicultural policies advocated by many West European governments often set migrant groups apart, as they clung on to guest worker illusions for too long and denied the reality of permanent settlement.[45] 'We asked for workers, we got people instead', as the Swiss writer Max Frisch summarized the guest worker conundrum back in 1967.[46] In the meantime, the illusion of temporariness would do a lot of damage, as it prevented governments from effectively addressing the real problems of long-term unemployment, welfare dependency and segregation that hit migrant communities disproportionately hard in the

1970s and 1980s, decades marked by protracted economic recession and mass unemployment.

So, multicultural policies stimulated segregation under the guise of tolerance, and delayed rather than stimulated the integration of migrant groups. This only started to change in the 2000s, when the realities – and real problems – could no longer be denied, and European governments started to accept the new reality of having become de facto immigration countries. In this light, Merkel's 2010 statement that 'Multikulti has failed' can be seen as a sign of finally coming to terms with that reality.

Short-term challenges, long-term successes

The idea that integration has 'failed' is a myth based on a failure to see a consistent pattern of long-term success, and on a one-sided focus on particular groups where problems persist beyond the first and second generations. It is easy to be blinded by the social problems and interracial tensions that often accompany the large-scale settlement of new groups with different religions, customs and habits. However, if we look at the longer term, most groups have fared remarkably well.

Lower-skilled immigrants from rural areas have often found it difficult to adapt to modern city life in a different country. In hindsight, the integration of lower-skilled, semi-literate workers who were recruited from Mexico to work in the US, from Pakistan and Bangladesh to work in the UK, and from Turkey and North Africa to work in Europe was bound to be a challenge, not only because they were often treated like guest workers who were not expected to stay in the first place, but also because they were catapulted from traditional peasant communities straight into modern Western city life.

Their migration was not only the crossing of a border, but also a radical, socially disruptive and emotionally unsettling transition from rural to urban life. It is a huge emotional stretch to migrate from Mirpur in rural Pakistan to Manchester, Birmingham or Bradford; from the Rif and Atlas mountains of Morocco and Algeria to Paris, Brussels or Amsterdam; from Central Anatolia in Turkey to Berlin and Frankfurt; or from Oaxaca in Mexico to Los Angeles. It would have felt like time travel. Having been uprooted, and working long hours, it is only to be expected that, in their free time, these workers would retreat into the familiarity of their own community to find comfort, safety and dignity amid a strange, bewildering and sometimes hostile world they did not really know, that seemed to have little interest in them and that expected them to return.

With the passing of time and the growing-up of children, however, communities inevitably take root in destination societies. Despite the struggles, alienation and conflict that immigration often involves, in the longer run most migrant groups succeed in adapting and adjusting to their new home. Almost unnoticeably, a few generations down the line, 'they' become 'us', adopting the language, habits and customs of their new homeland. This is what happens when migrants settle and have children, and their children have children too.

Things can change fast. What seemed unimaginable yesterday is easily taken for granted today. In the UK, since 2019, the Johnson and Truss governments have included a record number of ministers of Asian and also African ancestry – a sea change from the nearly all-white cabinets of just over a decade ago. This culminated with the appointment of Rishi Sunak as prime minister in 2022. Perhaps even more significantly, during the Euro 2020 tournament, descendants of Caribbean and South Asian migrant workers of the post-Second World War decades were waving English flags in the streets of English cities and towns – an unimaginable scene just a few decades earlier, when some of the same streets saw turbulent race riots.

Of course, this doesn't mean that racism is dead. Some would argue that the success stories of select groups of privileged migrants of a certain class background are not representative of the experiences of most migrant and minority groups and can actually serve as a fig leaf to conceal problems of racism, discrimination and segregation. However, it would also be too harsh to deny that real progress has been made.

At the same time, there are clear differences in experiences across destination countries. Immigrants seem to have generally fared better in societies that accept the permanent nature of immigration, facilitate access to citizenship, and remove barriers to work and entrepreneurship – as compared to reluctant immigration countries that deny the permanency of settlement, discourage migrants and refugees from working and push them into welfare dependency. For too long, governments have made excuses for not taking responsibility for the people they allowed to settle, looking the other way and ignoring long-term unemployment and social isolation.

They become more like us than we become like them

Despite the short-term challenges, the pattern of long-term progress is undeniable. As majority populations get used to newcomers, this usually takes away fear, and may even encourage the adoption of some habits. The first step towards real integration is when majority populations not only adapt and appreciate the foods of migrants, but also start to consider them as their own. Chicken tikka masala has become as quintessentially British as fish and chips (although some say it was actually invented in Britain), burritos and tacos have become as American as apple pie and coleslaw, and kebab and döner have become as German as bratwurst and sauerkraut. This is emblematic of the immigrant experience: those who seemed unassimilable strangers not that long ago have become part and parcel of destination societies.

However, if we look at things from a distance, such changes are rather superficial. While destination societies may adopt certain elements of the new cultures migrants bring – such as food, music and dress – this impact is not as profound as we tend to think. In this context, the Princeton sociologist Alejandro Portes has argued that, although large-scale immigration to the US and western Europe may appear to have fundamentally transformed the 'sights and smells' of cities, in reality these are 'street-level' changes. Immigration has, in fact, barely changed the deeper cultural, political and economic structures of destination societies.

Referring to the US, Portes argued that 'the fundamental pillars of American society have remained unaltered',[47] including the political and legal systems, the educational system, the dominance of English, and the basic values guiding social interactions. Although more and more individuals from non-white migrant-origin groups occupy high-ranking political positions, the systems themselves are essentially unaltered. Portes therefore questions the popular idea that immigration has fundamentally changed the American mainstream. For the same reasons, large-scale immigration seems to have left the fundamental pillars of European nations unchanged.

Although it is often said that integration is a two-way process, this cliché ignores the fact that immigrants have to make by far the biggest effort at adapting and fitting in. In other words, immigrants become more like us than we become like them.

In the same way that immigrant groups once considered unassimilable – such as Germans, Italians, Irish and Jews – are now fully considered as part of the 'mainstream', the evidence shows that most Latin American and Asian immigrants in the US, and Muslim, Caribbean and African immigrants in Europe, have become full members of destination societies. In fact, recent immigrant groups are assimilating at a similar – or even faster – pace to previous generations in terms of language, education and work, challenging popular claims that their cultures or religions stand in the way of integration. So, there's a good chance that the perceived 'problem groups' of today will be replaced by the newcomers of tomorrow, and that the migrants of today will start to complain about new immigrants coming in – usually the best sign of successful integration, and that 'they' have become 'us'.

Myth 11: Mass migration has produced mass segregation

'Ghetto Britain: Entire districts segregated', 'Ghettos in English cities almost equal to Chicago', 'The powder keg of the suburbs', 'An American-style urban revolt'.[1] Such headlines, featured in newspapers across Europe, resonate with broader fears that, with large-scale immigration, Europe has unintentionally imported American-style 'ghettos' onto its own soil. Although the integration of most immigrants has been rather successful, the experiences of some groups have proved less positive. Even though this is a 'minority within a minority', it is still a significant problem. Across north-west Europe, politicians, media and opinion-makers have expressed worries about racial and ethnic segregation hitherto unknown in Europe.

In the UK, riots broke out in 2001 between local white and South Asian communities in Oldham, Bradford, Leeds and Burnley, sparking widespread concerns about poverty, social isolation and segregation in northern industrial cities. In France, major riots starting in 2005 and 2007 among migrant youth equally awakened public attention to the long-term effects of immigration, and reinforced fears about ghettoization. These events resonated with images of long-term unemployment, poverty and crime among North and West African migrant youth living in the insalubrious high-rises of the *banlieues* – suburban housing estates built in the post-war period.

In Sweden in 2017, gang violence and violent clashes between immigrant youth and the police in the Stockholm suburb of Rinkeby made the international headlines. In 2018, the Danish government adopted controversial laws with the aim of 'abolish[ing] ghettoes by 2030', including measures to evict migrant families from social housing blocks in low-status neighbourhoods to shake them out of self-isolation and life in 'parallel societies'.[2] Similarly, in 2022 the Swedish followed suit as it proposed a 50 per cent limit on concentrations of people with immigrant backgrounds in so-called 'troubled areas'.[3]

The 9/11 terrorist attacks in 2001 on the World Trade Center in New York and the Pentagon in Washington, DC sparked fears in America and Europe that home-bred terrorists of Muslim immigrant backgrounds might pose a security threat from within. In Britain, worries about segregation mounted in the wake of the 7/7 bombings on the London transit system in 2005. In 2015 and 2016, a new wave of attacks occurred in Paris, Brussels, Berlin, Manchester and London. When it came out that the Bataclan and Charlie Hebdo attacks in Paris were perpetrated by young men who had grown up in the Brussels immigrant neighbourhood of Molenbeek, this increased concerns that such neighbourhoods had become breeding grounds for religious extremists.

Far-right nativist groups and proponents of the 'great replacement' conspiracy theory see all this as proof that immigration is a liberal plot to Islamize Europe and displace white voters. Most people understand that such radicalized youth only form a small fraction of immigrant-origin groups. However, these events did resonate with a more general feeling that, as the then chairman of the UK's Commission for Racial Equality, Trevor Phillips, stated in the wake of the 7/7 bombings, Britain had been 'sleepwalking [its] way to segregation' by ignoring problems for too long.[4]

In the US, concerns about segregation have always revolved around the historical Black–white divide rooted in centuries of slavery and racism, and this is still a problem in major US cities. However, the large-scale immigration of Latino workers has given rise to new concerns about the concentration of social problems, unemployment and violence in segregated neighbourhoods.

Media reporting and politicians' statements have given an impression that large-scale immigration has created permanent ethnic underclasses living parallel lives in segregated neighbourhoods marked by high unemployment, welfare dependency and poverty. It resonates with popular ideas that, as immigrants seem to cling on to their culture, language and religion, their increasing self-segregation obstructs integration, with closed immigrant communities becoming breeding grounds for social dysfunction, crime or religious fundamentalism.

How it really works

With some exceptions, segregation is not alarmingly high

As we have seen, the integration of the majority of migrants, including those of non-Western backgrounds, has been remarkably successful. However, optimistic averages about successful long-term integration conceal the fact that a significant minority of migrant-origin groups are clearly faring less well, as highlighted by high rates of school dropouts, unemployment and welfare dependency. We can also not deny that some immigrant neighbourhoods in Europe and America have become hotbeds of poverty and disadvantage. However, do such problems justify claims that, with large-scale immigration, segregation is on the rise?

The facts give reason to debunk such claims. First of all, levels of segregation among recent immigrant groups are generally not as high as many people think, and although there are real problems, they cannot be compared to historical Black–white segregation in the United States. Second, there is no evidence that ethnic and racial segregation is increasing, despite continued immigration.

Geographers have developed various ways of measuring residential segregation: the most used indicator is the segregation or dissimilarity index, which measures the distributions of population groups across residential areas of a city.[5] The segregation index reaches a value of 100 when groups are totally segregated, and 0 when all neighbourhoods have exactly the same ethnic and racial mix. Researchers consider values above 60 'high', values below 30 'low' and in-between values 'moderate'.[6]

Studies that have measured ethnic segregation vary in their findings, depending on the specific data and methods used, but they also show some consistent patterns. First, segregation in continental western Europe is generally lower than in the US, particularly when compared to Black–white segregation.[7] In 1980 the segregation index for Asians (from whites) living in major US central cities was 41, for Latinos it was 52, but for African Americans it was a staggering 75. By 2010, the latter value had dropped to 60, while the segregation index for Asians and Latinos had remained rather stable at levels of 39 and 51 respectively.[8]

Partly depending on urban planning and housing policies, segregation levels in Europe vary significantly across countries, cities and migrant groups. Contrary to the *banlieue* stereotype, French cities tend to have the lowest average segregation levels in Europe – for instance, 23 and 12 for Algerians and Portuguese in Paris, respectively. That does not mean that the problems in some *banlieues* are not real, but that the issues in some 'problem neighbourhoods' are not representative of the overall immigrant experience in France. Ethnic segregation is relatively low in Germany, with segregation levels for Turks in Düsseldorf and Frankfurt at 30 and 18.[9] Most Dutch cities have moderate levels of segregation – around 40 – such as for Moroccans in Rotterdam and Amsterdam, and Turks in The Hague. Only for some groups in some European cities – such as Moroccans in Brussels, North Africans in Antwerp, and Iranians in Stockholm – does segregation reach 'American' levels, with values between 50 and 60.[10]

Compared to continental Europe, levels of ethnic and racial segregation in the UK are higher, particularly among South Asian groups. This partly reflects generally higher levels of class segregation in the UK. As immigrant groups tend to be over-represented in low-income groups, class segregation tends to coincide with higher levels of racial and ethnic segregation.[11] It is therefore no surprise that some of the highest segregation levels are found among Bangladeshi and Pakistani communities in cities such as Birmingham, Bradford and Oldham. There, in the 1990s, segregation reached levels of between 60 and 80 – although levels in London were much lower. Black Caribbean and Indian-origin groups in the UK have similar segregation levels to most other immigrants in continental Europe.[12] This reflects their earlier arrival, smaller group size, higher income levels and more dispersed initial settlement patterns compared to more community-focused Pakistani and Bangladeshi groups.[13]

Not only is segregation in Europe generally not alarmingly high, but the evidence shows that since the 1990s, levels of racial segregation have actually decreased in most countries.[14] This reflects broader trends of integration and upward mobility, as migrants and minorities climb the economic and housing ladders. All across western Europe, the large-scale arrival of migrant workers and their families from the 1950s and 1960s initially went hand in hand with a concentration of migrant groups in ethnic enclaves, where housing was affordable and they could count on help from fellow countrymen and -women.

However, these trends have reversed in recent decades, with overall levels of ethnic segregation in Europe declining. As immigrants and their children climb the economic ladder, they can increasingly afford to rent or buy houses in middle-income neighbourhoods, leading to increased racial mixing. In the UK between 1991 and 2001, for instance, the average segregation indices among Bangladeshis living in large urban areas went down from 69 to 61, for Pakistanis from 56 to 51, for Indian-origin groups from 42 to 40, and for Black Caribbean populations from 43 to 37. Since 2001, this trend towards increased residential mixing between white British and other ethnic groups has continued.[15] This has also been the historical pattern in the United States, with immigrant groups initially clustering in typical immigrant neighbourhoods, before spreading out. For this reason, levels of residential segregation for Asians and Latinos have remained relatively stable despite continuing immigration.[16]

Empowerment through community life

While there is evidence that levels of racial and ethnic segregation have decreased rather than increased, we must also question the assumption that the concentration of ethnic groups in particular areas is necessarily a bad thing. Urban geographers have made a useful distinction between the 'ghetto' and the 'ethnic enclave'.[17] Ghettos are areas that are almost exclusively inhabited by one particular racial, ethnic or religious group; are the product of explicit discrimination and exclusion by majority groups, who refuse to have minorities live with them; and have become sites of multigenerational poverty – the archetypical examples being the Jewish ghetto in medieval Europe, African American urban segregation in the twentieth century, and the enduring situation of Romani people in Europe.[18]

The typical immigrant neighbourhoods of Europe, North America, Australia and New Zealand are ethnic enclaves: racially mixed areas, where groups concentrate together on a largely voluntary basis, and where such concentrations are generally a temporary, transient phenomenon. As long as it is largely a result of free choice to live together, rather than the result of discrimination and exclusion, the outcomes of ethnic clustering can actually be very positive.

First of all, the desire to live together emanates from a basic human desire to be to among people who speak the same language and who have similar lifestyles, customs and habits. Second, such clustering can in some ways advance integration, because community life can empower disadvantaged minorities. As immigrants and minorities are often confronted with exclusion and discrimination when trying to access good education, jobs and services, migrant community life has proved a vibrant 'emancipation machine', as it can enable them to overcome disadvantages and prejudice and achieve socioeconomic mobility through bonds of solidarity, self-help and entrepreneurship. The presence of large numbers of people with the same origin also provides an initial customer base for migrant businesses, and enables communities to establish schools, places of worship, sports clubs, trade unions, newspapers and various other organizations.

Entrepreneurship has proved to be an important route towards the economic and social mobility of migrant and minority groups who are confronted with structural unemployment, discrimination and limited access to job markets. Typical examples of migrant businesses include grocery shops, bakers, kosher and halal butchers, barbershops, dry cleaners, tailors, beauty parlours, coffeehouses, bars and restaurants.

Although such 'ethnic businesses' may initially mainly cater for the needs of their own communities, later they often start to serve customers from majority groups as the latter learn to appreciate the growing diversity of affordable options for grocery shopping and exotic foods. Migrant entrepreneurs can enjoy the advantage of being able to rely on the labour of family members, who often feel obliged to contribute to the family business and are motivated by feelings of solidarity to 'make it together'. In the initial settlement phase of new immigrant communities, entrepreneurship allows families to obtain assets, save money, provide a good education for children and eventually achieve middle-class status. Such businesses also create additional jobs for local workers and are a major factor in attracting new migrants from the same origin country, thereby accelerating the growth of migrant communities and further expanding the customer base.[19]

Once they have achieved middle-class status, and new generations have grown up, such groups typically rent or buy houses in middle-class areas and move out of immigrant neighbourhoods. This pattern of moving to higher-status areas is quite typical when we look at the settlement history of immigrant communities around the world. So, the initial clustering of migrants in particular neighbourhoods is no proof of 'ghettoization' – as media and politicians often claim.

Ethnic enclaves as emancipation machines

Ethnic enclaves can be veritable emancipation machines. Many working-class neighbourhoods in cities around the world have seen such a succession through the coming and going of new and old immigrant groups. The Lower East Side in New York City received successive waves of newly arrived immigrants – first Germans, then Italians and Jewish East Europeans, as well as Greeks, Hungarians, Poles, Romanians, Russians, Slovaks and Ukrainians. In a similar way, from the seventeenth century, the East End of London received successive immigration waves: Huguenot (Protestant) refugees fleeing repression by the French king between 1670 and 1710, Irish weavers from the early nineteenth century, Jews fleeing pogroms in Russia between 1875 and 1914, and Bangladeshi and Pakistani workers from the 1950s and 1960s.[20]

The Jewish experience of social mobility in Britain is a classic example of migrant success. The first generation of refugees managed to escape discrimination and badly paid and insecure factory jobs by becoming small entrepreneurs in the 'rag trade' (clothing manufacturing) or the retail sector. Putting a strong emphasis on education for their children, many of the second generation were able to move into business or white-collar employment, paving the way for professional careers for the third generation.[21] Bangladeshi people now live in the same areas of the East End, often working in the same sweatshops and worshipping in the same buildings. What is now Brick Lane Mosque was originally built in 1743 as a Protestant chapel for Huguenot refugees from France, then was converted into a synagogue for Jewish refugees from Russia and Central Europe in 1891, before it was turned into a mosque in 1976 after the arrival of Bangladeshi migrant workers from the Sylhet region in the Spitalfields and Brick Lane areas.[22]

So, we come from a much more segregated past than we think, as we have forgotten about past groups living in ethnic enclaves who have moved out and seamlessly blended in. This constant moving-out of old migrant groups reflects their success in achieving higher education and income levels, and broader integration processes. In other words, the arrival of new immigrants has been more than counterbalanced by the out-movement of long-term settlers.[23] This largely explains why racial and ethnic segregation has *not* increased, despite continuing immigration.

Allusions to racial segregation in the United States are sensationalist

There are more reasons why the experiences of immigrant neighbourhoods, both in Europe and North America, cannot be compared to racially segregated neighbourhoods in America, where the nature and level of segregation is of an entirely different scale and nature. Black–white segregation in the US was caused by explicitly racist policies of assigning separate and vastly inferior forms of housing, education and services to Black populations, based on racist beliefs that Black and white people should not mix.

In their landmark study *American Apartheid: Segregation and the Making of the Underclass*, published in 1993, sociologists Douglas Massey and Nancy Denton showed how segregation didn't happen spontaneously, or because African Americans didn't want to mix with whites, or because they happened to concentrate in poorer neighbourhoods.[24] Segregated African American neighbourhoods were *intentionally* created by white people during the first half of the twentieth century, to isolate the 6 million or so Black people who had moved from the rural South to the cities of the Northeast, Midwest and West as part of the Great Migration. Yet their hopes of emancipation were quickly dashed. Black workers were excluded from the unions of the American Federation of Labor,[25] while city councils passed laws to create separate neighbourhoods for Black and white residents, effectively 'creating a formal apartheid system'.[26]

Apart from violent attacks on Black people living in white areas, discrimination (in real estate and banking) was the most important institutional mechanism in achieving segregation. This happened particularly through racial redlining: lenders refusing to issue mortgages to borrowers living in Black or racially mixed neighbourhoods, as well as the denial of home insurance to Black residents in the suburbs, and the building of public housing in segregated districts. These practices became part of official federal policies during the New Deal, between 1933 and 1939.[27] As white Americans massively took advantage of federal lending programmes to buy new homes in burgeoning all-white suburbs where Black Americans weren't allowed to live, Black migrants coming in from the rural South moved into older homes in city centres. In the post-war decades, this led to extraordinarily high levels of segregation.[28]

However, these problems only got really bad from the 1960s onwards, when the jobs that had attracted Black workers from the South started to disappear as industries closed down or moved out of the city centres. As the Chicago sociologist William Julius Wilson documented in his book *The Truly Disadvantaged: The Inner City, the Underclass, and Public Policy*, this resulted in mass unemployment and rising poverty, as well as the departure of the rising Black middle classes to more affluent neighbourhoods, further depriving inner-city areas of community leaders and structures and exacerbating family dysfunction, high school-dropout rates, drug abuse and crime.[29]

Europe lacks such a recent history of official, government-endorsed racial segregation. For this reason alone, the problems of immigrant neighbourhoods in Europe – as well as in America – can therefore not be compared to Black segregation in the US, which was near-total and explicitly government-endorsed. The French sociologist Loïc Wacquant conducted extensive research on segregated American neighbourhoods, and Chicago's South Side in particular. Based on his knowledge of both French and North American segregation, Wacquant has pointed out why sensationalist comparisons between the French working-class *banlieues* – and European immigrant neighbourhoods more generally – and Black–white segregation in the US don't make much sense.[30]

First, segregated neighbourhoods in the US tend to be much bigger than the typical European immigrant neighbourhoods. Such neighbourhoods in Chicago, New York and Los Angeles have several hundreds of thousands of inhabitants and cover hundreds of square kilometres. The largest French *cités* never even reach one-tenth of that size. Second, the *banlieues* are mainly residential areas, with many people going elsewhere on a daily basis for work or shopping, as they generally only have to walk a few streets to leave their neighbourhoods. By contrast, the American 'ghetto' is a largely self-contained place – or, in the words of Wacquant, a 'black city within the city', where many people have little, if any, contact with other races or classes.[31]

Third, segregated neighbourhoods in America are largely monoracial, with Black Americans forming the overwhelming majority.

Typical *immigrant* neighbourhoods (in Europe and North America) are anything but uniform. Although some ethnicities may dominate, there is invariably a rich mosaic of ethnic, racial, religious and income groups – including white and middle-class – living next to one another.

Fourth, the scale and depth of problems of American segregated neighbourhoods are of an entirely different order than in Europe. Violence and crime in even the most notorious European immigrant neighbourhoods mostly concern theft, burglary, vandalism and the small-scale drugs trade, while armed robberies and lethal gun violence are actually quite rare.

It should be said, though, that the image of the American 'ghetto' has itself been sensationalized, based on harmful stereotypes that have been reinforced by popular media, racist politicians and prejudiced pundits.[32] As the American geographer John Agnew has stressed, the usual focus on Chicago and a few other notorious examples reinforces a picture of 'hyperghettoization' which is not representative of the overall experience of (often more mixed patterns of) racial segregation in the US.[33] America's ugly history of segregation came to change the very meaning of the word 'ghetto'. While it was originally associated with Jewish urban quarters in Europe and later also America, its connotation changed in the 1950s to conjure stereotypical images of run-down and crime-ridden African American segregated areas. Because of the racist connotations it accumulated, the term 'ghetto' is highly controversial, with many considering its usage slanderous and racist.[34]

Finally, the overall quality of public infrastructure, streets and housing in lower-income neighbourhoods is incomparably better in most European cities, largely thanks to higher public investments in social housing and public infrastructure. In the US, the degradation of working-class inner-city neighbourhoods was reinforced by a sharp decline in federal funding devoted to social housing. The subsidized public housing 'projects' of the post-Second World War era were of such bad quality, and so poorly managed and underfunded, that they quickly became 'last resort' poverty traps.

As we saw in chapter 9, social housing in Europe has also been partly privatized, but the overall size and quality of the social housing stock are much higher than in the US and still considered to be 'respectable'. They look better, are generally safe places for families to live, and have facilities such as playgrounds, parks, schools, commercial areas, public libraries and public transport. Still, in Europe the neglect and defunding of social housing together with growing inequality has created worrying forms of protracted segregation in particular neighbourhoods.

degradation of
public housing in US

From social housing to social dumping

On 14 June 2017, a fire broke out in the twenty-four-storey Grenfell Tower block in North Kensington, London. Seventy-two people died and seventy were injured, while hundreds of homes were lost. Most tenants were from low-income working-class backgrounds, and 85 per cent of the residents who died were from ethnic minority communities. An investigation revealed that cladding and insulation fitted in 2015 were flammable, and that this had caused the fire to spread so fast. Although the council knew the cladding did not comply with regulations, and was known to be dangerous on façades, it was nevertheless used to save costs. Much social housing in the UK still has flammable cladding or is unsafe in other ways.[35]

This illustrates the consequences of government neglect of social housing. On both sides of the Atlantic, the big social housing programmes of the mid-twentieth century were intended not to house the poor and destitute, but to provide decent homes to working-class families with regular jobs and incomes. In the US, this was part of the New Deal programme, while in Britain and the rest of Europe, post-war reconstruction efforts provided a huge impetus to pour government resources into social housing, which received support from across the political spectrum. However, from the 1960s, the departure of middle-class families to the suburbs – combined with the defunding of social housing – degraded some of these areas into 'social dumping' grounds where only the poorest, most marginalized populations wanted to live.

In Britain, some politicians have used the derogatory term 'sink estate' for a council housing estate that becomes run-down because it is starved of investment in amenities, infrastructure and public spaces.[36] As a result, social housing has increasingly degraded 'from a badge of citizenship to a symbol of segregation'.[37] The neglect, defunding and degrading of social housing has disproportionately affected migrants and minorities, as they have become over-represented in low-quality, unhealthy or dangerous social housing.

Urban planning and social housing policies have a large impact on the level and severity of residential segregation. In France in the post-Second World War decades there were severe housing shortages, and to resolve the problems of urban slums the government embarked on an ambitious programme to build affordable housing (*habitations à loyer modéré*, also known as HLMs) in the *banlieues* of large cities. However, as native working-class families often did not want to live in anonymous, unattractive high-rise estates on the peripheries of cities, immigrant families were settled there.

In the UK, social housing has generally taken the form of council estates, which are geographically segregated from the more affluent neighbourhoods where most houses are privately owned. In the post-war decades, new estates often took the form of mass-housing projects consisting of flats and tower blocks.[38] As many white British families moved out of such council estates from the 1970s, they were replaced by migrants and ethnic minorities. The same applies in inner-city areas traditionally inhabited by the British working class. So, what is essentially a class divide now looks like an ethnic divide.

Of course, moderate levels of ethnic clustering are not necessarily problematic, and in many cases community solidarity can empower migrant and minority groups through study, work and entrepreneurship. However, in some cases local experiences have created more problematic forms of protracted segregation. In Europe, more extreme forms of segregation are generally the unintended outcome of misguided urban planning in combination with particular historical circumstances that nobody foresaw.

For instance, residential segregation is a growing concern in Sweden, with cities such as Stockholm, Gothenburg and Malmö reaching some of the most extreme segregation levels in Europe. In some neighbourhoods, such as the Stockholm suburb of Rinkeby, over 80 per cent of the population is foreign-born. While the biggest groups are from Somalia, Iraq and Syria, Rinkeby is inhabited by a wide variety of nationalities. The roots of the segregation between native Swedish and immigrant populations are to be found in the Swedish housing policy of building social housing estates in isolated places – far from the city centre, employment opportunities and spaces for community activities.[39] Housing estates such as Rinkeby were part of the prestigious Million Program, in which the Social Democratic Palme government built nearly 1 million housing units for the Swedish working classes between 1965 and 1974.

As Swedish working-class families didn't want to live in the concrete, sterile, low-quality apartment buildings, they became a housing solution of 'last resort' for socially marginal groups, often living on benefits. From the 1980s, the government started to settle migrants and refugees in these neighbourhoods. It was also a matter of unfortunate timing – as asylum inflows peaked in 1992, the Swedish economy went through its worst crisis for decades, pushing newly arrived refugee families into unemployment and welfare dependence.[40] From the 1990s, the privatization of housing drove the poor out of the gentrifying city centres towards these neighbourhoods.[41] In Rinkeby, the resulting accumulation of poverty and social problems culminated in a surge of violence between youth gangs.

'Eyes on the street' and misguided urban planning

The most extreme and eye-catching problems with segregation seem to have emerged whenever governments have built large-scale, anonymous, low-quality housing estates where native workers do not want to live. These problems can easily be avoided by learning from the errors of the past. This is nothing to do with integration policies per se, but with sensible urban planning that fosters community life, social safety and some level of racial and class mixing. Across the Western world, misguided experiments with modern urban 'blueprint' planning in post-war decades had disastrous consequences in terms of the loss of community and the rise of social dysfunction and crime.

'Modern' urban planning focused on the geographical separation of the functions of living, shopping, working, leisure and traffic. In the name of urban renewal, slum clearance and modernization, urban planning in many Western cities has long focused on the construction of expressways and high-rises. As the American-Canadian journalist and urban theorist Jane Jacobs argued in her 1961 book *The Death and Life of Great American Cities*,[42] this turned out to be a catastrophic error, as it destroyed community life and prevented social control, turning dense, lively neighbourhoods into unsafe, eerie places where nobody likes to go and nobody likes to live. Instead of helping city-dwellers to continue living in their neighbourhoods, this literally destroyed these neighbourhoods (stigmatized as 'slums') and took the heart out of downtown communities.

Most people don't like to live in such anonymous places. High-rise buildings intersected by large green spaces inhibit community life and social control and lead to a lack of safety. Inspired by Jacobs's critique, urban planners have increasingly realized that crime is lower and people's perceptions of safety are higher when there is a geographical mixing of the prime social and commercial functions of housing, working, shopping and entertainment, because the constant presence of people and, as Jacobs aptly put it, 'eyes on the street' fosters social control. This prevents shopping centres and inner-city areas from becoming deserted, eerie-feeling or 'ghost towns' at night, where people don't dare to walk – even though they may look a bit scruffy. Likewise, the presence of small shops, restaurants and cafés in residential areas fosters liveliness and social connectivity.

This is why the rise of shopping malls and large supermarkets on the outskirts of big cities has had negative repercussions for social cohesion in inner-city neighbourhoods. As mom-and-pop stores and local bakeries and hardware shops closed down, neighbourhoods and towns also lost important social centres. The paradox is that old city neighbourhoods and urban slums that may *appear* run down often provide exactly the mixing of functions that tend to be fertile ground for community life and small-scale entrepreneurship typical of ethnic enclaves.

Increasingly, income segregation is the real problem

The evidence clearly defies the idea that the immigration of non-Western migrant groups has led to the formation of permanent ethnic underclasses living 'parallel lives' in urban ghettos. In some cases, segregation becomes protracted, with neighbourhoods turning into multi-generational poverty traps for marginalized minorities. However, this is not so much the result of the particular culture or religion of such groups, but rather of their economic marginalization combined with misguided urban planning policies that turned neighbourhoods into poverty traps.

For too long, governments have ignored and neglected these real problems. Clearly, denying or soft-pedalling these problems will not solve them, but likely make them worse. However, in order to effectively address such problems, we need to understand the structural causes of segregation, which are generally a combination of long-term unemployment, poverty, misguided urban planning and a failure to provide opportunities for the social mobility of marginalized groups.

In this respect, a highly relevant – and worrying – development is the growing class segregation across the Western world, in which rich and poor groups live increasingly separate lives. A range of studies from north and south Europe show that economic liberalization, growing inequality and the defunding and privatization of social housing have increased class-based residential segregation and growing alienation between economic elites (the most segregated group of all) and middle-income and poor families living in racially more mixed neighbourhoods and suburbs. It is in this intersection of racial exclusion and residential segregation that we find the worst instances of poverty – with income segregation hitting the most disadvantaged migrant communities – as well as some marginalized white groups – hardest.[43]

In the US, too, the importance of class inequality in explaining patterns of residential segregation has been increasing. As Douglas Massey and his collaborators showed, the outlawing of racial redlining and other discriminatory practices by 1977 prompted a decline in average levels of Black segregation. However, it paradoxically led to a concentration of problems in the largest 'ghettos' because of growing class segregation. As the new Black middle classes moved out, problems became increasingly concentrated among the poor Black families who were left behind. With numbers of Latinos growing from the 1980s, their racial isolation often increased too, while wealthier (often Asian) migrant groups moved into more affluent neighbourhoods. As income groups have become more and more segregated, this has resulted in 'polarized urban geography' marked by increasing concentrations of affluent whites and Asians living in wealthy coastal areas, alongside high concentrations of poverty among poor Black and Latino residents in older, declining industrial areas in the Midwest and the South, which also contain pockets of white and Asian poverty.[44]

These kinds of segregation have little do with migrant and minority groups supposedly clinging on to their culture, language or religion, unwilling to integrate, but with the inability of poor groups – irrespective of their ethnicity or race – to escape from these conditions. The causes of such protracted class segregation are *structural* and are linked to increasing income inequality and the liberalization of housing and rental markets. Ethnic segregation is decreasing as previous migrants climb the economic ladder, and recent migrants are becoming more diverse in class background. But because migrant and minority groups are still over-represented among lower-income earners, class segregation is disproportionately affecting them. So, indeed, what looks like a racial divide is essentially – and increasingly – a *class* divide. These new patterns of segregation continue to deny disadvantaged communities access to good education and career prospects.

If anything, this shows that we cannot decouple any debate on segregation from a broader debate on inequality.

Myth 12: Immigration sends crime rates soaring

'They're bringing drugs. They're bringing crime. They're rapists. And some, I assume, are good people.' This is how Donald Trump talked about Mexican immigrants during his campaign ahead of the 2016 presidential election. In his first year in office, Trump decried immigrant gang members saying that they 'don't want to use guns, because it's too fast and it's not painful enough. So they'll take a young, beautiful girl, 16, 15, and others, and they slice them and dice them with a knife because they want them to go through excruciating pain before they die. And these are the animals that we've been protecting for so long.'[1] In the UK, when immigration debates reached fever pitch ahead of the Brexit vote in 2016, UKIP leader Nigel Farage argued that: 'The free movement of peoples in Europe has become the free movement of criminals, Kalashnikovs and terrorists.'[2]

Politicians and media have commonly portrayed migrants and minorities as criminals, rapists and potential terrorists. In fact, opinion polls suggest that the biggest fear people have about immigration is not about immigrants taking jobs, driving down wages or undermining welfare, but that it will lead to more crime. A major survey conducted in 2010 revealed that one-third to a half of people in major Western immigration countries think that immigration increases crime, and between half and three-quarters think that illegal immigrants increase crime.[3] This resonates with deep fears about the development of gang culture in run-down immigrant neighbourhoods and urban 'ghettos'.

The idea that immigration makes our societies and streets less safe by bringing in crime is one of the oldest and most deep-seated fears about immigration. Gang- and mafia-like criminal activities have often been linked to immigrant and minority groups, such as African American and Latino 'gangs' in the US, and Albanians, Bulgarians and Moroccans in western Europe. Such groups are usually seen as being involved in illicit activities such as the drug trade, robbery, loan sharking, extortion and human trafficking. These problems seem to be perpetuated as criminal groups lure the next generations into delinquent lifestyles, discouraging community members from escaping from disadvantage through education and work.

Particularly in the US, illegal immigrants are often seen as a crime liability, because their underground, marginal lifestyles are thought to encourage them to survive by engaging in criminal activities. In Europe, besides fears that some migrant-origin Muslim minorities are terrorists or would support terrorism, there are concerns that misguided stereotypes about 'loose Western women' among young Muslims somehow give them a 'moral licence' to provoke, harass or sexually assault non-Muslim women in the street.

Although most people would reject racist bigotry that portrays entire groups as criminals, rapists and terrorists, the apparent over-representation of some immigrant and minority groups in criminal activities is a common source of concern. From this perspective, reducing legal and illegal immigration is an essential element of crime-fighting.[4]

How it really works

In general, immigration lowers violent crime

It is true that some migrant and minority groups are over-represented in crime statistics. It is also true that an above-average share of prison populations is of non-white background. And it is also true that some minority youth make (migrant and non-migrant) women feel less safe in the streets. Does that mean that immigration is leading to more crime? Or is this all about racial prejudice? Because this is such a loaded issue, it's important to look carefully at the evidence.

It is not easy to measure the relation between immigration and crime, if only because there are so many other factors – such as unemployment, income and education, as well as social control, cohesion and trust in communities – that tend to affect crime rates.[5] For instance, when immigrants settle in urban neighbourhoods that already had higher crime rates, correlations between immigration and crime can be spurious. As young men commit most crimes, an over-representation of migrants in crime statistics may just reflect the fact that many migrants are young men. To properly assess the impacts of immigration on crime, studies should control for such biases as best they can.

The most reliable way to do so seems to be by studying the relation between changes in immigration rates and changes in crime rates in the same geographical units (such as neighbourhoods, municipalities, states or countries) *over time*. Fortunately, in recent years several high-quality studies by sociologists and criminologists have been published on this issue. While findings vary depending on methods used and groups studied, there is no evidence that immigration drives up crime rates. In fact, many forms of immigration are associated with *lower* crime rates. This conclusion seems to hold for *violent* crime in particular. The paradox is that immigration often makes places safer.

The best research on this issue has been done in the US. Even though immigrants have on average lower levels of education and lower wages than the native-born population, most studies show that immigrants are generally less likely to commit crimes than the native-born. On average, neighbourhoods with high concentrations of immigrants have lower rates of crime and violence than comparable non-immigrant neighbourhoods.[6] Another pattern is that, if immigrants are involved in crime, it is *non-violent* crime such as car theft and burglary – particularly among unemployed and poor immigrants – and they are heavily underrepresented in violent crimes such as aggravated assault, rape and murder.[7] In the US, immigrants are also less likely to spend time in prison than the native-born. One study found that, among men between eighteen and thirty-nine years of age, incarceration rates among the foreign-born were one-quarter those of the native-born.[8]

All this evidence not only undermines the 'criminal alien' stereotype – it actually reverses it. Ramiro Martinez, a criminologist at Northeastern University, and his colleagues found that Haitian, Jamaican and Cuban immigrants had *lower* murder rates than the overall population, and that these rates had *decreased* after the 1980s as these immigrant groups became larger and more established.[9]

Robert Sampson, a criminologist at Harvard University, showed that crime rates strongly depend on the ability of neighbourhood communities to organize social control based on shared values. Because immigration generally has a positive effect on this ability, it therefore tends to reduce crime. For instance, Sampson and his colleagues found that Mexican Americans living in Chicago neighbourhoods were 45 per cent *less* likely to commit violence than third-generation native-born Americans. According to Sampson, this crime-reducing effect of

Do increased crime rates (less community control) go up with longer stayed immigrants?

immigration helps to explain why crime rates in cities such as Los Angeles, San Jose, Dallas and Phoenix *dropped* in times of high immigration; and why places of intense immigration, like New York and cities on the Mexican border, such as El Paso and San Diego, are actually some of the safest cities in the US.[10]

Compared to the United States, evidence from Europe is more scattered, but what is available equally challenges the idea that immigration increases violent crime. One major study analysing national-level data from twenty-one European countries found no relationship between immigration levels and the incidence of rape, sexual assault and homicide.[11] Another study that analysed trends of immigration and crime across England between 1971 and 2002 concluded that, in line with research from the US, neighbourhoods actually tend to become safer as more immigrants move in. It found that crime is significantly lower in ethnic enclaves where immigrants form at least 20 to 30 per cent of the population.[12]

This crime-reducing effect was found to be particularly large in ethnic enclaves where immigrants from the same ethnic background concentrate, presumably because of the social control such communities can typically offer. This resonates with evidence reviewed in the previous chapter that, contrary to the 'ghetto' stereotype, the type of ethnic enclaves where new migrants tend to concentrate often provide community life that fosters informal social control, solidarity and entrepreneurship. *against assimilation (segregation has less crime?)*

Hard-working, conservative and community-oriented

So, the available evidence does not sustain claims that immigration sends crime rates soaring – rather, it shows the contrary: immigrants generally have *lower* crime rates. It is not so difficult to explain this striking pattern. First of all, people don't generally migrate with the objective of becoming criminals, but with the objective of working, studying, joining family members, or a combination thereof. Because migration is costly and risky, and requires a considerable amount of planning and willpower, migrants are not a negative sub-selection of the populations of their origin countries. Instead, as we saw in chapter 8, immigrants tend to be a select group of rather 'exceptional people'[13] with particular attitudes and mindsets that make them more likely to succeed, and which are not typically associated with criminal behaviour.

The idea that immigration increases crime dates back to the early twentieth century, when US sociologists hypothesized that the settlement of foreign workers from Catholic countries such as Ireland and Italy would lead to 'social disorganization' and delinquency in the neighbourhoods where they settled. However, historical and contemporary studies have shown this belief to be largely wrong.[14] On the contrary, migrant workers typically come from socially conservative, community-oriented and religious backgrounds, and strongly adhere to traditional values of solidarity, respect and hard work.

Illegal immigrants have the lowest crime rates

Because they are generally keen on staying and obtaining permanent residency or citizenship, immigrants are often among the most law-abiding members of society. This applies even more for illegal migrants, whose prime objective is to stay out of sight of the police, as arrest may mean deportation and the loss of all possessions and investments that went into their migration. Such double punishment – arrest and deportation – provides a particularly strong incentive to lie low, work hard and avoid getting involved in any kind of crime.

It is therefore not surprising that, contrary to political claims, studies have found that the massive increase in immigrant detention and deportation by the US federal government did not have a significant effect on crime rates.[15] The irony is that illegal immigrants – the migrant category most often accused of being criminal – tend to be the least involved in criminal activities, and particularly in violent crime. Michael Light, a sociologist at the University of Wisconsin-Madison, has led several studies which undermine popular claims that illegal migration leads to more crime. One of his studies that analysed data from across all US states between 1990 and 2014 revealed that the size of the undocumented migrant population in a state does not increase crime, and suggested that it might even have a slightly crime-reducing effect.[16]

Using individual data on arrests from the Texas Department of Public Safety between 2012 and 2018, Light and his colleagues compared crime rates between illegal migrants, legal migrants and native-born US citizens. Their findings were remarkable. Illegal immigrants turned out to have the *lowest* crime rates, legal migrants were somewhere in the middle, while native-born citizens were twice as likely to be arrested for a violent crime compared to undocumented migrants, four times as likely to be arrested for property felony, and 2.5 times more likely to be arrested for drug crime. These results were consistent across a broad range of crimes, including homicide, assault, robbery, sexual assault, burglary, theft and arson – undocumented migrants had consistently lower crime rates than native-born citizens.[17] For *all* criminal convictions in Texas in 2015, convictions among illegal immigrants were 50 per cent below those of native-born Americans.[18]

The dark side of (downward) assimilation

The evidence is crystal clear: immigrants tend to be less criminal. But while first-generation migrants are generally less involved in violent crime, the picture can change when we look at the second generation. To a large degree this reflects integration assimilation, because non-migrants have higher crime rates than immigrants in the first place. Ironically, one of the 'downsides' of assimilation is that the longer migrant groups stay, the more their crime patterns start to resemble those of the native-born.

This typically involves the descendants of lower-skilled migrant workers who experienced what sociologists Min Zhou and Alejandro Portes have called 'downward assimilation'. Zhou and Portes have made a useful distinction between three main patterns of what they call 'segmented assimilation'.[19] From this perspective, the real question is not whether the children of immigrants assimilate (or integrate) – nearly all of them do – but to what segment of society they will assimilate.

The first trajectory is that of the children of skilled migrants, who often outperform native-born children at school and have successful professional careers. The second trajectory is the one of children of lower-educated migrant workers, who can rely on close family ties and supportive communities (often in ethnic enclaves) to help them work their way up through education, work and entrepreneurship, eventually enabling them to join the middle class.

The third, more problematic, pattern is that of downward assimilation. In this trajectory, parents are also lower-skilled migrant workers, but children fail to join the 'mainstream' middle class because a combination of discrimination, unemployment, poverty, segregation and weak community structures stand in the way of achieving success and often perpetuate disadvantage. Experiences of racism and exclusion can foster the development of adversarial subcultures among disadvantaged youth who have failed to move up the socioeconomic ladder and find themselves trapped in impoverished neighbourhoods.[20] This combination of factors seems to explain why some marginalized migrant and minority youth growing up in segregated inner-city neighbourhoods or dilapidated social housing blocs and *banlieues* in Europe try to find alternative careers in the criminal world or, sometimes, resort to religious fundamentalism.

A survey conducted by Portes and his colleagues among second-generation youths in Southern California and South Florida highlighted that, besides problems such as high school-dropout rates and early pregnancy, higher rates of arrests and imprisonment are indicators of downward assimilation. The research showed that second-generation Mexican and Caribbean youth were most likely to find themselves behind bars.[21] Higher parental education and stronger community cohesion seem to explain the lower imprisonment rates found among Chinese, Korean, Filipino American and Cuban American youth.

Importantly, though, the over-representation of some second-generation groups in crime statistics reflects class-related factors such as their social and economic status, not their race, ethnicity or religion. In general, crime rates are highest among men between eighteen and thirty-five years of age with low levels of education and earning low wages. Long-term unemployment in particular as well as family dysfunction and a lack of social control are powerful predictors of criminal behaviour.[22]

The main reason why certain second-generation groups are over-represented in crime statistics is that they form a growing share of disadvantaged working-class populations in Western countries. Again, it is class that trumps other explanations. Crime is not some inherent trait of people of particular ethnic, racial or cultural backgrounds, but rather an outgrowth of the economic marginalization of immigrant groups experiencing downward assimilation. The criminal reputation of certain marginalized migrant-origin groups therefore tends to fade as soon as (and if) they eventually find a way to climb the economic ladder and attain middle-class status. This is exactly what has happened with former working-class immigrant groups with criminal reputations, such as the Irish and Italians in the United States.

The vicious cycle of racial profiling and prejudice

On the night of 30 April 1999, Marianne Vaatstra, a sixteen-year old girl from a small village in the province of Friesland, in the Netherlands, went out partying with her friends but never came home. The next morning, she was found lying dead in the meadows. When the coroner reported to the press that Marianne had been raped and then had her throat slit, he added that cutting a victim's throat was not a typically 'Dutch mode' of killing. People were quick to blame the inhabitants of the local asylum seeker centre. This culminated in a wave of threats and violence towards refugees in the region, with one asylum seeker being stabbed with a knife.[23] I grew up in Friesland, and I vividly remember how everybody was talking about 'those' asylum seekers who 'must have done it'.

This negative sentiment turned national when far-right leader Pim Fortuyn stated that 'slitting a throat, that's not something a Frisian man would do'.[24] With the media portraying the asylum seeker centre as 'a hotbed of criminal activities', a TV crime show aired pictures of 'Middle Eastern' (Iraqi and Afghan) men as the likely suspects during prime time. Although subsequent DNA analysis ruled them out, it didn't dampen public suspicion that asylum seekers must have done it. After the case went cold for years, in 2012 a new DNA investigation provided irrefutable evidence that the perpetrator was a local farmer who lived two miles away from the crime scene. Local inhabitants reacted in shock and sometimes disbelief that a local farmer – a good father, family man and helpful neighbour – could have committed such a horrible crime.[25]

This is not an isolated case. Evidence shows that prejudice and racial profiling is another important reason why some minority and migrant-origin groups are over-represented in crime statistics. The reason is that, simply put, they have a higher chance of being arrested and sentenced. This can easily create a vicious cycle: as non-whites are more likely to be suspected, arrested and sentenced, the media attention this generates further reinforces prejudices against minorities, and young men in particular. Such prejudice increases the chance that the police are called in, and that members of certain groups are arrested, convicted and receive higher penalties for the same offence.

For instance, drugs used by middle-class youths living in affluent suburbs – or cocaine use by executives – are less likely to lead to arrest than street-level drug use by minority youths living in immigrant neighbourhoods. In the US, Black and Latino defendants have long stood a higher chance than whites of receiving prison sentences – and tend to receive longer sentences if imprisoned – although the gap appears to have been decreasing in recent decades.[26]

In all societies, young people – and men in particular – have tested out boundaries. Yet there are huge variations in how communities and law enforcement deal with this. In socially cohesive neighbourhoods, petty crime by youth is often solved without formal police involvement, through social control and corrections by parents and neighbours. And if the police are called in, they are likely to issue a stern reprimand to the offender or their parents.

In less affluent neighbourhoods, problems are less likely to be solved this way. If things get out of hand and if the police come at all, they are more inclined to arrest the offender. If the teen daughter of a white middle-class suburban family is caught shoplifting, she is more likely to get away without formal charges than a Black girl growing up in a low-income neighbourhood, whose parents do not have the accent or connections to convince store managers not to call in the police – or the police officers to not charge her.

Racial profiling and prejudice also mean that displays of wealth by non-whites are likely to draw the suspicion of the police. It is an all-too-common experience for Black drivers to be pulled over, particularly when they drive a fancy car. Racial prejudice affects the day-to-day lives of minorities in ways that many white people are not even aware of.[27]

Racial and ethnic prejudices also affect how the media report on crime. If a Black man kills another Black man, chances are higher this will be reported as 'gang violence' or some kind of 'drug killing', obviously lowering the chance such a case will be seriously investigated. If a white man kills scores of schoolchildren or shopping mall customers, this is often framed as mental illness. If a Muslim man commits a similar crime, journalists and pundits are often quick to frame it as a likely terror attack – leaving aside the question of whether suicide bombing could also be a case of mental illness. If a white man kills his wife, the media is more likely to interpret this as a case of mental illness or as a *crime passionnel*. However, if a Muslim man commits the same crime, the media is often quick to make a connection to religious fanaticism or 'backward' cultural practices such as honour killings.

Such stereotypes also permeate the movie industry. Black and other non-white actors often complain they are always cast as the criminal, gangster or drug dealer, while Albanians and other East European men are often cast as human traffickers and Muslims as religious fanatics or terrorists. The fear that immigrants increase crime is deeply ingrained into majority cultures, and resonates with deep-seated prejudices about 'foreign' men, stereotyping them as more aggressive, criminal and misogynist, and as sexual predators – or indeed traffickers – who particularly target white women, reflects age-old fears among majority groups that 'they' are taking 'our' women.

Over-prosecuted, under-protected

Racial profiling is real. And we have hard evidence to prove it. Until recently we lacked data to estimate the full extent to which racial profiling and prejudice contribute to perpetuating the 'criminal alien' stereotype. However, some studies have become available that provide more robust estimates. In 2022, Dutch sociologists Willemijn Bezemer and Arjen Leerkes published a study that compared the likelihood of being registered as a crime suspect among migrant and non-migrant youth with similar levels of self-reported criminal behaviour.[28] In the Netherlands, youths with a Moroccan or Caribbean background are six to seven times more likely to have been suspected of criminal behaviour than those of non-migrant origin. Amongst youth with a Surinamese or Turkish background, crime suspicion rates are four times higher.

However, their study found that only a small part – 13 per cent – of this over-representation of groups with a 'criminal reputation' in crime suspicion rates could be explained by real differences in criminal behaviour. Bezemer and Leerkes estimated that nearly half (46 per cent) of this over-representation could not be explained by factors such as criminal behaviour, socioeconomic position and other individual and neighbourhood-level factors. It is therefore likely that racial profiling and prejudice among police officers, as well as victims and witnesses of crimes, play a major role in explaining this over-representation. Comparing groups with similar levels of criminal involvement, those with secondary vocational education were four to five times more likely to be crime-suspected compared to similarly criminal youngsters in high-level pre-university education. To put it simply, higher-educated, predominantly white youths are more successful in staying out of trouble with the police. Immigrants and minorities are not only more likely to be arrested, but are also more likely to be charged for crimes and to be punished more harshly.

Victims of crime – whether this is domestic abuse, assault, rape or murder – are also less likely to receive police protection if they are minority members.[29] Fear and distrust of the police may prevent them from seeking and finding legal protection, particularly when they are migrants with undocumented status, as they may fear deportation if they report the crime to the police.[30] Minority groups are also less likely to be able to persuade law enforcement and justice systems to protect them from violent perpetrators, compared to middle-class groups who tend to be better at navigating their way through complex administrative systems and securing protection from the police. For instance, a victim of domestic violence will find it easier to have the perpetrator arrested and issued with a restraining order, and will more easily find a shelter, if she (or he) is living in a white affluent neighbourhood with a well-funded police department – as compared to a member of a minority group living in a run-down neighbourhood with underfunded social services and police.

Racist prejudice also means that non-white minorities are more likely to become the *target* of police violence. In May 2020, George Floyd, a forty-six-year-old African American man, was murdered by a police officer in Minneapolis, Minnesota. This incident, which triggered the global Black Lives Matter movement, was yet another illustration of the persistence of institutional racism and the difficulties of many majority groups to even acknowledge its existence. Obviously, such experiences reinforce distrust in the ability and willingness of the police to protect non-white minorities, and of politicians to really do something about it.

Crime rates have dropped as immigration has increased

So, the evidence undermines the myth that immigration has sent crime rates soaring. In fact, this myth is a double myth. The first part is that immigration increases crime. The second is that crime rates have gone up. In fact, the reverse is true: not only is there solid evidence that immigration lowers crime, but crime rates have actually gone down! A major study of trends in crime data between 1988 and 2004 across twenty-six Western countries showed reductions of 77.1 per cent in theft from cars, 60.3 per cent in theft from persons, 26 per cent in burglary, 20.6 per cent in assault and 16.8 per cent in car theft.[31] In the United States, between 1990 and 2013, violent crime and property crime went down by 50 and 46 per cent, respectively.[32]

Murder (homicide) rates have decreased in nearly all Western countries, too. For instance, between 1991 and 2019, intentional murder rates in the UK dropped from an annual rate of 1.0 to 0.5 per 100,000 inhabitants, while in Germany they dropped from 1.4 to 0.7 and in France from 1.7 to 0.8. Although murder rates are much higher in the US, the long drop in annual murder rates, from 10.2 per 100,000 inhabitants in 1991 to 5.4 in 2019 has been remarkable.[33]

Our societies have actually become safer while immigration populations have grown. This is largely a spurious correlation, however, as these drops in crime are mainly explained by factors such as income growth, better education, decreasing unemployment and population ageing.[34] However, in contrast to what politicians suggest, immigration has reinforced rather than decelerated the crime drop in Western countries, as immigrants are generally *less* criminal than the native-born. Crime is more prevalent among the second generation of some immigrant groups that experienced downward assimilation into adversarial urban subcultures that can become conducive to crime. However, there is no evidence that particular ethnic, racial or religious backgrounds are inherently more prone to criminal conduct. Because some immigrant-origin and minority groups are over-represented among the poor and the unemployed, these groups are also tend to be over-represented in crime statistics.

However, prejudice and racial profiling make minority groups a disproportionate target of arrest, sentencing and imprisonment, perpetuating a vicious cycle of prejudice, segregation and disadvantage. This is a serious problem, as it reinforces the feeling of being treated like second-class citizens, reducing trust among discriminated-against groups in the willingness of police and the government to protect them. It can further contribute to a culture of hostility, resistance and distrust towards the police, judiciary and governments. This is particularly true in a political climate where influential politicians and the media accuse migrants of committing the most heinous crimes.

This is not a reason to deny, trivialize or soft-pedal real problems that exist. The disproportionate involvement in crime or intimidating behaviour among some marginalized minority youth is a serious problem, not only because it can make neighbourhoods unsafe and unpleasant to live in, but also because it keeps putting these groups at a disadvantage. However, in order to effectively address and avoid such problems, it is important to understand their causes. Besides the problem of racial profiling, crime is strongly linked with economic marginalization and particularly the socially, morally and mentally crippling consequences of racist discrimination and long-term unemployment.

This shows these problems can only really be tackled if effective law enforcement is combined with policies that actively counter racial profiling and job market discrimination and give disadvantaged youth real opportunities for social mobility through education and work – regardless of their racial or ethnic background.

Myth 13: Emigration leads to a brain drain

'Brain drain can virtually rob the future of the poorest countries', claimed the United Nations Development Programme (UNDP) in 2007. This resonates with widespread concerns that emigration deprives developing countries of their 'best and brightest'. The idea that emigration leads to a brain drain is one of most common concerns about migration voiced by politicians, experts and international development agencies. The constant haemorrhaging of engineers, scientists and managers seems to continually frustrate efforts to stimulate innovation, entrepreneurship and economic growth in origin countries, while the departure of doctors, nurses, teachers and academics undermines efforts to improve healthcare, education and good governance.

This issue of 'brain drain' calls our attention back to the much-ignored 'other side' of migration. As such, this is a good thing. The almost-exclusive focus of debates on the consequences of *immigration* for destination countries goes along with a striking – and debilitating – neglect when it comes to the causes and impacts of *emigration* for countries of origin. As the Algerian sociologist Abdelmalek Sayad has argued, 'Every immigrant is also an emigrant' – but we typically ignore the second dimension.[1] This Western-centric receiving-country bias has haunted migration debates for too long already. After all, how can we really understand migration if we miss half the picture by ignoring the causes and consequences of migration from the perspective of origin countries?

With regard to the impact of migration on origin countries, the verdict is usually rather negative. Politicians in origin countries have often accused rich countries of robbing poor countries of their best and brightest. It indeed seems a gross injustice that cash-strapped governments must invest their meagre resources into educating and training new generations of leaders, only to see them poached away by corporations in rich countries sometimes even before they graduate. 'What may be good for you is bad for us' is the message to the governments of rich countries. In fact, to some, it is a continuation of colonial practices, in which rich countries continue to deprive poor countries of their most valuable human resources.

In the UK, for instance, the NHS has been accused of 'poaching' African nurses and doctors to fill increasingly urgent labour shortages. And it seems quite sickening indeed: Africans are delivering the most advanced care to the sick and elderly in rich countries while there are not enough doctors and nurses left in Africa to deliver the most basic health services to poor and starving populations. 'It is estimated that there are currently more Malawian doctors practicing in the northern English town of Manchester than in the whole of Malawi', a widely published report by the Global Commission on International Migration (GCIM) claimed in 2005, and with the increased dependency of Western healthcare systems on foreign doctors and nurses, things only have seem to have got worse since then.[2]

The 'brain waste' makes matters even worse – migrants doing jobs they are overqualified for as they are unable to get their diplomas and qualifications recognized. Engineers driving taxis, school teachers working in fish factories, and nurses working as cleaners is the reality for quite a few migrants. The message is clear: rich countries should stop these 'unethical' recruitment practices which 'cream off' the most talented members of poor societies, or compensate poor countries for their lost investment in education.

In destination countries, the brain drain argument makes many left-wing people, intellectuals and humanitarian organizations ambivalent about migration. They tend to welcome the diversity immigration brings but – aware they need to be concerned about the plight of the global poor – feel guilty and worry that immigration is leaving origin countries worse off. The brain drain is the most humanitarian-sounding argument against immigration: that it would not only be better for migrants, but also for origin countries as a whole, if migrants stayed home to help advance their own countries. Immigration restrictions curbing the recruitment of scarce talent would therefore even constitute an act of 'compassion' to poor origin countries.[3]

How it really works

Skilled emigration isn't very massive

Although governments of origin countries have good reason to deplore the large-scale departure of skilled workers, it would be unfair to blame the 'brain drain' for the structural problems that made these workers leave in the first place. Emigration did not cause the development problems that many poor countries face, such as economic stagnation, bad healthcare, bad education, high unemployment, huge inequality and rampant corruption. Such problems explain why young, talented people don't see a future in their own country and therefore opt to pursue a career abroad. In other words, they vote with their feet. So, in reality, we have turned the whole causality of the argument upside down: the brain drain is a symptom, not the cause, of development failure.

There are several reasons why it is unfair to blame emigration for development problems at home. First, skilled emigration is not as massive as the brain drain hypothesis suggests. The majority of international migrants are lower-skilled workers and their families, and the departure of the higher-skilled is only truly massive in a handful of generally small countries. Prominent emigration countries like Mexico, Morocco, Turkey and the Philippines typically have 5 to 10 per cent of their population living abroad – and only a minority of these migrants are higher-skilled.

In general, international migration does not take a very high share of the higher-educated. One study found that in two-thirds of these countries, less than 10 per cent of the higher-educated population had migrated.[4] Another study found that, on average, 6 per cent of the higher-educated population of low-income countries had migrated to Western countries. In sub-Saharan Africa, the poorest region in the world, this brain drain rate is 13 per cent; in Central America, 17 per cent. The brain drain is mainly a serious issue for small (island) states such as Jamaica, Antigua, Barbuda and Fiji, where 40 to 50 per cent of the higher-skilled population has emigrated.[5]

Most countries are relatively able to retain most of their higher-skilled citizens. So, the images of a massive emptying-out of talent are generally not correct. And the brain drain rates have gone down rather than up. Although the number of skilled migrants leaving developing countries has been increasing, the number of people in those countries who received a tertiary education has increased at a much faster pace – because of the massive expansion of schooling. Between 1990 and 2020, the share of young adults enrolled in higher education in developing countries soared from 8 to 35 per cent, the basis of which was laid by an increase in secondary-education enrolment rates – from 45 to 73 per cent – over the same period.[6]

One study published in 2017 and conducted by a group of researchers from across Africa assessed the retention of specialist surgical graduates from university training programmes in eight countries in East, Central and Southern Africa – Ethiopia, Kenya, Malawi, Rwanda, Tanzania, Uganda, Zambia and Zimbabwe – between 1974 and 2013. Of the 1,038 surgical graduates included in the study, no less than 85 per cent were retained in the country they trained in, and 93 per cent were retained within Africa, meaning that half of the 15 per cent that had left their country had emigrated to another country on the continent.[7]

While Zimbabwe had the lowest retention rate, with two-thirds of graduates staying, it was Malawi that had the *highest* retention rate, with 100 per cent of surgical graduates remaining in the country. This is interesting, as the quote about there being more Malawian doctors in Manchester than in the whole of Malawi is one of the most repeated 'facts' about the brain drain. This false statistic has taken on a life of its own and has been cited over and over again by politicians, journalists and activists. But despite its catchiness, this claim has always been a myth.[8]

In the 1970s and 1980s, some Malawian medical students received their training at Manchester University's medical school, creating a small cluster of Malawian students and doctors in Greater Manchester. At the time, Malawi had extremely low medical staff rates. In around 1985, there were twenty-one native-born doctors in Malawi and nineteen Malawian doctors in the UK. Many doctors in Malawi were immigrants themselves. The founding of the Malawi College of Medicine in 1991 led to an increase in the numbers of doctors trained as well as higher retention rates. In 2012, of the 618 doctors on the register of the Medical Council of Malawi, around thirty-four Malawian doctors were practising in the UK, of whom about seven were in the Greater Manchester area.[9]

According to the authors of the study, high surgical-graduate retention rates across the region show that the expansion of national training initiatives has been successful in addressing the surgical workforce shortage.[10] They therefore qualified the medical brain drain as a 'myth'. If there was ever such a thing as an African medical brain drain, medical emigration has effectively been decreasing – as it has from most other regions in the world. Global figures suggest that the Caribbean region has the highest rate of medical emigration, with 28.4 per cent of all physicians living abroad in 2014. In sub-Saharan Africa, between 2004 and 2014 the physicians expatriate rate decreased from 18.2 to 14.5 per cent.[11]

This does not mean that – particularly for smaller, low-income countries – the departure of the higher-skilled is not a problem. In some sectors, it can lead to real shortages. But the data shows that it is not such a massive phenomenon as the brain drain narrative suggests.

Don't blame migrants for problems that make them leave in the first place

Another problem with the brain drain hypothesis is the assumption that emigrants would have done jobs reflecting their qualifications and ambitions if they had stayed. This ignores the fact that many developing countries have high unemployment, particularly among their higher-skilled. In 2015, I participated in an analysis of survey data on education and work among youth in twenty-five developing countries. We found that youth unemployment was typically 20 per cent or higher in Latin America, the Middle East and North Africa. Unemployment was highest among the highly educated youth living in urban areas, particularly among young women in the Middle East and North Africa, where it reached levels of around 44 per cent.[12]

In 2021, a quarter of the youth were unemployed in countries like Morocco, Egypt, Turkey and Jamaica, and in some countries, such as Tunisia and Haiti, youth unemployment stood at around a third. While still at a somewhat lower level, youth unemployment has been rising fast in Central American countries like Honduras and Guatemala and South Asian countries like Pakistan, Bangladesh and Nepal.[13]

Because of the massive expansion of education in developing countries, the number of young people with university diplomas has been soaring, especially in middle-income countries. However, particularly in countries with stagnating economies, there are often not enough jobs for them, leading to increasing unemployment. A striking contrast is that while in rich countries unemployment tends to be highest among the lower-skilled, in developing countries unemployment is typically highest among the highly educated. This reflects an increasing gap between the number of graduates their education systems produce and the number of higher-skilled jobs available.

High unemployment rates in origin countries cast serious doubt on the assumption that emigration would mean an automatic loss. Many emigrants would either have been unemployed or underpaid if they had stayed. From a purely economic perspective, too, emigration can then be a positive thing, as it allows migrants' labour to be more productive in rich countries. More importantly, it allows migrants to earn a much higher income abroad, enabling them to remit money back home. In this way, both emigration and destination countries, as well as migrants themselves, are better off. So, what seems a drain at first sight can become a gain when re-examined.

But, more fundamentally, the point is that migration is not the cause of the structural problems that made people leave in the first place. To illustrate this argument, let's go back to the claim that emigration is causing the healthcare crisis in many African countries. Some African countries have indeed seen high levels of medical emigration. However, detailed statistical analyses by economist Michael Clemens failed to find a significant effect of medical emigration on health outcomes like infant mortality, vaccination rates and the prevalence of acute respiratory infections in young children.[14] More generally, staffing shortages in the public health sector were mainly caused by unattractive working conditions, low salaries, poor training facilities and a lack of career prospects. In fact, before leaving, many doctors worked in urban hospitals or private clinics or in non-medical jobs. The recruitment of fresh medical graduates by private hospitals offering better pay seems to be more of a cause of staffing shortages in public hospitals than does emigration.[15]

The main problem is often not a lack of doctors, but governments' failure to provide basic health services in slums and rural areas. Such basic health services, such as vaccinations, treatments for dehydration during diarrhoea, malaria prophylaxis and basic primary treatment for acute respiratory infections, do not require highly trained doctors and nurses in the first place. In sum, most doctors and nurses would not have provided such basic healthcare if they had stayed.

A brain gain with a brain drain

It is important not to trivialize the problem of the departure of skilled professionals. However, the point is that it would be wrong to blame emigration for the problems that made people leave in the first place. This is not a uniquely 'Third World' problem. The term 'brain drain' was coined after the Royal Society published a report in 1963 in which it expressed concerns about the migration of scientists from Britain to North America. The report prompted the Minister for Science to accuse the Americans of 'parasitising' British brains, prompting the *Evening Standard* to coin the term 'brain drain'.[16] Concerns over the British brain drain persisted into the 1970s and even the 1980s. However, the main reason why so much of Britain's talent was leaving in this period was a general lack of economic vitalism and career opportunities for young professionals. So, emigration was indeed a symptom, rather than a cause of these problems.

Another reason to question the brain drain hypothesis is that an emigration of lower- and higher-skilled workers can generate significant benefits, particularly in the longer run. What appears at first sight to be a loss can become a net gain over time. First of all, the large sums of money remitted by migrants are a vital lifeline that enables countless families and entire communities in origin countries to then improve their living standards and send their children to school. As we saw in chapter 6, in most emigration countries, remittances exceed development aid by many times and flow directly to those who need them most. A 2017 study of Mexican immigrants in the United States found that emigration to the United States led to an immediate fivefold increase of family income.[17]

Another positive effect of migration can be the brain gain. The term 'brain gain' was coined by economist Oded Stark and his colleagues to describe the positive impact that the prospect of emigrating can have on the motivation of people in origin countries to pursue and continue education.[18] The mechanism works as follows: if young people are exposed to emigrants' success, this can instil an awareness that obtaining degrees and skills will increase their chances of finding attractive jobs abroad, and that education is the safest avenue to securing visas that allow them to work and study abroad. The prospect of emigrating can therefore motivate young people to continue their education. Although a share of the higher-educated may end up emigrating, the majority will stay, so the *net effect* on origin-country education levels can be positive: the brain gain.[19]

One study found that migration of nurses from the Philippines to the US increased nursing enrolment and graduation rates in the Philippines at a much higher rate than actual emigration, thus increasing overall education levels in the Philippines.[20] Another study showed that when in the 1990s the British Army introduced education as a selection criterion for Nepalese men wanting to join the Gurkha units of the army, this motivated families to invest in schools and teachers so that their sons could still join. This increased the average education of young Nepalese men by more than a year, allowing even those not being selected for the army to get better jobs and increase their income.[21]

On top of this motivational effect, remittances give families the *resources* to invest in the education of their children. Study after study has shown that the top priority for migrants is to provide their children with a better education. A whole range of studies have found a positive effect of emigration and remittances on school retention and education levels in origin communities.[22] In El Salvador, for instance, remittances were found to have a significant effect on school retention. In urban areas, the effect of remittances was at least ten times greater than the effect of other income. In rural areas, the effect of remittances was about 2.6 times that of other income.[23]

I also made this observation during my own fieldwork. The survey I conducted among 500 families in the south Moroccan Todgha valley showed that remittances enabled children, and girls in particular, to stay in school. The interviews that one of the students in our team conducted with women 'left behind' by their émigré husbands revealed that they saw education as the most effective – and socially acceptable – way for their daughters to gain more independence.[24] So, the demonstration effect and remittances generated by emigration can simultaneously give people the aspirations and capabilities to achieve higher education levels.[25]

Emigration potentially helps to expand educational and skill levels in origin countries, as remittances allow parents to send their children to school. The supply of extra cash not only enables them to pay for school fees, books and school supplies; the flow of remittances also means that children don't have to drop out of school prematurely to work to feed the family, which is common among poor families.

Even for higher-skilled people who do have jobs, it can still make a lot of sense to emigrate and pick up manual jobs abroad, because it enables them to earn much more money and give their children a better future. It sounds unnecessarily harsh and impersonal to call this 'brain waste'. After all, such migrants use their brains rather well – it is often the best option they have, given the circumstances, a profoundly *rational* decision. Emigrating, even if this means working in 'lower' jobs, at least temporarily, is often a more attractive option than staying, because it represents the best hope for a better future for the family.

Emigration can stimulate growth in origin countries

So, the prospect of emigrating may increase aspirations to study, while remittances from abroad enable them to pay for such education. There are other ways origin countries may gain from higher-skilled emigration. We have seen how the image of university graduates abandoning their countries en masse after graduating is a bit simplistic. First, skilled emigration is not as massive as is often imagined. Second, many higher-skilled workers receive at least part of their education and training abroad. In fact, the desire to study abroad has led to a rapid increase in international student migration over recent decades.

Third, the brain drain hypothesis implicitly, and wrongly, assumes that people are lost forever once they have left. In reality, many migrants return to their origin countries after having accumulated knowledge, experience and money abroad. There, they put their money, knowledge and expertise to use by investing in all sorts of businesses – ranging from grocery shops, coffeehouses and transport companies to construction firms, factories and IT firms. The French economist Hillel Rapoport and his colleagues found solid econometric evidence that migrants play a positive role in diffusing knowledge and technologies back to their origin countries. The internet has greatly expanded the scope for such transnational entrepreneurship. Even many migrants who don't go back can invest and do business in origin countries while living abroad. And because of the personal connections it forges, immigration often increases trade between countries.[26]

Entrepreneurship in origin countries is another important way that what appears to be a brain drain can be converted into a significant brain gain. For instance, in the 1960s and 1970s, the rising emigration of the higher-skilled to the US was a major headache for the South Korean government. However, when Korea's high-tech sector took off and the country pursued democratic reforms, it was able to attract back experienced nationals from the US. Returning Koreans played a major role in business development and economic growth in later decades.[27]

A similar thing happened in India. After gaining independence from British rule in 1947, India set up Institutes of Technology in the 1950s to support national development. To the government's great frustration, many graduates emigrated to the US and other rich countries. However, many higher-skilled migrants later returned, which boosted the growth of India's economy. Investment by Indian IT professionals working in Silicon Valley has been a crucial factor in the rise of the Indian IT industry, which is now the second biggest in the world.[28]

The transformative power of social remittances

Emigration also affects social, cultural and political change in origin countries, as migrants not only send money but also bring back new ideas, norms and values. Sociologist Peggy Levitt coined the term 'social remittances' to describe the way in which emigration and the exposure to new ideas it brings can fundamentally change social relations and cultural norms and aspirations.[29] This can happen through ideas migrants bring back themselves, through their function as 'role models', or through the financial autonomy migration can give. For example, emigration can strongly improve the autonomy of women, particularly if women are able to gain an independent income by migrating themselves.

Emigration can also be a potent force for political change – for better or worse. Because migrants come from diverse ethnic, ideological and class backgrounds, it is difficult to generalize about the political impacts of migration. Depending on who migrates, political remittances can either challenge or reinforce the powers that be. There is evidence that students who studied in democratic countries can play a role in promoting democracy in origin countries.[30] However, political change is not necessarily about peaceful reform only, as emigrants come in all political colours. Exiles may also try to organize a revolution from abroad.

For this reason, dictators often have ambivalent attitudes towards emigration, torn as they are between courting and controlling their diaspora.[31] On the one hand, autocratic governments often see emigration as a useful political 'safety valve' to generate cash flow, reduce unemployment and, in this way, quell popular discontent. In the 1970s, the Marcos regime in the Philippines set up an extensive labour-export programme in a deliberate attempt to create an outlet for potential discontent by providing people with economic opportunities abroad.[32] On the other hand, autocratic regimes have been keen to prevent emigrants forming a political opposition from abroad by different kinds of 'remote control' – such as the setting-up of spying networks, and harassing or killing political exiles or intimidating their families back home.

Social remittances can also have a positive effect on demographic changes in origin countries. The French demographer Philippe Fargues discovered that decades of large-scale migration from Morocco to western Europe contributed to the diffusion and adoption of new marriage patterns and family norms, prompting Moroccan couples to marry at a later age, use contraceptives and have fewer children. This contributed to the spectacular drop in Moroccan fertility levels from over seven children per woman in 1970 to 2.3 children per woman in 2020.By contrast, in countries such as Egypt, where most migrants go to Saudi Arabia and other culturally conservative countries in the Gulf region, emigration has slowed down the fertility decline.[33]

However, emigration is not automatically a force for reform. It may actually consolidate power. Higher-skilled migrants in particular are often from middle-class or elite groups, who do not necessarily represent the views of the poor and the oppressed. Many African, Middle Eastern and Asian students attending Ivy League universities in the US or Oxbridge in the UK are from elite backgrounds. The knowledge and skills obtained abroad not only do necessarily contribute more equality and democracy, but can also be used for 'improving' authoritarian rule and perfecting oppression upon return. For instance, former Libyan leader Muammar Gaddafi sent his son, Saif al-Islam Gaddafi, his intended successor, to get a PhD at the London School of Economics in an apparent bid to give Libya a more acceptable image and a leader who spoke fluent English and knew the ways of the global elites.[34]

Emigration is neither the cause nor the solution of development problems

We cannot blame emigration for development problems such as poverty, inequality and corruption. In fact, 'brain drain' is an unfortunate term, as it automatically casts the departure of the highly skilled as a negative thing. The brain drain hypothesis not only overestimates the scale of higher-skilled emigration, but also ignores the long-term benefits that emigration can have for origin countries. Moving abroad enables people to acquire skills, knowledge and money they can reinvest back home, while emigration and remittances stimulate education in origin countries. Migration has enabled millions of young, ambitious people and their families to fulfil their dreams and achieve life-changing improvements in their living standards, housing, nutrition, health, education and overall future prospects. In developing countries, non-elite groups have good reason to pin their hopes on emigration.

Yet this does not mean that migration alone can set in motion processes of economic and human development. Emigration and remittances can be hugely beneficial for families and communities in places and regions of origin, but econometric research has failed to find a noticeable effect of emigration and remittances on national economic growth in origin countries.[35] While the brain drain hypothesis is far too negative, it is equally unrealistic to pin high hopes on emigration as a development 'game changer', as emigrants cannot be expected to change structural problems in origin countries. Emigration is neither the cause of nor the solution to development problems.

Since starting my fieldwork in Morocco thirty years ago, I have studied the development impacts of migration in various countries, including Turkey, Tunisia, Egypt, the Philippines and Mexico, and made extensive reviews of the research literature.[36] On that basis, I came to the conclusion that, despite its considerable benefits at the micro level for families and communities, it is an illusion that migration can fix structural development problems at the macro level, such as corruption, failing institutions and a general lack of confidence in governments.

Brain drain is a symptom, not the cause, of development failure. Migration can neither be blamed for a lack of development (brain drain), nor be expected to boost economic growth and development (brain gain) in unattractive investment environments. There is no automatic mechanism through which migration 'leads to' development. In fact, we can envisage two scenarios: a vicious and a virtuous cycle. If states fail to implement reform, migration is unlikely to fuel national development, and can instead help to sustain structural remittance dependency, underdevelopment and authoritarianism, despite the obvious benefits for migrants, their families and communities – as has been the case in Morocco, Egypt and the Philippines. However, if development takes a positive turn and reform occurs, migrants are likely to reinforce these positive trends through investing and returning – as seems to have been the case in in South Korea, Taiwan and India.

However, in the latter examples migration is still not the factor that triggers such reform. Rather, it is structural political and economic reform that enables migrants to trust that it is safe to return and invest. It is essential to get the direction of the causality right. Development is a condition for investment and return by migrants, rather than a consequence of migration. Instead of blaming emigrants for the conditions that make many people leave in the first place – or making them feel guilty for leaving – governments would be better advised to pursue structural reforms that give young people real opportunities at home and encourage emigrants to return and invest.

Myth 14: Immigration lifts all boats

We need immigrants to secure our competitiveness in a globalized economy. Immigrants not only fill urgent job shortages in vital economic sectors, they also bring new knowledge and ideas that boost innovation, productivity and growth.

This is the classic pro-immigration argument championed by business lobbies, liberals and pro-immigration groups. It is the complete opposite of the 'threat' narrative that casts migration as a major cause of a whole range of economic and social problems. According to this 'migration celebration' narrative, immigration is an unmitigated economic benefit for destination countries: everybody benefits from it.

It has also long been the dominant narrative in the classic immigration countries of the United States, Canada, Australia and New Zealand: immigrants are the hope of the nation. In 1989, Ronald Reagan voiced this belief when he exalted immigration as 'one of the most important sources of America's greatness', and claimed that 'thanks to each wave of new arrivals to this land of opportunity, we're a nation forever young, forever bursting with energy and new ideas, and always on the cutting edge, always leading the world to the next frontier . . . If we ever closed the door to new Americans, our leadership in the world would soon be lost.'[1]

The idea that immigration is a major boost for growth and innovation has also been a common talking point of the corporate sector and international organizations. However, according to this migration celebration narrative, immigration is not only beneficial to receiving nations, but also to origin countries, because the huge amounts migrants remit and the skills they acquire have the potential to reduce poverty and stimulate growth and innovation back home. After all, immigration provides a life-changing opportunity for countless people in developing countries to earn higher wages, advance their careers and improve the long-term well-being of their families. Freer circulation of higher- and lower-skilled workers would therefore help to fill critical labour shortages and boost growth in both origin and destination countries.

For this reason, many economists and liberal (and libertarian) politicians have adopted pro-immigration viewpoints. They believe that freer migration will lead to a 'more optimal allocation of production factors' – as it seems in everybody's benefit if workers go from places where unemployment is high and wages low to places where labour is scarce and wages are higher, because this will simultaneously increase the wealth of nations *and* the income and living standards of migrants and their families back home.

The World Bank has voiced this view as follows: 'The rich have many assets; the poor have only one – their labour. Because good jobs are slow to come to the poor, the poor must move to find productive employment. Migration is, therefore, the most effective way to reduce poverty and share prosperity, the twin goals of the World Bank.'[2]

Economists have estimated that even a modest liberalization of immigration policies could generate benefits that *by far* exceed the results of trade liberalization, aid or any other government interventions to stimulate growth.[3] The biggest growth opportunities in the world economy would therefore lie not in the mobility of goods or capital, but in the mobility of labour. It is the classic laissez-faire argument, applied to migration.

So, in this view, migration lifts all boats: immigration optimizes the matching of the supply and demand for labour, and increases employment and productivity while generating huge flows of poverty-reducing and growth-boosting remittances to origin countries. More liberal immigration policies are therefore a win-win-win strategy benefiting migrants as well as origin and destination countries. To enhance this triple win, we should open the doors for immigration of professionals, vital lower-skilled workers and high-potential refugees, while foreign students should be encouraged to stay and work after graduating.

How it really works

Immigration cannot solve global inequality

As we have seen in this book so far, there is no evidence that immigration has played any major role in undercutting wages or increasing unemployment. Neither is immigration a major cause of substandard education, overcrowded healthcare, welfare cutbacks, the lack of affordable housing or problems such as crime. However, as much as the migration threat narrative exaggerates the potential downsides of migration, the migration celebration narrative tends to overstate its benefits. In particular, it tends to ignore the fact that the economic benefits of migration tend to be unequally distributed between wealthier and poorer people in origin and destination countries.

While there can be little doubt that (freer) migration can considerably contribute to personal, national and even global prosperity, the crucial question is how these benefits are *distributed* between origin and destination countries, as well as between richer and poorer members within societies. With regard to international inequalities, there can be little doubt that destination societies reap more economic benefits from migration than origin societies. This is because the labour of migrants primarily boosts economic productivity and profits in destination societies. Immigration benefits growth in destination countries by expanding the size of their populations and economies and by stimulating innovation and investment.

However, as we saw in the previous chapter, studies have failed to find a positive effect of remittances on national economic growth in origin countries.[4] Although remittances and migrant investments can potentially enhance growth, emigration also means the loss of workers and human capital. As the two effects seem to cancel each other more or less out, the average economic effect of emigration on origin-country growth is near to zero. Although migration and remittances come with huge micro-level benefits for migrants and their families and communities, emigration is clearly not a development panacea.

Furthermore, remittances mainly benefit middle-income – and not the poorest – countries in the world. Of the $502 billion in remittances sent by migrants to developing countries in 2022, just $11 billion went to low-income countries. The bulk of remittances – $341 billion – went to lower-middle-income countries, and the remaining $150 billion went to upper-middle-income countries. If we adjust this in per capita terms, low-income countries receive $16 per year per person in remittances, against $101 and $60 respectively for lower- and upper-middle-income countries.[5]

This has to do with the 'selectivity' of migration: as we know, because moving abroad requires considerable resources, most international migrants come neither from the poorest countries nor from the poorest sections of origin-country populations. The most financially rewarding forms of migration – skilled migration to Western countries – are generally only accessible for better-educated, better-off groups. Migration involves considerable costs in the form of payments for passports, visas, recruitment fees and travel, or money to be paid to smugglers. When the 'poorest of the poor' migrate, this is generally within countries or to neighbouring countries. Middle-income groups living in middle-income countries are therefore the ones who reap most benefits from the most lucrative forms of long-distance migration.

More generally, the evidence highlights the fact that the transformative impact – whether positive or negative – of migration is not as big as many people think. The magnitude of migration is simply too small for that. Only 3 per cent of the world population are international migrants, and to put things even more in perspective, in 2022 all the money sent back by migrants to low- and middle-income countries was only 0.7 per cent of the total gross domestic product of these countries.[6] These facts alone should banish any illusions that migration and remittances can ever be the great global equalizer.

Immigration primarily benefits the affluent

The evidence also gives us reason to be sceptical about the claim that immigration is an unmitigated benefit for all members of destination societies. First of all, as we saw in chapter 8, the benefits of immigration for average-income earners are actually rather small. While immigration expands the *total* size of populations and economies of destination countries, its effect on *average* incomes or wages is relatively small. Immigration increases total productivity and consumption – the more immigrants, the more producers and consumers, and the bigger the economic pie – but the slice each person gets on average remains equally big, because immigration increases the size of the population as well.

Second, and most importantly, the evidence also shows that it is the affluent that reap most economic benefits from immigration – it makes their already bigger piece of the pie grow even larger. Although economists disagree about the impacts of immigration on *average* wages, with regard to the distribution of the economic benefits of immigration most studies show a rather consistent pattern: immigration increases higher incomes more than it increases lower incomes. There is no evidence that immigration massively undercuts wages. This is because immigrants generally don't compete for the same jobs as local workers. However, they don't benefit much from immigration either, as the wage effects of immigration on lower wages are often insignificant.

Immigration mainly benefits the wealthy, not workers. The lowest-income groups in destination societies, such as school dropouts, may actually lose out, as they are more likely to compete for the same jobs as immigrants. For that reason, former immigrants are most susceptible to finding their wages negatively affected by the arrival of new immigrants. Although these negative effects are not very large, most economic benefits of immigration clearly go to the wealthier members of destination societies. In other words, while immigration does not make poor people much poorer, it does help to make rich people a little richer.

It is not difficult to understand why the affluent reap most economic benefits from immigration. They own the businesses benefiting from the influx of labour and skills, while the immigration of private care workers such as nannies, cleaners and cooks enables well-off families to maintain their lifestyles. The owners of businesses that benefit most from the influx of migrant workers in terms of productivity and profits are generally among the wealthier members of society. Higher-income groups are also more likely to own stocks in such corporations, or have stakes in pension funds that have invested much of their money in these stocks.

Because domestic chores and care tasks are increasingly done by migrant workers – the new servants of our age – upper-middle-class and elite groups are more rested, can work more hours, be more productive, earn more money, buy bigger houses and nicer cars, and go on holidays more often. Higher-income groups are also the main clients of the various personal services delivered by migrant workers. Thanks to the availability of – documented or undocumented – migrant workers, they are able to outsource various household chores, ranging from cleaning, cooking, washing, ironing, gardening, shopping, delivery and personal care to dog walking for affordable prices.

Particularly in countries with weak or absent state-funded systems for child and elder care, such as in southern Europe, Britain and the US, immigrants fulfil an increasingly important role as care workers. Thanks to the influx of migrant workers it has remained affordable for middle-class groups to eat out – or have food delivered. The continuous influx of lower-skilled immigrants frees up time and energy that higher-income earners can spend on work and leisure. And so the cycle continues, as they need more migrant workers to build, maintain and guard their ever-bigger houses (and their gardens, and swimming pools). Migrant workers are also likely to run the hotel, taxi and restaurant services affluent people use while on their holidays or while working.

Ordinary citizens are most directly confronted with the social and cultural changes brought by immigration, because they often work in the same places as migrants and they are also more likely to have immigrants as neighbours – while affluent groups living in affluent neighbourhoods or 'gated communities' are not confronted with the consequences of immigration in their daily lives. However, this not only applies to lower-skilled immigration. The influx and settlement of higher-skilled immigrants alongside affluent native professionals in gentrifying inner-city areas may make long-time residents – migrant and native alike – feel less and less at home, or may even push them out of their own neighbourhoods, as they can no longer afford to pay the rent or because they are evicted to make place for newly built apartment buildings and shopping centres. Ordinary citizens have therefore good reason to be sceptical of corporate elites singing the praises of immigration.

How immigrants and chicken changed Albertville, Alabama

Although on a global or even national scale immigration is not as massive and transformative as we often think, the impacts of immigration can be quite life-altering on the local scale of neighbourhoods or towns. This is best illustrated when we zoom in on how immigration has concretely changed local communities. In 2017, *This American Life*, a public radio programme and podcast,[7] aired the documentary *Our Town* – produced by journalists Ira Glass and Miki Meek and based on eight months of research and over a hundred interviews – about what happened when large numbers of Latino migrant workers, mostly from Mexico, showed up in Albertville, a mountain town in northern Alabama. Back in 1990, 98 per cent of the 15,000-strong population of Albertville was white.

After just twenty years, this all-white town had become one-quarter Latino through the arrival of about 6,000 migrant workers.

Our Town gives an extremely insightful, vivid example of how immigration changes local communities in profound and complex ways that defy simplistic pro- and anti-immigration schemes. Most of the Latino workers came to work in the chicken processing plants in Albertville. These plants were built in the post-war decades to provide employment for local workers when the state of Alabama realized that cotton and corn were no longer bringing in enough for small farmers. Local farmworkers left the fields and started work in the plants, killing and processing chickens. In Albertville, the poultry plants became the biggest employers in town. For young people without high school diplomas, they offered decent jobs, benefits and retirement, and enough pay to buy a house. Until the 1980s, it was very easy to move from job to job, as labour demand was high.

However, in the mid-1990s, things changed with the arrival of a steady stream of Latino workers – mostly men, and mostly without their families. At the beginning, the newcomers were a novelty. But as their numbers kept on increasing, they sparked feelings of unease among the local workers, who suspected them of being illegal migrants. Local workers felt that they were cheating the system – breaking the law by sneaking across the border illegally. Most of the earlier migrants had been working in America for many years, and had been granted amnesty in 1986 with Reagan's Immigration Reform and Control Act (IRCA). They had moved from other parts of America, where they had been in agriculture and construction jobs, as the Albertville chicken plants gave more attractive and stable employment. This allowed them to bring over their families. Later, workers and families started to move there directly from Mexico.

Resentment set in towards the employers, as local workers suspected them of secretly encouraging the illegal migration of Latinos, as the migrants were willing to work double shifts, didn't complain and wouldn't join the union. Despite politicians' repeated promises to take aggressive action against the undocumented workers who were moving into poultry plants as well as carpet factories and hotel jobs across the US South, there was never a serious crackdown. Fines were low, the chances of being arrested were slim, and employers would help undocumented workers to hide during the few workplace raids that took place.

For long-time workers, it felt like immigrants were 'taking jobs that didn't belong to them' and that management had abandoned their loyal employees.

Background research led by economist Giovanni Peri for the documentary found no evidence that immigrants had literally taken away jobs from local workers.[8] The immigration of Latino workers was mainly driven by soaring labour demand, as the poultry business was booming in the 1990s and the supply of local workers was drying up, because long-time workers were starting to retire and many children with high school diplomas no longer wanted to work at the chicken plants because there were better opportunities. So, as demand went up, and local supply went down, Mexican and other Latino workers filled the gap.

However, for long-time residents still working at the plants it was a bitter pill to swallow. Over the previous decades, wage increases for local workers had been minimal – far too low to keep up with the rising cost of living. If local wages had kept up with inflation since the early 1970s, they should have been double what they were now. This was part of a nationwide trend in which the real wages of low-income earners, particularly those without a high school diploma, had dropped since the early 1970s. This decrease in real wages was not a natural phenomenon, but was caused by policy choices that lowered workers' protection and labour standards, weakened unionization, kept minimum wages below inflation levels and increased competition from abroad.[9] In the meatpacking industry more specifically, the closure of plants in urban union strongholds and their movement to non-union rural areas had contributed to pay cuts.[10] These developments obviously made these jobs less attractive to native workers, thus drawing in even more migrants who were still willing to do the work.

So, to get the main causality right: as the documentary highlighted, 'it wasn't immigrants that led to wage stagnation' but wage stagnation that drew in more foreign workers. Still, as the documentary highlights, for long-time chicken plant workers in Albertville, it was hard to see any benefits. Peri's research indicated that while immigration had not caused unemployment, it did decrease the wages of local workers without a high school diploma by up to 7 per cent – the equivalent of $23 a week, or almost $1,200 per year. This confirms general evidence that immigration does not depress the wages of most workers, except for those earners in the bottom 10 per cent.

A perfectly kept front lawn – not anymore

Thus, local workers are generally right if they say they don't see many economic benefits from immigration. But, as the *Our Town* documentary illustrates, it is not the economic consequences that necessarily anger local workers most. In fact, few would blame immigrants for declining labour standards. And on a personal level, many workers can empathize with migrants toiling to support their families. In Albertville, it was not so much that people personally hated individual immigrants. The resentment of local workers was rather directed towards the companies that seemed to have forgotten about them. The poultry industry had made huge profits, and workers felt they themselves were paying the economic, social and cultural price of immigration.

Feelings of alienation and annoyance were real. Long-time workers began to feel that they had become the new minority in their own workplace. In the early 2000s, just ten years after the arrival of the first Latino workers, they started to dominate the workforce. They wouldn't speak English, but rather stayed in their own groups, didn't interact with the American workers and wouldn't join unions. There were also annoyances outside the workplace, such as the driving habits of many of the Mexican workers, who often didn't have licences and frequently ignored traffic rules.

Starting in the late 1990s, when the Latino workers left the trailer parks and moved into rental houses – often with their families – the annoyances grew. The immigrant workers would park cars in front yards and leave garbage cans and trash strewn on the lawn, destroying the grass. To the great dismay of locals, many migrants didn't seem to have any interest in maintaining their rented houses and gardens. After all, they were in Albertville to make money – not to settle – and they came from places in the Mexican countryside 'where a perfectly kept front lawn was not a thing'.[11] Then there was a spike of drugs-related crime in Albertville – such as burglary, theft and car theft – linked to an epidemic in meth use that happened to coincide with the arrival of many immigrants. Newspapers and politicians were quick to make the link to Latino immigration, although Albertville migrant workers were rarely involved in such crimes.

Apart from such false allegations, the social and cultural changes were real, and a shock to many local workers. Things eventually came to a boiling point in the mid-2000s. In 2006, across the US, a wave of marches took place in support of President Bush's plan to create a path to citizenship for undocumented immigrants. In Albertville, too, local and migrant residents organized a march. Although the march was a success, the show of numbers also backfired by sparking an anti-immigration backlash among other local inhabitants, who started pressuring the government and Immigration and Customs Enforcement (ICE) to deport illegal immigrants. In 2008, Albertville elected a new mayor who ran on an anti-immigration platform. His policies included attempts to bar city contractors from hiring undocumented immigrants, to make English the official language and to ban taco trucks.

In 2011, Alabama's new immigration law, HB 56, was passed – the most extreme anti-immigration state law ever. It intended to make life in Alabama so unpleasant for immigrants that people would 'self-deport'. The law made it criminal for citizens to lodge undocumented migrants, rent them a house or transport them. But the main impact was not that migrants went back but that they stayed home and off the roads, while many Latino children no longer dared to go to school.

By 2012, things reversed course. HB 56 was ditched as it was found unconstitutional by the courts, and a new mayor was elected who emphasized the importance of integrating Latino residents into the community. As the documentary shows, the schools also developed into a countervailing force against polarization – as this is where white and Latino people would meet, and their children started to make friends – and they were quite successful. By the late 2010s, the 98 per cent graduation rate for Latino children was higher than the 92 per cent graduation rate for white children. This eventually changed how immigrants and Latinos viewed each other in the town, and immigrant families have become more settled into neighbourhoods and have made white friends. Immigration also gave a boost to local business, as Latino establishments have spread all over town.

There is more to life than GDP

While the Albertville case is unique, similar stories can be written about countless neighbourhoods and towns where large numbers of migrant workers – or refugees – arrived in a short period of time, whether in the American Rust Belt states, the mining and industrial towns of England

and Scotland, the French *banlieues* or the industrial heartlands of Germany, the Netherlands, Belgium, Switzerland, Italy, Austria and Scandinavia. For local workers, the social and cultural changes can be profoundly upsetting and sometimes alienating.

A one-sided focus on the economic impacts of immigration misses the point that immigration can be particularly upsetting because of the drastic impacts it can have on existing local lifestyles. In hindsight, it is not surprising that the sudden influx of 6,000 foreigners in a small town like Albertville initially led to feelings of unease, alienation and fear. And it should also not be surprising that such an influx can lead to resentment towards businesses and political leaders who don't seem to really care about local workers – treating them as disposable production units rather than as people and fellow citizens. The feelings of abandonment and betrayal are often real and palpable.

There is clearly more to life than GDP. Even in cases where the marginal economic impact of immigration is statistically positive, this is hardly ever a convincing argument to sway citizens who are disproportionately exposed to the social change migration brings on the local level – all the more so because pro-immigration elites rarely ever live in the same neighbourhoods or work in the same places as lower-skilled migrant workers do.

Economic 'facts' will not convince, not only because the size of such immigration-generated income gains are generally very small and mainly benefit the already affluent, but also because academic hair-splitting about the economic and fiscal impacts of immigration ignores the social and cultural consequences immigration can have at the local level. The argument that immigration contributes a certain fraction of a percentage point to GDP growth is as unconvincing as the argument that NAFTA contributes *x* dollars to the average American citizen or that EU membership adds *y* pounds in income for the average UK citizen. Such arguments are even less convincing in situations where real incomes have declined, labour standards have eroded and social security has been dismantled.

Claims that migration will 'lift all boats' therefore reflect elite views and corporate agendas, as they conceal that migration mainly privileges the already privileged. Economic elites benefit most from immigration, as they own the businesses with labour and skills shortages that need to be filled, while migrant workers in the care and service sectors allow the affluent to maintain their luxurious lifestyles. In origin countries, too, relatively better-off groups benefit most, because most migrants come from neither the poorest countries nor the poorest segments of populations. All of this reveals the need for more nuance in debates about immigration, and a careful balancing of the pros and cons of immigration by examining the different social, cultural and economic consequences – and how these differ across income groups.

Although it is a myth that foreign workers steal jobs or massively undercut wages, it is also true that local workers barely reap any direct economic benefits from immigration – and may in some cases even lose out – while they are also most directly confronted with the socio-cultural changes immigration brings to their daily lives. From this perspective, the corporate and liberal elites singing the praises of immigration can indeed appear out of touch about the real discomfort, social problems and tensions that immigration can bring. Ordinary citizens have therefore good reasons to ask: 'What's in it for us?'

Real Incomes vs. GNP

Myth 15: We need immigrants to fix the problems of ageing societies

We badly need more immigrants to combat the problems caused by population ageing. This is perhaps the most popular pro-immigration argument among opinion leaders. Politicians on the left and right have used the demographic argument to plead for more open attitudes towards immigration. And it all seems to make a lot of sense. After all, families in industrialized countries are having fewer children than ever, and labour shortages are more pressing than ever. Rapid ageing has also raised worries that the shrinking size of the working-age population will make it more and more difficult for governments to raise sufficient tax revenues to pay for the education and care of children and the healthcare and retirement pensions of the elderly. Ageing is seen as a particular threat to the viability of pension schemes, and a reason for increasingly costly healthcare.

Fertility levels in almost all high-income countries have dropped far below what demographers call the 'replacement level fertility' of 2.1 children per woman. (This is the number of children women should have on average to prevent the population from shrinking in the longer term.) In 2020, fertility rates in the UK, Germany and Canada stood at 1.5, 1.6 and 1.4, respectively. In the US, where fertility levels hovered around the relatively high level of 2 until recently, they have also dropped below replacement level since 2008 and reached 1.6 in 2020. Fertility drops are particularly dramatic in southern Europe and East Asia. In 1960, the average Italian and Spanish woman had 2.4 and 2.9 babies respectively – by 2020, this had dropped to 1.2 in both countries. Over the same period, Japanese fertility dropped from 2.0 to 1.6. In South Korea, fertility imploded from 6.1 to 0.8 – the lowest level in the world.

As Western populations are ageing and the baby-boom generation has started to retire en masse, death rates have already started to exceed birth rates in some countries. This means that *natural growth* – the annual number of births minus the annual number of deaths – has become negative.

Without immigration, the populations of Germany and Italy would already be shrinking, and in countries such as China, Japan and Greece, populations have actually already started to shrink in absolute terms.

Some governments, such as those of Sweden, Denmark, Iceland and France, have tried to fend off these problems by encouraging couples to have more babies – for instance by giving premiums to large families, tax breaks and generous provisions for pregnancy, passing parental leave legislation, and establishing government-subsidized childcare facilities. Although these have had some mitigating effect, even in these countries fertility levels have remained below replacement level since 2010, and reached levels of around 1.7 in 2020. Although 'babies, no immigrants' makes for an attractive slogan frequently recycled by anti-immigration politicians, pro-baby family planning policies have proved to have only marginal long-term effects.[1] This demographic transition seems impossible to reverse, because it has been a fundamental part of *structural* social, cultural and economic changes, such as women's emancipation and growing education, which seem almost impossible to reverse.

The seemingly unstoppable demographic decline of the West is expected to further increase labour shortages in a whole range of sectors, including agriculture, construction, care, hospitality and delivery. In this context, opening borders seems particularly important to ensure that we have enough people to care for our children, the elderly and the sick. There are already increasing shortages in the supply of young native workers able and willing to do the type of care and service sector jobs for which the need is likely to soar because of ageing. As the number of old people increases, we will need more and more nurses, doctors, cooks, cleaners and domestic workers.

The inevitable conclusion is that instead of curbing immigration, we badly need immigrants to rejuvenate our ageing societies. Given the low fertility rates and pressing labour needs, governments should be attracting immigrants in order to secure the vitality of their societies and economies. Instead of seeing refugees as a burden, we should see them as a vital source of human capital. Immigration is increasingly essential to ensure that the active, working-age population remains large enough to generate sufficient tax revenues to uphold pension and welfare systems. The immigration of workers seems especially vital to ensure future care for children, the elderly and the sick. In this way, the vicious cycle of ever-decreasing fertility levels can be broken and we can bolster the future vitality of our societies.

How it really works

Immigration is too small to fix the effects of ageing

The idea that immigration can fix ageing problems is among the most popular pro-immigration arguments. However, it is also very unrealistic. Migration cannot solve the structural demographic and economic problems of ageing societies. It is true that population ageing – in combination with economic growth, increasing education and women's emancipation – has exacerbated labour shortages, which, in their turn, have caused increasing immigration. However, that does not mean that immigration can solve these structural problems, simply because compensating for the demographic effects of ageing would require politically unacceptable and unrealistically high immigration levels.

The general scale of immigration is too small to counteract the structural effects of ageing. Migrants form only 3 per cent of the world population and between 10 and 15 per cent of the population of most destination countries. Back in 2000, the UN's Population Division published a study entitled *Replacement Migration: Is It a Solution to Declining and Ageing Populations?* It swept the whole 'we need more immigration to fix ageing problems' argument off the table.[2] The study worked out the levels of annual net immigration that would be required to compensate for the effects of future population ageing. To this end, it calculated the 'support ratio' by dividing the size of the old-age population (65 years or older) by the share of working-age population (15–64 years). It then calculated what levels of net immigration (the number of people entering minus the number of people leaving a country) would be needed to keep the support ratio stable.

For Germany, in order to keep the population constant until 2050, it would need a net immigration level of about 324,000 per year, which is more or less within the range of actual immigration levels to Germany over recent decades. Keeping the working-age population stable would require a net immigration of 458,000 per year, which is perhaps still realistic. However, because of the rapid pace of population ageing, maintaining the current support ratio would require a totally unrealistic net inflow of 3.4 million migrants *per year* to rejuvenate the population sufficiently to counterbalance the effect of ageing – more than ten times the recent levels of net immigration to Germany.

Calculations for other countries yielded similar patterns. For the United Kingdom, keeping the support ratio constant would require more than 1 million immigrants annually – more than five times the average net migration in 2011–21 of around 200,000. Keeping the demographic support ratio in the United States stable would require a total number of 593 million additional migrants from 1995 to 2050 – almost twice the total US population. This comes down to an average net migration of 10.8 million *per year*, more than ten times recent net immigration levels to the US. Doing the same trick in France would require an annual net immigration of 2.4 million, more than 20–40 times regular flows. Keeping support ratios in Japan stable would require 553 million immigrants between 1995 and 2050, more than four times the current population of the country.

These are obviously totally unrealistic scenarios. Besides the question of whether countries could really attract such huge numbers of immigrants (they won't), this would be politically unfeasible. The evidence is crystal clear: immigration can perhaps help to keep populations constant and fill some labour shortages, but it cannot reverse the structural shift towards ageing.

Immigrants get older, and have fewer babies, too

This raises the question *why* immigration barely has an effect on fertility levels and birth rates. As most immigrants are young and often come from countries where couples make more babies, why does this not have much lasting effect on fertility levels? As falling fertility rates have slowed down the growth of native populations in destination countries, immigration accounts for a larger share of population growth than was historically the case,[3] and as immigration populations have grown, why don't we see that fertility rates have increased? We would have at least expected some stabilizing effect.

The first part of the answer is that real-world immigration levels are not as massive as we often think, and are simply too low to make a real 'dent' in the demographic structure of populations. The second part is that, although immigrants may be relatively young when they arrive, they get older, too. So the support ratio compensating effect of immigration is only temporary. As they start ageing themselves, migrant workers and their families will ultimately also need care and will rely on pension systems. In other words, immigration can temporarily moderate but not solve the structural ageing of populations.

The third part is that immigrants are having fewer and fewer babies, too. A common stereotype is that immigrants from non-Western countries have big families. In fact, this idea is the misleading demographic assumption behind the 'great replacement' conspiracy theory, according to which immigration is a plot to replace and outbreed native white populations.

Even putting aside the paranoia of conspiracy theorists, the assumption that higher birth rates among migrants can compensate for ageing is simply at odds with the facts on the ground. The idea that immigrants have larger families is only true for some groups, but mainly in the short term. If migrant workers come in from developing countries with high fertility levels, they tend to arrive with larger families. In the first years after arrival, they often continue these high-fertility patterns. Particularly among young women who migrate after getting married, there can be a spike in fertility in the first years after arrival – presumably because immigrants are making up for the births that have been postponed.[4]

However, this is generally only a temporary phenomenon. There is extensive evidence showing that immigrants adapt to family planning habits and demographic norms of destination societies within two to three generations. Comparative research among lower-educated migrant-origin groups from high-fertility countries in six European countries showed that the second generation has much lower fertility rates than their parents, and this was expected to decline further in the third generation.[5]

For instance, the fertility rates of the UK-born children of migrants of Pakistani, Bangladeshi and Indian origins are 32 to 57 per cent lower than the same groups in the 1970s.[6] These declines are more rapid than fertility declines in origin countries.[7] In the US, birth rates among Latino immigrants fell 25 per cent between 2000 and 2017, and among US-born Latino women they have fallen to similar levels as birth rates among native whites.[8]

Although some migrant-origin groups still have above-average fertility levels, more and more migrants come from countries with low fertility levels while rising education levels of recent immigrants have also pushed fertility levels down. This reflects the growing immigration of skilled migrants from East and South Asia to North America and the increased migration from low-fertility countries in central and eastern Europe to western Europe. In fact, many recent immigrant groups have lower than average fertility rates than majority populations, particularly among higher-skilled immigrants. For example, fertility among Indian-origin communities in the UK was 1.67 as compared to 1.74 for white British populations in the 1998–2006 period. Likewise, Asian immigrants in the US have lower birth rates compared to native whites.[9]

An important reason why immigrant birth rates have declined rapidly is that overall fertility levels in origin countries have dropped and more and more women are migrating independently as workers or students, instead of the old pattern of housewives following their husbands. This means that new incoming migrants from Mexico and Guatemala to the US, and from Turkey and Russia to Germany, and from Nigeria and Ghana to the UK, already have higher levels of education and lower fertility preferences than their predecessors, even if they do manual jobs 'below' their education level. All these factors combined explain why, in many countries, there is barely any difference in fertility levels among native- and foreign-born populations, and why migrants may actually have lower fertility. This further undermines the myth that immigration can compensate for ageing.

Demographic factors do not cause migration

The idea that migration is a fix for demographic problems is also based on the rather naive idea that migration is somehow an automatic response to demographic imbalances in the world, and that it can therefore lead to greater demographic equilibrium between high- and low-fertility countries. This is linked to the popular idea that high birth rates and fast population growth in combination with poverty will generate 'population pressures' that will massively push people out from poor countries as they are pulled in by opportunities in countries experiencing declining fertility, ageing and even shrinking populations. This idea, also known as demographic determinism, is the basis of popular 'push-pull' models that see migration as being predominantly driven by demographic forces. But, despite the popularity of this view, this is not how migration really works.

In reality, there is no direct link between demographic factors and emigration. A few examples serve to illustrate that. First of all, emigration is highest from countries with moderate and rapidly falling levels of population growth. This has less to do with demographic factors than with the fact that these are typically middle-income countries where economic development and increasing education have led to a general expansion of people's aspirations and capabilities to migrate. In fact, countries with the highest population growth, such as those in sub-Saharan Africa, actually tend to have the lowest levels of long-distance emigration. Again, that has not much to do with demographics, but with the fact that most people are too poor to migrate.

So, high emigration is more common in countries where population growth is low or declining fast, rather than in countries with high population growth – where, according to misguided 'push-pull' models, emigration pressures should be highest. In fact, several countries, such as in eastern Europe, combine extraordinary low birth rates and rapidly ageing populations with very high emigration levels, the exact opposite pattern of what 'demographic determinism' would predict.

Also, from a destination-country perspective, there is no causal connection between demographic factors and immigration. Again, as the example of eastern Europe highlights, low fertility and rapid ageing can coincide with high emigration, mainly because of economic factors. The reverse is also possible. There are countries – such as Saudi Arabia, Qatar and the United Arab Emirates – that have long combined high birth rates with high immigration, although birth rates have been recently plummeting there, too. Finally, there are wealthy countries with extraordinarily low birth rates and relatively low immigration. Japan and South Korea are probably the best examples.

All of this highlights the absence of a direct link between demographic trends and migration. This defies narratives about migration that suggest that 'population pressure' causes migration – for instance, the widespread idea peddled by politicians, experts and pundits that population growth in sub-Saharan Africa will 'lead to' massive emigration – if that were the case, migration from Africa should currently be at its peak level, which is clearly not the case.[10]

People aren't being pushed and pulled around the world by demographic forces. In fact, this is one of the most pervasive migration myths endlessly recycled by politicians, media and pundits. People don't leave their countries because of population pressure; neither do they magically massively show up at the border to fill demographic deficits. People don't migrate to relieve their countries of birth surpluses and demographic pressures, and to provide demographic assistance to destination countries by filling in their birth deficit. Most people migrate because of job opportunities, to get an education, to join family, or, in a minority of cases, to flee violence and oppression. For this reason alone, it is an illusion that migration can 'fix' problems related to ageing.

The myth of unlimited labour supply

Another problematic assumption underlying the idea that migration can help solve ageing-population problems is the naive belief that there is somehow a quasi-unlimited supply of cheap labour 'out there' that can be tapped into at will. The assumption of 'unlimited labour supply' may have held in the past, but it is less likely to do so in the future, as it crucially ignores the fact that fertility rates are dropping fast in societies around the world. The same forces – urbanization, industrialization, modernization, education and women's emancipation – that have driven fertility decline in such countries have already led to extraordinary drops in birth rates in contemporary 'developing countries', suggesting that the two- or even one-child family seems to be increasingly becoming the international norm.

Fertility has declined rapidly in most origin countries, too. In the middle-income countries from which many immigrants originate, fertility levels have already dropped to near replacement level. In 2020, fertility was 1.3 in China, 1.6 in Brazil, 1.9 in Mexico and Turkey, 2.1 in India, 2.2 in Indonesia and 2.4 in Morocco – obviously destroying the stereotype that Muslims, Latinos and Chinese have lots of babies. This is also the case in religiously conservative countries such as Saudi Arabia and Iran, where fertility has plummeted from 7.6 and 7.3 in 1960 to 2.5 and 1.7 in 2020. In low-income countries, fertility levels are still well above replacement level, but have started to plummet as well. For instance, between 1986 and 2020, fertility in Ethiopia dropped from 7.4 to 4.2, and there is no end in sight.

As a consequence, world population growth is running out of steam. Although nobody can exactly predict future fertility rates, according to the 2022 Revision of World Population Prospects of the UN's Population Division, the world population will increase from the current 8 billion to 9.7 billion in 2050 to peak at levels of around 10.4 billion by the mid-2080s. A recent study carried out for the Club of Rome even predicts that world population will peak at around 8.8 billion before 2050.[11] Belying past doomsday scenarios about a 'population bomb', world population growth is slowing down much faster than expected, mainly because of fast increases in women's education, rapidly decreasing poverty and improved access to contraceptives.[12] All of these factors will end two centuries of fast global population growth, after which the world population will start to decline rapidly. In many regions of the world, and Europe and Asia in particular, the population is expected to shrink considerably in the coming decades. Africa is the only major world region where populations are expected to grow during the entire twenty-first century, although growth rates are declining there, too.

What is even more important than numbers are the underlying, fundamental shifts in the age composition of populations, and how this may affect global migration patterns. As fewer children are born, the share of under-fifteen-year-olds in the total population is dropping in most countries in the world. The share of young adults in the total population is dropping in all middle-income countries – the very countries that have produced most emigrants over past decades. Low-income countries in sub-Saharan Africa and Asia where fertility levels have only started to drop in recent decades are the only countries where future improvements in education, income and infrastructure are likely to increase the aspirations and capabilities to migrate among future cohorts of young adults.

The situation is quite different for the middle-income countries that have dominated global migration in recent decades, such as in Latin America, North Africa, the Middle East and South Asia. As these countries are starting to age themselves, this may decrease their future emigration potential, along with increasing immigration. Particularly if this demographic transition is combined with economic growth and increasing labour shortages, this may trigger a migration transition – with several countries turning into migration destinations and countries of net immigration. Such migration transitions have happened in the past in countries such as Spain, Italy, Ireland, Portugal, Greece, South Korea, Malaysia and Thailand. In some quintessential 'emigration' countries, this process might already be under way, as countries as diverse as China, Turkey, Mexico, Morocco, Brazil and Poland have started to attract significant numbers of immigrants in their own right.

Where will future migrants come from?

As large parts of the world are increasingly running out of children, and the pool of abundant labour sources is shrinking, the idea that migration can structurally compensate for population ageing is becoming an even more unrealistic proposition than it already was. Because of demographic change combined with economic development, the poorest countries in the world still have the highest future emigration potential. Most of these countries are located in sub-Saharan Africa, while pockets of extreme poverty also exist in countries such as Haiti, Afghanistan, Nepal, Pakistan, Cambodia and Myanmar. Although fertility levels are dropping in these countries, they are still well above replacement level, and it will take a generation or two before current reductions in the number of babies born will start to translate into a decrease in the number of young jobseekers.

However, as the emigration potential of low-income countries increases, that of current high-emigration middle-income countries may dwindle fast, and they may begin to attract migrants in their own right. Ageing is also starting to create labour shortages in middle-income countries where rural-to-urban migration as a source of labour is running out of steam. China, for instance, is facing increasing labour shortages because of a combination of fast economic growth and ageing. As the supply of rural-to-urban migrants is dwindling, and salaries rising, Chinese businesses may increasingly start to recruit foreign workers. Assuming future economic growth and political stability, China seems bound to become a major migration magnet, which is likely to affect migration patterns around the world in ways that are difficult to predict.

Across many other middle-income countries, a combination of ageing, women's emancipation and increasing education is causing the domestic supplies of lower-skilled workers to dry up, generating increasing demand for workers in care, construction, agriculture, industry and services. Even in countries like Morocco, Mexico and the Philippines, employers are starting to complain about the lack of young people wanting to do manual work, while affluent urban families are finding it more and more difficult to find young, uneducated, adolescent women from rural areas willing to clean their houses, cook and look after their children – as declining rural poverty has decreased the need to do such work and girls go to school for longer and longer. And this is set to become a global issue. The crucial question is therefore: where will these workers come from? While the global pool of abundant, cheap labour sources is shrinking, the global demand for migrant workers may further increase. Although it is impossible to predict the future, and much depends on political and economic developments, this means that employers in rich countries can no longer just take for granted that there is an unlimited supply of cheap labour willing to come whenever they snap their fingers. Particularly as middle-income countries start to attract more and more migrant workers, this may increase global competition for workers across skill levels, while the pool of potential labour exporters is dwindling. This may well increase the global demand for migrant workers while supplies run increasingly short.

This will likely cause a geographical reorientation of global migration flows, with countries such as Nigeria, Ethiopia, Indonesia, Myanmar, Nepal, Pakistan and Afghanistan increasingly entering the global migration stage. But we cannot assume that these migrants will automatically move to Europe and North America. This reveals a Euro- or Western-centric view of the world that is blind to rapidly changing migration realities on the ground. Apart from the fact that most migration occurs *within* regions, new global migration destinations have appeared on the horizon. African migrants have increasingly discovered the Gulf, China, India and even Latin America as destinations. New global cities have emerged in the Middle East (Istanbul, Dubai, Tel Aviv), Asia (Singapore, Hong Kong, Kuala Lumpur, Mumbai), Latin America (São Paulo, Mexico City) and Africa (Johannesburg, Lagos, Cairo), attracting growing numbers of migrants from futher afield.[13] More and more Asians are moving to countries within Asia, such as Japan, South Korea, Malaysia, Thailand and Singapore. The governments of Australia and New Zealand, too, can no longer just assume that Asian migrants will always want to come to their countries as soon as they open the door.

With global supplies of labour declining in the longer run, it is even more unlikely that immigration will be able to even partly compensate for the effects of population ageing, which is set to become a truly global phenomenon. The world population above sixty years old is projected to double from 1 billion in 2020 to 2 billion in 2050, while the global working-age population (15–59) will increase from 4 billion to 5.3 billion over the same period. All these senior people will need people to care for them.

As immigration cannot fix this problem, our societies will have to accommodate the consequences of population ageing in different ways. More generally, demographers agree that there is clearly no 'solution' to population ageing, which is to a considerable degree unavoidable and is not as disastrous as it's often portrayed.[14]

As is the case with so many migration myths, the idea that immigration is a solution to ageing is based on both an exaggeration of the (ageing) problem at stake as well as a huge inflation of the sheer magnitude and change potential of migration. While immigration can certainly help to fill the most urgent labour shortages, it will not be able to counter the structural, global trend towards people having fewer children and living longer. Rapid declines in global fertility levels question the assumption that there is a quasi-unlimited source of labour 'out there' into which rich countries can tap at will. The future political question may therefore no longer be how to stop migrants from coming, but how to attract foreign workers.

Migration Propaganda

Myth 16: Borders are closing down

Immigration policies have become more and more restrictive. Once upon a time, Western countries used to welcome workers, family members and refugees. However, since the 1980s governments have increasingly slammed the door shut as they have suspended recruitment programmes, introduced visa requirements, set up tougher asylum rules and severely curtailed family reunification. Destination-country governments have increasingly collaborated with countries of origin and transit to reinforce border controls by cracking down on smuggling and trafficking in order to curb illegal migration, prevent the arrival of asylum seekers and deport undocumented migrants.

This is the impression we're getting if we listen to politicians. After all, they love to talk tough on immigration. 'It's going to be a big, fat, beautiful wall!' Donald Trump famously promised voters.[1] 'We have more agents and technology deployed to secure our southern border than at any time in our history,' Barack Obama boasted.[2] British politicians, too, have incessantly stressed their determination to bring immigration 'back under control' or create a 'hostile environment' for illegal immigration. All over the West, politicians have vowed to seal off borders for illegal immigrants and to put fences up to prevent asylum seekers from entering. Particularly during election times, aspiring leaders usually promise us that they will clean up the mess left by their predecessors – that they will 'take back control of immigration' or 'repair our broken immigration system'.

All this reinforces the impression that borders are closing down. Time and again, using belligerent language, politicians have promised voters to 'fight', 'combat' and 'crack down' on illegal migration. This has gone along with the promise to introduce 'firm but fair' asylum policies to identify 'real' refugees and deport 'bogus' asylum seekers back home. At the same time, they promise to curtail the legal entry of lower-skilled migrants and their families. All of this reinforces the impression that governments are progressively tightening the screws of immigration systems.

How it really works

Most immigration policies have become more liberal

Everybody seems to agree on the 'fact' that borders are closing down. When I started following academic debates on immigration policies in the 2000s, I was intrigued to find out that despite the many articles and books written about this topic, nobody had actually tried to *measure* how immigration policies had evolved. This surprised me – because what reasons do we have to uncritically believe what politicians tell us? After all, we know there is often a huge gap between what politicians say and what they do, so why would we take for granted that what they say about migration they also do? Is it possible that politicians try to mislead us? A lack of data made it impossible to find out what was exactly going on, so I decided to collect this data myself.

In 2010, a generous grant from the European Research Council (ERC) allowed me to set up a research team at Oxford University's International Migration Institute (IMI), to analyse the evolution of immigration policies over the past century and to measure their effectiveness in impacting migration flows. The project, Determinants of International Migration (DEMIG), lasted from 2010 until 2015. For two years, we read large piles of reports, laws and regulations, to document major changes in migration policies. This resulted in a database – DEMIG POLICY – that captured 6,500 immigration and emigration policy changes in forty-five countries between 1900 and 2014.[3]

We assigned codes to every policy change, to indicate whether the policy change was restricting or relaxing immigration rules. Based on these scores, for each year we calculated what I will here call the Immigration Restrictiveness Index (IRI). An IRI score of above 0 means that restrictive policy measures exceed liberal policy measures. A score below 0 means that, on average, policies across all countries included in DEMIG POLICY have moved in a more liberal direction. The scores also give an indication of the degree of restrictiveness or liberalization. For instance, an IRI score of –0.5 means that, in that particular year, there were twice as many liberal policy measures compared to restrictive policy measures. By comparing IRI scores over the past century, we were able to track the changes in the overall restrictiveness levels of immigration.

Graph 13 summarizes the results of our analyses. It reveals a striking pattern: since the end of the Second World War, immigration policies have consistently moved in a more liberal direction – as the line stayed consistently below zero. We also conducted more specific analyses for specific regions. However, these yielded similar results for most Western countries.[4] This defies the common assumption – and politicians' tough rhetoric – that immigration policies have become more restrictive. On the contrary, for the past seventy years, most immigration rules have become more *liberal*.

Border enforcement went up while legal barriers went down

Our analysis showed that historical trends in immigration policies have not been linear. The graph reveals a big difference between the period before and after the Second World War. Immigration policies became more restrictive over the first half of the twentieth century, reflecting a general trend towards protectionism, nationalism and authoritarianism from the 1920s onward. This was also the time when the modern passport system was invented, and governments – which had previously primarily been concerned with controlling emigration – became increasingly preoccupied with immigration controls.[5]

These trends were reversed after the Second World War, at least in Western countries, as the US and its allies were determined to restore a liberal, pro-democratic world order. This went along with the establishment of the Universal Declaration of Human Rights, the foundation of the United Nations High Commissioner for Refugees and the international Refugee Convention. These conventions, as well as the enshrining of human rights in national legislature, automatically implied that migrants and refugees were given more rights. To align national legislatures with these new human rights principles, governments had no choice but to change their immigration laws and regulations.

As a result, between 1945 and the 1980s, Western liberal democracies embarked on a path of accelerated liberalization of immigration policies and a major overhaul of immigration regimes. This reflected the increasing commitment of governments to international human rights principles, such as the right to family life – which gave settled migrants

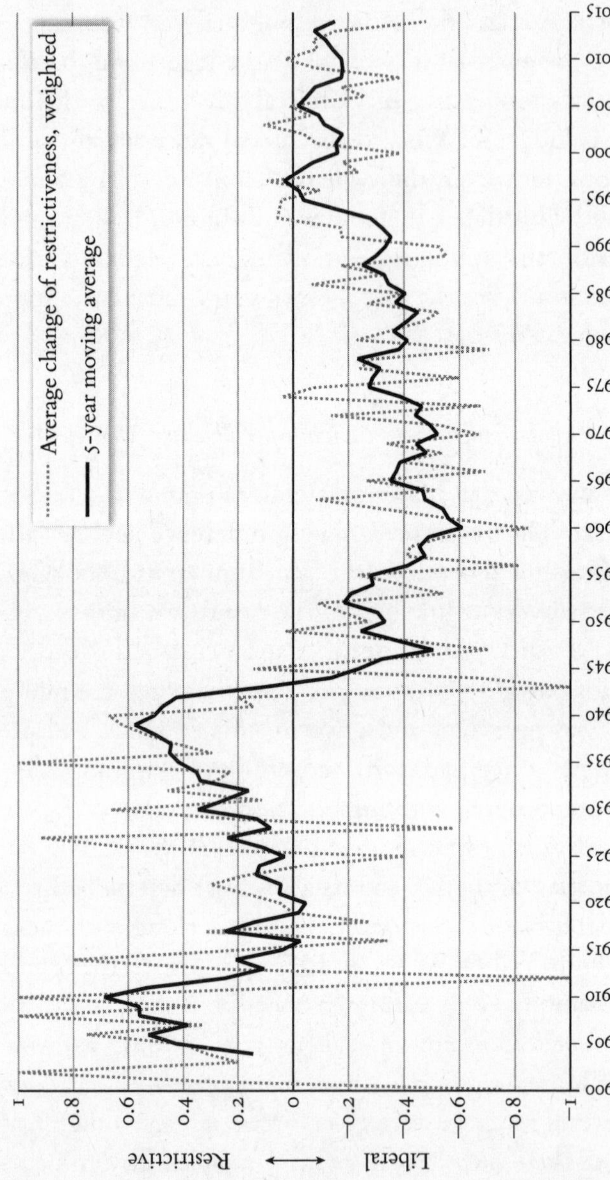

Graph 13: Yearly average of changes in migration policy restrictiveness in forty-five countries, 1900–2014. Values below zero signify that, on average, liberal migration policy changes have outweighed restrictive migration policy changes in that year.

the right to family reunification – and the right of refugees to apply for asylum.

Economic needs played an important role, too. As we saw earlier in this book, the expansion of legal channels for labour immigration was a response to the increasing demand for foreign workers in agriculture, construction and various industries and services. After 1989, the proportion of restrictive compared to liberal policy changes increased, which is visible in the upward trend of the line on the graph. At this time, governments were curtailing the immigration of family members of lower-skilled workers and adopting tougher asylum policies. On a par with visa restrictions for migrants from many non-Western countries, governments also introduced carrier sanctions that obliged airlines to check the immigration status of passengers prior to boarding. This measure was meant to block refugees from travelling to Western countries by plane and applying for asylum on arrival.

Despite efforts to prevent the arrival of illegal migrants and asylum seekers – the two main migrant groups habitually cast as 'unwanted' – the data shows that there has been a deceleration of liberalization since the 1990s rather than a wholesale reversal towards increasing restrictions. Governments may have tried to curtail but have not reversed or abolished the general right to family reunification introduced in the 1950s and 1960s; despite attempts to 'push back' asylum seekers, they have not withdrawn from the UN refugee convention; and asylum rejection rates in Europe have gone down rather than up. This overall trend is robust for the liberal democracies across western Europe, North America, Australia and New Zealand, and liberal policy changes have continued to outnumber restrictive policy changes in the decades after 1989. For instance, the collapse of communism led to a liberalization of immigration policies in former socialist states in central and eastern Europe. The enlargement of the EU over the 1990s and 2000s created a huge free migration space comprising more than 500 million people.

Contrasting their own 'we don't need migrant workers' narratives, politicians have endorsed the development of myriad immigration schemes for a broad range of lower- and higher-skilled jobs. In addition, the liberalization of labour market policies increased the leeway of employers and private agencies to recruit migrant workers. Compared to the days of official, government-orchestrated recruitment, this effectively decreased politicians' ability to control what was happening on the ground. Governments expanded the number of visas given to foreign workers, investors, intra-company transferees, au pairs, trainees and students. While since the 1990s restrictive measures have increasingly focused on border enforcement aimed at preventing the arrival of illegal migrants and asylum seekers, laws and regulations on the legal admission of foreign workers, family members and students have generally become more liberal, although perhaps at a slower pace than before.

Graph 14 illustrates this for the US.[6] Since the 1990s, and particularly since the 2000s, the numbers of temporary workers – usually coming in on H1B (skilled), H2A (seasonal agricultural) or H2B (seasonal non-agricultural) visas – intra-company transferees, investors and students, and their families admitted on temporary residency permits have increased, from around 1 million per year in the 1980s to 3 million in the 1990s, and reaching unprecedented levels of almost 7 million in 2019, just before the Covid-19 pandemic caused an immigration slump. This number far outstrips the number of legal permanent residence permits (green cards, the classic mode of entry into the US), which have averaged around 850,000 annually between 1975 and 2020, and the number of border apprehensions, which averaged around 1.1 million per year over the same period.[7]

This highlights the huge gap between politicians' tough-on-immigration rhetoric and the reality of immigration policymaking on the ground. In fact, the highest-ever levels of legal immigration in the US were reached during the Trump presidency. And immigration to post-Brexit Britain reached an all-time high during the Johnson premiership, with net migration topping 500,000 in the year ending June 2022.[8] We can see similar trends in many other Western countries. In fact, some of the countries where politicians have made the loudest noise about curbing immigration, such as Australia and the Netherlands, have seen strong increases in legal immigration.

The corporate push to open borders

The idea that immigration policies have become more restrictive is also based on the flawed assumption that borders were wide open in the past. That may have been true during particular episodes and for particular nationalities – such as the more or less free circulation of

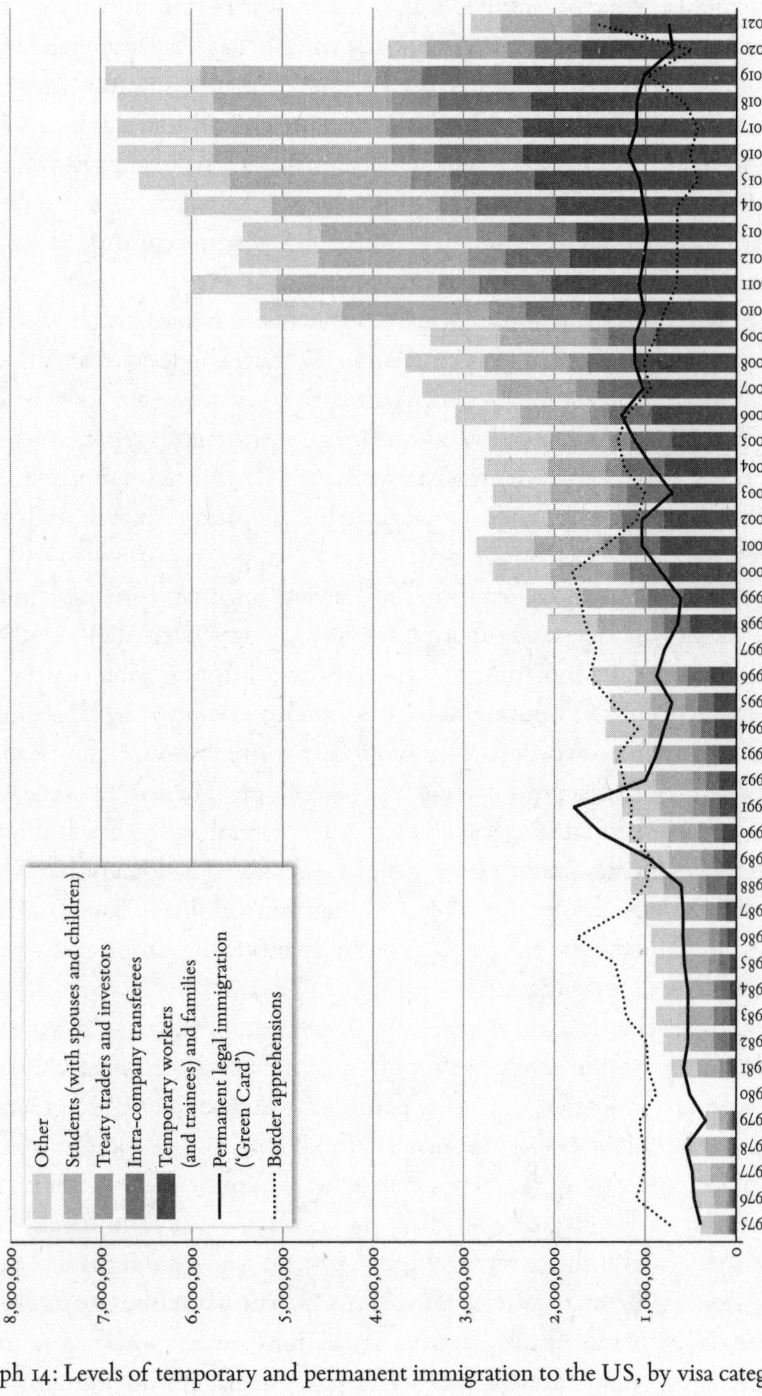

Graph 14: Levels of temporary and permanent immigration to the US, by visa category

Mexicans to the United States until 1965, and Caribbean, Pakistani and Bangladeshi workers to the UK in the post-war period until 1962 – but these are the exception rather than the rule. What has happened is that as some doors were closed (particularly with former colonies), governments opened others (think of free EU migration) and abolished visa requirements (for instance, in 2017 Ukrainians gained the right to enter the EU visa-free). At the same time, they outsourced worker recruitment to private agencies and made it much easier for various categories of higher- *and* lower-skilled workers to migrate.

So, we come from a more immigration-restrictive past than we usually imagine. Increasing immigration in Western countries over the past decades does not so much reflect a failure to control borders, but the fact that governments have allowed more and more immigrants to legally enter and stay. This raises the question of why this has happened. For what reasons have legal entry policies become more liberal, and why does political rhetoric suggest the complete opposite?

Political scientists have put forward several arguments to explain this 'discursive gap' between what politicians say and what they do about immigration. The most important one is that business lobbies pressure governments to relax immigration rules and to tolerate the employment of undocumented workers. This economic argument was first proposed by Gary Freeman, a political scientist at the University of Texas at Austin, who argued that political elites and the general public have different preferences with regard to immigration policies.[9] The idea is that political elites generally prefer liberal immigration policies for economic reasons, while the general public have more moderate, sceptical or negative opinions on immigration.

Political scientists use the concept of 'client politics' to explain why numerically small interest groups often gain disproportionate influence on political processes, at the expense of the wider public. Freeman applied the client politics concept to explain how corporate lobbies often dominate immigration policymaking, by arguing that immigration generates 'concentrated benefits' – especially for employers and investors – and diffuse, more indirect, costs borne by the general public.[10] Because of such concentrated benefits, 'special economic interests' generally gain the upper hand in immigration policymaking. Client politics have enabled corporate elites to push for liberal immigration policies behind closed doors, even if these are opposed by a generally more immigration-sceptical general public. This provides a powerful incentive for politicians who liberalize immigration policies to make the public believe that they are actually doing the opposite. They do so by creating a media circus and resorting to tough talk targeting the most vulnerable migrant groups – asylum seekers and illegal migrants – who represent a minority of all immigrants, as well as largely symbolic measures such as border walls. By deliberately creating an image of toughness, politicians are effectively putting up a smokescreen.

A smoking gun

The most convincing evidence of the huge gap between tough political rhetoric and the much more lenient practice is the general unwillingness of politicians to enforce laws that enable them to crack down on the employment of undocumented migrant workers.[11] The extraordinarily low levels of workplace enforcement provide evidence of 'smoking gun' calibre that governments are generally willing to turn a blind eye towards the employment of illegal migrant workers, whom politicians constantly say are 'unwanted' and for whom they aim to create a 'hostile climate', but who are actually very much in demand and therefore largely tolerated.

In reality, Western governments have done very little to stop illegal labour, especially in strongly liberalized free-market economies such as the US and UK and in the large informal economies of southern Europe. In the US it actually used to be legal to hire undocumented workers – who would be put on the regular payroll and pay taxes – until Reagan's Immigration Reform and Control Act provided amnesty to millions of undocumented workers but also prohibited hiring illegal immigrants. Yet, as it was easy to forge documents, the act failed to stop irregular employment.[12]

In 2004, Immigration and Customs Enforcement announced a new strategy of aggressive worksite enforcement. However, this was mainly window dressing, as there was no political will and no resources made available to actually enforce the law. Most of ICE's efforts are focused on border enforcement; only one-eighth of its total budget goes to domestic Homeland Security Investigations (HSI) investigations.[13] In 2022, HSI had roughly 10,000 employees,[14] compared to Customs and Border Protection's more than 60,000 agents.[15] Only a fraction of HSI's work is focused on worksite enforcement; ICE no longer publishes the exact amount, but in 2010, the number was $6 million – 0.1 per cent of its nearly $6 billion budget.[16]

While HSI's worksite-enforcement strategy officially focuses on 'the criminal prosecution of employers who knowingly break the law', actual enforcement levels have been almost laughably low. Since criminal penalties for employers were first enacted by Congress in 1986, few have been prosecuted. Prosecutions for employers have rarely exceeded 15–20 per year, except for brief periods in 2005 under President George W. Bush and in the first year of the Obama administration, when that number reached twenty-five. Of those prosecuted, only a handful saw actual jail time – fewer than five a year.[17]

Crackdowns are almost always symbolic, apart from a few highly publicized raids. Considering that there are an estimated 11 million US employers, the probability of apprehension is virtually zero. Chances of being apprehended are particularly low among white employers, as employers with minority surnames accounted for 85 per cent of the total number of convictions.[18]

Fines are also largely symbolic. In 2020, fines for knowingly hiring or continuing to employ undocumented workers ranged from $583 to $4,667.[19] In addition, fines recommended by ICE agents are normally negotiated down between agency attorneys and employers. The amount payable is so low that employers view the tiny chance of being charged as a normal risk and a cost of doing business.

For immigrants themselves, enforcement levels are slightly higher, but are still very small considering the large number of workers. Between 2009 and 2018, worksite arrests ranged from 120 to 779 individuals each year,[20] out of a population of around 11 million undocumented immigrants. This means that one out of every 14,000 to 92,000 undocumented migrants was arrested at worksites even during Trump's widely publicized 'crackdown'. In fact, the chance of being arrested for working illegally is in the same range as that of being struck by lightning.[21]

Don't ask, don't tell

In the UK, too, there is a huge gap between politicians' tough talk and the tellingly low levels of workplace enforcement. In 1996, the UK first made the employment of undocumented immigrants illegal through introducing employer sanctions. In 2016, the government passed new legislation to criminalize irregular work, this time targeting employees. This went along with ever-tougher political rhetoric about creating a 'hostile environment' for illegal migration. However, the actual data shows that efforts to combat illegal work have always been weak, and that enforcement levels have in fact been going *down* instead of up.

Two years after the 2016 policy's implementation, government records indicated that there were zero convictions under its law.[22] Furthermore, fines for working illegally have dropped markedly, while 'enforced removals' (deportations) are down, too.[23] In the UK, work-site enforcement falls to the Home Office's Immigration Compliance and Enforcement Team, also dubbed 'ICE'. Home Office immigration control consists of three directorates: Visas and Immigration, Border Force and ICE. While Visas and Immigration has 8,000 staff and an £800 million budget, enforcement has less than half that budget and only 1,208 full-time employees – and the gap in support is widening. Between 2015 and 2020, the immigration enforcement directorate had an 11 per cent reduction in its budget to £392 million, and a 5 per cent reduction in its headcount.[24]

In stark contrast to the harsh political rhetoric, British ICE's actions against employers have always remained symbolic. The Home Office does not publish data on the number of employers arrested or prosecuted, but when it was forced to release data in a freedom of information request submitted by *People Management*, it was confirmed that the numbers are indeed minuscule. In 2015–16 only twelve employers were prosecuted, and in 2016–17 just three.[25] Enforcement numbers against illegal workers also dropped, with arrests declining from 7,253 in 2013 to 1,634 in 2018–9.[26] Over the same period, the number of illegal working inspections (raids) carried out by ICE went down from 7,846 to 2,987.[27]

About half of all working inspections were to restaurants and fast-food outlets, while shops accounted for a quarter. ICE deployments have declined across the board, but nowhere as dramatically as in government offices, hospitals, care homes and private residences. This suggests that the authorities have increasingly shied away from cracking down on sectors where illegal workers are seen as having much-needed skills and meeting employers' pressing demands.

While the gap between tough political *rhetoric* and lenient policy *practice* seems extreme in the US and the UK, the situation is not fundamentally different in most other Western countries. A largely similar situation prevails in Spain, Portugal, Italy and Greece, with their large informal sectors that heavily depend on migrant labour. Enforcement levels *appear* somewhat higher in countries such as Germany, France and the Netherlands and in Scandinavia. However, in these countries, too, actual enforcement levels remain rather low, particularly in sectors where labour needs are high and the massive rounding-up of undocumented workers would provoke public outrage or pushbacks by powerful corporate players.

In December 2022, there was public outrage in France when it appeared that the construction company building the Olympic Village in Paris had hired illegal workers from Mali, Morocco, Turkey and other countries, but everybody also understood that, without them, the show couldn't go on.[28] Further illustrating the huge discursive gap between politicians' tough talk and much more lenient practices on immigration, there have been regular 'scandals' when the press found out that some of the most hard-line immigration politicians turned out to employ illegal migrants as nannies, cleaners, gardeners or construction workers.

Across the West it's an open secret that many cleaners, nannies and caregivers, as well as agricultural and construction workers, are in fact working illegally. Employers often prefer not to even know the immigration status of their workers. It's the migration equivalent of 'don't ask, don't tell'. In Europe, undocumented migrant domestic workers have an almost zero chance of being arrested and deported. There is no support for the police to raid individual houses to arrest illegal migrants working as domestic workers, nannies or caregivers – not only because these are police-state practices that few people would endorse, but also because it is an open secret that these workers are very much needed.

Better human rights means more migrant rights

Pressing labour shortages, economic interests and corporate lobbies explain to a great extent why governments have facilitated the legal entry of workers and collectively turned a blind eye to the deployment of illegal workers. However, there is more to immigration than business lobbies and class warfare. Besides client politics, immigration policies have also become more liberal because democratic governments thought this was morally the right thing to do. This was part of a general post-war spirit that was in favour of international collaboration and respect for human rights. As a consequence, democratic states voluntarily committed themselves to a series of international human rights obligations and refugee conventions – which automatically *also* tie their hands in attempts to control immigration.[29]

The disastrous experiences with economic protectionism and racism in the 1930s and the atrocities of the Second World War created a determination to prevent this from ever happening again. After the defeat of Nazism and Fascism, a post-war spirit of international collaboration created the momentum for the establishment of the United Nations and the Bretton Woods Institutions (such as the World Bank and the International Monetary Fund) as well as the enshrining of fundamental human rights, including for migrants and refugees, in international and national law. The war experience and the right to national self-determination also accelerated the end of European imperialism and the rapid dismantling of the British, French, Dutch, Portuguese and Belgian colonial empires.

The adoption of the human rights and refugee conventions and their subsequent enshrinement in national and international law had unforeseen implications for immigration policies, as it tied governments' hands by limiting their own freedom in terms of migration policymaking. Governments had less leeway to refuse the entry and stay of immigrants as it could violate fundamental human rights. The inclusion of fundamental rights, and the right to seek refuge and the right to family life in particular, also made it more difficult to deny entry to asylum seekers and the family members of migrant workers. Although this was not the intention, changes in national legislation and international human rights obligations also pushed governments to expand the rights of family and asylum migrants, and limited governments' freedoms in prohibiting their arrival and settlement and enforcing their return.

Greater attention on race equality from the late 1960s also obliged traditional countries of European settlement – the United States, Canada, Australia and New Zealand – to abolish racist 'whites only' immigration policies. This greatly facilitated legal immigration from Asia and other non-European origin countries.

In the US, the 1965 amendments to the Immigration and Nationality Act removed the discriminatory national-origins quota system, which favoured European immigration. These amendments were seen as part of civil rights legislation that aimed to root out racism. The removal of such rules unintentionally created a worldwide immigration system,[30] which facilitated growing immigration from Asia and Africa. Similar abolitions of whites-only immigration rules encouraged non-European immigration in Canada, Australia and New Zealand. However, as many doors were opened, others were partly closed. For instance, the introduction of worldwide quotas in the United States restricted previously free immigration and circulation from Latin American and Caribbean countries.[31]

Moral, diplomatic and practical arguments pushed governments to overhaul immigration policies in a more liberal direction. Increased general respect for human rights as well as diplomatic and trade interests made it less and less acceptable for governments to indefinitely deny long-time immigrants permanent residency status or citizenship, or to prohibit their families from joining them. Various attempts made by European governments to drastically curtail the general right to family reunification were overturned by national and European courts as they were seen to conflict with fundamental human rights – and similar legal protection mechanisms have often curtailed governments' freedoms to infringe on the rights of asylum seekers, despite politicians' repeated promises on such issues.[32]

This trend towards liberalization is also visible in citizenship reform. European countries which had long opposed the idea of being immigration countries, such as Germany, were eventually compelled to change immigration and citizenship laws and bring them in line with what was increasingly seen as the international standard for liberal democratic systems. Another sign of this liberalization was a growing acceptance of dual citizenship, despite the backlash in a few north-west European countries.

Despite political rhetoric against illegal immigration, in practice governments have regularly held legalizations or 'amnesties', giving legal status to undocumented migrants. Large-scale illegal migration to southern European countries in the 1980s and 1990s led to legalizations from which more than 3.2 million foreigners benefited.[33] Since 1986, Italy has had six legalization programmes resulting in the regularization of about 1.4 million migrants. Between 1985 and 2005, Spain had twelve legalizations, granting legal status to over 1 million immigrants.[34] In the

US the situation is different. Since the Reagan administration granted amnesty to some 2.7 million undocumented, mostly Mexican, migrants in 1986, there has been a continuous political stalemate on this controversial issue. Nevertheless, in the US, too, the reality on the ground has pushed the executive to deal with the most pressing humanitarian issues. For instance, in 2012 the Obama administration enacted the Deferred Action for Childhood Arrivals (DACA) policy, which allowed hundreds of thousands of undocumented immigrants, mostly Latinos, who had come to the US as children, to remain, work and study without fear of deportation.

These examples highlight that increased commitment to international human rights obligations and humanitarian concerns pushed democratic governments to also expand the rights of migrants and refugees. If governments were to treat such vulnerable groups too harshly, they would run the risk of incurring the wrath of human rights organizations, churches, opinion leaders and celebrities. Politicians must strike a careful balance between maintaining an image of being firmly in control and preserving their humanitarian credentials.

The immigration trilemma

Despite the tough political rhetoric, a combination of business lobbies and human rights obligations helps to explain why entry policies for most types of migrant have generally become more liberal rather than more restrictive. At the same time, the public has remained concerned about controlling immigration. Political scientist James Hollifield has therefore argued that modern democracies are trapped in a 'liberal paradox'. This paradox is the unresolvable tension between the need for liberal states to remain open to trade, investment and migration in order to maintain a competitive advantage, and the need to protect the rights of their citizens.[35]

Unlike the movement of goods and capital, the movement of people involves great political risks as governments are keen to maintain sovereign control of their borders to protect the rights and preferences of their citizens. The central challenge then becomes how to maintain economic openness and at the same time respect the preferences of citizens, while also respecting the fundamental human rights of foreigners.

This creates a triple bind or a 'trilemma' between three political objectives that seem impossible to reconcile in a satisfactory manner. One way in which politicians have tried to find a path around this trilemma is to prevent the spontaneous arrival of asylum seekers and illegal migrants, in an effort to escape the fundamental human rights they are entitled to once they have reached the national territory. Ironically, the expansion of rights to protection for refugees and other vulnerable groups such as minors has therefore strengthened the incentive for states to prevent their arrival in the first place, and to collaborate with countries of origin and transit to prevent this from happening.

Politicians may also try to make a lot of noise about the closure of some entry channels, while at the same time opening others – although the latter usually get hardly any media attention. For instance, Brexit marked an end to free EU mobility to the UK, but at the same time Britain resurrected its dormant temporary worker programmes, progressively relaxed entry requirements for migrant workers, opened new channels for Hong Kongers and abolished visas for citizens from Guyana, Colombia and Peru in 2022. So, once again, while some doors are closed (often with much pomp and circumstance), others get opened (usually more covertly).

Another way politicians have tried to find a way around this trilemma is to adopt tough rhetoric and to resort to highly visible border-enforcement measures such as building walls and fences. As sociologist Douglas Massey put it, the main reason why elected leaders revert to often ineffective (but symbolically powerful) enforcement measures such as border walls is to create the *appearance* of control.[36]

It is the symbolic function that counts, as a focus on border enforcement and belligerent rhetoric helps to project an image of decisiveness and boldness. While border enforcement targets asylum seekers and illegal migrants, it leaves the general set of rules and regulations for (the numerically much more important) legal immigration unaffected. As the vast majority of migrants cross borders legally, 'getting tough' on immigration provides politicians with an opportunity to portray themselves as crusaders who will root out the malign practices of smugglers and traffickers and protect the nation from foreign invaders. What actually happens on the ground is less important to them.

This strategy may help to conceal, but will not resolve the immigration trilemma. You cannot have economic liberalization *and* liberalize immigration policies *and* satisfy citizens' wishes for less immigration. One of the three has to go. So, the most attractive option for politicians is to *suggest* that they clamp down on immigration through bold acts of political showmanship that conceal the true nature of immigration policies.

Myth 17: Conservatives are tougher on immigration

Most people believe that left-wing, liberal politicians are in favour of immigration, and that right-wing, conservative politicians want to reduce immigration. This resonates with how liberals and conservatives tend to view themselves. People who *see* themselves as 'progressive' or 'left-wing' tend to be positive about immigration and diversity and in favour of generous refugee policies. By contrast, people adhering to conservative values are often less enthusiastic about immigration, particularly if immigrants come from a different ethnic or religious background.

Immigration hard-liners often portray left-wing politicians as 'soft' on immigration. In Europe, conservative parties have blamed the left for the 'failed integration' of former migrant workers because of their alleged naive enthusiasm for immigration, diversity and multiculturalism. How much this idea has got under the skin of many left-wing politicians is visible in their eagerness to show off their tough-on-immigration credentials in an attempt to appeal to more centrist voters.

During his tenure as prime minister, Tony Blair repeatedly boasted about his tough line towards 'bogus' asylum seekers and illegal migration and emphasized how 'soft' on immigration the Tories actually were. In 1999, for instance, Blair criticized the Conservatives for voting to restore benefits to asylum seekers and arguing against his government's proposals to remove support from families whose claims were rejected.[1] More recent Labour leaders such as Jeremy Corbyn have also done their best to show a desire to bring immigration 'back under control'. President Obama, who was nicknamed 'deporter in chief' by critics, prided himself on his commitment to border enforcement, as the number of deportations reached an all-time high under his presidency.

The urge that progressive politicians feel to fight this soft-on-immigration image proves how much this belief has taken hold. And opinion polls prove it. In 2008, a poll showed that only 5 per cent of British voters thought that Labour had the best policies on immigration, against 46 per cent for the Conservatives.[2] This shows that most people believe that there is a left–right divide in political attitudes towards immigration and related issues of race, diversity and identity – as part of an increasingly polarized debate between pro- and anti-immigration camps, in which the left is imagined to be pro and the right to be anti, and this is also how the media tends to report on these issues.

How it really works

There is no left–right divide on immigration

There is often a discursive gap between what politicians say and what they do about immigration. We should therefore be careful in taking the tough talk of immigration hard-liners at face value. So, why would we take for granted that the right wing is anti-immigration and the left wing is pro-immigration because we're being told so? This categorization has always struck me as a bit simplistic. After all, corporate lobbies who generally favour immigration have significant influence on political parties, and particularly conservative parties. And trade unions, traditionally allied to the political left, have always been suspicious or sometimes outright hostile towards the recruitment of foreign workers.

This question started to intrigue me around 2013. I had been living and working in Oxford since 2006, during times when debates about immigration in Britain had reached fever pitch, with politicians on the left and right outbidding each other to show their seriousness in tackling the migration issue – with the left being put on the defensive to fight the image of being 'soft' on immigration, and the centrist Lib Dems the only party to adopt a more overtly pro-immigration standpoint. But knowing how big the gap between rhetoric and practice can be, I started wondering to what extent left- and right-wing politicians and parties really differed when it came to the actual laws and regulations on migration they adopted.

Luckily, I had the data that enabled me to answer this question. As part of the Determinants of International Migration (DEMIG) project, we had just compiled a database containing information on the evolution of migration policies in the Western world.[3] We had originally collected this data to measure the evolution and effectiveness of migration policies. However, I realized we could also use the data to test whether right-wing governments were tougher on immigration compared to left-wing governments.

Together with my Oxford colleagues Mathias Czaika and Katharina Natter, we merged DEMIG POLICY with existing databases containing information on the political colour of national governments. We also made a crucial distinction between immigration and integration policies. *Immigration policies* are about the right to enter a country – laws and regulations about visas, work permits, family reunification and asylum. *Integration policies* are about the rights that already settled migrants can claim, such as access to education, healthcare, permanent residence, and citizenship. We then distinguished two other policy categories: *border controls*, such as the construction of border fences, border patrols and passport checks, and *exit policies*, such as return programmes and deportations.

Using this data, we measured whether right- and left-wing governments differed in terms of immigration policy restrictiveness. Graph 15 reports the most important result, which was confirmed by regression analyses we conducted for a study published in 2020.[4] It shows the restrictiveness of policies adopted by Western governments between 1975 and 2012, depending on the political orientation of the parties in government. Using the Immigration Restrictiveness Index (IRI) mentioned in the previous chapter, values above 0 indicate that, on average, more restrictive policies were adopted. Values below 0 indicate a tendency towards more liberal policies.

The analyses show two clear patterns. First, the evidence confirms the finding of the last chapter: immigration regimes have generally become more liberal. While border controls and exit policies (such as deportation) have become more restrictive, the actual package of laws and rules that regulate the legal entry, stay and integration of immigrants has generally become more liberal. Second, there is no big difference between left- and right-wing parties when it comes to the restrictiveness of the immigration policies they adopt. Right- and left-wing parties do not enact opposite reforms on immigration – most of the differences we found were small and generally statistically insignificant. This suggests that the political ideology of parties in power plays only a very limited role in explaining the restrictiveness of immigration policy reform.

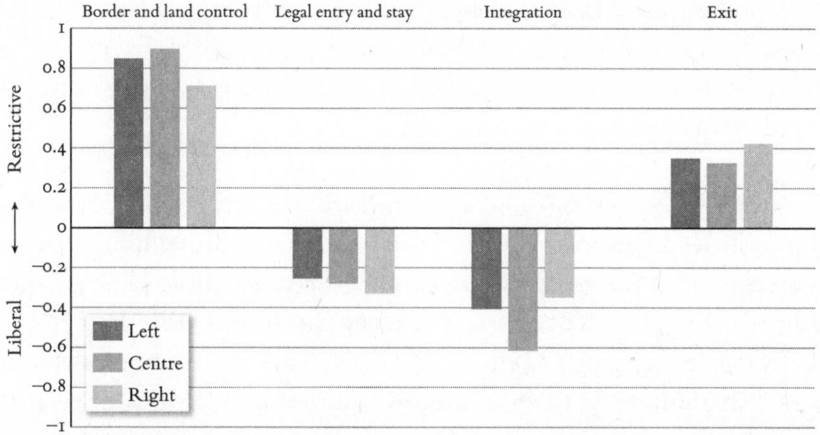

Graph 15: Comparison between ideological orientation of governments and immigration policy restrictiveness in twenty-one Western countries[5]

The results of our analysis surprised me. I had expected to find that differences in policy practices between right- and left-wing governments were smaller than the rhetoric suggested. However, I had not expected that there would be hardly any differences at all. Although left-wing-dominated governments were slightly more liberal on issues like access to citizenship and the rights given to asylum seekers, the differences were significant but small. With regard to entry rules for labour and family migrants – the very core of immigration policies – we did not find any significant differences between left- and right-wing governments at all.

So, behind the rhetoric and headlines, there is barely a noticeable difference between right- and left-wing parties when it comes to policy *practices*. On the whole, ideological differences between political parties have hardly any influence on the kind of policies governments actually adopt. Other factors turn out to be much more important. Economic ups and downs have a strong and significant effect on immigration policies. Economic growth and the resulting labour shortages increase corporate pressures on governments to allow more migrant workers in, and are also likely to reduce popular opposition against immigration. During economic downturns and rising unemployment, calls by labour unions and conservative groups to stop recruitment and limit inflows tend to gain force. So, business cycles affect the political willingness to allow more immigrants, largely irrespective of the ideological colour of the parties in charge.

Political parties are divided internally on immigration

How can we explain this absence of a clear right–left divide in immigration policies? The answer is that the immigration issue divides parties *internally*, with the main divide running between those close to their parties' economic tradition and those closely aligned with their parties' sociocultural ideology. Left-wing parties have to accommodate the conflicting interests of labour unions who traditionally favour restrictive policies, and liberal and human rights groups favouring more open policies. Right-wing parties are divided between business lobbies favouring immigration and cultural conservatives asking for immigration restrictions.[6] This can create 'strange bedfellow' coalitions of immigration sceptics and immigration enthusiasts, for example labour unions and cultural conservatives arguing in favour of immigration restrictions, and businesses lobbies and human rights groups arguing in favour of liberal policies.

Left-wing politicians may talk softer than they act on immigration to preserve their humanitarian credentials, while right-wing politicians may do the reverse to preserve their tough-on-immigration reputation. Over the past thirty years in the US, Republication *and* Democratic presidents have progressively intensified border enforcement, while workplace enforcement was as much a joke under Trump as it was under previous presidents. In practice, such strange bedfellow coalitions have often blocked law enforcement. For instance, in 1995, the US Commission on Immigration Reform, which was mandated by Congress in 1990, came up with recommendations for more effective immigration policies. Arguing that 'reducing the employment magnet is the linchpin of a comprehensive strategy to deter unlawful immigration',[7] it proposed a national computerized system – better known as E-Verify – to check whether workers' IDs and social security numbers were valid.[8]

The commission wanted it to be mandatory, but then an 'almost laughably' broad coalition rose up against it, including the National Rifle Association (NRA), the American Civil Liberties Union (ACLU), business lobbies, church groups and Latino communities, who all portrayed it as an 'unwanted Big Brother government intrusion'.[9] So, only a voluntary programme moved forward, which was ineffective as it couldn't prevent migrant workers from using fake IDs or somebody else's papers.[10]

This exemplifies the fact that the complex realities of immigration policymaking don't fit easily within simplistic left–right-wing schemes. Both Republican and Democratic politicians have championed immigration reforms that typically reflect trade-offs between different positions and interests on immigration. The immigration reforms themselves often reflect this ambiguity, as they are usually 'mixed bags' of liberal and restrictive policy measures. For instance, Ronald Reagan's 1986 Immigration Reform and Control Act legalized millions of undocumented immigrants but simultaneously made it illegal for employers to hire undocumented immigrants, and introduced tougher border controls. In 2007, the bipartisan Comprehensive Immigration Reform Act of 2007, which was strongly endorsed by Republican president George W. Bush but failed to pass Congress, proposed providing legal status and a path to citizenship for millions of undocumented immigrants – alongside increased border enforcement, the introduction of a new guest worker system and the introduction of a points-based system to facilitate skilled migrants.

Democratic politicians have not necessarily been more lenient on immigration issues, and their policies are also mixed bags of restrictive and liberal actions. While deportation reached an all-time high under President Obama in 2012, he also enacted the Deferred Action for Childhood Arrivals (DACA) policy, which protected young undocumented migrants from deportation.

In Britain, too, parties are divided *internally* on the immigration issue. Both the Labour and Conservative parties have traditionally been torn on immigration, and have supported both restrictive and liberal policies in the past. Such intra-party divisions became apparent around the 2016 Brexit vote. Brexit, in which the immigration issue took centre stage, split the Conservative and Labour parties right through the middle. While business-minded Conservatives tended to oppose Brexit, Conservatives who were more preoccupied with British sovereignty and identity tended to be in favour of leaving the EU. In the Labour Party, the trade union wing of Labour and leaders such as Jeremy Corbyn – who tend to see the EU and the associated free trade and free movement as a neoliberal project – have always been rather Eurosceptic, even if they were officially in favour of 'Remain'. However, middle-class and urban-based Labour voters and politicians are generally more pro-EU and pro-immigration. Brexit almost tore Labour apart because of immigration, as they were unable to formulate a truly unified position.

Why labour unions are torn about immigration

So, historically, sceptical or hostile attitudes towards immigration have been anything but the exclusive domain of the right. The ambiguous position of trade unions towards labour immigration is a case in point. For trade unions, immigration has always been an extremely divisive issue. Their default position has been to see the recruitment of migrant workers as a corporate strategy to import cheap labour, divide the working class (between native and foreign workers), break the power of unions and keep wages down.

The initial reflex of unions is therefore to be against large-scale immigration, as they fear it will harm their bargaining power. This has a long history. In the early twentieth century, US trade unions turned against Black internal migrants from the US South. When, between 1914 and the 1950s, millions of African Americans fled segregation and economic exploitation in the Southern states for better wages in the industrial cities of the North, they were excluded from membership of the unions of the American Federation of Labor. This had to do with racism but was also because employers were suspected of recruiting Black workers as strike-breakers. American trade unions were also highly critical of the Bracero programme that recruited 4.5 million guest workers from the Mexican countryside between 1942 and 1964, out of fear that immigration would displace domestic workers and hold down wages.[11]

In Europe, trade unions and the parties associated with them were critical of the recruitment of guest workers and demanded safeguards, such as equal pay and conditions that would not undermine the position of local workers. One of the motives for European industries to purposefully select lower-skilled and often illiterate workers in rural areas of North Africa and Turkey was the desire for a compliant conservative workforce that was not liable to join trade unions or communist parties – those with diplomas were generally seen as potential troublemakers.[12]

While generally opposing the organized recruitment of foreign workers, unions also feel the urge to defend the rights of foreign workers who are already present – and, if possible, to unionize them, to prevent employers driving a wedge between native and foreign workers. This puts labour unions in a painful, difficult-to-resolve split between their deep suspicion towards the large-scale recruitment of migrant workers and their natural reflex to defend the rights of all workers, whether native or foreign. Social democrat and labour parties, the traditional allies of unions, are also involved in a never-ending struggle to balance nationalistic sentiments ('own workers first') with the ideal of international class solidarity.

Unions usually become staunch advocates of the equal rights of migrants once the reality sinks in that they won't go back. For instance, beginning in the early 1980s, the American Federation of Labor and Congress of Industrial Organizations (AFL-CIO) supported sanctions against businesses employing undocumented workers. However, in 2000 they renounced their support for the enforcement of employer sanctions, as AFL-CIO had come under new leadership, emerging from unions with large numbers of immigrant members, including many undocumented workers. This faction had close ties to the US Conference of Catholic Bishops, which supported the legalization of undocumented migrants.[13]

So, the typical pattern is one of initial opposition, followed by a subsequent drive to incorporate foreign workers. Such a turnaround generally happens once unions realize workers won't return and are 'there to stay', at which point trade unions start to consider – and treat – migrant workers as their new constituencies. In western Europe, too, labour unions and labour parties often opposed guest worker policies in the 1960s and 1970s. When pushed, they only agreed with recruitment on the condition that foreign workers would get salaries and labour rights on a par with native workers. In more recent years, unions have often argued that free migration within the EU mainly serves corporate interests, by giving businesses access to cheap labour in eastern Europe – which, in their view, undermines the position of local workers through the exploitation of foreign workers. But, at the same time, they feel the need to defend the rights of exploited migrant workers.

Why conservatives are torn about immigration, too

As much as labour unions are divided on immigration, groups of people often seen as 'conservative' are often torn between a certain fear of too much cultural change and their often religiously inspired humanitarian impulse. This further undermines the entire idea that we can make a simple moral divide between anti-immigration conservatives and pro-immigration lefties. Religion is perhaps the best example. Although many people see religion as a 'conservative' thing, all world religions stress the value of compassion towards the weak and vulnerable, and urge believers to welcome strangers and protect the prosecuted.

The Torah, the Hebrew bible (the Old Testament for Christians), mentions the word 'stranger' (gûr גּוּר or gēr גֵּר) almost fifty times, and stresses the obligation to treat strangers with dignity, hospitality and active support. The Vayikra, the third book of the Torah (known to Christians as Leviticus) says that: 'The alien who resides with you shall be to you as the citizen among you; you shall love the alien as yourself, for you were aliens in the land of Egypt' (Leviticus 19:34). The Israelites themselves were 'strangers' during their enslavement in Egypt and captivity in Babylon.

According to the gospels, Jesus was unequivocal about the need to 'love your neighbour as yourself' (Mark 12:30–31). Because in the New Testament, 'stranger' and 'neighbour' are synonymous, this implies that these moral principles also apply to people you don't know. Jesus said that those sitting at his right who will go to paradise are 'blessed' because 'I was hungry and you gave me food, I was thirsty and you gave me drink, I was a stranger and you welcomed me' (Matthew 25:35).[14]

Islam calls on Muslims to grant *istijara* (إستجارة) – asylum – to those who seek it. Qur'anic verse 9:6 specifies that this right to seek protection extends to *musta ʾmīn* (مستأمن), or non-Muslim foreigners. Muslims are commanded to protect and help 'those oppressed men, women and children who cry out "Lord, rescue us from this town where people are oppressors!"' (Q4:75).The Hindu concept of *vasudhaiva kutumbakam* (the world is one family) rejects boundaries of nationality, ethnicity and religion, while *dharma* – which requires that 'one should never do that to another which one regards as injurious to oneself' – compels Hindus to respect and fulfil the needs of refugees.[15]

Many people of faith take such principles very seriously. People who may have rather 'conservative' opinions on issues like abortion, divorce, the role of women or same-sex marriage can also see it as a fundamental religious duty to welcome immigrants and protect refugees, particularly when they arrive on their doorstep. There is research evidence showing that religious people are not necessarily more opposed to immigration, and that those who practise their religion (praying and churchgoing) tend to have more positive attitudes about immigration policies and issues like the establishment of an asylum seeker centre in their community.[16]

Churches have often been at the forefront of protecting the rights of migrants and refugees and preventing them from being wrongfully deported. One of the first acts of Pope Francis in 2013 was to visit the Italian island of Lampedusa, where many migrant boats arrive, where he said mass for migrants and refugees, condemning the 'global indifference' to their plight.[17] The Church of England has been one of the most ardent critics of the harsh refugee policies of successive Conservative- and Labour-led UK governments.

More than criticizing governments, churches and religious organizations also see it as their duty to show compassion by reaching out through concrete action. Spontaneous actions to give shelter to refugees and undocumented migrants in communities are often led by religious groups. Alejandro Olayo-Méndez is an assistant professor at the Boston College School of Social Work. He is also a Jesuit priest who has done clinical work with immigrant and refugee communities, and he was my DPhil student at Oxford. His doctoral research took him back to his native Mexico, where he documented the important role that faith-based organizations played in running a nationwide network of shelters that provide safety, food and assistance to Central American, Cuban, Haitian and Venezuelan migrants and refugees on their way to the US, and protect them from violence, kidnapping and extortion by criminals, gangs and the police.[18]

When I visited El Paso, Texas, on the US–Mexico border with Alejandro in January 2023, we met Ruben Garcia, a layman who, for the past forty years, has served as the director of Annunciation House. This Catholic organization operates several houses of hospitality for refugees and immigrants right on the border. He told us that Annunciation House supports asylum seekers and refugees as they transition to their destinations. Sometimes, this work includes helping them to find services in places initially not so welcoming of migrants. 'We have helped people to settle in cities like Omaha, Nebraska, which is very conservative.' In places like this, they have worked through education and information with some faith-based communities to be more receptive and support asylum seekers. There is always an initial hesitation but through time they have embraced the newcomers and made them part of their community.

Throughout history, churches have been refuges for the persecuted – sacred places that the police do not dare enter. In Morocco, Protestant and Catholic churches have played a vital role in helping to grow communities of refugees and migrants from sub-Saharan Africa, and protecting them from racist attacks and violence and arrest by the police.[19] In the US, nine faith-based agencies – Evangelical, mainstream Protestant, Catholic and Jewish – work with the government to help find housing and jobs for refugees and to arrange English classes.[20]

In 2020, conservative evangelical groups were horrified by the Trump administration's practice of separating nearly 4,000 children from their parents at the border – with officers yanking away babies and crying toddlers clinging to their parents' legs.[21] As part of Trump's 'zero tolerance' policy to arrest and detain anyone crossing the border without authorization, parents were detained and the children were sent to faraway childcare facilities. Often, for months onward, children were not told where their parents were or what would happen, and vice versa. This sparked widespread protest by leaders of Jewish, Mormon, Catholic, Protestant and evangelical Christian groups, calling out such policies as going against the teachings of their faiths.[22] Eventually, this pushed the administration to reverse course, even though the policy had already caused much trauma.

The urgent need to go beyond the pro/anti framing

The reality clearly defies the stereotype of a world divided by right-wing immigration hardliners and left-wing open-border enthusiasts. The ambivalent feelings and emotions immigration typically evokes on a personal level are also reflected on the political level. On average, right-wing governments do *not* adopt more restrictive immigration policies compared to left-wing governments. This highlights the increasing gap between the tough immigration rhetoric adopted by politicians and their much more lenient policy practices. In reality, there is no clear left–right divide in immigration policymaking, as the issue divides political parties *internally*. We can find similar ambivalence within trade unions, religious organizations and all across society.

This illustrates the danger of reducing immigration debates to an opposition between pro- and anti-immigration camps. The whole framing of migration debates in pro- and anti- terms is deeply problematic for various reasons. Such framing, which dominates the media, is simplistic and does not do any justice to the complexity of real-life immigration policymaking and the moral and practical dilemmas this raises.

First of all, it works to polarize and to block any evidence-informed debate, as it pushes both sides to only cherry-pick facts that serve their argument and hampers our ability to really listen to each other's thoughts, concerns and emotions about this important issue. Second, the fear of sounding soft on immigration has devolved into a never-ending contest of who can sound harshest on illegal immigration. Politicians have indulged in various forms of immigration scaremongering and immigrant scapegoating, and this is irresponsible behaviour because of the proven ability of xenophobic rhetoric to sow hatred and division by setting population groups against each other and emboldening far-right nativist groups.

In what world do we live where politicians *pride* themselves on building walls and fences that keep refugees out? Irrespective of what you think about such issues, or if you think such measures are to some extent a 'necessary evil', we should at least expect politicians to behave more responsibly by showing a bit more modesty, humility and empathy – and to stay away from using divisive rhetoric.

For decades now, the public has been more and more decoupled from the realities of immigration policymaking. Politicians on the left and the right are misleading the public about the true nature of their immigration policies. This is disingenuous. But it also highlights the hole politicians dug for themselves as they got caught up in their own lies.

This rhetorical sham distracts attention away from the real issue and the real problems that exist and need addressing, and obstructs any real, nuanced debate on the pros and cons of immigration that would be more representative of the mixed feelings most people have on the topic, and that would also be more helpful in devising policies that are based on a real understanding of how migration works and the dilemmas it creates.

For thirty years, immigration debates have increasingly been held hostage by the far right, as it has made mainstream politicians fearful about sounding 'soft' on immigration. This has made them increasingly afraid to tell the truth about migration and to be honest about the difficult dilemmas it poses. Instead, they indulge in attacks and counterattacks. But that's not a debate. We can – and should – do so much better.

Myth 18: Public opinion has turned against immigration

'We must stop the migrant invasion.' 'Enough is enough!' 'Britain is full and fed up.' 'Xenophobia on the rise in France.'[1] Such headlines seem to support the widespread idea that public opinion in Western countries has increasingly turned against immigration. This is also how politicians tend to frame it: 'We will crack down on immigration because this is what the people want.' It reflects the popular idea that mass immigration is exceeding the absorption capacity of destination societies, and that this would explain mounting opposition against uncontrolled immigration.

This has been the central claim of populist and far-right politicians for decades – the people want less immigration, but mainstream politicians have ignored them. The rise of far-right politicians like Jean-Marie and Marine Le Pen in France, Filip Dewinter in Belgium, Geert Wilders in the Netherlands, Nigel Farage in the UK, Donald Trump in the US and Giorgia Meloni in Italy seems to have finally woken up the political establishment to the need to take public opinion seriously by carrying out their wish to limit immigration and secure their countries' borders.

There seems to be an increasing sense that mainstream politicians have for too long ignored growing dissatisfaction about immigration out of a misplaced fear of sounding racist, and that this has enabled far-right politicians to mobilize the votes of people who feel that their concerns are not being taken seriously by out-of-touch political elites. In order to prevent further polarization and social division on this issue, politicians should therefore finally be taking people's dissatisfaction seriously by drastically curtailing immigration.

This sentiment that 'we should finally listen to ordinary people' to win back their votes – which has become quite prominent in progressive and left-wing circles – was voiced in 2018 by Hillary Clinton. Contemplating her election loss against Donald Trump, she said that immigration was inflaming voters and contributed to the election of

Trump and Britain's vote to leave the EU. She therefore argued that Europe must curb immigration to stop right-wing populists. 'I think Europe needs to get a handle on migration because that is what lit the flame,' she said, calling on leaders to send a stronger signal that Europe was 'not going to be able to continue to provide refuge and support'.[2]

Across Europe, many mainstream politicians have adopted the anti-immigration talking points that used to be the exclusive domain of the far right. The message politicians try to send is 'we hear you', suggesting that they have finally understood what people really want. Not everybody has joined this chorus. Human rights activists and liberals have argued that politicians are playing with fire if they take over xenophobic rhetoric to win elections, arguing that this will only reinforce prejudice, hatred and violence. They would rather argue that we should counter xenophobia by informing the public about the facts and the positive contributions migrants and refugees make to destination societies.

However, despite this disagreement, both camps actually share the same underlying belief that it is a fact that public opinion has increasingly turned against immigration.

How it really works

Public opinion has grown more positive on immigration

Is xenophobia really on the rise? Interestingly, both anti- and pro-immigration camps often claim so, and many opinion-makers believe so, too, but what does the evidence say? Fortunately, there is a wealth of opinion polls and surveys that can give us an instant answer on that question, and what they reveal is that people's opinions on immigration tend to be rather nuanced. But, most importantly, they show that there is no evidence that public opinion has generally turned against immigration. While public *concerns* about immigration fluctuate with economic cycles, political debates and the occurrence of border crises, public *opinion* on issues like immigration, race and diversity has remained strikingly stable in the longer run. In many countries, long-term trends have in fact rather been towards more favourable opinions about immigration.

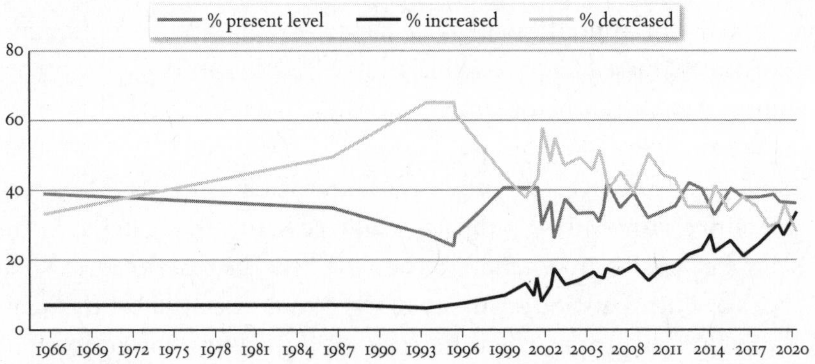

Graph 16: Views on immigration in the US, 1966–2020. Respondents to this poll were asked: 'In your view, should immigration be kept at its present level, increased or decreased?'[3]

For instance, successive polls by Gallup have shown that the share of Americans in favour of higher immigration levels remained rather stable between 1966 and 2002, at around 7 per cent, after which it started to rise to around 34 per cent in 2020. As Graph 16 shows, the share of Americans in favour of less immigration rose from 33 to 65 per cent between 1966 and 1993, but then declined to levels of 28 per cent in 2020. The share of people favouring immigration at the present level remained rather stable, at around one-third of all Americans, during the entire 1966–2020 period. Currently, each of the three positions on immigration receives support from about one-third of the US population.

These trends towards increased support for liberal immigration policies exist across party lines. According to surveys conducted by the Pew Research Center, the share of self-declared Republican or Republican-leaning adults in favour of increased immigration rose from 15 to 22 per cent between 2006 and 2018. Among Democrat or Democrat-leaning people, support for increased immigration grew from 20 to 40 per cent. Over the same period, support for decreased immigration fell from 43 to 33 per cent among Republicans, and from 37 to 16 per cent among Democrats. Opinion research challenges the common idea that there is growing polarization on migration issues across party lines – when we don't look at political rhetoric but at what actual voters think. Although clear party differences exist within electorates, it is not true that the general public has turned against immigration – what we rather see is that support for immigration has increased in a period in which immigration has increased.[4]

Similar trends can be observed in the UK, where opinion research clearly refutes the idea that public opinion has turned against immigration. For instance, a study by Oxford University's Migration Observatory showed that public attitudes towards immigration in the UK have generally grown more favourable over the past decades. Their analyses of European Social Survey (ESS) data showed that on the question of whether people of a different race should be allowed to come and live in Britain, the percentage of people answering 'a few' or 'none' was consistently hovering at around 50 per cent between 2002 and 2012, but subsequently dropped to 43 per cent in 2014, to 32 per cent in 2016, and further to 26 per cent in 2018.[5] An analysis of the Ipsos MORI trend survey indicated that 64 per cent of British respondents were negative about the impact of immigration in 2011. This share had dropped to 28 per cent in 2018, while the percentage of people with positive attitudes increased from 19 to 48 per cent.[6]

Remarkably, this positive turn in attitudes towards immigration was happening exactly during the time that debates on immigration reached fever pitch in the run-up to the 2016 Brexit referendum. This shows the importance of not conflating public concern and political rhetoric about immigration with public *opposition* to immigration, as they are not the same thing. Public interest in immigration fluctuates with economic cycles, political debates and media hype. Public and political interest in immigration does not automatically mean that people have turned against it. While political and media interest in immigration is typically highly volatile, public opinion is much more stable. We also saw this after the European 'refugee crisis' of 2015, which had no noticeable effect on the attitudes of Europeans towards immigrants.[7] This shows that the general public is much more level-headed than politicians are about immigration issues.

Data from across Europe also belies the idea that xenophobia is increasing. A study of the European Social Survey data showed that, between 2002 and 2018, people in many destination countries – including the UK, Germany, Ireland, Belgium, Spain, Portugal and Sweden – became more positive towards immigration, whereas in other countries – including the Netherlands, Denmark and Switzerland – things remained rather stable. Only a minority of countries – Bulgaria, Greece, Hungary and Italy – showed a downward trend.[8] Analyses of another survey, the Eurobarometer, showed that, in Europe, young people increasingly co-identify as 'European'.[9] Such changes seem to largely reflect a *structural*, more permanent shift in attitudes, which demographers call 'cohort effects'. This means that young people nowadays have more positive opinions about immigration and diversity issues than their parents did when they were young themselves.

Most people have rather nuanced opinions about immigration

Perhaps the most important teaching from the public opinion research is that in most high-immigration countries, people seem to have rather nuanced and often ambivalent views on immigration and diversity. Only a minority of people are strongly opposed to immigration or have explicitly racist views. High-earning, highly educated young urbanites are generally positive about immigration.[10] Opposition is usually strongest among older white social conservatives with lower levels of education and income. A recent study on Japan and Germany suggests that anti-immigrant sentiment is particularly high among low-income groups with 'left-wing' opinions about the responsibility of governments to protect local workers.[11] These groups typically feel that they have lost out from economic liberalization, and feel left behind by political elites.[12] In Europe, the divide in attitudes towards immigration of highly educated young adults and lower-educated seniors is particularly high in the UK, Sweden and France.[13]

Besides considerable division along generational and educational lines, attitudes vary towards different types of migrants, with the strongest opposition focused on illegal immigrants, refugees and lower-skilled workers.[14] The generally higher acceptance of higher-skilled compared to lower-skilled workers outweighs factors such as country of origin, race or religion.[15] However, detailed research based on focus-group interviews in Britain reveals a more nuanced picture: most people are favourable towards migrants who are self-supporting through employment and tax payments – they support immigration that is economically beneficial rather than necessarily higher-skilled.[16] This is demonstrated by high support for lower-skilled migrants filling urgent labour needs such as in agriculture.

As one study put it, most people are, in fact, 'balancers', who see both pros and cons, and can therefore be put neither in the pro- nor the anti-immigration camp.[17] This is confirmed by analyses of the World Value Survey, showing that, across the West, people hold diverse and seemingly contradictory attitudes towards immigration – for instance, they can support restrictions while also acknowledging the positive economic and cultural impacts of immigration. Roughly half of people form a 'conflicted' middle, who are neither strongly for nor strongly against migration.[18]

All of this challenges the narrative of a growing public divide on immigration. Overall the polarization about immigration is rhetorical and political – it does not reflect actual trends in public opinion. A Eurobarometer survey from 2017, which focused on immigration, is another excellent source of European public opinion based on polls across all EU member countries. Graph 17 shows people's opinions about the impacts of immigration on their societies. Around 54 per cent of all citizens from the EU28 (the UK was still included) had a moderately to very positive opinion about the impacts of immigration on society. Meanwhile, 29 per cent had a 'neither positive nor negative' opinion, while 17 per cent had a more negative opinion.

In the longer run, contact with immigrants reduces xenophobia

It is common to think that xenophobia is a response to immigration: by this logic, the more immigration, the stronger the opposition. In fact, the evidence seems to show rather the opposite. Opinion research reveals the following paradox: anti-immigration attitudes are often strongest in countries and regions with the fewest immigrants. Societies with a longer history of immigration are generally more open to it, while younger people are also more positive about diversity and immigration.

The data from various surveys suggests that people tend to have more negative opinions about immigration and integration in East European countries with relatively low levels of immigration, such as Bulgaria, Hungary and Slovakia. This does not necessarily mean that eastern Europeans are inherently more racist, but that many people are simply not familiar with immigrants. Support for immigration is generally higher in many countries with longer histories of large-scale immigration,

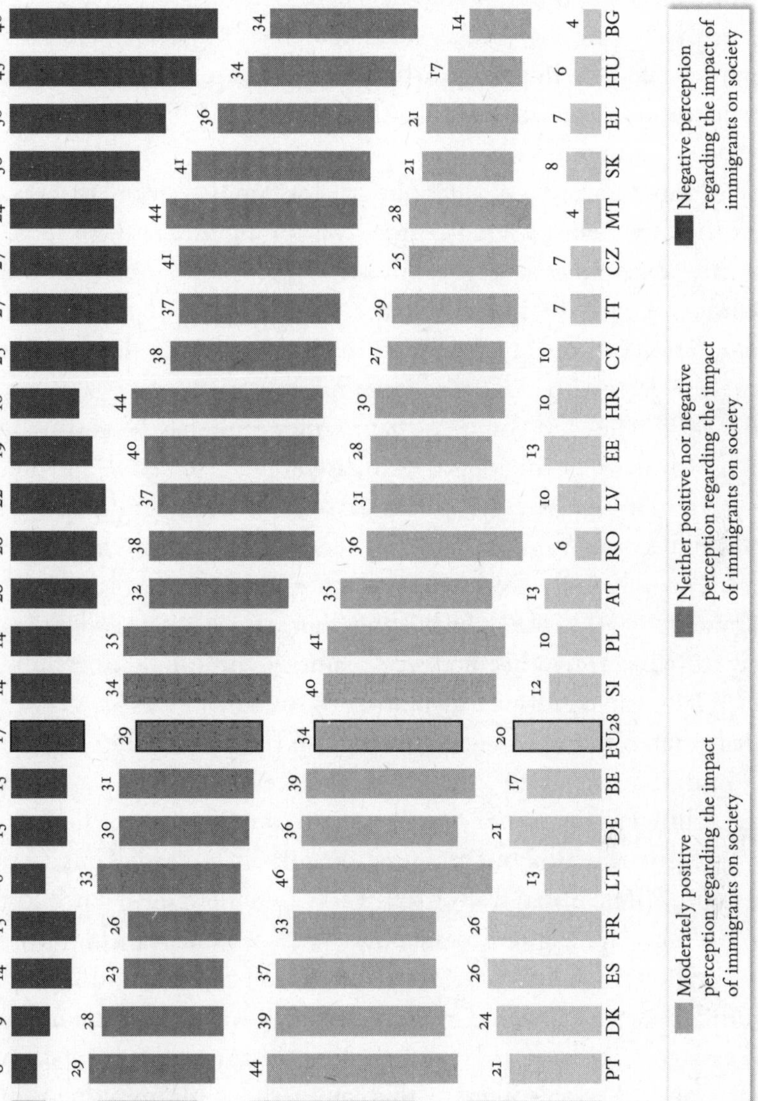

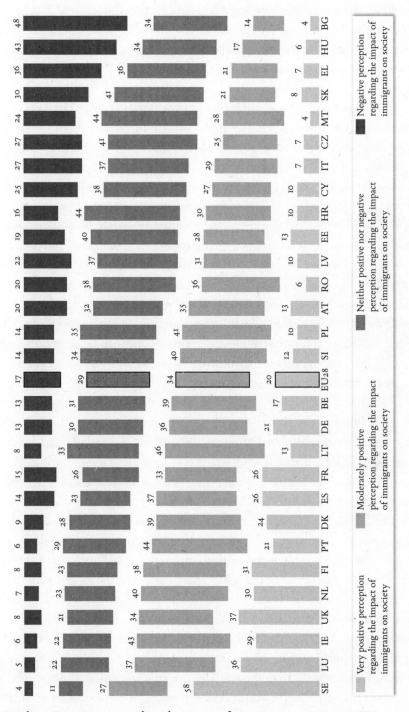

Graph 17: Perceptions regarding the impact of immigrants on society in EU countries (including the UK)[19]

such as the United States and Canada but also the United Kingdom, Germany, Spain, the Netherlands and Sweden. However, there are some outliers. Particularly in Italy, and to some extent also France, public opinion is more negative than one would have expected based on recent immigration levels.

The most negative evaluations of immigration seem to prevail in countries that lack a long history of immigration but which have recently experienced large influxes of asylum seekers and illegal migrants, such as Malta and Greece. This suggests that the impact of immigration on anti-immigrant sentiment may be non-linear – first rising, then decreasing. Initially, large influxes of migrants and refugees can raise worries and concerns that immigration may be getting out of hand. However, in the longer term, as people get used to the presence of foreigners and start to create personal ties with migrants, as the stranger becomes familiar, as 'they' become 'us', this tends to reduce fears. This is broadly consistent with the 'contact hypothesis' in psychology and social science, which argues that actual contact and interaction tend to reduce prejudice between majority and minority groups, and which has been confirmed by numerous studies.[20]

It is therefore important to distinguish short- and long-term effects of immigration on public opinion. The difference may partly explain why, following the rise of East European immigration to the UK after 1995, negative views about immigration initially increased, but decreased after 2010.[21] The initial fear of strangers often melts away once foreigners become colleagues, neighbours and classmates. In this way, immigration may have contributed to a greater acceptance of 'the other'.

Border communities are often remarkably welcoming to immigrants and refugees, because they share a long history of cohabitation and migration. All of this suggests that familiarity with immigrants breeds contentment rather than contempt, particularly in the longer run; however, this is not an *automatic* outcome. If the majority don't meet migrants and minorities in their daily lives, prejudice and racism may well persist. This highlights the dangers of residential and school segregation in perpetuating prejudice, as well as of the harm done by incendiary rhetoric from politicians and opinion leaders. Some of the most negative opinions about immigration can be found in countries where politicians' anti-immigrant rhetoric has taken on particularly harsh forms and seems to have become self-reinforcing, such as in Italy and Hungary, where leading politicians have espoused virulent xenophobic rhetoric for years.

So, growing familiarity with immigrants usually takes the edge off xenophobia and racism, particularly when new generations grow up having never known anything else and having gone to school with immigrant kids. Such mingling also encourages the development of social ties. This undermines the claim that large-scale immigration has created an anti-immigration backlash among the general public. It is inflammatory rhetoric by politicians, pundits and media, not immigration, that has emboldened nativist groups and racist violence.

Despite progress, racism and prejudice are still major problems

So, public opinion seems to have become less, rather than more, xenophobic and racist. In the 1960s, anti-racism was given major impetus through the US civil rights movement, which stimulated the rise of similar anti-racist movements in the UK and throughout the Western world. In recent years, the Black Lives Matter movement has given yet more impetus to the anti-racist struggle. Younger generations seem to have become more aware of the entanglement of racism with European and North American legacies of colonialism and slavery, which may help to explain why opinions about people of other races, cultures and religions have grown more positive, despite – or rather because of – increasing levels of immigration and settlement.

However, despite the progress that has been made, racism, segregation and discrimination are still formidable problems that exclude racial minorities – both migrant and non-migrant – and continue to put them at a structural disadvantage. There is no space in this book to do full justice to these problems, but what the evidence presented shows is that migrants and non-white minorities continue to experience substantial discrimination, particularly in job hiring and access to housing, while racial profiling by the police and government institutions is still very common. Although overt displays of 'Jim Crow' racism and explicit discrimination have become less and less acceptable, conscious and unconscious racist prejudice still play major roles in perpetuating disadvantage. As scholars like Philomena Essed and Eduardo Bonilla-Silva have extensively demonstrated, racial prejudice affects the day-to-day lived experiences of minority groups in negative and painful ways that are often not visible to white people.[22]

Racism goes down as immigration goes up

There is no proof that 'the people' have massively turned against immigration or that racism and xenophobia are on the rise. Rather, people have moderate, mixed opinions about immigration – and indeed people tend to be more level-headed about immigration than politicians often are. At the same time, it is important not to be naive. Racist prejudices arising from the legacy of colonialism and slavery – and which are deeply ingrained in people's minds and institutions – cannot be rooted out with the stroke of a pen, but it is important to acknowledge the real gains that have been made. Equally important is not to automatically equate concerns about immigration, or wanting less immigration, with racism – which is the error pro-immigration advocates have often made, and which *also* contributes to the polarization that has haunted migration debates for too long.

Racism is not about migration per se. It is often directed at people who are not migrants at all, such as African–Americans or Native Americans in the US or Romani in Europe, and Jews throughout Western history. But it is often historically intertwined with human mobility, such as the European invasion of other continents and the subjugation and enslavement of non-European peoples. Modern racism has its roots in colonialism, and the concomitant need to invent an ideology that would justify the denial of human rights to non-European peoples through their dehumanization. Only by casting people's cultural and genetic features as 'inferior' could Europeans justify their 'civilizing mission'. The control of non-white labour was always central to the colonial economies – and the consequences of this unequal treatment can still be felt today.

Racism is still a formidable problem – as we have seen in this book, it seriously reduces people's chances of obtaining a good education, internships and jobs, prevents access to better housing, and limits their ability to escape poverty, social isolation and segregation. Migrants and ethnic minorities also remain the disproportionate target of institutional discrimination and racial profiling. This highlights the continued need to raise awareness of the damage racism continues to inflict on societies, and continue fighting discrimination by securing equal opportunities.

On the other hand, the evidence gives no reason to succumb to doom-and-gloom visions about growing racism and xenophobia. It is easy to forget that in earlier periods, politicians and even academics used openly racist language against immigrants and minorities. We come from a deeply racist past, when fears about the 'Black Peril', Jewish conspiracies and invasions by 'racially inferior' migrants threatening to dilute the 'superior' white race were commonplace.

We have come a long way since the late nineteenth century, when Max Weber called Polish migrant workers a '*tiefstehende Rasse*' that threatened to displace German farmers, and since the early twentith century, when Edward Ross argued that white Americans were committing 'race suicide' by admitting southern Europeans and those of 'African, Saracen, and Mongolian blood', and Edwin Grant, another sociologist, called for 'a systematic deportation' to eugenically cleanse America of the 'Scum from the Melting-Pot' (see chapter 4).

In 1968, the British Conservative member of parliament Enoch Powell gave his infamous 'Rivers of Blood' speech to warn against the dangers of the mass settlement of immigrants – from the Indian subcontinent and the Caribbean – which would make Englishmen feel like 'strangers in their own country'.[23] Powell claimed that immigrants had arrived 'with a view to the exercise of actual domination, first over fellow-immigrants and then over the rest of the population' and that 'it is like watching a nation busily engaged in heaping up its own funeral pyre'.[24] Powell predicted that, if nothing was done to stop immigration and send back migrant workers, Britain could expect US-style interracial violence.

The South Asian and Caribbean descendants of the migrants Powell was fomenting against are now largely considered a full part of the British nation – and in recent decades, many have reached the highest political, economic and academic echelons. There has been a broad trend away from the overt racism, prejudice and discrimination that were still common not that long ago. On a more sceptical note, one could perhaps say that as 'old migrants' have increasingly become part of 'us', politicians have found new targets – in the case of the UK, asylum seekers, illegal migrants and East European immigrants. While this is partly true, it would be too harsh to deny the real progress that has been made.

Though racism and racist violence by nativist groups remain huge problems, the evidence challenges the assumption that people have become *increasingly* racist or xenophobic. This shows that tough-on-immigration politicians often make a caricature of public opinion, as it is simply not true that public opinion has massively turned against immigration.

The evidence also questions the idea that xenophobia is the result of increasing immigration and diversity. In fact, it rather suggests that we have to turn the causality upside down. In the longer run, immigration and the resulting growing familiarity with different people and cultures tend to *decrease* xenophobia and lead to more positive attitudes towards immigrants and minorities. If anything, this exemplifies the extraordinary absorption capacity of destination societies to deal with immigration. When people get used to the presence of immigrants and the racial 'other', opinions tend to get more subtle, particularly in the longer term. The more people see, meet and get to know immigrants and minorities, the less likely they are to resort to xenophobic extremism. This gives reason for hope and reasoned optimism about the potential for better, more nuanced ways to discuss – and deal with – issues of immigration race and diversity.

Myth 19: Smuggling is the cause of illegal migration

Media images and political rhetoric often convey apocalyptic visions of an increasingly massive exodus of people fleeing poverty and war at home, and desperately trying to enter the West via dangerous overland journeys through forests and deserts or by cramming themselves into unseaworthy boats that can barely stay afloat. These narratives also depict migrants and refugees as victims of 'unscrupulous' and 'merciless' criminal gangs and ruthless mafias. By painting rosy pictures about life and work in the Wealthy West, these criminals trick poor people into paying large sums of money to get smuggled across borders, but instead of providing a safe passage, they force migrants into treacherous and potentially lethal situations, often abandoning them on the way.

Smugglers and international crime syndicates seem to be running massive scams – cashing in, but failing to deliver the services they have promised. Many migrants and refugees get stuck in countries of transit, as they run out of money to migrate any further, and often fall victim to abusive police and violent gangs. Every year, thousands of migrants die from thirst while trying to pass through the desert into the United States, or from drowning while crossing the Mediterranean into Europe. Those lucky enough to make it to the Wealthy West then find their dreams shattered as they are forced to work in exploitative and slave-like conditions by abusive employers. The grim reality of being a *clandestino* is a far cry from the dreams sold by unscrupulous smugglers.

The narrative of smugglers preying on the vulnerability and desperation of migrants and refugees has come to dominate our collective imagination when it comes to illegal migration. Politicians have indulged in showing moral outrage about these practices, and have vowed to root them out. This resonates with the widespread idea that smugglers' criminal activities are the root cause of illegal migration and the large-scale arrival of asylum seekers at the border. Or, as the United Nations Office on Drugs and Crime (UNODC) summarized: 'The system of migrant smuggling . . . has become nothing more than a mechanism for robbing and murdering some of the poorest people of the world.'[1]

According to the International Organization for Migration (IOM), smuggling is 'a global threat to migration governance, national security and the well-being of migrants', while 'criminal networks profit significantly from this situation'.[2] In 2021, UK Home Secretary Priti Patel vowed to 'smash the criminal gangs who cause such misery', reiterating her determination to 'break their business model'.[3] Across the Atlantic, we hear similar rhetoric: in 2022, the Biden administration launched an 'unprecedented' operation to disrupt human smuggling networks and prevent Central American 'migrant caravans' from moving north, boasting of an 'all-of-government effort to attack the smuggling organizations'.[4]

The conclusion seems clear: we should combat smuggling to prevent criminals from further abusing poor people who harbour unrealistic expectations about life and work in the West. This view has united governments and international organizations in their determination to win the war against smuggling. Politicians often talk about the need to undermine the business model of smugglers by stepping up border controls and introducing harsher punishments. As part of such crackdowns, since the early 1990s governments have invested more and more money, equipment and personnel into border enforcement. Countries have criminalized the provision of assistance to illegal migrants by humanitarian organizations or individual citizens. Governments have built border fences, and been involved in 'pushbacks' by towing back migrant boats or deporting asylum seekers back across borders.

How it really works

Smuggling is a reaction to border controls, not the cause of illegal migration

The suffering of migrants and refugees in the various borderlands of the world is a pressing humanitarian problem. Although illegal migration represents a minority of all migration globally, this can never be a reason to trivialize or diminish the agony, suffering and exploitation of vulnerable groups of migrants and refugees. However, notwithstanding politicians' repeated promises, nearly four decades of anti-smuggling crackdowns have failed to stop illegal migration, while the suffering of migrants and refugees has intensified rather than diminished. Why have governments failed to stop migrants from crossing borders illegally? Why have anti-smuggling crackdowns utterly failed to produce any tangible results?

This is not a moral or ethical question, but a question about the long-term *effectiveness* of such policies, which surprisingly few journalists ever ask about. Why has the US failed to stop people from crossing borders despite almost forty years of increasing resources poured into fences, and border patrols to track down smugglers? Why has the UK never managed to prevent migrants and asylum seekers from crossing the Channel, despite draconian measures to secure British borders? Why has 'Fortress Europe' turned out to be a pipe dream? Does this mean that we should do our best to seal off our borders and introduce even harsher punishments for smugglers? Should we just invest yet more money and resources in border enforcement?

The evidence shows that increased border enforcement is not only unlikely to solve the problem, but is actually likely to make things worse. The idea that smuggling crackdowns will reduce illegal immigration is based on false assumptions about the causes of illegal migration. While politicians and international organizations perpetuate the myth that smugglers are responsible for the suffering of migrants and refugees, the truth is that smuggling is a reaction to border controls, not the cause of illegal migration.

Since the 1990s, persistent demand for migrant workers in agriculture, construction and services in destination countries has not been matched by legal migration opportunities for migrant workers. In contrast, governments have tried to prevent them from arriving. They have primarily done so by introducing travel visa requirements for migrant workers who could previously come and go freely, and enforcing those requirements by increasing border controls. As we know, the growing mismatch between labour demand and border policies has prompted increasing numbers of workers to cross borders illegally, or to overstay their visas or temporary work permits.

Although travel visas are not formally about immigration, governments use them to block the entry of visitors they see as potential overstayers. Using data we collected at Oxford University's International Migration Institute (IMI) for the DEMIG project (see chapter 16), map 4

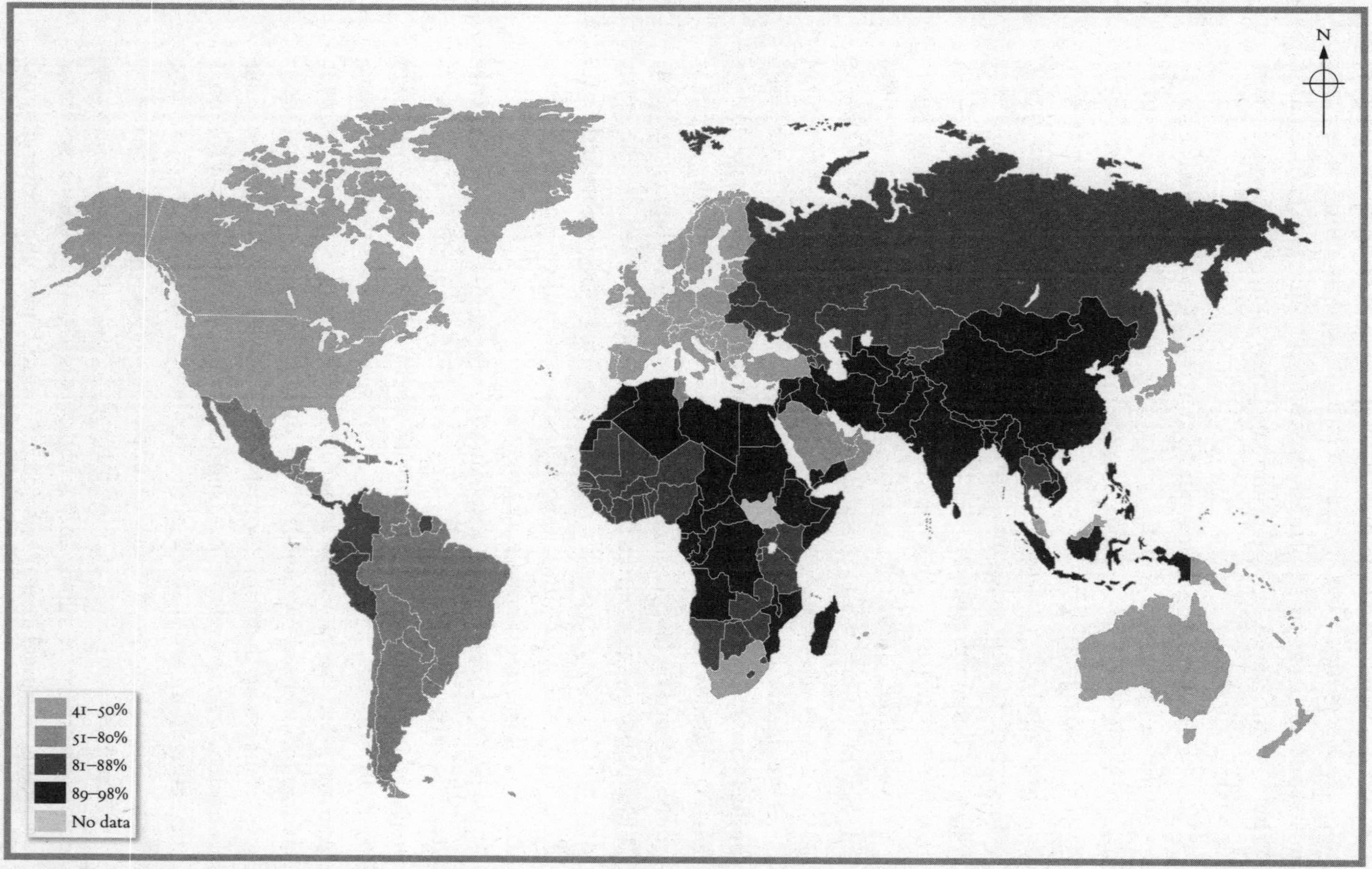

Map 4: Travel visa restrictiveness – degree to which citizens of each country need a visa to travel[5]

shows the degree to which citizens of each country in the world need a visa to travel to other countries. A score of 50 means that citizens of a particular country need a visa for half of the countries of the world; a score of 100 means they need visas for all countries.

The map shows a clear pattern. Citizens of large parts of Africa as well as the Middle East and South and South East Asia need a visa to travel to the large majority of other countries. While Latin Americans have comparatively high travel freedoms, they do face considerable travel restrictions to key Western migration destinations. For instance, because of visa requirements since 1965, Mexicans and other Latin Americans can no longer enter the US freely, a policy increasingly enforced since 1986.

Governments tried to prevent asylum seekers from arriving by compelling airlines to check passports and visas before passengers were allowed to board planes. Such carrier sanctions prompted asylum seekers to join illegal migrants in their overland and maritime journeys. Governments reacted by further ramping up border enforcement. The result was that migrants and refugees started to buy the services of smugglers in order to cross borders. As border enforcement made it more and more difficult to cross borders without being detected, migrants became even more dependent on the services of smugglers. So, the introduction of visas drove migration underground. For example, boat migration across the Channel to the UK in the early 2020s was dominated by Albanians, mainly because Albania is the only country in western and central Europe whose citizens still need a visa to enter the UK.

Because governments keep on recycling the same failed solutions to the same problems, they not only fail to address the problems, but actually make matters worse. Instead of eradicating smuggling, increased border enforcement has made labour migrants and refugees only *more* dependent on smugglers. The militarization of border controls has also prompted refugees and migrants to take longer and more dangerous routes, and to pay increasingly large sums of money to smugglers in order to make ever-longer journeys. In the absence of legal migration channels, border controls *increase* migrants' dependence on smugglers. Governments therefore seem caught in a vicious cycle of more border enforcement → more smuggling → more border enforcement → more smuggling, and so on, from which it seems difficult to escape.

Gap years no more

So, the policies implemented to 'solve' the problem of illegal migration are themselves *part of the problem*. For instance, the starting shot of trans-Mediterranean boat migration was fired in 1991, when Spain and Italy introduced visa requirements for North Africans as part of the Schengen agreement.[6] Before that, Moroccans, Tunisians and Algerians could travel freely to southern Europe, to go on holiday, explore opportunities or work for a few months or years. And so they did, in significant numbers. This migration was largely 'circular', meaning that most North Africans would travel back and forth a lot – Moroccans mainly to Spain, and Tunisians often to Italy.

During my research stays in Morocco, I spoke with men who were middle-aged but who in their younger years would often hop on the ferry from Morocco to Spain – eight miles across the Strait of Gibraltar – for extended trips, often for a combination of pleasure and work. They might spend a few weeks or months on a farm or a construction site before returning home – and then go back the next year, which was easy as no visas were needed. Their accounts of these trips were generally ones of adventure, discovery and falling in love, their eyes glowing with nostalgia.

This has always struck me as not entirely unlike the way young Westerners often have gap years abroad after finishing secondary school, to explore what life and the world have to offer. Western youth still enjoy this huge privilege – freedom of mobility – while hardly being aware of it. And this is what my Moroccan friends would tell me when I was young and I told them that Morocco was such a beautiful country: 'But you can come and go whenever you want. For us, this is like a prison, we can't just get out.'

For many, being young is about exploring the world and discovering what life has to offer. When my Moroccan colleague, geography professor Mohamed Berriane, did research on migrants from Senegal and other West African countries in Morocco, he discovered that many of these young men and women – who are usually portrayed as poor and destitute, or as victims of traffickers and smugglers – cast their own migration as an 'adventure': trying out life in a different country, often working along the way, seeing how far they can go, not sure about where they will end up and whether to stay or go.[7] Given the close historical and religious connections between the countries, it has always been completely normal for Senegalese to travel to Morocco – for work, study, or pilgrimage – and they don't even need a visa; although attitudes seem to have hardened, with European governments putting pressure on Morocco to stop what they frame as 'transit migration'.

How migration was driven underground

Until the border was closed in 1991, young Moroccan men would have seen their migration to Spain as a largely temporary venture. This circular migration had many advantages. Migrants could benefit from the job opportunities and higher salaries abroad, while spending the rest of their time with family at home, where life was cheaper. Because they did not need a visa, only a passport to cross borders, they could easily re-migrate to Spain if they needed extra cash. All it took was a ferry ticket. For this reason, Moroccan immigrant communities in Spain remained very small, as most had little reason to stay permanently or bring their families over.

Before 1991, these open borders worked like a revolving door, with migrants constantly travelling back and forth between Africa and Europe – and there was barely any permanent settlement in Spain. However, increasing immigration restrictions stopped these revolving doors from working, as they threw a spanner in the flexible mechanism of constant coming and going. With the introduction of Schengen visas in 1991, free entry into Spain and Italy was blocked, and as it was difficult to get visas, North Africans started to cross the Mediterranean illegally in *pateras* (small fishing boats). This was initially a small-scale, relatively innocent operation run by local fishermen in need of extra cash.

However, when Spain started to install early-warning quasi-military border control radar systems along the Strait of Gibraltar in the 1990s, crossing the Mediterranean or the land borders with Ceuta and Melilla – two Spanish exclaves on the Moroccan coast – became more difficult. The time of Moroccan 'gap years' in Spain was over once and for all. Smuggling professionalized, and migrants started to fan out over an increasingly diverse array of crossing points on the long Mediterranean and Atlantic coastlines. The diversification of crossing points continued over the 2000s, when migrants started to cross not only from Morocco and Tunisia, but also Algeria and Libya to Italy and Spain, and from the West African coast towards the Canary Islands.

This unintentionally increased the geographical area that border control agents 'had' to cover, spanning almost the entire Mediterranean coastline and measuring 28,600 miles in total, islands included.[8] Increased border enforcement also meant that the business of smuggling became more professional, while the length, cost and risks of migration increased, with growing numbers of migrants dying on the journey. The diversification of smuggling routes went along with a diversification of origin countries. In the 1990s, most people crossing the Mediterranean were young North Africans attracted by labour shortages in the booming agriculture and construction sectors of Italy and Spain. Since the 2000s, an increasing number of aspiring migrant workers from sub-Saharan African countries such as Senegal, Mali, Guinea, Ghana and Nigeria have joined this cross-Mediterranean boat migration.[9]

Over the 2000s, these labour migrants were increasingly joined by refugees fleeing conflict and oppression in countries like Somalia, Eritrea and the Democratic Republic of Congo, as they could no longer travel by plane to Europe to apply for asylum because of carrier sanctions. While prospective migrant workers would continue to try to sneak across borders without being detected, refugees would apply for asylum on arrival. However, as Spain and Italy signed 're-admission agreements' with Morocco and Tunisia – in which the latter countries agreed to take back illegal migrants who entered Europe from their territories – more and more aspiring migrant workers who did get caught at the border applied for asylum upon arrival to avoid deportation.

From 2014, increased maritime border patrolling in the Mediterranean caused yet another reorientation of smuggling routes – towards Turkey, the Balkans and central Europe. This was reinforced by the large-scale movement of Syrian refugees from Turkey to Greece in 2015 and 2016. Increased border enforcement in the Aegean Sea after 2016 would again reorient smuggling routes to the central Mediterranean – from Libya and Tunisia to Italy and Malta, from Morocco to Spain, and from the West African coast to the Canary Islands.

Map 5 shows how increasing border controls unintentionally led to a huge diversification of terrestrial and maritime migration routes beyond the initial main crossing point across the Strait of Gibraltar separating

Morocco and Spain.[10] So, massive investments in border enforcement did not stop smuggling, but rather set in motion an endless cat-and-mouse game between border patrollers and smugglers, who constantly shifted routes and strategies to keep their business going.

Growing dependency on smugglers

Across the Atlantic, in almost exactly the same way as in the Mediterranean, the militarization of border controls on the US–Mexico border since the 1990s has increased the reliance of migrants and refugees on smugglers ('coyotes') to cross borders, while increasingly long waiting lists for family reunification have also prompted family members of US migrants to cross borders illegally. Increasing border controls has led to a diversification of migration routes, with migrants and smugglers undertaking longer and more dangerous journeys – such as through the Sonoran Desert – while costs have gone up accordingly.[11]

Successive US governments have pressed for Mexico to prevent the movement of Central Americans over its territory in exchange for financial support. As a result, migrants and asylum seekers have increasingly become the target of systematic violence by state agents and criminal gangs. However, instead of solving any of these problems, border enforcement has only increased migrants' dependency on smuggling services and made them more vulnerable to violence, exploitation and abuse – whether by smugglers, police or border guards, or temporary employers for whom many work to pay for the next leg of the journey in Mexico.[12]

For the same reason, successive UK governments have failed to stop illegal migration across the English Channel. Tougher entry restrictions for prospective migrant workers, asylum seekers and people seeking to join family members have increased the number of migrants trying to cross the Channel illegally, often hidden in trucks on UK-bound ferries or on the train through the tunnel connecting France and Britain.

Since the 1990s, this has prompted the establishment of spontaneous border camps in northern France for people waiting for an opportunity to cross. Attempts to crack down on illegal migration across the Channel, and the razing of the border camps, have not stopped migrants from trying to cross the border but rather have led to a rerouting of migration routes. In the 2010s, growing numbers of migrants and asylum

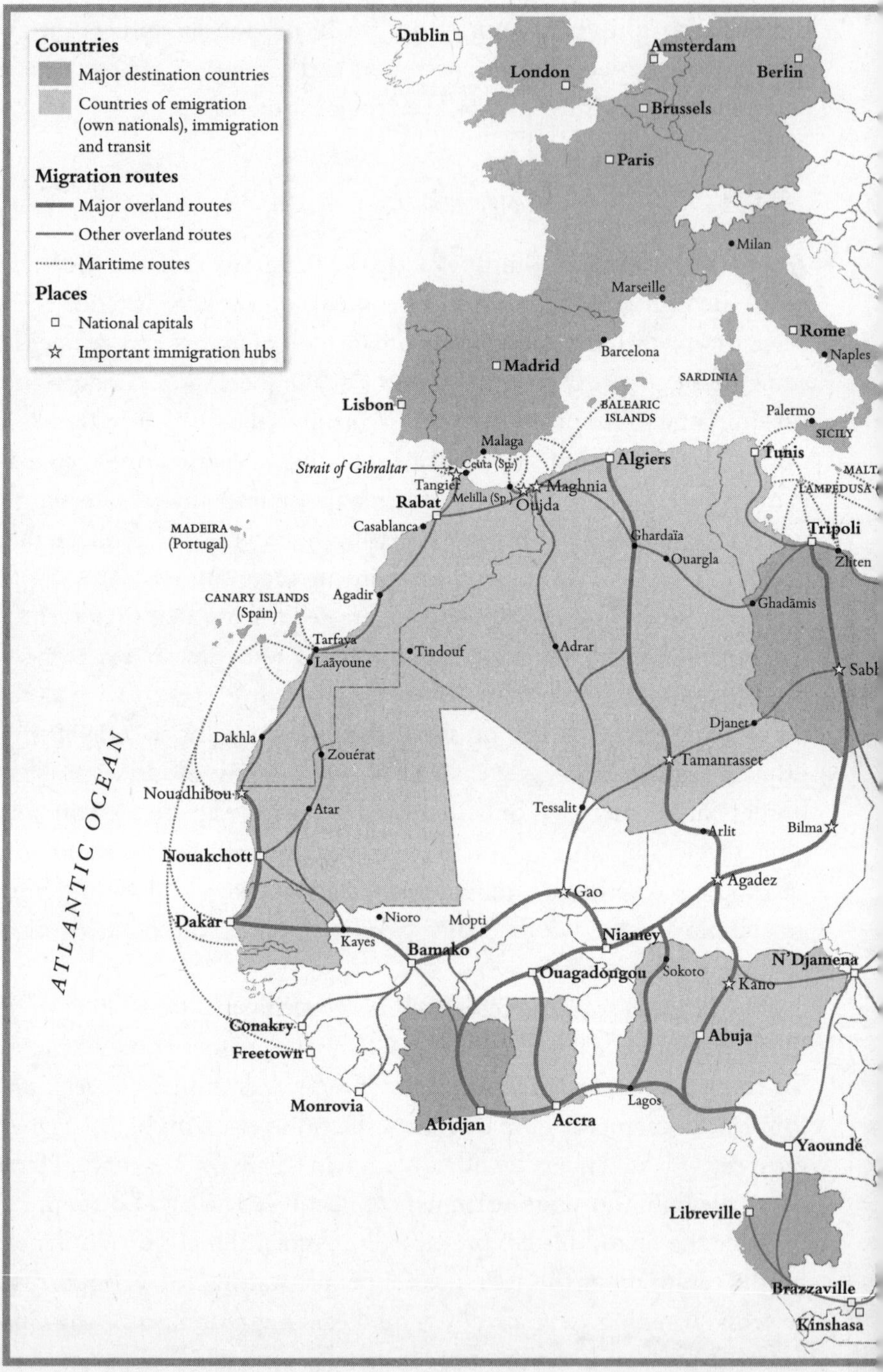

Map 5: Overland and maritime migration routes to North Africa, the Middle East and western Europe[13]

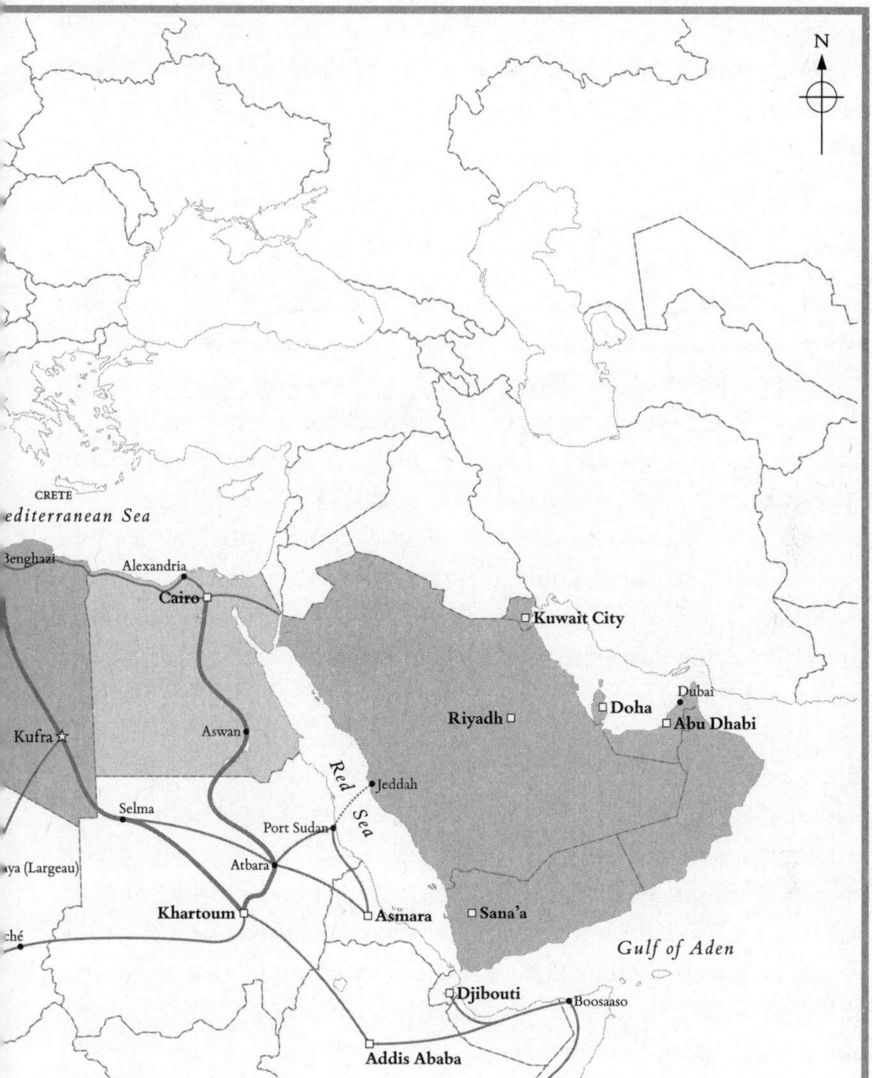
N
CRETE
editerranean Sea
Benghazi
Alexandria
Cairo
Kuwait City
Dubai
Doha
Abu Dhabi
Riyadh
Aswan
Kufra
Red Sea
Jeddah
Selma
Port Sudan
Atbara
ya (Largeau)
Khartoum
Asmara
Sana'a
Gulf of Aden
ché
Djibouti
Boosaaso
Addis Ababa
gui
Mogadishu
INDIAN OCEAN
0 400 800 km
0 200 400 600 miles

seekers tried to embark as stowaways on UK-bound ferries from Belgium and the Netherlands, instead of leaving from France. Since Brexit, a growing number of prospective migrant workers and asylum seekers have embarked on smaller, smuggler-operated boats leaving from the French coast.

Smuggling is not the same as trafficking

The image of smugglers tricking migrants and refugees into dangerous journeys is generally misleading. Media and politicians contribute to this misunderstanding by systematically confounding smuggling with trafficking. These two terms are often equated, but mean quite different things, and to understand the causes of illegal migration it is crucial to get the distinction right. In fact, trafficking does not have to involve any migration at all. As we will see in the next chapter, trafficking is about the severe exploitation of vulnerable workers through deceit and coercion. Smuggling is about service delivery, with migrants and refugees voluntarily paying money to smugglers to cross borders safely and avoid being caught by the police, border guards or criminals. The vast majority of illegal border crossings involve smuggling, with migrants and refugees buying services that help them to cross closed borders.

This is a very important distinction because it is a source of many misunderstandings about migration, and the media consistently gets it wrong. For instance, in October 2019, thirty-nine aspiring migrant workers from Vietnam were tragically found dead inside a truck trailer in Essex in south-east England. Soon, media reported that they were 'trafficked' to Britain via China and France, whereas in reality this was about smuggling, with migrants and their families paying large sums of money to make the passage to the UK, where they planned to work. So, when the news media and politicians report that 'migrants are being trafficked', that generally doesn't make much sense, as it gives the impression that migrants are being forced to cross borders – as if it were against their own will, as if they were passive victims or a piece of merchandise.

Smuggling is a form of service delivery

As with most forms of illegal, uncontrolled service delivery, there are regular cases of deceit, violence and extortion, and the most dramatic cases are what we typically hear about in the media. These are the stories of people being abandoned by smugglers in the middle of the desert or the sea, or of smugglers setting up rackets with police and border guards. As routes get longer, and risks increase, sometimes things go horribly wrong, as in the case of the fifty-three Mexican and Central American migrants found dead in a hot, airless tractor-trailer in San Antonio, Texas, in June 2022,[14] and the thousands of migrants and refugees dying in the desert or drowning in the sea every year.

However, the key point is that such experiences are not *representative*. Most migrants will eventually slip through borders without being detected. Although deceit does occur and accidents do happen – particularly when border enforcement forces them to use longer and more dangerous routes – smugglers generally have an interest in delivering, as their reputation enables them to stay in business. In addition, migrants usually demand safeguards. It is quite common for migrants to give only part of the smuggling fee upfront, and the other part upon arrival. Payment in instalments ensures that services are delivered.

Another common misunderstanding is that smugglers are part of international organized crime or centralized, hierarchical, mafia-like structures or criminal gangs. Gang violence is a serious problem, and Mexican drug cartels are increasingly involved in kidnapping migrants and refugees for ransom. Practices of extortion, threat and killings also cause internal displacement within Mexico.[15] However, numerous studies from around the world have shown that gangs or mafias do not generally organize smuggling. In fact, the very reason migrants buy the services of smugglers is to keep themselves away from criminals, as well as the abusive state agents that often collaborate with them. Smugglers' core business is to provide migrants with a safe passage, which is why migrants are willing to pay for their services.[16]

Smuggling is generally about families helping each other, or local operators running small-scale operations. Several studies by Gabriella Sanchez, an anthropologist who has done extensive research on the US–Mexico border, have shown that most smugglers are small operators, and are often former migrants themselves. Contrary to common stereotypes, Sanchez found that women and children play an important role in smuggling operations, recruiting customers, negotiating fees and payment plans, withdrawing smuggling payments from banks, caring for migrants, and driving or guiding groups of border crossers through the desert.[17] She also found that, worldwide, most people convicted for smuggling are in fact independent operators, working on behalf of friends and family members seeking to be with their loved ones, or they are migrants themselves trying to reach a destination.[18]

Julien Brachet, a French geographer who spent years doing fieldwork in towns and oases in the Sahara Desert, found that for migrants from sub-Saharan African countries who try to cross the Sahara on their way to North Africa through countries like Niger and Libya, the biggest dangers they face are abusive or corrupt policemen, border agents and soldiers, who exact informal tolls and bribes and may strip migrants of money and essential assets such as mobile phones.[19]

Brachet's research has also confirmed that, contrary to the stereotypical images of international mafias, smugglers tend to be small-scale operators who have a good knowledge of local routes and circumstances. They are often former nomads, migrants or ex-migrants, who sometimes cooperate with corrupt police and border officials. For decades, local traders and truck drivers have played an important role in smuggling migrants across the Sahara Desert. Such operators combined people smuggling with other business – typically cross-border trade and the smuggling of goods. This kind of mixed transport has become less usual because of the EU-driven hardening of border controls in the Sahara, and the subsequent professionalization of people smuggling. Migrants typically keep paying smugglers for one difficult leg of the journey at a time.[20] In North and West Africa, people who smuggle migrants in *pateras* and *pirogues* (fishing boats) are often current or former fishermen.[21]

Migrants are not stupid

Ultimately, the question is not whether smugglers are 'good' or 'bad'. Some are good people, some are bad people, many are trustworthy, others will try to deceive you, others are volunteers, some are criminals. The bottom line is that smugglers provide a service that migrants and refugees are willing to pay for. Cases that reach the media – when things go wrong, when boats sink, when migrants are abandoned in the desert – are not representative. In the vast majority of cases, smugglers deliver their services. Rather than criminals who trick migrants into dangerous journeys, smugglers are the only hope – or a necessary evil – for people aspiring to cross borders.

Smuggling doesn't necessarily have to involve payment. Driving a family member, friend or acquaintance across borders is probably the most common form of smuggling. In Morocco, a popular and relatively safe way to move illegally to Europe is to hide in the vehicles of family members when they return from their summer holidays. When I interviewed young would-be migrants in Morocco, they listed a whole range of possible legal and illegal migration methods – ranging from visa overstaying, document forgery, travelling with papers of 'lookalike' persons, hiding in trucks, cars or vans – and they would carefully balance their options, often indicating that the smugglers' boats were generally the least preferred option.

Smuggling can also happen voluntarily, out of humanitarian motives, without any payment. Humanitarian activists or ordinary citizens often assist migrants and refugees to cross borders, sometimes simply by giving them a ride. In August 2016, Cédric Herrou, a French farmer, was arrested because he had helped migrants and asylum seekers to cross the French–Italian border. He was a smuggler, too.[22] And so were the people who helped Jews escape Nazi-occupied territory during the Second World War. And those who helped people escape from the Eastern Bloc during the Cold War.

For most people who engage with smugglers, emigration is not an act of desperation, but a deliberate investment in a better future which requires careful planning. As harsh as it may sound, even the risk of dying is not a significant deterrent. The International Organization of Migration has estimated that, between 2014 and 2022, at least 53,000 migrants died while trying to cross borders: half of them (26,000) in the Mediterranean, the most lethal border area in the world; 12,000 in Africa; and 7,400 in the Americas.

But that hasn't deterred migrants from crossing – if anything, it has made them more dependent than ever on smugglers to *avoid* dying en route or being caught. When Senegalese economist Linguère Mously Mbaye analysed survey data she collected in Dakar, she found out that prospective migrants who planned to undertake the dangerous trip to the Canary Islands across the Atlantic were aware of the risk of dying but were willing to take it. She also found they had remarkably realistic expectations about the wages they could earn in Spain and France, their favoured destinations. This showed that their migration was a rational, deliberate undertaking, for which they had prepared carefully, and that they were drawn by real work opportunities.[23]

For refugees, smugglers are often the only hope to get out. As authoritarian regimes want to prevent people from fleeing, many refugees need to hire smugglers to leave their country. Only by using smugglers' services have refugees all over the world been able to escape violence and persecution by brutal dictatorships. For instance, many Iranians who fled the Ayatollah regime used smugglers to cross deserts and mountains in an attempt to escape to Afghanistan. Most smugglers will charge refugees as they charge other migrants, but sometimes people will smuggle refugees voluntarily. In those cases, smugglers can be true heroes.

The real migration industry

Because smuggling is a reaction to border controls, there is no point blaming smugglers for causing illegal migration, as this will not solve any problems. So why do governments continue to recycle costly policies that have proved to be ineffective and even counterproductive, and which come with a high human toll? First of all, it reflects the unwillingness and inability of governments to align their migration policies with the economic reality on the ground. The truth is that, in the absence of legal migration channels and the ability to freely circulate as in a not-too-distant past, labour demand is the driving force making migrants cross borders illegally. It is then much more convenient for politicians to blame smugglers instead of pointing the finger at themselves – and taking responsibility for getting us into this mess.

Another part of the answer is that blaming smugglers is an effective strategy to divert attention away from the interests of the multibillion-dollar military-industrial complex in border controls. Governments have invested massive amounts of taxpayers' money in border surveillance. Businesses involved in building, maintaining and operating electronic border surveillance systems, walls and fences, patrolling vessels and vehicles, the migrant detention and deportation industry as well as the military have a vested interest in making the public believe that we are facing an impending migration invasion and that we therefore need to be 'fighting' and 'combating' smugglers, as if we are indeed waging a war.

This reveals the contours of the real migration industry. Not smugglers, but arms and technology companies have reaped the main windfalls from the West's fight against illegal migration. According to a series of investigations by the Migrants' Files – a consortium of European journalists – EU countries paid €2.3 billion in taxpayer money to border enforcement between 2000 and 2014, while deportations had a price tag of at least €11.3 billion.[24] A further billion euros was spent on coordination efforts to control European borders, mainly through Frontex, Europe's border agency. Between 2012 and 2022, the annual budget of Frontex ballooned almost ninefold, from €85 to €754 million.[25]

Four leading European arms manufacturers – Airbus (formerly EADS), Thales, Finmeccanica and BAE – and technology firms like Saab, Indra, Siemens and Diehl are among the prime beneficiaries of EU spending on military-grade technology supplied by these privately held companies. Frontex employs over 1,900 staff members, more than 900 of whom are part of the European Border and Coast Guard standing corps, to be deployed in Frontex operations on the ground. For its 2021–7 budget cycle, the EU plans to expand this standing corps to around 10,000 border guards. In total, the EU budget for 'migration and border management' for 2021–7 is €22.7 billion, up from €13 billion in 2014–20.[26]

Across the Atlantic, an even bigger migration industry has emerged on the US–Mexico border. In a 2013 study, the Migration Policy Institute (MPI), a migration think tank based in Washington, DC, calculated that the US government spent $187 billion on federal immigration enforcement between 1986 and 2012. To put this into perspective, the $18 billion spent on border enforcement in 2012 alone was 24 per cent higher than the combined costs of all other principal federal criminal law enforcement agencies (FBI, Drug Enforcement Administration, Secret Service, US Marshals Service and Bureau of Alcohol, Tobacco, Firearms and Explosives).[27] And, as in Europe, costs have continued to rise: in 2018, the US border enforcement budget rose to $24 billion – now 33 per cent higher than other criminal enforcement agencies.[28] The 2018 FBI budget was $8.5 billion, three times lower than the border enforcement budget.

So, on both sides of the Atlantic, massive investments in border controls have created a hugely profitable market for the private companies implementing them. However, a focus on border enforcement alone is bound to fail as long as it ignores the real causes of illegal migration. The truth is that as long as there is demand for migrant workers, as long as politicians turn a blind eye to the illegal employment of migrant workers, and as long as violent conflict occurs, people will keep on finding ways across borders. The more governments try to prevent this, the more migrants become dependent on smugglers.

It is an illusion that the long US–Mexico and Mediterranean borders can be completely sealed off. This doesn't mean that immigration policies are a total failure. As we have seen, the large majority of people migrate legally. And for the most part, migration controls work. The point is more that destination-country demand for lower-skilled workers will inevitably continue to produce illegal migration as long as governments don't provide legal ways of entering. Even totalitarian states cannot achieve total migration control. One way or another, migrants will continue to find ways to get in, with smugglers helping them.

As long as people have good reasons to migrate, border controls will clearly not deter them from coming. There is no easy 'solution' to this problem, but the solutions of the past have been a waste of taxpayers' money and have not only been ineffective but have made problems worse. The fact is that migrants and refugees use smugglers' services because of a lack of legal migration channels. Immigration restrictions and border controls increase the market for smuggling and the costs and dangers of overland and maritime journeys. This has led to increased suffering and a rising death toll, but it hasn't deterred migrants from coming over in the past, and it's unlikely to do so in the future. Policies to 'combat' smuggling are bound to fail, because they are among the very causes of the phenomenon they pretend to 'fight'.

Myth 20: Trafficking is a form of modern slavery

In *Taken*, a blockbuster action movie released in 2008, Kim, the seventeen-year-old daughter of American ex-CIA officer Bryan Mills (played by Liam Neeson), is abducted by Albanian traffickers while on holiday in Paris. Bryan travels to Paris, where he heroically manages, after killing scores of Albanian traffickers, to rescue Kim – who has been drugged into semi-conscious subservience – from being auctioned off as a sex slave to an Arab sheikh on a luxury yacht moored in the Seine.

This is the common understanding many people have of trafficking. Another widespread image is of poor teenage girls and young women in developing countries, who are tricked into migrating to cities or Western countries based on false promises about nice jobs and glamorous lifestyles, only to find themselves coerced into sex work or other forced labour in the most appalling circumstances. Every year, international trafficking rings allegedly smuggle large numbers of illegal workers across borders – to the Gulf, Europe and America – where they are forced to work in agriculture, mines, sweatshops, restaurants, domestic service, beauty parlours and brothels.

Trafficking is reported as being a multibillion-dollar industry run by international mafias who ruthlessly exploit some of the most vulnerable people in the world. Characterizing trafficking as the 'multibillion-dollar sale of people', the United Nations Office for Drugs and Crime (UNODC) has claimed human trafficking is the third-largest criminal industry in the world, after arms and drug dealing, and that the global trafficking industry makes an estimated $32 billion annually through sexual exploitation, forced labour, domestic servitude, child begging and the removal of organs.[1]

According to the US Institute Against Human Trafficking, there are 'hundreds of thousands, and potentially over a million' victims trapped in the world of sex trafficking in the US alone.[2] Recent estimates of the numbers of 'modern slaves' have sent shockwaves through the international community. In 2017, for instance, the UN's International

Labour Organization (ILO) and Walk Free, an anti-slavery NGO, published a joint report – funded by Walk Free – that claimed that an estimated 40.3 million people, women and children in particular, are living in some form of modern slavery.[3] According to the report, most 'modern slaves' are involved with cleaning houses and flats, producing clothes, picking fruits and vegetables, fishing, mining minerals and working in construction. This prompted Andrew Forrest, an Australian billionaire and founder of Walk Free, to declare: 'We now have the largest number of slaves on Earth that we've had in human history.'[4]

In 2019, the *Guardian* newspaper used these numbers to argue that the current number of 'modern slaves' is 'more than three times the figure during the transatlantic slave trade'.[5] This claim was based on estimates that 12 million Africans were forcibly taken to the Americas through the transatlantic slave trade – compared to 40.3 million 'modern slaves' now.[6] This resonates with news headlines about the severe exploitation of Asian and African domestic workers in Arab Gulf states who find themselves locked up, beaten, raped or even murdered by their employers. In recent years, news about the horrific treatment of construction workers in Arab Gulf states – such as those building the football stadiums for the 2022 World Cup in Qatar – led to eruptions of international outrage.

Everybody seems to agree that human trafficking is one of the most brutal, evil and heinous forms of crime. International outrage has prompted politicians, philanthropists and international organizations to vow to eradicate modern slavery by viciously cracking down on trafficking syndicates, and by putting in all efforts to rescue trafficking victims from the tentacles of criminals, pimps and abusive bosses. The message is clear: we need to take bold action now to save innocent victims from the criminals who exploit them. There is no time to lose: we need to end slavery *now*.

How it really works

Trafficking is not the same as slavery

It seems difficult to disagree with slogans like 'we need to end slavery now'. Who could possibly condone the kidnapping of teenage girls and young women by criminals who sell them into sex slavery? How can we justify that millions of people are forced to work long hours and live in perpetual fear of violence, rape and other forms of abuse?

Since the 2000s, the United States government has played a leading role in combating trafficking around the world and pressuring governments to comply with its standards through the Trafficking in Persons Office of the State Department. Anti-trafficking charities and NGOs have proliferated, in both rich and poor countries. Governments around the world and organizations including the International Labour Organization and the International Organization for Migration have taken a major interest in the issue and received massive funding for anti-trafficking programmes.

However, despite all these efforts, decades of anti-trafficking campaigns have failed to produce any noticeable results. In fact, the evidence shows that anti-trafficking campaigns have not only been ineffective, they have actually made the lives of alleged victims *more* miserable – by failing to provide effective protection and *increasing* their vulnerability to abuse and exploitation.

I first found out about this when I did research on the sex trafficking of Nigerian women in Italy and other European countries. In 2006, I went to Abuja, Nigeria's capital, where I interviewed government representatives, anti-trafficking organizations and humanitarian NGOs who were involved with this issue. To my astonishment, I found out that many alleged trafficking victims who were 'rescued' in Italy and flown back to Nigeria did everything they could to get back to Italy to resume their work.[7]

This showed that, despite the exploitation they may have endured, Nigerian sex workers couldn't just be reduced to victims in need of 'saving'. On the contrary, most of them were voluntary migrants and didn't consider themselves victims. Their reality was clearly more nuanced than the horror stories of girls and young women being lured into migrating illegally and sold off into sex slavery. And this didn't turn out to be an isolated case, but a common pattern: alleged victims of trafficking often don't *want* to be rescued, to the extent that one of the slogans of anti-anti-trafficking activists has even become 'rescue us from our rescuers'.

As this is a complex and sensitive topic, with so much confusion and distortion around it, it's perhaps most useful to start by pointing out what trafficking is *not*. Trafficking is rarely ever about young women being kidnapped by criminals to be sold off into sex slavery. Images and movies about teenage girls and young women being snatched from the street, forced into vans, locked up in brothels, drugged and chained to beds and forced to have sex have little to do with the reality of trafficking. There is also no evidence for the stereotype that human trafficking is a multibillion industry run by shadowy mafias and international criminal cartels trafficking large numbers of innocent women and girls across borders. The 'Hollywood version' of trafficking is the product of our imagination, and it has very little to do with the real world.[8]

The reality of trafficking is also at odds with stereotypes about poor women and men from 'Third World' countries being forcibly smuggled across borders to work as 'modern slaves' in domestic servitude, agriculture, construction and sweatshops in the West or Arab countries. Trafficking is also not about smuggling. There is immense confusion in the media and politics between smuggling and trafficking. Smuggling is a form of service delivery for which migrants pay voluntarily in order to cross borders. As we will see, trafficking is about severe labour exploitation, often happens in the context of legal migration, and doesn't have to involve migration at all.

Trafficking generally is also not about desperately poor rural families in the Global South selling their children – girls and boys – to traffickers transporting them to the big city to be resold into domestic servitude, sex slavery or forced labour in mines or on farms. Field studies done by researchers who have actually talked to presumed trafficking victims have shown that, for the vast majority, work done by minor migrants in developing countries is generally much more voluntary than it's usually framed, and that their labelling as 'modern slaves' doesn't make much sense.[9]

The whole idea of trafficking being literally about the buying, smuggling and selling of human beings, which comes down to treating other people like private property – as in slavery – is a myth. For that reason, it is inappropriate to equate the situation of exploited workers to the historical experiences of Africans who were violently abducted and shipped to the Americas to be sold off as slaves to plantation owners. Slavery implies that people can be treated by their owners or dominators as they wish with impunity, and be bought and sold at markets. By portraying trafficking victims as 'modern slaves', anti-trafficking activists and organizations not only distort the truth, but also trivialize the injustice, cruelty and violence suffered by the victims of the transatlantic slave trade and other historical forms of slavery, in which people and their descendants were reduced to property and subjected to systematic violence, rape and murder. This is why the comparison with slavery is not only inappropriate, but also unethical.

Trafficking is about the severe exploitation of vulnerable workers

In reality, trafficking is not about abduction or sex work, but about the severe exploitation of vulnerable workers through deceit and coercion. Perhaps the biggest misunderstanding – and source of much misery for exploited workers – is that trafficking often only 'counts' if victims are abducted, beaten, chained and locked up, or forced to do sex work against their own will. In fact, there seem to be no independently confirmed cases of kidnapping where victims were subsequently sold to third parties for the purposes of sex slavery or other forms of forced labour. But trafficking can involve being pressured or coerced into exploitative and dangerous situations from which the victim cannot escape. Most confirmed cases of sex trafficking seem to be an extension of various forms of domestic abuse and parental neglect, combined with other circumstances such as poverty and drug use.

These generally have nothing to do with migration or being abducted in the first place. A common pattern of sex trafficking is minors (usually teenage girls) fleeing broken or abusive homes who are 'groomed' by men posing as boyfriends but who, often after a 'honeymoon phase', subsequently start abusing them, by putting them under psychological and economic pressure to do sex work. For instance, in 2012, nine men received heavy jail sentences for their involvement in a child sex abuse ring involving forty-seven teenage girls from vulnerable backgrounds in Rochdale and Oldham in Greater Manchester, England between 2008 and 2010. The perpetrators initially groomed the girls by giving them presents, small amounts of money, alcohol and drugs, but subsequently pressured them into having sex and 'passed them around' while intimidating and bribing them into keeping quiet about being raped and forced into prostitution.[10] These are the worst cases of abuse, but they have little to do with Hollywood images of criminal gangs abducting girls off the street in broad daylight to be sold off as sex slaves. It is bad enough as it is.

In most confirmed trafficking cases, there was some level of initial consent among the victims, but they found themselves subsequently trapped in situations of exploitation and abuse from which they found it impossible to escape because of the threat of violence or because they had nowhere to go. Neither is trafficking necessarily about sex work or illegal migration. In fact, as documented by migration researchers Bridget Anderson and Ben Rogaly, many cases of extreme labour exploitation and forced labour in the UK involve migrant workers who entered the UK perfectly legally and were formally employed, often in the public sector.[11] Many other trafficking cases do not involve migrants at all.

Anti-trafficking policies are often counterproductive because they automatically assume that a particular type of work – particularly sex work, or women doing domestic work in the Gulf countries – must be forced, without properly investigating why, under what circumstances and with what level of consent migrants do this work. In this context, Janie Chuang, a professor of law at the American University and a trafficking expert, has argued that the use of increasingly vague and loose definitions of trafficking has led to 'exploitation creep', where voluntary migration and precarious work are lumped together into the same 'trafficking category'.[12]

As part of a race for funding and attention, anti-trafficking NGOs have been tempted to put more and more categories of vulnerable workers under the 'modern slavery' heading. This has hugely inflated numbers of alleged trafficking victims. But it also means that in most concrete cases of severe exploitation, workers do not receive protection when they try to find legal recourse, as their experiences almost never fit the sensationalist 'sex slave' stereotypes.

To illustrate this, Chang cites an example of approximately 300 Filipino teachers who paid roughly $17,000 each in previously undisclosed fees to a recruiter for jobs teaching in Louisiana public schools under the H1B visa programme. The recruiter threatened to have the teachers deported unless they committed to work one more year, for which they had to pay the recruiter 10 per cent of their salaries and additional recruitment fees, plus mandatory payments of hundreds of dollars of above-market costs for their mandatory substandard housing. Despite the fact they were trapped by this insurmountable debt and the recruiter's repeated threats of deportation and lawsuits, the teachers lost the initial lawsuit as jury members found that their experience didn't fit the stereotypical 'modern slavery' image of trafficking being about violence, imprisonment and illegal immigration.[13]

The 'stranger danger' inflation of trafficking statistics

So, trafficking is not about abduction, slavery, smuggling or even migration, but about abusive labour relations based on extreme power inequalities. This is in line with the official 2000 United Nations Protocol to Prevent, Suppress and Punish Trafficking in Persons, whose definition of trafficking is quite vague but revolves around coercion and the abuse of power, and which does not presume that initial consent disqualifies a person from being a trafficking victim.[14] In that sense, the etymology of the term 'human trafficking' is very unfortunate, as it evokes trade in illegal goods, like drugs and arms trafficking, in which the merchandise are goods that have no agency. For that reason, the transatlantic slave trade was human trafficking – literally the trade in human beings – as people were being reduced to goods and treated as private property, as if they were cattle.

In fact, the origins of the modern term 'trafficking' go back to the myth of 'white slavery',[15] which was deliberately created by whites in the post-abolition US of the late nineteenth century to raise suspicion about Black men allegedly abducting and sexually abusing innocent white women. This deeply racist narrative and the ensuing moral panic about Black men being sexual predators and 'taking' white women was the source of much cruelty and even led to public lynchings. The prejudices on which this narrative was based fed straight into contemporary stereotypes about trafficking as portrayed in movies like *Taken* – with 'dark' (Black, Arab, Albanian) men generally seen as the abusers, and innocent white, or Asian, women as the usual victims. It also reinforces the usual conflation of trafficking with sex slavery in the media.

These kinds of fears and stereotypes lead to the sort of moral panic that totally misrepresents the nature and causes of severe labour exploitation. The anti-trafficking industry has fabricated an image of trafficking that confirms our worst 'stranger danger' fears and conflates sex work and slavery, but that has generally little to do with reality. To attract publicity and money, they have taken an interest in misrepresenting the issue and hugely inflating the numbers. Ronald Weitzer, a professor of sociology at George Washington University and an expert on sex trafficking, has criticized anti-trafficking organizations for making up numbers, describing this activity as 'guesswork', and the mass media for uncritically reporting these unverified numbers.[16] After a long investigation into the issue, journalist Michael Hobbes similarly concluded that 'the internet is awash in exaggerated, misleading and downright fabricated numbers' about children being forced into the sex trade.[17]

The real numbers are much smaller than such claims. In the US between 2000 and 2015, federal prosecutors took on a yearly average of forty-three cases involving the sex trafficking of minors.[18] As reported by sociologist Julia O'Connell Davidson, in the UK the actual number of trafficking prosecutions is tiny compared to the usual claims made about trafficking.[19] Even if we assume that these numbers are underestimates, the overall scale is a far cry from the usual claims about millions of 'modern slaves' that come in handy to raise attention and funding, but perpetuate misconceptions of trafficking that stand in the way of effectively helping victims of severe labour exploitation, whether they are migrants or not.

Debt repayment is not the same as trafficking

Sensationalist portrayals of trafficking are not based on a true understanding of how people end up in situations of severe labour exploitation, and critically fail to acknowledge how workers might voluntarily opt to stay in such situations, as the alternative is arguably worse. This typically leads to the kind of misguided anti-trafficking operations that don't help actual victims of trafficking, but make them worse off by depriving them of their livelihoods. The main problem here is that governments and anti-trafficking NGOs exaggerate the true scale of trafficking by mislabelling most forms of migration involving sex work, smuggling or some form of debt repayment as non-consensual criminal acts. Migrant workers mislabelled as trafficking victims therefore resist being 'rescued' as this usually implies deportation and loss of income.

A common source of misunderstanding on this issue is the usual conflation between debt repayment and trafficking. Crucially, paying back debts to employers and recruiters isn't automatically the same as being trafficked. Debt repayment is a very common part of contractual arrangements between migrants and recruitment agencies, in which migration debts are for instance being repaid through salary deductions during the first months or sometimes years of employment. Sometimes, however, arrangements become so exploitative that the workers have no reasonable option of walking out or going back home without facing severe consequences – such as violence, threats to family members back home, imprisonment or deportation. At that point, when people can no longer choose not to pay their debts, and are coerced into continuing to do the work or find their most basic rights violated, it crosses the line between debt repayment and debt bondage.

Certainly it is not easy to draw a sharp line between forced labour and extremely poor working conditions.[20] Many labour situations – whether involving migrants or not – are clearly exploitative or even abusive, but that does not automatically make the workers trafficking victims. The fact alone that migrants pay back debts to recruiters, smugglers or employers does not make them 'modern slaves' in need of rescuing. Each year, millions of migrants around the world borrow money to move abroad. This is a largely *voluntary* affair. Nobody forces them to do so. Taking on debts is the way millions of poor people create a better future for themselves by migrating to the West, the Gulf and other wealthy countries – mostly legally, sometimes illegally.[21] Migrants are very keen to pay off their debts to set themselves free and be able to earn more money to send home. It would therefore be nonsensical to unilaterally cast such migrant workers as victims, since they would not consider themselves as such. Having made a huge investment of time, effort and money, many would do anything to avoid going home empty-handed, and have a strong interest in staying and paying off their debts.

In practice, rescuing means deportation

This brings us back to the case of Nigerian sex workers in Italy and elsewhere in Europe. Why do so many of them resist being 'liberated'? Each year, thousands of women from Nigeria are believed to be trafficked for sex work in Europe. For decades now, foreign donors, governments and many NGOs have run campaigns aimed at 'combating' such trafficking. However, in practice such campaigns have consistently failed. The main reason is that these women's decision to migrate was generally a voluntary one, based on a desire to create a better future and to provide for their families.[22]

Nigerians began migrating to Italy in the 1980s in response to a rising demand for workers in agriculture and services. Female sex workers were one of the many groups that migrated, and they tended to work independently. In the early 1990s, the introduction of travel visas and other immigration restrictions made emigrants, including sex workers, more and more dependent on large loans in order to pay for their journey. This created a market for intermediaries. Initial contact with recruiters is usually made through relatives, friends or acquaintances, who put prospective sex workers in touch with a 'madam' who organizes and pays for the journey. The migrant and the madam conclude a 'pact', which obliges debt repayment in exchange for a safe passage to Europe.[23]

In Europe, the women work under the supervision of the madam. Contrary to the idea that they were deceived, they actually knew what kind of work they were going to do, although they were not always fully aware of the difficult conditions in which they would have to work and the exact size of their debts. Importantly, however, this work offers some real career prospects. After repaying their debt in one to three years, the women are free, and it is fairly common for them to become madams themselves.[24]

The Nigerian government came under intense international pressure to do something about this. The Nigerian Women Trafficking and Child Labour Eradication Foundation (WOTCLEF) has run awareness campaigns to warn young women about the dangers of trafficking. In 2003, the National Agency for the Prohibition of Traffic in Persons (NAPTIP) was established to implement new anti-trafficking laws. Collaborating with organizations like IOM and UNICEF, NAPTIP was involved in the deportation of hundreds of alleged trafficking victims back to Nigeria.

However, these operations were ineffective and made the sex workers worse off. One problem was that Italian law enforcement did not distinguish between traffickers and trafficking victims, and simply labelled both as 'illegals' without further investigation. This meant that when the Italian authorities did 'sweeps' (raids), the madams were flown together with sex workers on the same deportation flight back to Nigeria.[25]

However, the biggest problem was that the supposed trafficking victims did not want to be 'rescued' in the first place. Even in the case of severe abuse, they were generally not willing to denounce traffickers, because neither the Italian nor the Nigerian government provides any form of protection or alternative employment for trafficking victims. This has drawn the criticism of Nigerian human rights NGOs, which accuse the government of being more concerned with putting on a good show and laundering its negative image abroad than protecting the alleged trafficking victims themselves.[26]

While most women involved didn't see themselves as victims, even those who needed help were not well protected and feared deportation, and they generally didn't want to denounce their madams. Their migration was not as involuntary as the slogans peddled by politicians and anti-trafficking agencies suggest. In reality, these women are actors and victims at the same time, reflecting the ambiguity of so many precarious migrant workers who voluntarily sign up to work, which despite its exploitative nature still offers a real prospect to improve their long-term well-being and is a generally much better option than staying at home.

Most sex workers are voluntary workers

Trafficking is often associated with sex work, and particularly sex workers who are migrants, but there is a clear danger in automatically conflating sex work and trafficking. Julia O'Connell Davidson argues that this conflation is driven by a coalition between radical feminists and the religious right that sees any form of sex work as inherently oppressive and morally reprehensible – and that assumes that women and girls who do sex work are routinely subject to rape, beatings, imprisonment and torture.[27] This sits uncomfortably with evidence suggesting that most workers enter the sex trade voluntarily, because it allows them to earn much more money than other jobs that are available to them.

For instance, based on 100 interviews he conducted with migrant sex workers across the gender spectrum in London, sociologist and film-maker Nicola Mai concluded that most had entered sex work of their own free will. Many had originally come to the UK – mostly from eastern Europe – to be cleaners, work in coffee shops or restaurants or various other casual jobs. However, bad working conditions and low salaries drew them into the sex trade, which allowed them to escape from poverty, earn much more money and gain independence.[28] Contrary to pervasive stereotypes about 'pimps', many prostitutes work independently or in collectives with other sex workers.

Mai found that these migrant sex workers often provided for their families back home. If they felt exploited, it generally had more to do with unsatisfactory payment and working conditions than being literally forced through physical violence or threats. Most migrant sex workers were driven by aspirations to improve the living conditions of their families, explaining their willingness to do what many perceive to be unattractive, degrading or immoral jobs. This is not to glorify sex work, but to acknowledge a hard economic reality.

Anti-trafficking in practice: brothel raids and deportation

Anti-trafficking 'rescue operations' don't solve the problems of exploitation but generally make the presumed victims worse off because they deprive them of their livelihoods. Sex workers are already a group that is vulnerable to abuse and exploitation, by clients, pimps and police. This is particularly the case in countries where sex work is criminalized, and sex workers therefore risk being fined, jailed or abused by police. Among migrant sex workers, those without residency papers are most vulnerable, as they generally don't seek help for fear of being arrested and deported.

In practice, the term 'rescue operation' is a euphemism for police crackdowns on sex work. The 'rescuing' work of anti-trafficking NGOs around the world usually comes down to orchestrating brothel raids in collaboration with the local police. As most sex work is entered into voluntarily, in practice only very few (if any) of the sex workers 'rescued' by anti-trafficking raids fit the tight criteria of trafficking victims. The large majority of sex workers who don't fit the 'victim' bill run the risk of being arrested, fined or imprisoned, while migrant sex workers usually face deportation. It is these fears that prevent real trafficking victims from seeking help and protection from the police.

In the UK, brothel raids are the Home Office's most common way of running anti-trafficking operations. As UK law defines a brothel as a residence from which two or more sex workers work, many raids take place in workers' private homes. These 'rescue missions' are often humiliating experiences, leading to imprisonment or deportation. However, the operations only result in the identification of a tiny number of trafficking victims.

For instance, in December 2013, more than 200 police clad in riot gear with dogs raided walk-up apartments of self-employed sex workers in Soho, London, kicking in doors, slapping closure notices up, seizing property and money, and throwing (predominantly East European) women out onto the street in the freezing cold. Some immigrant women were taken into custody and interrogated on the pretext that they might be victims of trafficking or rape, despite their protestations that they were not being forced to work. This led to the removal of women as potential trafficking victims, although no evidence of trafficking was found, while other evictees found themselves forced to work on the streets.[29] Sex worker organizations claimed that the real goal of such operations is to arrest, detain and deport women, who find their savings, jewellery and other possessions confiscated.[30]

Stereotypes about members of certain groups of non-white women doing lower-skilled service jobs can also lead to their being mislabelled as migrant sex workers and, therefore, trafficking victims. In 2019, police raided a Miami South Beach massage parlour – leading to nationwide news headlines about sex trafficking rings and what the police believed to be the horrible exploitation of women brought from China 'under false promises of new lives and legitimate spa jobs'.[31] However, later investigations revealed that, although the police had thought the workers looked Chinese and assumed they were migrants, virtually all the massage parlour workers were American citizens – albeit of Chinese descent. They had moved to Miami from other US states after having found these jobs through online forums. It turned out the massage parlour was not a brothel, but an actual massage parlour. Still, the arrested workers felt under pressure to fabricate stories and allege that they had been trafficked, as this was the only way to avoid arrest and imprisonment.[32]

This is a general pattern. Wanting to avoid prison or deportation often presses women to twist their stories and claim to have been abducted, deceived, raped and horribly abused in other ways to prevent arrest and, in the case of undocumented migrants, in the hope of qualifying for asylum. Such pressures – also known as 'conformity bias' – contribute to the inflation of trafficking statistics and the reproduction of stereotypical images of trafficking that have very little to do with reality. In this way, the trafficking myth is being perpetuated.

Inflating numbers doesn't solve problems, it makes them worse

Hundreds of millions of workers are exploited around the world. The real difficulty is to objectively determine when the line is crossed from 'voluntary' to 'forced' labour. However, the fact of being exploited is not the same as being forced to work. And this is also the problem with the 40.3 million 'modern slaves' claimed by the ILO and Walk Free.[33] This number has been so endlessly recycled by the media, politicians and anti-trafficking activists that it has reached the status of an unquestionable 'truth'. However, besides the highly questionable methods used to produce such numbers,[34] there are more fundamental problems with the 'modern slavery' claim.

To illustrate this, it is useful to break down the ILO number. Of those 40.3 million 'modern slaves', 14.5 million are women and girls described as 'trapped' in servile roles in forced marriages. Another 24.9 million are labelled by ILO as 'forced labourers'. This number includes 4.8 million (19 per cent) who are sexually exploited and 4.1 million (17 per cent) people who are in forced labour for governments, such as the military, public works and forced prison labour. The remaining 16 million (64 per cent) are labelled 'victims of forced labour exploitation in economic activities such as agriculture, construction, domestic work and manufacturing' who experience various forms of exploitation such as the charging of excessive fees, withholding wages, retaining identity documents or threats of violence, dismissal or denunciation to authorities.[35]

Half of the workers labelled as 'victims of forced labour exploitation' by the report are workers paying back debts through working. However, it is questionable whether we can automatically label such workers as 'modern slaves' or 'forced labourers', as this denies the possibility that workers still see a material interest in doing such work despite being exploited. In fact, many labour relations have an exploitative dimension. It is a common practice among migrant workers to voluntarily take on debts to finance their migration and to repay them through work. This is not to trivialize the situation of exploited workers, but to avoid using sensationalist labels that stigmatize workers, deny their agency, and usually inform policies that make exploited workers *worse off*.

Rescue us from our rescuers

The mislabelling of migrant workers as trafficking victims has prompted governments to shut down entire migration channels. Rhacel Parreñas, professor of sociology at the University of Southern California, has done extensive research on the experiences of Filipina migrant workers around the world. In 2011, Parreñas published a book, *Illicit Flirtations*, based on her fieldwork among what the US State Department considered in the mid-2000s to be the largest group of sex-trafficked people in the world: migrant Filipina hostesses in Japan.[36] The State Department portrayed these hostesses as being forced into sexual exploitation by *yakuza* – members of Japanese organized crime syndicates.

In 2005 and 2006, Parreñas worked alongside these women as a hostess in a Tokyo working-class club. She expected to find that they were modern slaves tricked into forced sex work. However, after many interviews, and by working as a hostess herself, she found out that Filipina hostesses had come to Japan voluntarily and that no one had forced them. They were neither drugged, nor taken on a plane, nor trapped in the hostess clubs.

Parreñas also discovered that the vast majority went to Japan in the full knowledge that they would have to flirt with customers at a club. She also found out that clubs neither required hostesses to engage in sex work nor forced them into sexual exploitation. This does not mean that abuse did not occur; Parreñas saw many hostesses facing huge limitations on their freedoms. Middlemen would often withhold their passports, ask large fees, retain salaries until the end of their three- or six-month contracts, and penalize those quitting before their contract ended.

Although many would consider such exploitation proof that the Filipina hostesses were trafficked, Parreñas's research showed that they still considered it their own choice to enter into a relationship of debt because of the potential financial gains, and they generally did not regret their choice. For them, as for so many migrants entering into debt repayment situations, migration was essentially an investment in a better future. These Filipina hostesses – who usually came from poor families – had agreed to their relationship of indenture prior to migrating.

While labour relations can be seen as exploitative, the 'modern slaves' label denies the fact that, given the limited opportunities they had in the Philippines, migrating was still a much better option than staying. Their migration was their best bet on a better future, and for many poor Filipinas, migration as a hostess has been a very effective road out of poverty. It would thus be one-sided to portray these women as victims only.

Because they automatically label such women and others like them as victims, anti-trafficking policies tend to have negative consequences for the alleged trafficking victims they 'rescue'. In the case of the migrant Filipina hostesses in Japan, their marking as trafficking victims immediately affected their situation in a negative way, as pressure by the State Department on Japan to tighten border rules resulted in a drastic decline in the numbers of hostesses by around 90 per cent – from 82,741 in 2004 to 8,607 in 2006.

The State Department championed this as a victory in the war on trafficking. Yet it was a huge setback for the Filipina hostesses, who deeply resented the 'rescue' that they felt had been imposed on them, because working in Japan was their sole path of economic mobility out of a lack of options back home. Their 'rescue' and subsequent denial of re-entry into Japan did not rescue them but instead resulted in the loss of their occupation and income. For those still wanting to migrate, it meant that they had to do so illegally, which only made them more dependent on middlemen, smugglers and employers.[37]

The evidence highlights the huge mismatch between the claims of anti-trafficking campaigners and realities on the ground. The human trafficking panic has done nothing to help victims of severe labour exploitation, while also legitimizing police operations against sex and migrant workers. Migrant workers who are mislabelled as trafficking victims resist being 'rescued', as this usually implies deportation and a loss of investment and income; ironically, the victimization of vulnerable workers by anti-trafficking campaigns makes them even more vulnerable and generally worse off. By criminalizing precarious work but failing to stop abusive employers, anti-trafficking policies have perpetuated a vicious cycle of abuse, exploitation and stigmatization.

Ultimately, trafficking is not about migration or particular forms of (sex) work, but about the severe exploitation of workers. As Cathryn

Costello, professor of refugee and migration law at Oxford University, has argued, criminalizing forced labour therefore seems like a 'spectacular sideshow compared to the real event, enforcing decent working conditions for all'.[38] Only by giving real victims of trafficking real protection, punishing abusive employers and providing viable alternatives in terms of work and opportunities can we find a way out of severe cases of labour exploitation.

Myth 21: Border restrictions reduce immigration

It seems like a no-brainer: the best way to reduce immigration is to make it more difficult for migrants to come.[1] Stricter entry rules – for instance, more stringent requirements for income, jobs, housing and knowledge of the language and culture of the destination country – will bring down immigration of migrant workers and their family members. Additionally, visa requirements will prevent asylum seekers from arriving at airports and land borders, while stricter border enforcement will prevent people from crossing borders illegally.

By raising costs and erecting legal barriers to migration, fewer people will qualify for entry. The more borders are open, the more people will come – so the reverse applies too: the more difficult it is to cross borders, the fewer people will come. This was the logic behind Brexit: leaving the EU seemed the only way to bring previously free immigration from eastern Europe back under control. It is also the logic behind Europe's efforts to prevent migrant boats crossing the Mediterranean, and the efforts of successive US administrations to prevent unlimited inflows of migrants and refugees across its border with Mexico.

This is part of a much longer trend in which Western countries have sought to limit immigration from former guest-worker countries since the 1960s and 1970s. In 1964, Congress cancelled the Bracero guest worker programme with Mexico, and in 1965 it placed the first-ever numerical limits on immigration from Latin America and the Caribbean. Reagan's 1986 Immigration Reform and Control Act granted an amnesty to undocumented workers, but it was also the start of a massive surge in funding for enforcement along the Mexico–US border.[2]

Since West European countries cancelled guest worker agreements in the wake of the 1973 oil crisis, they also sought to limit the immigration of workers and their family members from Turkey, North Africa and elsewhere through the imposition of visa restrictions. Over the same period, the old imperial powers of West Europe – Britain, France, the Netherlands, Spain and Portugal – ended free movement from former colonies. In the UK, the Commonwealth Immigrants Act 1962 imposed restrictions on the previously free entry of citizens of former British colonies. The 1971 Immigration Act and the 1981 British Nationality Act put Commonwealth citizens on a par with foreigners, while the UK introduced travel visas for most Commonwealth citizens in 1986.

The paradox is that while immigration policies have *generally* become more liberal, Western countries have simultaneously put an end to the previously free entry of guest workers and citizens of former colonies. Confronted with critiques that these policies are ineffective and inhumane, politicians usually respond that 'we have no choice', that these policies are a 'necessary evil' to prevent borders from being overrun and immigration and asylum systems from being overwhelmed. They would argue that immigration would undoubtedly be much higher *without* border restrictions and it would therefore be naive to plead for 'open borders', because this would be tantamount to opening the floodgates.

How it really works

Border restrictions produce more immigration

The underlying logic seems simple and straightforward: the higher the costs and risks of migrating, the lower the number of people who can afford to migrate and qualify for visas and residence permits. And the more walls and fences we build, the lower the number of people who can illegally cross borders. However, if that were true, how can we then explain that immigration to the US and western Europe has continued to rise over the past decade? And how can we explain the striking fact that this increase happened *in particular* from the origin countries targeted by immigration restrictions?

Despite the suspension of free movement, the US immigrant population born in Latin America and the Caribbean grew from 3.1 million in 1970 to 25.4 million in 2017. Over the same period, the non-European-born immigrant population living in western Europe, including the UK, increased almost fivefold, from 5.5 million to 26.4 million. In the UK alone, the number of immigrants born outside Europe rose from 1.5 million to 5.4 million, while the Europe-born immigrant population in the UK rose at a much slower pace, from 1.5 million to 3.5 million – despite the introduction of free EU movement in 1993. Despite – or, as we will see, probably partly *because of* – Brexit, UK legal *net* migration hit a whopping 504,000 in the year ending June 2022,[3] up from levels of about 275,000 in 2019[4] – the highest figure ever recorded.[5]

This raises serious doubts as to whether immigration restrictions have been effective. The idea that higher costs and risks will reduce immigration may seem logical at first, but this is not how migration works in reality. The evidence shows that ill-conceived immigration restrictions have not just been ineffective, but have been *counterproductive* by paradoxically leading to *more* immigration.

This is because immigration restrictions trigger unforeseen behavioural responses, as migrants defy and circumvent new immigration rules by finding legal loopholes, adjusting the timing of their migration or deploying new ways of crossing borders. The net result of these unintended effects is an accelerated growth of permanently settled migrant communities – the exact opposite of what these policies aimed to do.

The waterbed effect

The first such unintended consequence is that immigration restrictions tend to divert migration to other geographical routes or destinations. This is known as the 'waterbed effect'. When you push down on one side of a waterbed, the pressure will cause other parts to rise. Something similar happens when governments start to restrict immigration at particular crossing points or to particular countries. The result is often not that migrants cancel their migration plans, but rather that they seek out alternative routes.

For instance, when France, Belgium and the Netherlands introduced immigration restrictions for Moroccan immigrants in the 1980s, this prompted a partial reorientation of Moroccan emigration to Spain and Italy, which had visa-free entry until the early 1990s. Recent attempts by EU countries to curtail immigration from South Asian countries such as Nepal and Pakistan and from West Africa prompted increasing legal migration to southern and eastern European countries such as Italy, Spain, Portugal, Greece and Poland, where it is easier to obtain visas. While migrants use these countries as an entry and transit point to reach destinations in northern Europe, southern European countries have also evolved into new destinations in their own right.[6]

Immigration restrictions can also prompt already-resident migrants to resettle. Restrictions on family migration in the Netherlands prompted significant numbers of Dutch Moroccans to temporarily migrate to Belgium, which had fewer restrictions on marriage migration. Once their Moroccan spouses had established legal residence in Belgium, they relocated back to the Netherlands. This so-called Belgium route facilitated the continuation of marriage migration to the Netherlands. In a similar way, strict rules on marriage migration in Denmark prompted international couples living in Copenhagen to settle in Malmö, in Sweden, located only forty kilometres away over the bridge across the Sound strait.[7]

Besides the rerouting of legal migration, the waterbed effect has also constantly frustrated various governments' attempts to stop illegal immigration. At the US–Mexico border, increased border enforcement and the building of fences did not stop people from crossing; rather, it prompted migrants and coyotes (smugglers) to use longer and more dangerous routes through the desert. Another consequence was that migration costs went up, with coyote costs rising from $550 in 1989 to $2,700 in 2010 (almost a tripling of costs when adjusted for inflation).[8] The use of more dangerous routes also led to an increasing death toll, from an estimated 72 in 1994 to between 365 and 482 annual deaths in the 2000s.[9]

In a similar way, the introduction of visa restrictions by Spain and Italy in the early 1990s for North African workers launched the phenomenon of Mediterranean 'boat migration'. When Spain introduced visas in 1991, Moroccan migrants started to pay fishermen to smuggle them across the Strait of Gibraltar – the fifteen-mile-wide sea strait separating Africa and Europe – on small boats called *pateras*. When, in response, Spain started to patrol its sea borders more intensively, this did not stop the arrival of *pateras* but prompted a geographical diversification of terrestrial and maritime crossing points, first from eastern Morocco to Spain, and later from Libya and Tunisia to Italy, from the West African coast to the Canary Islands and from Turkey to Greece.

So, on either side of the Atlantic, border enforcement has not stopped the arrival of asylum seekers and illegal migrants. Instead, governments and border control agencies have been caught up in an endless cat-and-mouse game, in which migrants and smugglers constantly try to outsmart border controls. Likewise, in Britain, increased efforts to reduce the number of migrants crossing the Channel from France prompted migrants and smugglers to switch methods – such as illegally hiding in trucks – or to embark on UK-bound ships from Belgium and the Netherlands instead of France. From 2020, the combined effects of Brexit, pressing labour shortages and the end of free EU immigration led to a surge of boat crossings across the Channel.

Driving migration underground

A second unintended effect of border restrictions is that migrants switch to other legal channels ('category jumping') or start crossing borders illegally. The most typical example of such 'category jumping' is the switch from the labour to the family channel. This was an important reason why migration from Latin America to the US continued after the 1976 Immigration Act tried to restrict inflows, as migrants increasingly relied on family reunification and marriage as ways to enter and stay.[10]

Likewise, the continuation of immigration through the 1970s and 1980s from North Africa and Turkey to western Europe, and from South Asia to Britain, was largely facilitated by a switch from the labour to the family channel in response to the suspension of recruitment. To the great frustration of governments, such 'chain migration' continued throughout the 1990s and 2000s via the marriages of second-generation youth to community and family members still living in origin countries, which couldn't be stopped because it would violate the fundamental human right to family life.

Immigration restrictions also tend to drive migration underground into illegal channels. This happens especially when economic demand for migrant workers outstrips legal migration levels – explaining the surge of illegal migration from Mexico and Central America to the US and from North Africa to southern Europe since the 1990s. This also tends to increase migrants' dependency on smugglers to cross borders safely and without being caught.

Even a perfectly sealed-off border wall will not stop illegal migration. This is because visa overstaying is the biggest source of illegal stay. Many undocumented migrants arrived legally as tourists or temporary workers and subsequently *become* illegal after their visas or residence permits expire. When legal immigration channels are being shut down but labour demand remains high, increased visa overstaying is the usual reaction. For the US, about 40 per cent of all illegal migrants are estimated to be visa overstayers.[11] In Italy, overstayers represent an estimated 60–65 per cent of all illegal migrants, and in Japan it is 75–80 per cent.[12] In the run-up to Brexit, the number of foreigners needing a visa but who the Home Office did not record as departing the UK on time nearly doubled from 50,000 in 2016–17 to 92,000 in 2019–20.[13]

Such data doesn't include citizens of countries who don't need a visa to travel. Brazilians, for instance, don't need a visa to travel to the UK and most of continental Europe, and there is little preventing them from doing informal work and overstaying the maximum allowed duration for tourist visits of 180 days.[14] 'Visa runs' are another common strategy to circumvent immigration restrictions, and these are particularly attractive for migrants living in neighbouring countries. In this case, de facto migrant workers who have entered on tourist visas make brief trips in and out of the destination country to renew the maximum allowed period of stay for foreign tourists or visitors.

'Now or never' migration

A third unintended effect of the introduction of border restrictions is the occurrence of pre-emptive 'migration surges', which happen in anticipation – or rather out of fear – of future immigration restrictions. This is a classic example of how border restrictions can produce *more* immigration. Many people harbour vague (or more concrete) plans to explore new horizons abroad, but never execute them. If migration is free, the possibility of moving elsewhere is in the back of many people's minds as one of the many options in life – comparable with how most people think about moving within their own country, or within free-movement areas such as the European Union or, in the past, in open-border areas such as between Mexico and the United States and between Morocco and Spain.

However, such relaxed attitudes usually change when migration is no longer free. This typically turns migration from one of the many options in life into an obsession. If people suspect that, in the near future, migrating might no longer be free, this may create a migration fever, with anybody harbouring even vague aspirations of migration seizing their chance before it's too late. This can lead to 'now or never' migration surges that totally counteract the purpose of immigration restrictions.

One of the most spectacular 'now or never' migration hikes on record happened when Suriname became independent from the Netherlands in 1975. After 1965, migration from Suriname to the Netherlands had been growing slowly; as full Dutch citizens, Surinamese people could freely move there. Political worries about the free inflows of Surinamese people created the political momentum to accelerate plans for Surinamese independence, because the only way to stop free immigration was to 'de-Dutchify' the Surinamese. Although the Labour-led Den Uyl government couched this in anti-colonial language, the main goal behind the rush to make Suriname independent was to stop immigration.[15]

As independence was rushed through, many Surinamese hastened to emigrate as they grew increasingly insecure about the country's future stability. As Graph 18 shows, fears of future immigration restrictions and the eventual introduction of visas in 1980 triggered a huge migration

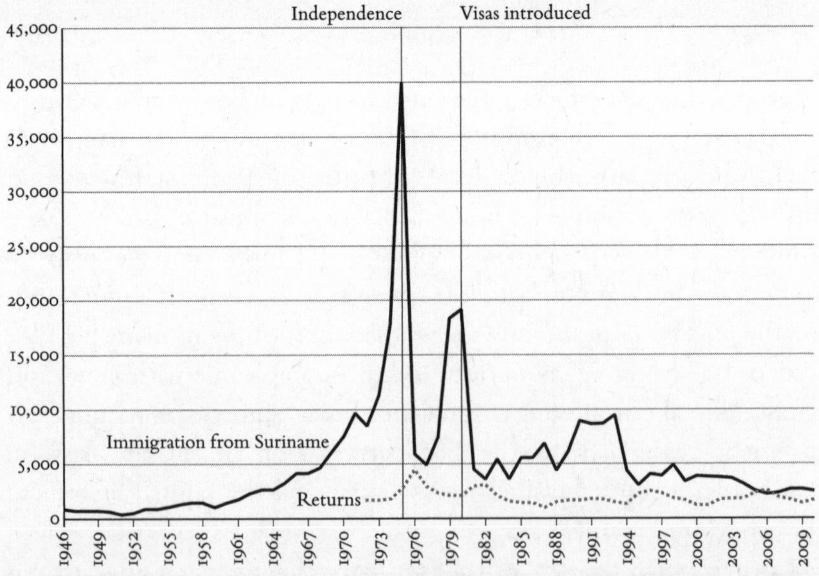

Graph 18: An example of 'now or never' migration spikes between Suriname and the Netherlands

surge, during which around 40 per cent of Surinamese natives moved to the Netherlands in the timespan of less than a decade. This migration surge led to an increase in the number of Surinamese in the Netherlands, from 39,000 in 1973 to 145,000 in 1981. So, rather than curbing immigration, the border closure backfired by triggering mass migration and permanent settlement in the Netherlands, tying the nations together closer than ever.[16]

A decade earlier, a similar migration surge happened in Britain, before the 1962 Commonwealth Immigrants Act came into effect. Until then, citizens of the British Commonwealth – mostly comprising former colonies – had full rights to permanently settle in the UK. Worries about unrestricted immigration prompted Parliament to end this. However, what politicians did not anticipate was that the announcement of the Act in 1961 would trigger an immigration surge, as Caribbean, Indian and Pakistani migrants rushed to 'beat the ban'. As meticulously documented by the geographer Ceri Peach, fears that the border would shut down only reinforced people's determination to get in, and this quadrupled the net inflow from India from 5,800 in 1960 to 23,750 the following year, while immigration from Pakistan – then still including Bangladesh (which became independent in 1971) – rose tenfold from 2,500 to 25,100, and migration from the West Indies surged from 16,400 to 66,300. This consolidated the permanent settlement of large South Asian and Caribbean immigrant communities in the UK, which was further reinforced by a subsequent switch to family migration, fuelling legal migration far into the 1970s and 1980s.[17]

How border restrictions produce more migration

The fourth and last unintended effect of border restrictions is their tendency to discourage return and to interrupt circulation by pushing temporary migrants into permanent settlement. Without border restrictions, migration patterns look like a revolving door, as migrants are free to travel back and forth between origin and destination countries. This constant coming and going is what migration researchers call 'circular migration'. Free migration tends to closely follow business cycles: during periods of high economic growth and growing labour shortages, immigration goes up, and during periods of recession and increasing unemployment, fewer immigrants will come and many migrants will return.

Such circulation is the norm for what is by far the most important and freest form of migration: internal migration. Migration between regions of the same country tends to be very fluid, highly circular and very responsive to economic cycles. A good example is the circular flows between Puerto Rico and the US mainland, with Puerto Ricans – as US passport holders – often leaving to work for a number of years on the mainland before returning to the island, and then perhaps moving back again.[18]

Under open-border regimes, international migration patterns strongly resemble the continuous back-and-forth movements of people *within* countries. Such circular migration was common for Mediterranean guest workers to north-west Europe, between Morocco and Spain and Tunisia and Italy before 1991, and for Mexicans coming and going to the United States until 1986, as border enforcement was minimal. Immigration restrictions have the unfortunate tendency to interrupt such free circulation, as they discourage return migration. So, the more difficult it is to enter, the more migrants will want to stay. The more migrants have invested in passports, visas or smugglers, the stronger the incentive not to go back, out of fear that that decision will be irreversible.

Because politicians, experts and the media have become totally obsessed with how many people are *coming*, they miss half the picture by neglecting to consider how migration restrictions affect the number *going back* and, more generally, the entire back-and-forth pattern of circular migration. Border restrictions typically prompt migrants to cancel return plans, as more migrants decide to stay on the safe side of the border. Depending on which effect is stronger, this makes the effect on net migration (immigration minus emigration) theoretically ambiguous. Often, the return-deterring effect of border restrictions is higher than their inflow-reducing effects. If visas, walls and fences stop more people from going back than from coming in, the effect on *net* immigration, and therefore the growth of migrant communities, may therefore paradoxically be *positive*.

So, immigration restrictions interrupt circular migration not so much by keeping people out as by keeping them in. This is why immigration restrictions often lead to *more* permanent immigration. The fear of not being able to migrate again explains why many Turkish and North African guest workers in north-west Europe cancelled their return plans and decided to stay after the 1973 oil crisis prompted the introduction of immigration restrictions, and why so many South Asian – and, more recently, East European – workers decided to stay put when successive British governments tried to slam the immigration door shut. The tendency of migration restrictions to push temporary migrants into permanent settlement is further reinforced by family reunification or 'chain migration', because the decision to settle permanently usually leads to a decision to let spouses and children come over. As governments lack the legal means to stop family reunification, the decision to end free movement leads to more migration while accelerating the growth of permanently settled migrant communities.

How Brexit accelerated immigration

As part of the Determinants of International Migration (DEMIG) project I led at Oxford University's International Migration Institute (see chapter 16), my colleague Mathias Czaika and I quantified the effect of border restrictions on in- and outflows of people.[19] We analysed data reported by thirty-eight Western countries on yearly inflows and outflows from about 190 origin countries all over the world between 1973 and 2011, yielding about 90,000 yearly 'bilateral' (country-to-country) migration-flow data points.

Our analyses revealed that, on average, the immigration-reducing effect of visa restrictions is largely or entirely cancelled out by their return-reducing effect. Visa requirements decreased inflows from origin countries by 67 per cent on average, but decreased return flows to the same origin country by 88 per cent on average, yielding an overall average reduction of the rate of coming and going back ('circulation') by 75 per cent. This confirms that immigration restrictions can paradoxically produce an *increase* in net migration, and push temporary migrants into long-term settlement.

Particularly in established migrant communities where networks are strong and family and friends can provide various forms of assistance to new migrants, the return-reducing effect is often bigger than the inflow-reducing effect. The tendency of border restrictions to increase net migration is particularly strong in the short and medium term. While the return-reducing effect of immigration restrictions is almost immediate, the effect on inflow takes a long time to materialize, mainly because networks continue to facilitate migration through the family channel. Our analyses revealed that it takes on average five to six years for the immigration-reducing effect of the introduction of visas to become statistically significant. Ten years after the introduction of visas in previously open migration corridors, inflows were reduced by an average of just 20 per cent. This explains the typical pattern – and paradox – of accelerated growth of immigrant communities after border restrictions are introduced.

Our analyses also found that visa restrictions reduce the responsiveness – or 'elasticity' – of migration flows to economic conditions down almost to zero. If borders are open, levels of immigration and emigration strongly correlate with business cycles. If borders are closed, immigrants no longer come and go with ups and downs in the economy, but rather stay put during economic crises. For instance, when the global recession of 2007–2008 sent the Spanish economy into a tailspin, immigrants from EU countries such as Romania went back home. However, immigrants from non-EU countries such as Morocco and Ecuador preferred to stay.[20]

This shows the difficulty of curbing migration in established migrant corridors, where family and community networks have given migration dynamics their own momentum. In a pattern that defies intuition, the circulation-interrupting workings of border restrictions explain why migrant communities have seen an accelerated growth – not so much despite, but *because of*, growing migration restrictions.

For that reason, it is highly uncertain whether Brexit will reduce migration to the UK – the effect actually seems to be the opposite. As could have been predicted from previous experiences, Brexit has motivated East Europeans not so much to go back as to stay put, thereby unintentionally stimulating permanent settlement according to the 'once in, never out' principle. By 30 June 2020, no fewer than 609,000 Romanians and 185,000 Bulgarians had filed applications for the EU Settlement Scheme, a transitionary scheme allowing EU migrants to stay in the UK after Brexit. The number of applications was higher than the 450,000 Romanians and 121,000 Bulgarians that were estimated to actually live in the UK. In essentially the same way as South Asian and Caribbean migrants rushed to beat the ban imposed by the 1962 Commonwealth Immigrants Act, Brexit seems to have prompted EU immigrants to stay – rather than go back – to secure their future residency rights.

How US border enforcement backfired

So, to summarize, immigration restrictions in previously free migration corridors often backfire because of: (1) migrant workers switching to the family, asylum or illegal channels; (2) the constant rerouting of migration itineraries; (3) the triggering of 'now or never' migration surges; and (4) their tendency to interrupt circulation and push migrants into permanent settlement. And these effects often reinforce each other.

The case of Mexican migration to the US is the best-researched example of how the unintended consequences of border restrictions can completely backfire. Douglas Massey, co-creator of Princeton's Mexican Migration Project (MMP), has led yearly surveys since 1982 on both sides of the border, yielding a unique data set, which in 2019 contained information on the migration experiences of 29,000 households. This allowed Massey and his colleagues to analyse in great detail how border reinforcement impacted migration between Mexico and the US.[21]

In a striking parallel with Europe's failed effort to stop workers and their families from coming and staying, the research showed that US immigration policies have completely backfired. Since the 1986 Immigration Reform and Control Act, successive administrations have drastically increased border enforcement and stepped up efforts to deport foreigners. However, instead of curbing inflows, these restrictions set off a chain of events that produced more rather than less Latino immigrants, and transformed Mexican migration from a largely circular flow of male workers going to three states into an 11-million-strong population of settled families living in fifty states.

While border enforcement stopped circular flows by discouraging migrant workers from returning to Mexico, their subsequent decision to settle triggered large-scale family migration and encouraged naturalization as a pre-emptive strategy to ensure residence rights and avoid deportation. Immigration restrictions also encouraged temporary migrants to overstay their visas, increasing the size of the undocumented migrant populations. And border enforcement drove migration underground, as US labour demand remained high and politicians were not willing to curtail illegal employment through worksite enforcement. As a result, between 1986 and 2008 the undocumented migrant population in the US grew from 3 million to 12 million, despite – or rather because of – a fivefold increase in the number of border patrol officers and a twenty-fold increase in funding for border controls.

Closed borders lead to migration obsession

Another way of studying the paradox of border restrictions producing more migration is to look at the 'other side' of migration by studying this phenomenon from the perspective of origin countries. For her doctoral research, my former Oxford colleague Simona Vezzoli compared the emigration histories of Guyana, Suriname and French Guiana[22] – neighbouring countries that have a lot in common in terms of history, society, economy and geographical location, but that have strikingly different emigration experiences.

Guyana and Suriname gained independence from Britain and the Netherlands in 1966 and 1975 respectively. French Guiana never became independent and is still a French *département* – in other words, a piece of EU territory in South America. For Guyana and Suriname, independence meant that it was much harder for people to emigrate to their former colonizer or other Western countries. By contrast, as full French citizens, the French Guianese can move to mainland France and anywhere else in the EU, whenever they like.

However, while Guyana and Suriname were exposed to stringent migration restrictions, no less than *half* of the population of Guyana and Suriname has migrated abroad – from Guyana mainly to the US, and from Suriname almost exclusively to the Netherlands. By contrast, emigration from French Guiana has remained very low, with less than 5 per cent of its population estimated to live abroad. Anxious of getting locked up within their own borders, many Guyanese and Surinamese got obsessed with emigrating and they did everything they could to get out. As French passport holders and EU citizens, French Guianese citizens have freedom of mobility. This explains their relaxed attitudes towards migration, strongly contrasting with the quasi-obsession with seizing any opportunity to get out that still prevails in Guyana and Suriname.

Opening the floodgates?

Another way of studying the effect of immigration restrictions is to turn the analysis around and look at what happens when governments *open* borders. Does this lead to uncontrolled mass immigration, as politicians often claim? Is this tantamount to opening the proverbial floodgates?

The removal of migration barriers between 1989 and 2007 within an expanding European Union is the single biggest real experiment in human history to test what would happen if all border restrictions were lifted. Together with my colleagues Simona Vezzoli and María Villares-Varela at Oxford University, I analysed the migration data we gathered as part of the DEMIG project to and from twenty-five EU countries between 1952 and 2010. Our goal was to find out how migration flows within, towards and from the EU reacted to the removal of migration barriers.[23]

When the Berlin Wall came down in 1989, many politicians and experts feared that this would lead to massive East–West migration waves. In May 2004, eight central and eastern European countries plus two Mediterranean countries (Malta and Cyprus) joined the European Union. Romania and Bulgaria followed suit in 2007. This sparked fears that western Europe would be inundated with East European migrants.

So, what happened? Graph 19 shows migration trends for the EU as a whole.

The dotted line shows that intra-European migration peaked in 1964 and 1969 at levels of 876,000 and 850,000. This mainly reflects labour migration from Portugal, Spain, Italy and Greece to northern Europe. After the 1973 oil crisis, the South–North guest worker migration largely came to a halt, with intra-European migration dropping to around 290,000 in 1983.

It is often believed that the fall of the Berlin Wall and the collapse of communist regimes in central and eastern Europe 'caused' a peak in migration. However, as the graph shows, East–West migration had already been building since the mid-1980s, particularly from Poland to western Europe. This culminated during the fall of the Berlin Wall when intra-European migration peaked at 743,000, reflecting increasing migration – particularly from Poland, but also from the Baltic states, Hungary, Romania and Bulgaria. This 'Berlin Wall effect' largely petered out after 1993, with intra-European migration stabilizing at lower levels of around 500,000 per year. From 2000, intra-EU migration started to increase again but was barely affected by EU enlargement, which only caused a minor bump in intra-EU migration. It is a myth

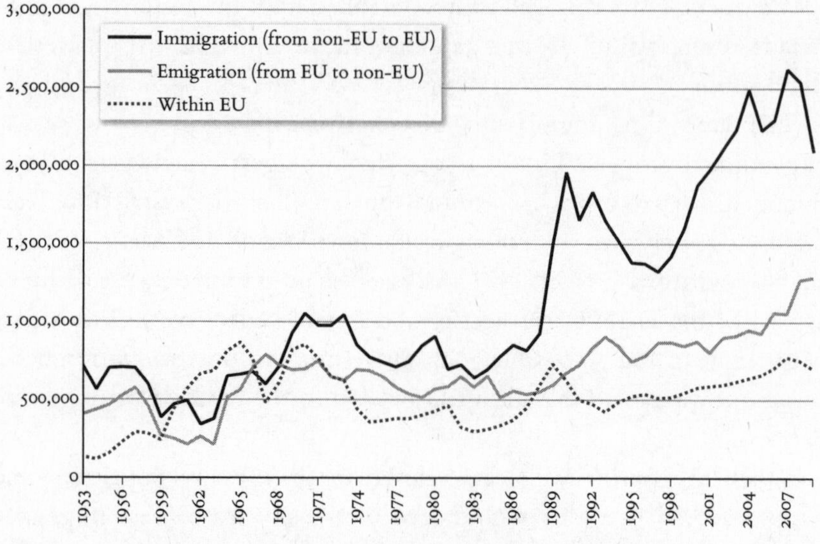

Graph 19: Annual migration from, to and within the European Union, 1953–2010[24]

that EU accession of East European countries caused a massive migration hike to the UK. In reality, Polish emigration to the UK had already been steadily increasing from 1998 in response to pressing labour shortages, and the accession barely affected this trend.[25]

Looking at the longer-term patterns, it is remarkable how small the effect of the EU enlargement and the introduction of free movement has actually been – considering the existence of considerable income differences in the EU. The 2004 and 2007 enlargements had a much lower effect on migration than is often thought – in fact, they barely affected long-term migration trends. This confirms a more general insight from the DEMIG project: while border opening can lead to a temporary spike in people rushing to cross borders out of fear that they may close again, such 'now or never' migration rushes are generally short-lived, after which immigration usually subsides to lower levels and becomes more circular in nature, as people gain confidence that the border will remain open and therefore adopt more relaxed attitudes towards migration.

Another striking trend was that the tightening of external EU borders coincided with a structural *increase* in non-EU immigration. While migration rates within the EU have remained strikingly stable, immigration from countries outside the EU increased rapidly, from levels of between 500,000 and 1 million over the 1970s and 1980s to levels between 2 and 2.5 million in the 2000s – a trend that would continue in the 2010s.[26] The graph also shows a growing gap between inflows and return flows (outflows). This bifurcation of immigration and emigration illustrates the unintended but consistent tendency of immigration restrictions to interrupt circulation. In parallel with developments on the Mexico–US border, this shows the introduction of visas and increased border controls do not stop migrants from coming, but rather discourage them from returning.[27]

The migration paradox

I once took a ride in a long-distance taxi on a desert road in the deep south of Morocco. These privately run 'grand taxis', as they are called there, work on a fill-up-and-go basis and provide essential long-distance transport between towns and cities. The taxis are usually old Mercedes and Peugeots brought by migrant workers. Ahmed, the driver, asked me what I was doing in life. When I told him that I was a migration researcher, he exclaimed, 'I am a migrant too!' He enthusiastically pulled out an ID card. It was his permanent Italian residence card. Showing it to me, he exclaimed, 'When I got this, I went back!'

Ahmed explained that, years ago, he had moved to Italy illegally and found a job as a farm worker. He was one of the many Moroccans who moved to southern Europe in the 2000s, attracted by soaring labour demand in sectors such as agriculture and construction. As he was in Italy illegally, Ahmed couldn't go back to Morocco, so he stayed put for years. However, he eventually managed to obtain legal residence during one of Italy's many regularization campaigns. For him, this residence status was a hard guarantee that he could always come back to Italy. This made him feel safe to return and join his wife and children in Morocco, where he invested his savings in his taxi business. Ahmed told me he went to Italy every year around harvest time, to work for a few months for the same farmer he had known for years and who had helped him to obtain his residency card. This enabled him to earn some extra money for his family, his children's education and his taxi business.

Ahmed's story illustrates a fundamental research insight: decisions to return depend on the prospect of re-migrating in the future. If there are no entry barriers, and people feel free to travel back and forth, migrants are more inclined to return home. Border closures tend to interrupt circulation and stimulate permanent settlement. Hence, the freer people are to stay and go where they want, the less obsessed they are with leaving and the higher the chance that they will return. The more restrictive immigration policies become, the more migrants want to stay.

Policies that attempt to restrict migration have failed to deliver because they are not based on a proper understanding of how migration really works. Because of the one-sided focus and virtual obsession with how many people are coming, politicians are blind to the effects of such policies on returns and the overall pattern of circulation. The evidence shows that it is impossible to reconcile the political wish to reduce inflows with the wish to encourage circulation and the return of migrant workers.

Myth 22: Climate change will lead to mass migration

'The great climate migration has begun', 'Climate crisis could displace 1.2bn people by 2050', 'Migration will soon be the biggest climate challenge of our time'.[1] These are just some of the headlines that have appeared in major international newspapers. They reflect a widely shared belief that climate change will lead to mass migration. A broad coalition of journalists, politicians, climate activists and migration experts have claimed that the effects of global warming will lead to massive movements of climate refugees.

Some experts have already linked recent migration surges at the Mexico–US border and in the Mediterranean to changes in weather patterns linked to climate change. They claim that the effects of global warming, especially on sea levels, rainfall patterns and temperature, as well as extreme weather events such as hurricanes, intense rains and heatwaves, will lead to growing conflict and unprecedented population displacements. The message is alarming, if not apocalyptic: if we don't do something now, we may all get swamped by a rising tide of migrants desperately scrambling to reach the shores of the West.

This idea is anything but new. Back in 1995, Norman Myers, an influential biodiversity specialist, claimed that growing distress and disaster in developing countries caused by climate change had already prompted about 25 million 'environmental refugees to make their way, usually illegally'. Predicting numbers would increase to 200 million by 2050, Myers warned that 'today's stream will surely come to be regarded as a trickle when compared with the floods that will ensue in decades ahead'.[2]

Myers's prophecy set in motion a steadily growing stream of publications, documentaries and political speeches that have given credence to an increasingly apocalyptic set of scenarios. In 2005, the United Nations Environmental Programme (UNEP) warned that 50 million people could become environmental refugees by 2010.[3] In 2007, Christian Aid, a UK-based development NGO, escalated dramatic forecasts of future population displacements up to 1 billion by 2050, in a report called

Human Tide: The Real Migration Crisis.[4] In 2022, the Institute for Economics and Peace claimed that over 1 billion people are at risk of being displaced by 2050 because of environmental change, conflict or civil unrest.[5]

Politicians have also jumped on the climate migration bandwagon. In 2015, European Commission president Jean-Claude Juncker declared that 'climate change is one of the root causes of a new migration phenomenon' and that 'climate refugees will become a new challenge – if we do not act swiftly'; and in 2021, the Biden administration warned that 'climate-change related displacement is . . . a current and future security risk'.[6]

The spectre of massive waves of climate refugees has become the newest 'truth' about migration everybody seems to believe. In many ways, climate migration seems the ultimate migration challenge of the future. Much media attention has focused on the fate of 'sinking islands' in the Pacific, such as the Maldives and Tuvalu, widely seen as the first victims of climate change. We are told that rising sea levels are forcing more and more people to relocate – the world's first climate refugees. Experts have claimed that a series of devastating climate-change-related hurricanes in Central America have spurred migration to the US, and that protracted droughts are forcing more and more Africans onto boats in desperate attempts to reach Europe. From this viewpoint, countering climate change by reducing carbon emissions is the only way to prevent a human tide of climate refugees from overwhelming Western countries.

How it really works

Climate change is real, but will not lead to mass migration

Climate change is real. Since the start of the Industrial Revolution in the late nineteenth century, average global temperatures have risen by 1.1°C, and according to estimates by the Intergovernmental Panel on Climate Change (IPCC) they are likely to rise a further 1.0–1.8°C in a very low greenhouse gas emissions scenario, 2.1–3.5°C in a moderate scenario, or as much as 3.3–5.7°C in an extreme scenario.[7] All climate change models agree that average temperature will particularly rise in temperate and polar zones – up to 7°C in more extreme scenarios.

Because of the complexity of climate systems, we cannot predict exact impacts, but there is widespread consensus among climate scientists that global warming will lead to significant changes in climates around the world. While rainfall may increase in various polar, temperate and tropical zones, large parts of southern Africa, the Mediterranean, Latin America and Australia are likely to get dryer. Scientists also expect that climate change will increase the occurrence of extreme weather events such as hurricanes, droughts, floods and heatwaves.[8]

The melting of temperate glaciers and ice caps in Antarctica and Greenland, as well as 'thermal expansion' caused by higher water temperatures, will accelerate the process of sea level rise. Between 1901 and 2018, sea levels rose by 15–25 centimetres, but the rate of sea level rise has recently been accelerating from 1.3 millimetres per year between 1901 and 1971 to an average speed of about 3.7 millimetres (3.2–4.2) per year between 2005 and 2018. In 2023, the IPCC projected that if countries make rapid cuts to carbon emissions, sea levels will rise by 28–55 centimetres by the end of the century. If emissions remain very high, sea levels may rise by 75–100 centimetres until the end of the century. Sea levels will not rise uniformly everywhere on earth, and may even drop slightly in some locations, such as the Arctic, but they will rise much faster elsewhere. Unless better flood defence systems are built, sea level rise is expected to increase flooding and damage from extreme weather events such as storm-surges and hurricanes.[9]

Global warming is one of the most pressing issues facing humanity, and the lack of willingness from governments and the international community to address it effectively – particularly through reducing carbon emissions – is a valid source of major public concern and global protest. However, to link this issue with the spectre of mass migration is a dangerous and misleading practice based on myth rather than fact. Forecasts of massive climate migration ignore scientific knowledge on the nature and causes of both environmental change and human migration, and the complex, indirect and two-way relationship between both. They also ignore empirical evidence showing that environmental stresses such as droughts, floods, hurricanes and wildfires are unlikely to generate massive international migration.

A closer look at the models used to forecast massive climate migration reveals their pseudoscientific nature. The typical approach of apocalyptic climate migration forecasts has been to map climate-change-induced developments (such as sea level rise, drought or desertification) onto settlement patterns to predict future human displacement. For instance, if climate change models predicted a sea level rise of (say) 50 centimetres, it would be possible to map all coastal areas affected by this and work out how many people lived in such areas. The assumption then is that all these people would have to move. The same reasoning is used for the effect of droughts, with climate migration models assuming that an *x* reduction in rainfall will lead to a *y* increase of migration from rural areas.[10]

With my own background in environmental geography, I have always been flabbergasted at how naively some serious research organizations buy into such 'deterministic' reasoning, which assumes a one-on-one relation between the environment and migration, in which 'environmental pressures' are somehow assumed to automatically generate movement – while geographers have long observed that people have historically shown huge resilience in coping with scarcity and environmental threats.

Paradoxically, people have historically often moved *towards* – instead of from – places with the greatest environmental hazards, such as river valleys and coastal areas, because these also tend to be the most fertile and prosperous areas – so the exact opposite of the climate refugee forecasts. In fact, over the past century, many people have voluntarily migrated from rural places to areas of greater environmental vulnerability, such as urban areas located near the coast, built on floodplains or in fertile delta areas, such as the Indus delta in Pakistan, the Ganges-Brahmaputra delta in Bangladesh and India, the Mekong delta in Vietnam, the Nile valley and delta in Egypt, and the Niger delta in Nigeria. They have done so because of the improved livelihood opportunities they can expect to find there, despite the high population densities and environmental hazards (particularly flooding) they often encounter. This highlights the danger of making a direct, simplistic link between the climate, the environment and migration.

'The good land is there where the flood is'

Scientific evidence undermines the idea that climate change will lead to mass migration. In 2010 and 2011, I participated in a study for the UK Government Office for Science on the links between migration and global environmental change.[11] The project, which involved some 350 experts and climate and migration researchers from more than thirty countries, was the most extensive scientific review that had ever been conducted on this topic. Based on a review of global evidence, the project concluded that environmental factors were but one of the many factors affecting migration, and that most displacement would be local and short-term.

Because migration is driven by many factors, it can rarely be reduced to the effects of just one form of change, such as climate change or other environmental factors. The environment is but one of the many factors that shape migration, and this effect is indirect rather than direct. This makes it difficult to directly attribute migration to climate change and other environmental factors. In fact, migration is likely to continue regardless of climate and the environment, because migration is mainly driven by powerful economic, political and social processes, such as labour demand (in destination areas) and development (in origin areas) or violence. This challenges the popular idea, for example, that migration within Bangladesh is an 'obvious example' of mass displacement due to the sea level rise. After all, much of this rural-to-urban migration would have happened anyway as part of large processes of urbanization, modernization and industrialization. In other words, migration is likely to continue regardless of climate and environmental change.[12]

The paradox is that the most fertile agricultural lands also tend to be most prone to flooding. For this reason, throughout history, people have settled in low-lying areas despite the risk of seasonal flooding and the usual inconveniences such as hot and sticky weather, mosquitoes and waterborne diseases such as malaria. The Limpopo valley in southern Mozambique is a fertile agricultural area that is subject to regular, sometimes disastrous flooding, which occasionally drives farmers from their fields and homes. However, few people bother moving out of the valley permanently, because that is where the water and fertile lands are – by contrast, they return as quickly as possible. Or, as local farmers would say, 'The good land is there where the flood is.'[13]

For this reason, people are not keen to abandon their lands in fertile river valleys and delta areas. They have historically learned to cope with seasonal and occasional flooding so it becomes a way of life – for instance, by building dykes, mounds, houses on stilts or even floating homes. In fact, fertile soils and abundant water are the very reasons that river plains and delta areas have always attracted people, have high population densities and were the cradles of early states and civilizations. Seasonal flooding is a blessing and a curse, because sediment transported by the river water also fertilizes the soil. Without regular floods, soils would become unfertile, while in dry climates salt accumulations would make them sterile.

Lands are rising as the seas are rising

Dramatic forecasts of massive climate migration are based on the assumption that sea level rise will drive people out of coastal areas. However, we cannot just assume that low-lying areas will simply be submerged. This is mainly because processes of sedimentation – leading to land growth – can counterbalance the effects of erosion and sea level rise, which lead to land loss. Sediment is small parts of rocks, soil, dead plants and animals, such as shells and coral, which have been eroded by strong flows of water, glaciers and winds. Because rivers start to flow more calmly as they reach the sea, sediment is deposited on riverbeds, floodplains and seabeds, causing existing coastal lands to rise and new lands to form in the sea. Likewise, tidal currents and waves erode and deposit sediment.

Land rise because of sedimentation explains why studies of satellite images have shown most deltas, mangroves and other coastal marshlands in the world have actually been growing, not shrinking, over the past decades, despite the rise in sea level. While it is uncertain whether land gains will be able to keep up with accelerated sea level rise in the future, such evidence shows the naivety of the simplistic 'lands will be flooded' narrative and the importance of understanding changes in the natural and human-driven supply of sediment by rivers and tides.[14]

Because of the constant interplay between erosion and sedimentation, delta areas are continuously reshaped by shifting patterns of land formation and erosion. Strong sea currents usually cause erosion and land loss in some places but sedimentation and land gains in others. While islands disappear, others are created. Analysis of satellite images in Bangladesh – which is mostly located in what is the world's largest delta (the Ganges-Brahmaputra delta) – has revealed that, in the period between 1985 and 2015, the rate of land area growth (through sedimentation) in coastal areas slightly outpaced the rate of erosion. So, despite sea level rise, Bangladesh was gaining rather than losing land. Net land gains between 1985 and 2015 were estimated to be 237 km^2, or 7.9 km^2 per year.[15]

Of course, local erosion of coastal land forces some people to move – though this has nothing to do with images of massive climate displacement, but with short-distance mobility – to places where land is gained, or to towns or cities. For instance, Bangladeshi peasants who have to move because of sea erosion generally move only a short distance. As the landscape is a highly dynamic river delta where land is gradually disappearing in some places, while reappearing in other places, people may even try to resettle in places of origin.[16]

The evidence also counters the stereotype that the Pacific islands are massively 'sinking' into the ocean. Again, this is because the effects of sea level rise and erosion are counterbalanced by the sedimentation of material generated by the surrounding reef, such as dead coral, weathered shells and dried-up microorganisms. One study that analysed land growth and land loss of thirty Pacific and Indian Ocean atolls – comprising 709 islands in total – revealed that 89 per cent of islands were either stable or had grown in land area, while only 11 per cent had decreased in size.[17] In Tuvalu, a small Pacific nation often singled out by the media as one of the first nations to disappear entirely due to sea level rise in the future, a recent study found that between 1971 and 2014, eight of Tuvalu's nine atolls and almost three-quarters of the 101 reef islands had *grown* in size. This *increased* Tuvalu's total land area by 3 per cent, even though in Tuvalu sea levels rose at twice the global average.[18]

So, in many coastal areas and island nations of the world, sediment supply has so far counterbalanced or even outpaced sea level rise. This undermines the entire assumption – and popular media narratives – that climate-change-related sea level rise is already a significant driver of current migration in delta areas such as Bangladesh or the Pacific islands. This doesn't mean that there's no possibility that future sea levels will outpace land gains through sedimentation. But we cannot just assume that land will simply be submerged because sea levels are rising. And it's clearly nonsensical to link recent and current migrations to climate-change-driven sea level rise.

Environmental hazards can trap poor people into immobility

There are five main reasons to be sceptical about popular claims that climate change will lead to mass migration. First, climate change, however serious, is a slow-onset phenomenon, which gives people time to adapt to resulting environmental stresses, such as to sea level rise or increasing droughts. Second, people can use various adaptation strategies, such as flood defence systems (levies, mounds, dykes, polders) or the introduction of irrigation and drought-resistant crops to cope with environmental stress. Third, in cases of floods and other environmental havoc, the vast majority of people move over short distances, such as to the next neighbourhood, village or town. Fourth, most displacements tend to be temporary, because most people wish to return home as soon as possible. Fifth, most people living in the poorer countries of the world do not have the resources to move over large distances.

We can therefore not simply assume that environmental stresses will automatically 'push' people out. A wide range of studies has shown that people generally prefer to stay home in the wake of natural shocks, and will do everything they can to stay put. In situations where agricultural productivity is affected, families with sufficient assets may adopt the migration of one or several members to town or cities as a strategy to earn extra income. However, such moves are more likely to be internal and temporary than international and permanent, as people generally prefer to stay close to home and long-distance migration is expensive.[19]

The idea that climate change will lead to mass migration is based on popular 'push-pull' models that naively assume that migration is somehow a linear function of poverty, violence and other forms of human misery. However, as we know, migration requires considerable resources, particularly long-distance migration from rural areas to cities or abroad. Extreme poverty – whether caused by environmental stress or other factors – actually tends to deprive vulnerable people of the means to travel and migrate over large distances, and they might therefore find themselves trapped where they are, unable to flee.

When Hurricane Katrina hit New Orleans in 2005, large parts of the city were flooded. The disaster displaced more than a million people in the Gulf Coast region and killed more than 1,000 people. African Americans were over-represented among the victims. This was because they often lived in the low-lying neighbourhoods most prone to flooding, while many of them didn't have cars or the social connections that enabled wealthier people to flee and find temporary lodging with friends or family living outside of the city.[20]

Following the same logic, when peasants become impoverished because of droughts, this may actually deprive them of the resources needed to move, trapping them in situations of extreme vulnerability.

Detailed studies fail to find a simple causal link between environmental stress (whether linked to climate change or not) and migration.[21] A severe drought in rural Mali, for instance, was found to increase short-distance, temporary migration to nearby towns to supplement family income, but did not increase long-distance and international migration.[22] In Malawi, droughts and floods have been shown to decrease out-migration from rural areas to cities.[23] Similarly, droughts in Burkina Faso have been shown to *reduce* international moves to Côte d'Ivoire.[24]

In my own research and fieldwork on migration in Morocco, I observed that only a few people living in the poorest, most remote and ecologically marginal oases in the deep south and Atlas mountain areas had migrated to Europe, mainly because people lacked the money, diplomas and connections needed for international migration. Most people migrated to nearby towns or cities within Morocco such as Casablanca, Marrakesh or Tangier. By contrast, populations of relatively prosperous, water-abundant and well-connected agricultural areas have been over-represented in emigration to Europe.[25]

So, scarcity and poverty – whether linked to environmental or other factors – may actually *prevent* people from migrating, certainly over long distances. It is therefore not surprising that field studies as well as large-scale empirical studies of global migration trends have failed to find any clear effect of climatic factors such as rainfall, temperatures and natural disasters on long-term trends of international migration, and actually suggest that they may decrease rather than increase long-distance emigration.[26] This evidence defies simplistic reasoning and models assuming that climate change will automatically 'push' people to migrate. In fact, depending on circumstances, environmental stress can lead to more or less migration.

The myth of advancing deserts

Another popular idea is that 'desertification' is a major cause of migration, particularly from African countries. The idea is that deserts are advancing rapidly, and that the resulting increases in droughts will be a major cause of migration by 'pushing' people out of rural areas. Again, this idea crumbles in the face of evidence. First of all, there is no conclusive evidence that deserts are expanding. For instance, analyses of satellite images suggest that parts of the Sahel zone – the semi-dry region south of the Sahara Desert – have in fact been 'greening' in recent decades, particularly because of increased tree cover.[27]

This confirms a large body of research and a general consensus among geographers that 'desertification' rarely ever complies with the stereotypical images of 'advancing deserts', but is generally a local phenomenon of land degradation largely caused by human intervention, such as the cutting-down of trees and shrubs, or land and water management practices leading to erosion or water scarcities. While geographers have questioned the very existence of desertification – encapsulated by the mediagenic but highly misleading image of 'advancing deserts' – and therefore even called it a 'myth', real cases of environmental degradation in dry areas are almost always primarily human-made and can generally not be attributed to the climate.[28]

As my own research on land and water management in North African oases has shown, the crisis of traditional oasis agriculture is almost exclusively the result of social, economic and political changes, partly brought about by migration. In Morocco, these changes include the departure of peasants' sons to work and study in cities, the emancipation of former serfs and sharecroppers who used to do most agrarian labour, and the rapidly decreasing economic importance of agriculture – with almost all families now gaining the lion's share of their income through non-agrarian jobs. The number of hands available and willing to do farm work has decreased, alongside a general disaffection with agriculture.

These social and cultural changes have also led to the dysfunction of traditional village institutions which organized land and water management. Together with growing labour shortages, this has often resulted in a lack of collective maintenance, the neglect of irrigation systems and decreased efforts to till the soil, to climb, maintain and pollinate date palms and to prevent erosion and sand encroachment of the fields and irrigation canals. In many places, traditional agriculture has suffered from mechanical water pumping for urban use and modern agriculture. This has resulted in falling underground water tables and the drying-up of wells, small rivers and other natural water sources. Particularly in smaller, marginal oases without perennial water sources, all of these factors have contributed to a lack of maintenance of collectively managed irrigation systems and a generalized neglect or even abandonment of land.[29]

If anything, this example highlights the complex nature of the links between the environment and migration. It also shows how deceptive first impressions can be, and that causal links may actually be the reverse of what they appear to be. The mediagenic sight of abandoned fields, cracked earth and dried-out palms sends a powerful image of 'dying oases' – and it's tempting for journalists and other visitors to believe that's why people are leaving. However, in this case, the causality rather runs the other way around: it is not the desert that is pushing people out, but people who are withdrawing from agriculture. This highlights the human and political causes of desertification. What may appear to be migration caused by climate-change-induced droughts is in fact an agrarian and ecological crisis caused by people.

Sinking lands or rising seas?

The climate refugee narrative also ignores evidence that the sinking of land, not rising sea levels, is the main cause of growing flooding hazards in several agricultural plains and coastal cities like Jakarta, Manila, Bangkok, Dhaka, New Orleans and Venice. As part of a process that physical geographers call 'land subsidence', the sinking of land is mainly caused by groundwater extraction for irrigation, industry and urban use. When swampy soils are drained, they tend to become more compact, causing land to subside. This is particularly true for soils with high organic content, and peat soils in particular, where the exposure to oxygen because of drainage causes organic matter to decompose. Certain types of rock also become more compact when water is withdrawn. The weight of the building mass may further contribute to the resulting process of soil compaction. Draining swamps helps to prevent waterborne diseases like malaria from spreading, and makes life in cities more pleasant. Drainage enables agriculture on soils that otherwise would have been too wet and swampy. However, drainage also accelerates land subsidence, which again increases the risk of flooding, which again increases the need for drainage, potentially creating a vicious circle.[30]

For instance, the Indonesian capital of Jakarta has been struggling with increased flooding. This even prompted the Indonesian government to build a new city, Nusantara, as its capital, set to be inaugurated in 2024. Although the media and politicians have routinely blamed sea level rise for growing flooding hazards, land subsidence is the main culprit. The speed of land subsidence in some coastal parts of Jakarta has reached up to 150 millimetres per year. By comparison, the average yearly rate of sea level rise is currently around 3 millimetres per year.[31] Several other big cities around the world are sinking because of land subsidence: Bangkok at a rate of 20–30 millimetres per year, Manila at rates of up to 45mm per year, and Ho Chi Minh City at rates of up to 80mm per year.[32]

So, again, what *appears* to be a natural disaster caused by climate change has been almost completely human-made. In the same vein, the construction of houses, hotels, industries and roads, and the clearance of mangrove forests, are generally the most direct cause of coastal erosion in the Pacific and many other areas of the world, which further questions the popular 'sinking islands' narrative. More generally, this highlights the human and political causes of most environmental hazards, which particularly hit the poor and vulnerable – and which climate migration narratives conceal.

Blaming the climate

For all these reasons, it is unlikely that climate change will 'lead' to large-scale international migration, let alone on the massive scale predicted. In some cases, this has already put the organizations making such claims to shame. When the massive climate migrations of 50 million people predicted by UNEP in 2005 had failed to materialize (in fact, populations turned out to be growing in the regions it identified as environmental danger zones, such as coastal urban areas), UNEP distanced itself from its earlier claims and deleted a rather apocalyptic climate refugee map it had published earlier on its website.[33]

However, such experiences have not stopped prestigious international organizations from producing pseudoscientific climate migration forecasts. In 2021, the World Bank attracted much international publicity with a report called *Groundswell*, which estimated that climate change could force up to 216 million people to move within their countries by 2050.[34] However, the study did not provide any details on the actual parameters it used to reach these estimates, reducing their models to a 'black box'. While this goes against all standards of scientific transparency, from the text of the report I inferred that the Groundswell models were based on the simplistic assumption that *x* decreases in water availability and crop productivity will push *y* amount of people to leave their homes.

Although the assumptions and methodologies underlying such

forecasts are highly problematic – and while empirical evidence clearly defies such claims – the question remains: why then is this myth being propagated by international organizations, researchers, climate activists and various pressure groups? The main explanation seems to be that doomsday scenarios of massive climate migration serve powerful political agendas both on the left and the right. For left-wing groups, the fabrication of the climate migration threat serves to direct attention to the issue of climate change, and heightens the urgency to address this. For right-wing groups, it serves to raise the spectre of future mass migration, and the need to step up border controls to prevent such an imagined deluge. For researchers, international organizations and governments, the climate migration narrative serves to attract media attention and funding.

By making a simplistic link between climate change and migration, politicians, media and experts deflect attention away from the human-made nature of many environmental hazards such as droughts and floods, but also from the failure of governments to protect the people who are most vulnerable to such hazards – whether related to climate change or not. If people are displaced or die as a result of a natural disaster, this is not just the direct consequence of the disaster, it also reflects the inability of governments to help people cope with such stresses, with measures such as flood defences, timely evacuation efforts and building regulations. Poverty, poor housing and weak public services explain why the damage and the number of people injured and dying are much higher when a hurricane hits a poor country like Haiti than much wealthier countries like the US. And, as shown by the example of Hurricane Katrina, even in rich countries, poor people are much more likely to lose their homes, get injured or die when disaster strikes.

This makes it of course very tempting for politicians to blame 'the climate' or other external environmental factors 'beyond their control', because this deflects the attention away from their inability or unwillingness to protect people from environmental hazards. In Africa and the Middle East, politicians often invoke 'drought' and 'climate change' to explain away a whole range of perceived problems in rural areas – from low agrarian productivity, economic stagnation and rural-to-urban migration – which have little if any direct relation to climatic factors. For the same reason, it is misleading to identify climate change as a major cause for growing migration from Central American countries to the US, as it obscures the economic and political causes of such migrations.

Governments, not the climate, displace people

Governments can also use climate change as an excuse to displace people. For instance, the government of the Maldives, a Pacific nation, has recycled older, highly controversial proposals for the 'resettlement' of its population – presently dispersed over 200 inhabited islands – onto 10–15 islands. But the real motive behind efforts to evict native populations from islands has always been economic, because the Maldives government finds it too costly to provide services and resources to such geographically dispersed populations. In recent years this view has gained renewed popularity, although it is now cast in environmental terms, with the government using sea level rise as an excuse to 'evacuate' islands.[35] But this also seems to conceal a hidden agenda – to sell entire islands, reefs and lagoons to the Saudi royal family as part of a large tourist development plan. The sea-level-rise argument comes in handy as an excuse to evict populations, so that developers can have free rein to build luxury resorts on the vacated islands.[36]

Governments, not the climate, displace people. The climate-migration narrative distracts attention away from the political causes of most displacement. Apart from conflicts and persecution, development projects – such as dams, mining, airports, industrial areas, middle-class housing complexes and tourism – are a major cause of displacement. So-called development-induced displacement is the largest single form of forced migration, leading to the internal displacement of an estimated 10–15 million people per year[37] and mainly affecting groups such as slum dwellers, the urban poor in general, indigenous peoples and other ethnic minorities. Displacees tend to be among the most vulnerable people, unable to defend themselves and often barely being compensated for the loss of livelihood.

Climate change mitigation can become a cause of displacement in itself. In China, hydropower, irrigation and water-transfer projects are an integral part of climate change mitigation and adaptation strategies, but they also displace a large number of people whose villages disappear under the water. Ironically, wildlife conservation and other environmental protection projects are also estimated to prompt the displacement – or forced settlement in the case of herders ('pastoralists') and nomadic peoples – and the loss of land and property for hundreds of thousands of people each year.

The fabrication of a migration threat

Climate change is real. The forecasted acceleration of global warming will have severe effects on production and livelihoods and the overall stability of planetary ecosystems, which may reach a dangerous tipping point. Urgent action is needed to prevent irreparable damage. However, apocalyptic forecasts of massive climate migration clearly lack any empirical basis, and are based on simplistic assumptions about the relationship between environmental change and migration. The climate change narrative also deflects attention away from the fact that most environmental hazards are human-made, and that governments, not climate change, are the main causes of environmental displacement.

To argue in favour of cutting carbon emissions by raising the spectre of massive climate migration is therefore a typical case of 'being right for the wrong reason'. The use of baseless apocalyptic migration forecasts to support the case for urgent action on climate change is not only intellectually dishonest, but also puts the credibility of organizations using this argument – as well as the broader case for climate change action – seriously at risk.

Most importantly, the adverse consequences of climate change – just like any other cause of economic stress and human suffering, such as violence, oppression and poverty – will most severely affect the most vulnerable populations, who lack the means to move out and who are most likely to get trapped in life-threatening situations. Genuine concerns about the environmental effects of climate change should therefore focus on those unable to move at all.

The Road Ahead

This book set out to present a holistic vision of migration – not as a problem to be solved, or as a solution to problems, but as an *intrinsic* part of broader processes of social, cultural and economic change that affect our societies. The evidence presented shows the need to go beyond the usual framing of migration debates in simplistic and polarizing pro- and anti-terms, and to not focus on what migration ought to be, but rather on what migration *is*, in terms of its actual trends, patterns, causes and impacts. Understanding the inevitability of migration, and its central role in economic development and social transformation, will lead us to a totally new way of understanding human mobility – a new paradigm on the very nature and causes of migration that belies almost everything that we are usually told on the subject. As Ronald Skeldon observed, 'Migration *is* development'; it is a process that benefits some people more than others, that can have downsides for some, but that cannot be thought or wished away. The power of a scientific, and above all nuanced view of migration as development helps us to understand and – to a certain extent – predict how migration will evolve as our societies and economies change.

Looking to the future, I hope that the information in this book will help you to analyse the news more critically, and to take with a pinch of salt the baseless claims often made by politicians, media and humanitarian organizations about migration having reached yet another all-time high, or about the waves of migrants and climate refugees yet to come, or about the success of their policies. I hope it will prompt you to ask yourselves on what assumptions such claims are made, and what interests drive these parties to make such claims.

As we have learned, media and humanitarian organizations tend to focus on the most dramatic stories, such as when boats sink, people die in the desert or migrants suffocate in lorries. This is not to detract from the seriousness of such cases – rather, it is to be aware of how they are used to create a one-sided view of migration as a 'desperate flight from misery', which unduly reduces migrants to victims who need to be rescued from smugglers and traffickers. There are countless other stories of people for whom (even illegal) migration enabled them to provide a much better future for themselves and their families, and these should not be buried under sensationalist headlines.

Furthermore, claims about policy successes should also be scrutinized in detail. For instance, in 2016 politicians claimed that the 'deal' between the EU and Turkey had successfully curbed Syrian refugee migration to Greece. The media swallowed the story hook, line and sinker, failing to notice that numbers had already drastically come down *before* the policy came into effect.[1] And for what exact reasons do politicians call preventing refugees from finding safety a 'success'? When immigration goes down, this usually has more to do with a change in circumstances – like rising unemployment in destination countries or the end to a conflict – than with policies, although politicians will always try to take the credit.

But perhaps the best example of the lack of a critical attitude is the consistent failure of the media to notice that the same tough-on-immigration politicians who boast about building walls and fences have consistently turned a blind eye to the large-scale employment of illegal workers. An awareness of the discursive gap between what politicians say and do about immigration will help us – ordinary citizens, and the journalists who report on these issues – to hold them to account more effectively, as will an understanding of why policies in this area have either failed or backfired over the last half a century.

What conclusion can we draw from all the evidence? First of all, *there is no need for panic*. The evidence clearly dispels the idea that we are living in times of an unprecedented migration or refugee crisis. Migration is neither at an all-time high nor accelerating. Migration is not spinning out of control. No massive waves of desperate migrants are about to crash onto our shores. Nor did immigration cause unemployment, job insecurity, wage stagnation and the lack of affordable housing, education and healthcare. Likewise, there is no evidence that immigration causes crime or is a threat to welfare provisions or social cohesion. Once we realize this, we will understand that immigrant scapegoating is just that – an age-old strategy used by politicians to deflect the attention away from their own complicity in creating these problems, and an excellent opportunity to present themselves as strong leaders fighting against a fabricated external enemy.

On the other hand, there is reason for concern. Evidence shows that most economic benefits of immigration go to the already affluent, while the social problems that immigration can bring have been disproportionately put on the shoulders of ordinary citizens who have already seen their job security, purchasing power and living standards erode over the past decades. Although immigration did not cause these latter problems, people have good reason to ask: 'What's in it for us?' Things were made worse as politicians – who clung on to guest worker illusions and therefore ignored problems for too long – failed to take responsibility for the migrant groups they let in, giving rise to situations of protracted segregation and discrimination that are very real and hard to deny.

In any case, we have reason to be hopeful about the prospect of having more nuanced debates in the future, because opinion research shows that most people have nuanced views about migration and are much more level-headed than many politicians are about this issue. There are no easy solutions to complex migration problems, but once we do away with unnecessary panic and fear, which have already paralysed discourse for too long, we create space for an informed debate about the benefits and downsides of immigration, and how to design better and more effective policies that work better for *all* members of our societies and avoid the errors of the past.

Given all the evidence, and given the current state of debates on the subject, the key question is how we might begin to design these policies. I didn't write this book to give policy advice; social scientists cannot, nor should they, dictate the direction in which our societies should move, as this should be the subject of informed democratic debate. What researchers *can* do is share fundamental insights about the nature, causes and impacts of migration; about which policy goals are realistic, and which are not; and, based on research and past experience, which policies work to achieve these goals, and which policies don't work, or are even counterproductive.

As this book has shown, liberal democracies are caught in a 'migration trilemma' between (1) the political wish to control immigration, (2) economic interests in more migration, and (3) fundamental human-rights obligations towards migrants and refugees. These conflicting policy goals seems impossible to resolve satisfactorily, and that largely explains why immigration policies can be incoherent and therefore often ineffective or even counterproductive.

The main way politicians have tried to resolve this triple bind is by creating an appearance of control, by using tough-on-immigration rhetoric and through largely symbolic measures such as the building of walls and fences and the occasional workplace crackdown, while at the same time facilitating legal entry and tolerating illegal immigration in practice. This is clearly not the way forward. As we have seen, this may help politicians to win elections but has never solved any problems – in fact has made them *worse* – while irresponsible rhetoric has created a climate in which the far right feel emboldened, and racism, polarization and intolerance can thrive. To counter this, the next time a politician vows to crack down on illegal migration, they should be interrogated on why they let employers get away with hiring undocumented workers and exploiting migrant workers more generally, and what alternative policies they propose to deal with labour shortages.

A second way out of the migration trilemma proposed by many politicians and experts is temporary migration. This would allow governments to fill urgent labour needs but avoid the potential problems permanent settlement brings in the eyes of many people. However, such proposals ignore a century of migration scholarship demonstrating that this is not a realistic solution for most types of migration. Research has shown that temporary migration schemes can only work for particular forms of seasonal work, such as in agriculture. Most employers don't like high turnover and prefer experienced, trusted workers to stay. In practice it is very difficult for governments to enforce return – and, as we know from past experiences with guest workers in Europe and America, efforts to close borders without addressing labour demand are likely to backfire by discouraging return and pushing workers into permanent settlement, ironically triggering even more migration through family reunification.

Immigration almost always goes along with some degree of permanent settlement. Even Gulf countries that don't care much about migrant rights have found it increasingly difficult to prevent long-term settlement, as their economies have become structurally dependent on migrant labour and migrants stay longer and longer. Migrants are not only economic 'factors of production', but also *people* who create social ties and bonds with colleagues and local populations; who make friends, fall in love, get married and have children. And the moment children are involved, settlement generally becomes permanent – as they quickly adopt the language and customs and naturally see as their home what is perhaps still a strange country to their parents.

It is very likely that this social reality will increasingly impose itself on Japan, South Korea and Arab immigration societies, as it has done in Europe's reluctant immigration countries in the recent past. In that sense, 'there is nothing more permanent than a temporary worker', as migration researchers sometimes quip. The paradox is that the more governments want them to go, the more migrants tend to stay. The policy implication is that, *if* governments decide to let migrant workers in – or tolerate illegal immigration – they should also accept the fact that many will stay and eventually bring their families. And as we have also learned from previous experiences, stubbornly denying such realities will create much bigger problems with integration and segregation later on.

As a more radical way out of the migration trilemma, some pro-immigration liberals and economists have proposed an 'open borders' solution. There is certainly evidence that freer mobility can be very beneficial and doesn't necessarily lead to mass migration. As we've learned from the largely free and uncontrolled migrations of the past – between Mexico and the US, Turkey and Germany, and Morocco and Spain – free migration tends to be highly circular (with workers going back and forth) and is less likely to push migrants into permanent settlement as it increases the chances migrants return after a while. In fact, because of these mutual benefits, not only the EU but also many other regions in the world – such as ECOWAS (in West Africa), MERCOSUR (in Latin America) and ASEAN (in South-East Asia) – have already introduced free movement or are in the process of doing so.

However, to expect that this will happen on a global scale anytime soon is unrealistic. The open borders proposition is vague, and could mean several different things – for instance, there is a big difference between visa-free travel, the right to reside and the right to work. Visa-free travel for tourist and business purposes is easiest to implement – and this is where we have recently seen most progress – as it does not come with more fundamental rights typically associated with citizenship, such as the right to reside, work and access public services.

It is therefore difficult to have truly open borders without some kind of joint citizenship, which gives all residents of regional unions the same rights, as in the case of EU citizenship. This inevitably implies some degree of erosion of national sovereignty, and this is exactly why EU free movement was such a hot-button issue in the UK during the Brexit campaign. In addition, we need to be critical towards 'free movement' agendas as they are often driven by corporate lobbies that disregard issues of labour exploitation and integration, raising inevitable questions about social justice and labour standards. The freeing up of migration is therefore inevitably going to be a slow, incremental and politically controversial process, with many bumps in the road and likely turnarounds.

Slogans like 'open borders' are therefore as impractical as 'closed borders' as a concrete guide for migration policies. Immigration will always need some degree of regulation. However, we can and should learn a lot from past and contemporary experiences with free migration, to take away unfounded fears that a certain liberalization of border regimes – for instance, lifting visa restrictions – would be tantamount to 'opening the floodgates'. In fact, as has been shown, the effect may paradoxically be the opposite: though such liberalization can initially lead to a migration hike, it almost always subsides to a lower level and becomes more circular once people gain confidence that if they leave they can come back again.

So, what should we do? Ultimately, the answer to that question depends on the kind of society we live in. Yet given the current liberal order of our societies and economies, we can make some important observations. First of all, it's important to emphasize that the large majority of people cross borders legally. These regular migrations rarely ever reach the headlines, but knowledge of this should be a healthy antidote against media images and political rhetoric suggesting that borders are beyond control.

Although we – and perhaps this book, too – focus (too much) on the areas where policies have failed, it is also important to acknowledge the huge progress that has been made. In a marked contrast from the situation just a few decades ago, almost all Western countries have embraced the fact that they have become de facto immigration countries. The days in which leading European politicians declared a state of 'zero immigration' or repeated mantras that 'we are not an immigration country' are long over.

Since the 1990s, we have seen a growing acceptance of these new realities, for instance in the liberalization of immigration policies to accommodate the growing demand for labour at various skill levels, and the increasing popularity of points-based immigration policies based on the Canadian and Australian models. As part of the same trends, and pushed by corporate lobbies, successive US governments have expanded the number of work visas issued to higher- and mid-skilled workers. Despite a – largely rhetorical – backlash against multiculturalism, most Western states have eased access to citizenship. Germany is the best example of a complete turnaround in immigration policy: although it was once in denial about the permanent nature of the settlement of millions of Turkish workers, and had one of the most restrictive citizenship laws until the 1990s, Germany is now a European forerunner in designing immigration policies where migrants and refugees feel more welcome and can gradually earn their way into permanent residence and citizenship.

The increasing acceptance of the immigration of skilled workers, investors and students presents a marked contrast to attitudes towards asylum seekers and lower-skilled workers, who are generally seen as less welcome or even greeted with hostility. These are the officially 'unwanted' migrants – and here lies the main tension between economic and political *reality* and economic *policy*.

With regard to refugees and asylum seekers, any sensible discussion on this topic is often paralysed by the perception that refugee migration is spiralling out of control, or akin to an exodus or foreign invasion. Contrary to the myths peddled by media, politicians and international organizations, the evidence shows that there is neither a long-term increase in refugee migration nor evidence that the Western world is being overwhelmed by floods of refugees, with refugees numbering only 0.3 per cent of the world population, or about 10 per cent of all international migrants, and 80–85 per cent of refugees already staying in origin regions.

The welcoming European response to the millions of Ukrainian refugees fleeing the Russian invasion in 2022 showed that ultimately this is about political will, not about numbers. Seven years earlier, popular support for Germany's relative openness towards Syrian refugees was undermined by most other European governments having a free ride on Germany's hospitality,[2] not because one of the world's richest economic blocs, comprising half a billion people, couldn't numerically handle such a refugee inflow. Hence, refugee crises are not crises of numbers but *political* crises rooted in governments' unwillingness to coordinate their efforts in the spirit of international solidarity.

It goes without saying that, in the longer term, conflict prevention is by far the best policy. Although Western countries individually have limited powers to effect such a radical global change, it would certainly be a good idea to refrain from unnecessary and illegitimate military interventions or attempts at destabilizing regime changes that are likely to produce large-scale refugee movements.

The more immediate question is how to maintain public support and create a political will for refugee protection. Politicians have a responsibility to maintain public support by ceasing their narratives about 'bogus' asylum seekers or comparing refugee flows to foreign invasions. Similarly, journalists should ask critical questions when such demagogic comparisons are made, and refugee and humanitarian organizations ought not to exaggerate refugee numbers, as it undermines support for refugee protection by sustaining a false image that a rising tide of desperate people are flocking to the West.

Apart from that, public support for asylum systems stands or falls with the ability of these systems to distinguish between people who have a valid reason to seek protection, and those who don't; and those whose claims are rejected should be sent back home. This requires governments to invest sufficient resources in a careful investigation of asylum claims. Superficial 'quick and dirty' investigations, motivated by deterrence and a drive to generate high rejection rates, tend to backfire as they lead to endless appeals procedures. The unfortunate – and very costly – result is that asylum seekers are left in a legal limbo zone that can last for years, often involves their detention and exclusion from work, often exacerbates trauma and has severely damaging consequences for their social and economic integration. Although it's an illusion to think that refugee-status determination can ever be perfect, governments bear a responsibility to mobilize their institutional capacities and to set up functional, credible and efficient asylum systems that give asylum seekers access to legal counsel and create clarity about the outcome as soon as is responsibly possible.

This leaves us with the biggest conundrum in migration politics: how should we deal with the immigration of lower-skilled workers? It is here that the discursive gap between what politicians say and do has been the biggest. The trends that have decreased the supply of native-born people willing and able to do manual jobs in agriculture, construction, industries and domestic work – such as population ageing, increasing education and women's emancipation – are relatively autonomous, largely irreversible and therefore difficult to influence via government policy. At the same time, ageing and the rise of the double-income family model have increased the demand for all kinds of service-sector work, particularly in child, health and elder care, food processing, warehousing, hospitality, transport, domestic work and education.

This has created a persistent demand for labour, which largely explains why lower-skilled immigration has continued in defiance of tough political rhetoric. Immigration restrictions and border enforcement have failed to stop migration as they don't address the real root cause of immigration – and, as this book has shown, in many ways the elephant in the room of migration debates: persistent labour demand. Ill-conceived immigration restrictions have therefore backfired, as they have triggered 'now or never' migration hikes, interrupted circulation, pushed migrants into permanent settlement, encouraged illegal migration, forced people to take greater risks when crossing borders and hire the services of smugglers to cross borders undetected.

Politicians vowing to destroy the 'business model' of smugglers are not to be believed, as they know themselves that it's their own policies that effectively created and sustain this business model in the first place. In that sense, these policies were always bound to fail, because they are among the very causes of the problems they pretend to solve.

Meanwhile, the repeated reluctance of governments to acknowledge the de facto permanent nature of their settlement – for guest workers in Europe, Caribbean and South Asian migrants in the UK and (often undocumented) Latino migrants in the US – and the related failure or unwillingness to address the real problems they encountered, exacerbated problems of social isolation and segregation. This has particularly affected those members of the second generation who experienced 'downward assimilation' and feel rejected by mainstream society. We risk making the same errors again. Today, many migrants do essential work, but often we treat them like servants, like a disposable workforce. Looking away will not make them go away, but rather will encourage their marginalization. In this way, politics of denial risk creating a new underclass mainly consisting of non-white workers.

Historical experiences have shown that even the most disadvantaged migrant groups have an extraordinary ability to emancipate themselves through hard work, study and entrepreneurship, despite the racist discrimination they often encounter. However, the condition is that they are given fundamental rights and offered pathways to permanent residence and citizenship. Nothing is more psychologically demoralizing, socially devastating and economically damaging than to leave migrants – and asylum seekers – in undocumented status and legal limbo zones for years or even decades, where they often cannot legally work to build a new future. The consequences for illegal workers are particularly devastating: children are separated from their parents, migrants can't visit their families back home (for a wedding, a religious celebration or a funeral) out of fear of not being able to go back again, and people live in constant fear that they may one day be deported and separated from their families.

As part of the War on Immigration, Western countries have pressed transit countries to collaborate with border enforcement. This means that Central American, Cuban and Venezuelan migrants and refugees transiting through Mexico must fear being chased by the police or being kidnapped and extorted by violent gangs. It means that African migrants and refugees are beaten up, raped, imprisoned and punished with forced labour by Libyan security forces, with the blessing – and the financial assistance – of the EU. It means that each year, and in breach of international law, tens of thousands of asylum seekers are 'pushed back' into often inhumane and dangerous situations. And it means that we confine asylum seekers for years on islands or in prisons, with nowhere to go, living in a legal limbo and constant uncertainty, which only aggravates the trauma they have already been through.

Many would argue that it's the migrants' own fault – that they bear responsibility for having migrated illegally, and that they should face the consequences. However, this argument would only be credible if governments and policies were consistent; in practice, tough-on-immigration rhetoric entirely contradicts the large-scale toleration of the deployment of illegal migrants. The truth is that entire sectors of economies throughout the industrialized world have become largely dependent on a (legal and illegal) immigrant workforce that exists and is unlikely to disappear magically one day. No matter what they say on television, no serious politician in the US really believes that the 11 million undocumented migrants will all be rounded up and deported. After tolerating this situation and after having benefited from migrant labour for so long, destination-country governments and societies cannot pretend that they don't also bear some responsibility for the situation we now find ourselves in. So, some form of amnesty is inevitable, but the longer politicians keep on denying the reality on the ground and fail to take responsibility, the longer the unnecessary suffering will endure and the bigger the damage will be.

So where does that leave us? The evidence shows that governments cannot design effective immigration policies if they are not in line with social and economic realities. The mismatch between the reality of labour demand and the lack of legal immigration pathways has produced illegal migration and has made migrant workers more vulnerable to abuse and exploitation by employers and traffickers. However, this does *not* mean that immigration policies should only be driven by corporate interests, or that governments should let more migrants in whenever business lobbies ask for it. Such corporate logic has dominated immigration policymaking over recent decades as part of broader economic liberalization and labour market deregulation; for instance, private agencies have increasingly gained ground in recruiting temporary workers, so the private sector – rather than governments – have increasingly been put in charge of regulating immigration. These corporate interests can help to explain the liberalization of immigration policies and the toleration of illegal immigration; as the great migration scholar Stephen Castles once observed, there is a fundamental mismatch between the decades-long trend towards economic liberalization on the one hand, and the wish for less immigration on the other. So, politicians – and societies at large – cannot have their cake and eat it.

The implication of this insight is not that we should continue on the current path, but that governments can only effectively influence migration if they change the economic realities that influence labour demand and, hence, immigration. This is the golden rule of successful immigration policymaking. To be effective, immigration policies should be consistent with general economic policy, and labour market policy in particular. Policies that at first glance appear to have nothing to do with immigration can actually have a huge influence.

For instance, it is not a coincidence that countries without government-subsidized elder and childcare facilities – such as Spain, Italy and also Germany – have high immigration of au pairs, domestic workers and caregivers for the elderly. It is also not a coincidence that universities in countries that have defunded higher education – such as the US and the UK – have become increasingly dependent on the immigration of fee-paying international students. Likewise, there is a link between the growing dependence of Britain's National Health Service on foreign nurses and doctors, and the failure of its own education system to train enough medical staff in the UK.

More generally, it is not a coincidence that countries with some of the most liberalized labour markets – such as the US, the UK and the Netherlands – have shown so little appetite to rein in employers' hiring of legal and illegal migrant workers. And one of the reasons for the general unwillingness to enforce labour law through workplace raids is a dislike of 'Big Brother' government intrusion that is deeply embedded into democratic societies in general and American and British culture in particular.

If governments are really serious about wanting more control over – or lower levels of – immigration, this inevitably means that they will have to pursue drastic economic reform and re-regulate labour markets, which will require a fundamental change in economic policy, and perhaps also lower economic growth in general. In other words, pursuing this kind of reform will necessitate a radical rethinking of some of the core principles that have guided economic and labour market policy over the last half-century.

For example, to what extent can we sustain the horticulture, food processing and hospitality sectors, which have become dependent on the continuous inflow of foreign workers? To what extent is it a good idea – and sustainable – that our universities are increasingly being bankrolled by fee-paying foreign students?

How much do we want to live in societies where busy, double-income couples increasingly outsource household chores – cleaning, cooking, washing, ironing, gardening and house maintenance – to migrant workers? Do we really want to create a society where elites are being served by a new underclass that mainly consists of migrant workers? Do we increasingly want to outsource the care of children and the elderly to foreign workers, or do we think that governments should be responsible for providing subsidized care facilities?

These are just some of the fundamental questions we need to ask ourselves – questions that will have indirect but significant implications for immigration. This is all the more important for the future, as we cannot assume the existence of an unlimited supply of cheap labour 'out there' in poor countries willing to come whenever we snap our fingers. In fact, because of global demographic changes, and as many parts of the world are running out of children and ageing is becoming a worldwide phenomenon, the future question may no longer be how to stop 'them' from coming, but how to attract migrants who are still willing to do the jobs that native workers shun.

In the end, we do have real choices, but these require a real commitment to pursue fundamental economic and social reforms. Japan can perhaps serve as a good example: despite its traditional resistance against immigration, it has not been able to escape the fact that industrial, ageing economies will inevitably attract a significant number of immigrants, and it is gradually coming to terms with that reality by accepting more immigrants – although often under the euphemistic guise of 'traineeships'. On the other hand, Japan still has a *much* lower immigration rate than almost any other industrialized society.

To understand this, we should not only look at its relative geographical isolation and cultural factors, but also at the ways in which Japan has partly dealt with labour shortages and ageing. Besides heavily investing in automation and robot technology, and having a much more regulated labour market than most Western countries, Japan has addressed ageing by having older members of its workforce increasingly work into their seventies. Japan also seems to have chosen – or rather, accepted – a scenario of low economic growth, which is, as we know, a fairly sure bet to reduce immigration.

The example of Japan as a wealthy society with *relatively* low levels of immigration shows this type of model to be a real possibility, even though it would probably take decades of structural reform to achieve in other places. We should be under no illusion that immigration will stop, but long-term structural reform has the power to influence the demand for migrant labour – and, hence, immigration – in the longer term.

The real question is whether most Europeans and Americans want to live in such a society. I suspect that is not the case. For instance, when the French go on strike to resist government plans to increase the pension age, they may be unwittingly choosing higher future dependence on migrant workers. As long as Western governments see maximizing economic growth as a top priority of public policy and keep on deregulating labour markets, this will undoubtedly only reinforce labour shortages and therefore immigration.

If politicians are really serious about decreasing a seemingly unsustainable dependence on immigrant workers, this requires fundamental changes in economic and labour market policy. For example, they can choose to increase pension age to counter the effects of ageing, or to stop subsidizing sectors that almost exclusively depend on migrant labour, or to encourage part-time work to enable parents to take care of their own children, cook their own food and tend their own gardens. If governments are serious about 'taking back control', they should re-regularize labour markets and rein in the gig economy.

To begin with, when debating migration we must acknowledge that it benefits some people more than others, and can sometimes even cause harm; this helps us to understand why some people feel more positively about migration than others. The fact that those who are already affluent reap most of the economic benefits of immigration, while local workers are most directly confronted with the day-to-day consequences, is of the utmost social and political salience. It means that we cannot divorce debates about immigration from broader debates about inequality, labour and social justice. After all, the way governments deal with immigrants is almost automatically also the way they treat *workers*.

Most problems experienced by migrant workers are related to job insecurity, bad working conditions and low pay, and though migrant workers are even more vulnerable to exploitation and discrimination than native workers, fundamentally this comes down to issues of labour rights that concern *all* workers. Trafficking is not about migration, or doing particular kinds of (sex) work, but about the severe exploitation of vulnerable workers, irrespective of whether they are migrants or not. Policies to protect vulnerable workers can therefore only be effective if they provide whistle-blowers with safeguards and provide better protection of rights or genuine opportunities – instead of 'rescue operations' that make workers *worse off* by deporting them and depriving them of their livelihoods.

So, while politicians' anti-immigration rhetoric tries to drive a wedge between native and migrant workers by insinuating that immigration causes all these problems, this obscures the fact that native and migrant workers share a common interest as *workers*, and it is government policy – not migrants – that has caused problems such as growing inequality, decreasing job security and wage stagnation. We cannot address the exploitation of migrant workers if we don't also ensure sure that all lower- and mid-skilled workers can earn a decent wage – and, more generally, restore the dignity of manual labour, particularly in the care sector and other services and industries that cannot be automated or outsourced and that we are likely to need more than ever in the future.

We should be under no illusion that this will eliminate the demand for migrant workers, but restoring the dignity of work will help to motivate some members of the native-born workforce to do such jobs, and it will better protect native and migrant workers alike. Such policies will also spread the benefits of migration more equally to all members of society, instead of primarily to the already affluent.

All of this shows that we cannot decouple immigration debates from debates about economic policy, labour standards, inequality, welfare, education and how we treat the sick and elderly. Any real debate on migration will therefore inevitably be a debate on the type of society we want to live in.

Notes

Reader's note

1 H. de Haas et al., 2019, 'International Migration: Trends, determinants, and policy effects', *Population and Development Review*, 45/4, pp. 885–922.

Myth 1: Migration is at an all-time high

1 IOM, 'Migration in the World', https://www.iom.sk/en/migration/migration-in-the-world.html [retrieved 26 September 2022].

2 UNHCR Staff, 'UNHCR's Grandi: Political inaction deepening displacement crisis', 10 October 2022, https://www.unhcr.org/news/stories/2022/10/634436c54/unhcrs-grandi-political-inaction-deepening-displacement-crisis.html

3 There are significant data gaps in migration data from earlier decades – meaning that much movement went unrecorded. Graph 1 is based on the author's calculations of data extracted from the Global Migrant Origin Database (World Bank) and the Global Migrant Origin Database (United Nations Population Division).

4 L. Potts, 1990, *The World Labour Market: A History of Migration*, London, Zed Books; Virginie Chaillou-Atrous, 'Indentured Labour in European Colonies during the 19th Century', https://ehne.fr/en/node/12279 [accessed 6 November 2018]; M. Shimpo, 1995, 'Indentured Migrants from Japan', in R. Cohen (ed.), *The Cambridge Survey of World Migration*, Cambridge, Cambridge University Press.

5 O. Chudinovskikh and M. Denisenko, 'Russia: A Migration System with Soviet Roots', Migration Policy Institute [website], 18 May 2017; M. Ellman, 2007, 'Stalin and the Soviet famine of 1932–33 revisited', *Europe-Asia Studies*, 59, pp. 663–93; T. Kuzio, 2002, 'History, memory and nation building in the post-Soviet colonial space', *Nationalities Papers*, 30, pp. 241–64; G. Uehling, 2004, *Beyond Memory: The Crimean Tatars' Deportation and Return*, Houndmills: Palgrave Macmillan.

6 A. McKeown, 2004, 'Global migration, 1846–1940', *Journal of World History*, 15, pp. 155–89; A. McKeown, 2010, 'Chinese emigration in global context, 1850–1940', *Journal of Global History*, 5, pp. 95–124.

7 D. S. Massey, 1988, 'Economic development and international migration in comparative perspective', *Population and Development Review*, 14, pp. 383–413.

8 Author's calculations based on data provided in *L'Italia in 150 anni: Sommario di statistiche storiche 1861–2010*, Roma, Istituto Nazionale di Statistica, 2012.

9 P. E. Lovejoy, 1989, 'The Impact of the Atlantic Slave Trade on Africa: A Review of the Literature', *The Journal of African History*, 30, pp. 365–94.

10 Hein de Haas, Stephen Castles and Mark J. Miller., 2020, *The Age of Migration: International Population Movements in the Modern World*, London, Bloomsbury, 6th ed.

11 Ibid.

12 Ibid.

13 Bell and Charles-Edwards estimated the global number of internal migrants at approximately 763 million in 2005. Based on interpolated estimates of the global migrant population in 2000 and 2010, there were an estimated 189 million international migrants in the same year, thus four times lower than the number of internal migrants. M. Bell and E. Charles-Edwards, 2013, *Cross-National Comparisons of Internal Migration*, New York, UN Population Division.

14 X. Li and D. Wang, 2015, 'The impacts of rural–urban migrants' remittances on the urban economy', *Annals of Regional Science*, 54, pp. 591–603. Based on 2020 census data, there would be 376 million internal migrants. See Kam Wing Chan, 2021, 'Internal Migration in China: Integrating Migration with Urbanization Policies and Hukou Reform', KNOMAD Policy Note 16.

15 The size of the arrows is indicative of the size of migration flows, and the size of the circles is an approximation of the size of immigrant populations.

16 See M. Bell et al., 2015, 'Internal Migration and Development: Comparing Migration Intensities around the World', *Population and Development Review*, 41(1), pp. 33–58; Tony Champion et al. (eds.), 2018, *Internal Migration in the Developed World: Are We Becoming Less Mobile?*, London and New York, Routledge; R. Skeldon, 2019, 'A classic re-examined: Zelinsky's hypothesis of the mobility transition', *Migration Studies*, 7(3), pp. 394–403.

17 K. Schewel, 2018, *Ziway or Dubai: Can Flower Farms in Ethiopia Reduce Migration to the Middle East?*, Geneva, International Organization for Migration.

Myth 2: Borders are beyond control

1 David Cameron, BBC News interview, 30 July 2015, https://www.bbc.com/news/av/uk-politics-33714282

2 'Leaders at EU Summit Vow to "Regain Control" of Borders', *New York Times*, 17 December 2015.

3 Remarks by President Trump, 4 January 2018, https://trumpwhitehouse.archives.gov/briefings-statements/remarks-president-trump-vice-president-pence-meeting-immigration-republican-members-senate/

4 Asher McShane, 'Invasion of the South Coast', LBC, 31 November 2022, https://www.lbc.co.uk/news/britain-facing-invasion-south-coast-asylum-broken-suella-braverman/

5 *Time*, 28 August 2006, p. 6, quoted in D. S. Massey et al., 2016, 'Why border enforcement backfired', *American Journal of Sociology*, 121, pp. 1557–600.

6 Philippe Fargues and Christine Fandrich, 2012, *Migration after the Arab Spring*, Florence, Migration Policy Institute, European University Institute.

7 'Gaddafi wants EU cash to stop African migrants', BBC News, 31 August 2010, https://www.bbc.com/news/world-europe-11139345

8 Natalie Kitroeff, '2 Hurricanes Devastated Central America', *New York Times*, 4 December 2020.

9 Philippe Fargues, 2017, *Four Decades of Cross-Mediterranean Undocumented Migration to Europe: A Review of the Evidence*, Geneva, International Organization for Migration; Hein de Haas, 2008a, *The Myth of Invasion: Irregular Migration from West Africa to the Maghreb and the European Union*, IMI Research Report, International Migration Institute, University of Oxford.

10 According to DEMIG C2C data, average total immigration from non-EU28 countries to the EU between 1997 and 2011 stood at 1,924,742; according to Eurostat data, total immigration from non-EU28 countries between 2013 and 2019 was 2,069,948. Inflows fluctuated strongly with economic trends – reaching 2.5 million in years of strong economic growth and high labour demand in the EU, and dropping below 1.5 million during economic downturns.

11 F. Düvell, 2011, 'The Pathways in and out of Irregular Migration in the EU: A Comparative Analysis', *European Journal of Migration and Law*, 13(3), pp. 245–50.

12 Peter William Walsh and Madeleine Sumption, 'Recent estimates of the UK's irregular migrant population', Migration Observatory, University of Oxford, 11 September 2020.

13 Mark Lopez et al., 'Key facts about the changing US unauthorized immigrant population', Pew Research Center, 13 April 2021.

14 Ibid.

15 Based on DEMIG C2C data, between 1997 and 2008, average yearly African emigration to Europe, North America, Australia and New Zealand was 422,770, of which 310,927 was to Europe. Based on apprehension data, the number of unsolicited border crossings from Africa across the Mediterranean was 42,363 over the same period. This would imply that roughly nine out of ten Africans moving out of Africa left the continent legally. The real proportion of illegal crossings is likely to be higher as many crossings go undetected. On the other hand, a significant proportion of unsolicited arrivals, particularly in Italy, concern asylum seekers from non-African countries such as Afghanistan, Iraq and Syria. Furthermore, data on legal inflows is incomplete, particularly for large destination countries like France and the UK. It is therefore safe to say that the overwhelming majority of Africans leave the continent legally.

16 C. Peach, 2006, 'South Asian migration and settlement in Great Britain, 1951–2001', *Contemporary South Asia*, 15(2), pp. 133–46.

17 This recruitment happened through a specialized recruitment office, BUMIDOM (Bureau des migrations d'outre-mer). See S. Pattieu, 2016, 'Un traitement spécifique des migrations d'outre-mer: le BUMIDOM (1963–1982) et ses ambiguïtés', *Politix*, 4, pp. 81–113.

18 Ministère des Armées, 'Les soldats d'Outre-Mer pendant la Seconde Guerre mondiale', Chemins de Mémoire, https://www.cheminsdememoire.gouv.fr/fr/les-soldats-doutre-mer-pendant-la-seconde-guerre-mondiale

19 Peach, 2006.

20 L. Thomas, 'Puerto Ricans in the United States', Oxford Research Encyclopedias [online], 2015.

21 M. M. B. Asis, 2016, 'The Philippines' Culture of Migration', Migration Policy Institute.

22 De Haas et al., 2020.

23 Ibid.

24 Ibid.

25 H. van Houtum and R. Bueno Lacy, 2019, 'The migration map trap. On the invasion arrows in the cartography of migration', *Mobilities* 15(2), pp. 196–219.

Myth 3: The West is facing a refugee crisis

1 'More than 100 million now forcibly displaced: UN report', UN News, 16 June 2022, https://news.un.org/en/story/2022/06/1120542
2 Alan Travis, 'UN refugee chief chides Blair for slating convention', *Guardian*, 29 October 2003.
3 D. S. FitzGerald, 2020, 'Remote control of migration: Theorising territoriality, shared coercion, and deterrence', *Journal of Ethnic and Migration Studies*, 46(1), pp. 4–22.
4 Ibid.
5 UNHCR refugee statistics [accessed 15 September 2022].
6 *UNHCR Global Trends: Forced Displacement in 2018* (Geneva: UNHCR, 2018).
7 UNHRC refugee statistics [accessed 13 February 2023].
8 Data analysis based on asylum data downloaded from Eurostat [accessed 27 May 2021].
9 'Asylum and refugee resettlement in the UK', Migration Observatory, 19 August 2022, https://migrationobservatory.ox.ac.uk/resources/briefings/migration-to-the-uk-asylum [accessed 27 May 2021].
10 'Asylum Denial Rates Continue to Climb', TRAC Immigration, https://trac.syr.edu/immigration/reports/630/ [accessed 16 June 2023].
11 T. J. Hatton, 2020, 'Asylum recognition rates in Europe: Policies and performance', *European Journal of Political Economy*, 102267.
12 See also T. J. Hatton, 2009, 'The rise and fall of asylum: What happened and why?', *Economic Journal*, 119, F183–F213.
13 S. Fransen and H. de Haas, 2022, 'Trends and Patterns of Global Refugee Migration', *Population and Development Review*, 48(1), pp. 97–128. Source of 2021 data: www.unhcr.org/globaltrends
14 Ibid.
15 Forcibly displaced flow data. UNHCR Refugee population statistics database [retrieved 12 June 2022].
16 P. Gatrell, 2007, 'Introduction: World Wars and Population Displacement in Europe in the Twentieth Century', *Contemporary European History*, 16(4), pp. 415–26. 'The Turkish–Greek conflict', ICRC, 25 January 2005, https://www.icrc.org/en/doc/resources/documents/misc/5gke3d.htm
17 Stephen R. MacKinnon, 2008, *Wuhan, 1938: War, Refugees, and the Making of Modern China*, Berkeley, CA, University of California Press; Micah

S. Muscolino, 2010, 'Refugees, Land Reclamation, and Militarized Landscapes in Wartime China: Huanglongshan, Shaanxi, 1937–45', *Journal of Asian Studies*, 69(2), pp. 453–78.

18 Rudolph J. Rummel, 1998, *Statistics of Democide: Genocide and Mass Murder since 1900*, Münster, Germany, Lit Verlag.

19 Malcolm J. Proudfoot, 1956, *European Refugees: 1939–52: A Study in Forced Population Movement*, Evanston, IL, Northwestern University Press.

20 R. J. Rummel, 1992, *Democide: Nazi Genocide and Mass Murder*, New Brunswick, NJ, Transaction Publishers.

21 S. Prauser and E. A. Rees (eds.), 2004, *The Expulsion of the 'German' Communities from Eastern Europe at the End of the Second World War*, Florence, European University Institute; Philipp Ther, 1996, 'The Integration of Expellees in Germany and Poland after World War II: A Historical Reassessment', *Slavic Review*, 55(4), pp. 779–805.

22 Eugene Kulischer, 1948, *Europe on the Move: War and Population Changes, 1917–1947*, New York, Columbia University Press, pp. 302–4; cited in Peter Gatrell, 2007, 'Introduction: World Wars and Population Displacement in Europe in the Twentieth Century', *Contemporary European History* 16(4), pp. 415–26.

23 Peter Gatrell, 2000, 'Forced Migration during the Second World War: An Introduction', Gale, https://www.gale.com/intl/essays/peter-gatrell-forced-migration-second-world-war-introduction

24 B. Khadria, 2008, 'India: Skilled Migration to Developed Countries, Labour Migration to the Gulf', in S. Castles and R. Delgado Wise (eds.), *Migration and Development: Perspectives from the South*, Geneva, International Organization for Migration.

25 M. Hamoumou, 1990, 'Les harkis, un trou de mémoire franco-algérien', *Esprit*, pp. 25–45; A. Moumen, 2010, 'De l'Algérie à la France. Les conditions de départ et d'accueil des rapatriés, pieds-noirs et harkis, en 1962', *Materiaux pour l'histoire de notre temps*, 3, pp. 60–68.

26 H. de Haas, 2022, 'Bevolking en Migratie', in Bart van Heerikhuizen et al. (eds.), *Samenlevingen: Inleiding in de Sociologie*, Groningen/Utrecht, Noordhoff Uitgevers bv.

27 The UK government tried and failed to convince the Indian government to receive these refugees, and eventually grudgingly allowed them to come. See also 'Ugandan Asians dominate economy after exile', BBC News, 15 May 2016.

28 This data was drawn from the UCDP/PRIO Armed Conflict Dataset, see Fransen and De Haas, 2022.

Myth 4: Our societies are more diverse than ever

1 For instance, in his 1993 book *Clash of Civilizations*, Samuel Huntington predicted that future wars would be fought not between countries, but between cultures. He identified Islamist extremism as the biggest threat to Western domination of the world.

2 Theresa May's speech to the Conservative Party Conference, see https://www.independent.co.uk/news/uk/politics/theresa-may-s-speech-to-the-conservative-party-conference-in-full-a6681901.html

3 De Haas et al., 2020.

4 J. Lucassen and L. Lucassen, 2009, 'The mobility transition revisited, 1500–1900: What the case of Europe can offer to global history', *Journal of Global History*, 4(3), pp. 347–77.

5 M. M. Ghaill, 2000, 'The Irish in Britain: The invisibility of ethnicity and anti-Irish racism', *Journal of Ethnic and Migration Studies*, 26(1), p. 417; L. Ryan, 2007, 'Who do you think you are? Irish nurses encountering ethnicity and constructing identity in Britain', *Ethnic and Racial Studies*, 30(3), pp. 416–38.

6 Cited in D. S. FitzGerald, 2014, 'The Sociology of International Migration', in C. B. Brettell and J. F. Hollifield (eds.), *Migration Theory: Talking across Disciplines*, London, Routledge, pp. 115–47; H. W. Smith (ed.), 2011, *The Oxford Handbook of Modern German History*, Oxford, Oxford University Press.

7 De Haas et al., 2020.

8 Y. Gastaut, 2004, 'Les bidonvilles, lieux d'exclusion et de marginalité en France durant les trente glorieuses', *Cahiers de la Méditerranée* 69, pp. 233–50.

9 A. Leizaola, 2002, 'Le Pays Basque au regard des autres', *Ethnologie française*, 32(3), pp. 429–38; G. Noiriel, 2007, *Immigration, antisémitisme et racisme en France (XIXe–XXe siècle): discours publics, humiliations privées*, Paris, Fayard.

10 See, for instance, S. Bonjour, 2009, *Grens en gezin: Beleidsvorming inzake gezinsmigratie in Nederland, 1955–2005*, Amsterdam University Press.

11 W. Mieder, 1993, '"The Only Good Indian Is a Dead Indian": History and Meaning of a Proverbial Stereotype', *Journal of American Folklore*, pp. 38–60.

12 Russel Thornton, 1990, *American Indian Holocaust and Survival: A Population History since 1492*, University of Oklahoma Press.

13 US Census Bureau 2021 data, https://www.census.gov/programs-surveys/decennial-census/data/datasets.html [retrieved 29 November 2022].

14 'History of lynching in America', NAACP [website], 27 November 2022, https://naacp.org/find-resources/history-explained/history-lynching-america
15 A. Harrison (ed.), 1992, *Black Exodus: The Great Migration from the American South*, University Press of Mississippi; I. Wilkerson, 2021, *The Warmth of Other Suns: The Epic Story of America's Great Migration*, Penguin; 'The Great Migration (1910–1970)', National Archives, https://www.archives.gov/research/african-americans/migrations/great-migration [accessed 3 December 2022].
16 Racial intermarriage became legal throughout the US in 1967 following a landmark Supreme Court decision in the *Loving v. Virginia* case.
17 See E. Lee, 2007, 'The "yellow peril" and Asian exclusion in the Americas', *Pacific Historical Review*, 76(4), pp. 537–62.
18 De Haas et al., 2020.
19 A. Chin, 2005, 'Long-run labor market effects of Japanese American internment during World War II on working-age male internees', *Journal of Labor Economics*, 23(3), pp. 491–525; K. Zong and J. Batalova, 2017, 'Chinese Immigrants in the United States', Migration Policy Institute.
20 A. Kibler, 2008, 'Speaking Like a "Good American": National Identity and the Legacy of German-Language Education', *Teachers College Record*, 110(6), pp. 1241–68; L. W. Grosghal, 'Chronicling America's Historic German Newspapers and the Growth of the American Ethnic Press', National Endowment for the Humanities [blog], 2 July 2014, https://www.neh.gov/divisions/preservation/featured-project/chronicling-americas-historic-german-newspapers-and-the-grow; 'During World War I, US government propaganda erased German culture', NPR, 7 April 2017, https://www.npr.org/2017/04/07/523044253/during-world-war-i-u-s-government-propaganda-erased-german-culture
21 H. H. Charles, 2021, *America's Dark History: From Columbus to Trump*, Wipf and Stock Publishers.
22 M. R. di Nunzio (ed.), 2006, *Woodrow Wilson: Essential Writings and Speeches of the Scholar-President*, NYU Press, p. 412. See also R. Perrucci and C. C. Perrucci, 2009, *America at Risk: The Crisis of Hope, Trust, and Caring*, Rowman & Littlefield Publishers.
23 At the time, the term 'Hun' was often used as a shorthand for savage or brutal behaviour. See Pearl James, 2019, *Picture This: World War I Posters and Visual Culture*, University of Nebraska Press, p. 61. See also Charles, 2021.

24 Brent Staples, 'How Italians Became "White"', *New York Times*, 21 October 2019. See also J. Guglielmo and S. Salerno (eds.), 2003, *Are Italians White?: How Race Is Made in America*, New York, Routledge.

25 *New York Times*, 16 March 1891.

26 FitzGerald, 2014.

27 Ibid.

28 *Time*, 28 August 2006, p. 6; quoted in D. S. Massey et al., 2016.

29 Jörg Blech, 'Die Mär von der vererbten Dummheit', *Der Spiegel*, 30 August 2010.

30 See L. P. Moch, 2012, *The Pariahs of Yesterday: Breton Migrants in Paris*, Duke University Press; D. Violain, 2003, *Bretons de Paris: des exilés en capitale*, Paris, Parigramme.

31 Benedict Anderson, 1983, *Imagined Communities: Reflections on the Origin and Spread of Nationalism*, London, Verso.

32 D. Mack Smith, 1960, 'Italy', in J. P. T. Bury (ed.), *The New Cambridge Modern History*, vol. 10, Cambridge, Cambridge University Press, pp. 552–76.

33 A. Green, 2001, *Fatherlands: State-Building and Nationhood in Nineteenth-Century Germany*, Cambridge, Cambridge University Press.

34 Charles Tilly, 1975, *The Formation of National States in Western Europe*, Princeton, Princeton University Press, p. 42.

35 I. Ahmed, 2002, 'The 1947 partition of India', *Asian Ethnicity*, 3(1), pp. 9–28; Haimanti Roy, 2012, 'Partitioned Lives: Migrants, Refugees, Citizens in India and Pakistan, 1947–65', University of Dayton, History Faculty Publications, Paper 21, http://ecommons.udayton.edu/hst_fac_pub/21

36 Data retrieved from Bundeszentrale für politische Bildung 2021; 'Soziale Situation in Deutschland; Spät-Aussiedler', www.bpb.de [retriered 8 October 2022].

37 De Haas et al., 2020.

38 Christopher Moseley, 2010, *Atlas of the World's Languages in Danger*, Paris, UNESCO; K. L. Rehg and L. Campbell (eds.), 2018, *The Oxford Handbook of Endangered Languages*, Oxford University Press; P. Ladefoged, 2003, *Preserving the Sounds of Disappearing Languages*, https://linguistics.ucla.edu/people/ladefoge/Preserving%20sounds.pdf; Nina Strochlic, 'The Race to Save the World's Disappearing Languages', *National Geographic*, 16 April 2018, https://www.nationalgeographic.com/culture/article/saving-dying-disappearing-languages-wikitongues-culture; Rachel Nuwer, 'Languages: Why We Must Save Dying Tongues', BBC Future, 5 June 2014,

https://www.bbc.com/future/article/20140606-why-we-must-save-dying-languages

39 Map based on https://www.pewresearch.org/short-reads/2013/07/18/the-most-and-least-culturally-diverse-countries-in-the-world/. This map draws on the cultural diversity index developed by Erkan Gören. See E. Gören, 2013, 'Economic effects of domestic and neighbouring countries' cultural diversity', Center for Transnational Studies, University of Bremen Working Paper No. 16.

40 R. D. Putnam, 2000, *Bowling Alone: The Collapse and Revival of American Community*, New York, Simon & Schuster, p. 140. In 2010, this percentage was 33 per cent. See J. M. Twenge et al., 2014, 'Declines in trust in others and confidence in institutions among American adults and late adolescents, 1972–2012', *Psychological Science*, 25(10), pp. 1914–23.

41 F. Sarracino and M. Mikucka, 2017, 'Social capital in Europe from 1990 to 2012: Trends and convergence', *Social Indicators Research*, 131(1), pp. 407–32. See also F. Sarracino, 2012, 'Money, sociability and happiness', *Social Indicators Research*, 109(2), pp. 135–88.

42 M. Abascal and D. Baldassarri, 2015, 'Love thy neighbor? Ethnoracial diversity and trust reexamined', *American Journal of Sociology*, 121(3), pp. 722–82; D. Baldassarri and M. Abascal, 2020, 'Diversity and prosocial behavior', *Science*, 369(6508), pp. 1183–7; T. Van der Meer and J. Tolsma, 2014, 'Ethnic diversity and its effects on social cohesion', *Annual Review of Sociology*, 40(1), pp. 459–78.

43 Jan Mewes et al., 2021, 'Experiences Matter', *Social Science Research*, 95.

44 Putnam, 2000, pp. 358–63.

45 Richard Wilkinson and Kate Pickett, 2009, *The Spirit Level*, London, Allen Lane, pp. 52–4.

46 C. Kesler and I. Bloemraad, 2010, 'Does immigration erode social capital?', *Canadian Journal of Political Science*, 43(2), pp. 319–47.

47 A. Alesina and E. La. Ferrara, 2005, 'Ethnic Diversity and Economic Performance', *Journal of Economic Literature*, 43(3), p. 794.

48 R. Alba, and J. W. Duyvendak, 2019, 'What about the mainstream? Assimilation in super-diverse times', *Ethnic and racial studies*, 42(1), pp. 105–24; J. Duyvendak et al., 2011, 'A Multicultural Paradise? The Cultural Factor in Dutch Integration Policy', in *Bringing Outsiders In: Transatlantic Perspectives on Immigrant Political Incorporation*; see also J. Duyvendak and J. Kesic, 2022, *The Return of the Native: Can Liberalism Safeguard Us Against Nativism?*, Oxford University Press.

Myth 5: Development in poor countries will reduce migration

1 P. L. Martin and J. E. Taylor, 1996, 'The Anatomy of a Migration Hump', in *Development Strategy, Employment, and Migration: Insights from Models*, Paris: OECD Development Centre, pp. 43–62.

2 'Migration at the Social Summit', *Migration News*, April 1995.

3 H. de Haas, 2008b, *Irregular Migration from West Africa to the Maghreb and the European Union*, Geneva, International Organisation for Migration.

4 H. de Haas, 2007, 'Turning the tide? Why development will not stop migration', *Development and Change*, 38(5), pp. 819–41.

5 'President Juncker launches the EU Emergency Trust Fund to tackle root causes of irregular migration in Africa', press release, European Commission, 12 November 2015.

6 'West African leaders meet on migration crisis', CGTN News, 30 October 2016. https://www.youtube.com/watch?v=ZF1VaFuHoao

7 National Security Council, *Strategy for Addressing the Root Causes of Migration in Central America*, https://www.whitehouse.gov/wp-content/uploads/2021/07/Root-Causes-Strategy.pdf

8 De Haas, 2007.

9 See H. de Haas, 1998, 'Socio-Economic Transformations and Oasis Agriculture in Southern Morocco', in H. de Haas and P. Blaikie (eds.), *Looking at Maps in the Dark*, Utrecht/Amsterdam, KNAG/UvA; H. de Haas, 2003, *Migration and Development in Southern Morocco*, PhD thesis, Nijmegen, Radboud University Nijmegen; H. de Haas, 2006, 'Migration, remittances and regional development in Southern Morocco', *Geoforum*, 37, pp. 565–80.

10 H. de Haas, 2021, 'A theory of migration: the aspirations-capabilities framework', *Comparative Migration Studies*, 9(1), pp. 1–35.

11 H. de Haas, 2023, 'La géographie changeante des migrations marocaines', *Géographie du Maroc.*

12 M. L. Flahaux and H. de Haas, 2016, 'African migration: Trends, patterns, drivers', *Comparative Migration Studies*, 4, pp. 1–25.

13 H. de Haas, 2010, *Migration Transitions: A Theoretical and Empirical Inquiry into the Developmental Drivers of International Migration*, IMI working paper 24, Oxford: International Migration Institute, University of Oxford.

14 Ibid.

15 These findings were also confirmed by studies that estimated net migration flows between census years and that followed the actual evolution of

emigration trajectories of countries over the post-Second World War period. See M. A. Clemens, 2014, *Does Development Reduce Migration?*, Washington, DC, Center for Global Development; M. A. Clemens and H. M. Postel, 2018, 'Deterring emigration with foreign aid: An overview of evidence from low-income countries', *Population and Development Review*, 44(4), p. 667; M. A. Clemens, 2020, *The Emigration Life Cycle: How Development Shapes Emigration from Poor Countries*, Bonn, Center for Global Development and IZA; H. de Haas and S. Fransen, 2018, *Social Transformation and Migration: An Empirical Inquiry*, Amsterdam, International Migration Institute, University of Amsterdam.

16 W. Zelinsky, 1971, 'The Hypothesis of the Mobility Transition', *Geographical Review*, 61, pp. 219–49.

17 R. Skeldon, 1990, *Population Mobility in Developing Countries: A Reinterpretation*, London, Belhaven Press; R. Skeldon, 1997, *Migration and Development: A Global Perspective*, Harlow, Essex, Addison Wesley Longman.

18 T. J. Hatton and J. G. Williamson, 1998, *The Age of Mass Migration: Causes and Economic Effects*, Oxford and New York, Oxford University Press.

19 De Haas, 2008a.

20 In a seminal paper published in 2002, the Norwegian migration researcher Jørgen Carling was the first to make a distinction between aspirations and 'abilities' in migration processes, coining the concept of 'involuntary immobility' to describe the phenomenon of the growing numbers of people living in poor countries who have the aspiration, but do not have the ability, to migrate. See J. R. Carling, 2002, 'Migration in the age of involuntary immobility: Theoretical reflections and Cape Verdean experiences', *Journal of Ethnic and Migration Studies*, 28(2), pp. 5–42. In my own work, I developed the capabilities-aspirations model to study the reciprocal links between migration and development in origin societies.

21 Economists call this 'opportunity costs'. In addition to the real costs long-distance migration usually involves, these opportunity costs further exclude the poorest of the poor from migration opportunities.

22 H. de Haas et al., 2020, *Social Transformation*, International Migration Institute working paper no. 166, Amsterdam, University of Amsterdam.

23 R. Rhoda, 1983, 'Rural development and urban migration: Can we keep them down on the farm?', *International Migration Review*, 17(1), pp. 34–64.

24 S. Elder et al., 2015, 'Youth and rural development: Evidence from 25 school-to-work transition surveys', Geneva, ILO; K. Schewel and S. Fransen,

2018, 'Formal education and migration aspirations in Ethiopia', *Population and Development Review*, 44(3), p. 555.

25 A. L. Mabogunje, 1970, 'Systems approach to a theory of rural-urban migration', *Geographical Analysis*, 2(1), pp. 1–18.

26 Clemens, 2020.

Myth 6: Emigration is a desperate flight from misery

1 Helen Dempster and Jasper Tjaden, 2021, *Are Public Information Campaigns for Migrants Effective? Lessons for the Biden Administration*, Center for Global Development.

2 Ibid. See also Ruiz Soto et al., *Migration Narratives in Northern Central America*, Washington DC, Migration Policy Institute.

3 T. G. Blanchette at al., 2013, 'The myth of Maria and the imagining of sexual trafficking in Brazil', *Dialectical Anthropology*, 37(2), pp. 195–227; Blanchette and A. P. Da Silva, 2012, 'On bullshit and the trafficking of women', *Dialectical Anthropology*, 36(1), pp. 107–25; R. Weitzer, 2000, 'The social construction of sex trafficking: Ideology and institutionalization of a moral crusade', *Politics & Society*, 35(3), pp. 447–75.

4 Ibram X. Kendi, 'The day shithole entered the presidential lexicon', *The Atlantic*, January 2019.

5 O. Stark, 1978, *Economic-Demographic Interactions in Agricultural Development: The Case of Rural-to-Urban Migration*, Rome, FAO; O. Stark, 1991, *The Migration of Labor*, Cambridge and Oxford, Blackwell; H. de Haas, 2010, 'Migration and development: A theoretical perspective', *International Migration Review*, 44(1), pp. 227–64; E. J. Taylor, 1999, 'The new economics of labour migration and the role of remittances in the migration process', *International Migration*, 37(1), pp. 63–88.

6 Philip Martin, 'Farm Workers in Mexico and Turkey', Wilson Centre, 29 September 2020, https://www.wilsoncenter.org/article/farm-workers-mexico-and-turkey

7 Melissa Montalvo, 'Thousands of farmworkers will get pay raises thanks to a lawsuit', 2 December 2021, https://calmatters.org/california-divide/2021/12/california-farmworkers-pay-raise/

8 Mark Hugo Lopez and Mohamad Moslimani, 2022, 'Latinos See U.S. as Better Than Place of Family's Ancestry for Opportunity, Raising Kids, Health Care Access', Pew Research Center. https://www.pewresearch.org/

race-ethnicity/2022/01/20/latinos-see-u-s-as-better-than-place-of-familys-ancestry-for-opportunity-raising-kids-health-care-access/

9 Author's calculations based on data extracted from the World Development Indicator database.

10 World Bank Remittance Trends 2006.

11 D. Kapur, 2003, 'Remittances: The new development mantra?', paper prepared for the G-24 Technical Group Meeting, 15–16 September, New York and Geneva, United Nations.

12 See D. Ratha, 2013, 'The Impact of Remittances on Economic Growth and Poverty Reduction', Washington, DC, Migration Policy Institute; J. Frankel, 2011, 'Are bilateral remittances countercyclical?', *Open Economies Review*, 22(1), pp. 1–16. Whether this counter-cyclical effect occurs also depends on business cycles in destination countries, which affects migrant earnings and, hence, their ability to remit money. See I. Ruiz and C. Vargas-Silva, 2014, 'Remittances and the business cycle: A reliable relationship?', *Journal of Ethnic and Migration Studies*, 40(3), pp. 456–74.

13 See Peach, 2006; R. Ballard, 2002, 'The South Asian Presence in Britain and its Transnational Connections', in H. Singh and S. Sertovec (eds.), 2002, *Culture and Economy in the Indian Diaspora*, London, Routledge; Mohamed Berriane et al., 2015, 'Introduction: Revisiting Moroccan migrations', *The Journal of North African Studies* 20(4), pp. 503–21; F. Riosmena and D. S. Massey, 2012, 'Pathways to El Norte', *International Migration Review*, 46(1), pp. 3–36.

14 R. Ballard, 2003, 'A case of capital-rich under-development: The paradoxical consequences of successful transnational entrepreneurship from Mirpur', *Contributions to Indian Sociology*, 37(1–2), pp. 25–57.

15 'How the city of Mirpur became Little England', BBC News, 5 March 2012, https://www.bbc.com/news/magazine-17156238

16 Ibid.

17 De Haas, 2006; de Haas, 2003; de Haas and T. Fokkema, 2010, 'Intra-household conflicts in migration decision making: Return and pendulum migration in Morocco', *Population and Development Review*, 36(3), pp. 541–61.

18 Dovelyn Rannveig Mendoza, 2009, *Guiding the Invisible Hand: Making Migration Intermediaries Work for Development*, New York, UNDP; Mendoza, 2020, *Shifting Labor Frontiers: The Recruitment of South Asian Migrant Workers to the European Union*, Amsterdam, FNV and ISSG.

19 Ibid.

20 Mendoza, 2011, *Labour Migration from Colombo Process Countries: Good Practices, Challenges and Ways Forward*, Geneva, IOM; Mendoza, 2020.

21 Mendoza, 2020.

22 Mendoza, 2011, *Running in Circles: Progress and Challenges in Regulating Recruitment of Filipino and Sri Lankan Labor Migrants to Jordan*, Washington, DC, Migration Policy Institute.

23 Mendoza, 2009; Mendoza, 2020.

24 OFW Statistics, https://www.dmw.gov.ph/archives/ofwstat/ofwstat.html [accessed 14 April 2023].

25 Mendoza, 2006, *Remittances and Development: Trends, Impacts, and Policy Options*, Washington, DC, Migration Policy Institute.

26 Mendoza, 2020.

27 See also K. Hewison, 2004, 'Thai Migrant Workers in Hong Kong', *Journal of Contemporary Asia*, 34(3), pp. 318–35.

28 Mendoza, 2012, *Regulating Private Recruitment in the Asia-Middle East Labour Migration Corridor,* Washington, DC, Migration Policy Institute.

29 K. D. Schewel, 2019, *Moved by Modernity: How Development Shapes Migration in Rural Ethiopia*, PhD thesis, University of Amsterdam; Schewel, 2022, 'Aspiring for Change: Ethiopian Women's Labor Migration to the Middle East', *Social Forces*, 100(4), pp. 1619–41.

30 Ibid.

Myth 7: We don't need migrant workers

1 Sky News, 9 December 2019, https://news.sky.com/story/general-election-pm-vows-to-reduce-immigration-despite-questions-over-points-based-system-11880941

2 Estimates calculated by the author on the basis of data drawn from the UN Population Division (2020). Immigrant population data for Germany and Italy was accessed from national statistical offices [accessed 17 April 2023].

3 See K. D. Schewel, 2020, 'Understanding immobility: Moving beyond the mobility bias in migration studies', *International Migration Review*, 54(2), pp. 328–55; M. Czaika and C. Reinprecht, 2022, 'Why do people stay put in environmentally stressful regions?', *Regional Environmental Change*, 22(3), pp. 1–12. R. Faini and A. Venturini, 2001, *Home Bias and Migration: Why Is Migration Playing a Marginal Role in the Globalization Process?*, CHILD Working Paper 27, Centre for Household, Income, Labour, and Domestic Economics.

4 M. Czaika and De Haas, 2012, 'The role of internal and international relative deprivation in global migration', *Oxford Development Studies*, 40(4), pp. 423–42.

5 H. de Haas et al. (2019), 'International migration: Trends, determinants, and policy effects', *Population and Development Review*, 45(4), pp. 885–922.

6 Clemens, 2020.

7 Statistisches Bundesamt [retrieved 8 October 2021].

8 See M. Czaika and H. de Haas, 2017, 'The effect of visas on migration processes', *International Migration Review*, 51(4), pp. 893–926; M. Czaika and C. Reinprecht, 2020, *Drivers of Migration: A Synthesis of Knowledge*, IMI Working Paper Series 163, University of Amsterdam, International Migration Institute.

9 Apprehensions by Spanish border guards reached a peak of almost 40,000 when unemployment hit an all-time low around 2006. After the 2008 economic crisis they plummeted to 32,000 in 2013 as Spanish unemployment peaked at 26 per cent, after which border apprehensions rebounded with economic recovery and growing labour demand, to peak at 65,000 in 2018. A. Villareal, 2014, 'Explaining the Decline in Mexico-U.S. Migration: The Effect of the Great Recession', *Demography*, 51, pp. 2203–28.

10 Eurostat, 'First permits by reason, length of validity and citizenship' [accessed 26 March 2021].

11 Mendoza, 2018, *Triple Discrimination: Woman, Pregnant and Migrant*, Washington, DC, Fair Labor Association.

12 Kim Parker, 2021, 'What's behind the growing gap between men and women in college completion?', Pew Research Center.

13 Esteban Ortiz-Ospina et al., 2018, 'Women's employment', OurWorldInData.org [online resource].

14 B. Anderson, 2000, *Doing the Dirty Work?: The Global Politics of Domestic Labour*, Palgrave Macmillan; R. Parreñas, 2015, *Servants of Globalization: Migration and Domestic Work*, Stanford University Press.

15 M. Ambrosini, 2013, *Irregular Migration and Invisible Welfare*, Basingstoke, Palgrave Macmillan; Ambrosini, 2015, 'Irregular but tolerated: Unauthorized immigration, elderly care recipients, and invisible welfare', *Migration Studies*, 3, pp. 199–216; H. Lutz and E. Palenga-Möllenbeck, 2010, 'Care Work Migration in Germany: Semi-Compliance and Complicity', *Social Policy and Society*, 9(3), pp. 419–30.

16 American Staffing Association, 'Staffing Industry Statistics', https://americanstaffing.net/research/fact-sheets-analysis-staffing-industry-trends/staffing-industry-statistics/#tab:tbs_nav_item_1 [accessed 3 December 2022];

IBIS World, 2022, 'Employment Placement Agencies in the UK - Market Research Report', https://www.ibisworld.com/united-kingdom/market-research-reports/employment-placement-agencies-industry/ [accessed 3 December 2022].

17 M. Berghege et al., 'Ik had mijn eigen huid in mijn handen', *De Groene Amsterdammer*, 17 May 2019.

18 F. Fasani and J. Mazza, 2020, *Immigrant Key Workers: Their Contribution to Europe's COVID-19 Response*, IZA Discussion Paper No. 13178; K. Pandey et al., 2021, 'Essential and expendable: Migrant domestic workers and the COVID-19 pandemic', *American Behavioral Scientist*, 65(10), pp. 1287–301.

Myth 8: Immigrants steal jobs and drive down wages

1 Drew Desilver, 'For most workers real wages have barely budged for decades', Pew Research Center, 7 August 2018, https://www.pewresearch.org/fact-tank/2018/08/07/for-most-us-workers-real-wages-have-barely-budged-for-decades/

2 L. Mishel and K.-F. Gee, 2012, *Why Aren't Workers Benefiting from Labour Productivity Growth in the United States?*

3 L. Mishel, Economic Policy Institute, Working Economics Blog, 2 September 2021, https://www.epi.org/blog/growing-inequalities-reflecting-growing-employer-power-have-generated-a-productivity-pay-gap-since-1979-productivity-has-grown-3-5-times-as-much-as-pay-for-the-typical-worker/; 1 December 2020, https://www.epi.org/blog/wages-for-the-top-1-skyrocketed-160-since-1979-while-the-share-of-wages-for-the-bottom-90-shrunk-time-to-remake-wage-pattern-with-economic-policies-that-generate-robust-wage-growth-for-vast-majority/

4 D. Blanchflower and S. Machin, 'Falling real wages', *CentrePiece*, Spring 2014, https://cep.lse.ac.uk/pubs/download/cp422.pdf

5 T. Piketty, 2014, *Capital in the Twenty-First Century*, Harvard University Press.

6 CNN, *Lou Dobbs Tonight*, Interview with Bernie Sanders, 25 June 2007, https://www.youtube.com/watch?v=38M9vfg4TPE. See https://www.vox.com/2016/2/12/10981234/bernie-sanders-lou-dobbs

7 L. McCluskey, 2016, 'The free movement of labour is a class question', Institute of Employment Rights, https://www.ier.org.uk/comments/len-mccluskey-free-movement-labour-class-question/

8 In economic jargon, the difficulty of disentangling cause and effect is also known as the 'endogeneity' problem.

9 J. Batalova and J. Zong, 2017, 'Cuban Immigrants in the United States', Migration Policy Institute; D. W. Engstrom, 1997, *Presidential Decision Making Adrift: The Carter Administration and the Mariel Boatlift*, Rowman & Littlefield.

10 D. Card, 1990, 'The impact of the Mariel boatlift on the Miami labor market', *ILR Review*, 43(2), pp. 245–57.

11 G. J. Borjas, 2017, 'The wage impact of the Marielitos: A reappraisal', *ILR Review*, 70(5), pp. 1077–110.

12 M. A. Clemens and J. Hunt, 2019, 'The labor market effects of refugee waves: reconciling conflicting results', *ILR Review*, 72(4), pp. 818–57. Clemens and Hunt argued that the results of Borjas's study were caused not by immigration, but by improved sample coverage of Black male lower-skilled workers who were previously undercounted in workforce surveys since the year of the Mariel boatlift. Because average wages among the lowest-skilled Black workers were 49 per cent lower than wages of their non-Black counterparts, the expansion of sample coverage, not immigration, would explain the drop in recorded wages.

13 G. Peri and V. Yasenov, 2019, 'The labor market effects of a refugee wave synthetic control method meets the Mariel boatlift', *Journal of Human Resources*, 54(2), pp. 267–309.

14 J. Hunt, 1992, 'The impact of the 1962 repatriates from Algeria on the French labor market', *ILR Review*, 45(3), pp. 556–72.

15 R. M. Friedberg, 2001, 'The impact of mass migration on the Israeli labor market', *Quarterly Journal of Economics*, 116(4), pp. 1373–408.

16 A. Glitz, 2012, 'The labor market impact of immigration: A quasi-experiment exploiting immigrant location rules in Germany', *Journal of Labor Economics*, 30(1), pp. 175–213.

17 S. Tumen, 2016, 'The economic impact of Syrian refugees on host countries: Quasi-experimental evidence from Turkey', *American Economic Review*, 106(5), pp. 456–60. See also E. Ceritoglu et al., 2017, 'The impact of Syrian refugees on natives' labor market outcomes in Turkey: Evidence from a quasi-experimental design', *IZA Journal of Labor Policy*, 6(1), pp. 1–28.

18 Ibid.

19 For major studies and overviews, see G. J. Borjas, 2003, 'The Labor Demand Curve is Downward Sloping: Reexamining the Impact of Immigration on the

Labor Market', *Quarterly Journal of Economics*, 118(4), pp. 1335–74; D. Card, 2009, 'Immigration and inequality', *American Economic Review*, 99(2), pp. 1–21; C. Dustmann et al., 2016, 'The impact of immigration: Why do studies reach such different results?', *Journal of Economic Perspectives*, 30(4), pp. 31–56; G. I. P. Ottaviano and G. Peri, 2012, 'Rethinking the effect of immigration on wages', *Journal of the European Economic Association*, 10, pp. 152–97; UNDP, 2009, *Overcoming Barriers: Human Mobility and Development*, New York, UNDP.

20 National Academies of Sciences, Engineering, and Medicine, 2017, *The Economic and Fiscal Consequences of Immigration*, Washington, DC, The National Academies Press.

21 K. Semple, 'A Somali Influx Unsettles Latino Meatpackers', *New York Times*, 15 October 2008; 'Somalis replace Hispanic workers at Iowa plant', NBC News, 29 July 2008; Chico Harlan, 'For Somalis, hope falls to the cutting floor', *Washington Post*, 24 May 2016.

22 C. Dustmann et al., 2005, 'The impact of immigration on the British labour market', *The Economic Journal*, 115(507), pp. F324–F341; C. Dustmann et al., 2008, 'The labour market impact of immigration', *Oxford Review of Economic Policy*, 24(3), pp. 477–94; C. Dustmann, T. Frattini, and I. P. Preston, 2013. 'The effect of immigration along the distribution of wages', *Review of Economic Studies*, 80(1), pp. 145–73.

23 Dustmann et al., 2013.

24 I. Goldin et al., 2011, *Exceptional People: How Migration Shaped Our World and Will Define Our Future*, Princeton and Oxford, Princeton University Press.

25 P. Moser et al., 2014, 'German Jewish émigrés and US invention', *American Economic Review*, 104(10), pp. 3222–55.

26 R. Vartabedian, 'Who got America to the moon? An unlikely collaboration of Jewish and former Nazi scientists and engineers', *LA Times*, 1 March 2020.

27 See J. Hunt, 2011, 'Which immigrants are most innovative and entrepreneurial? Distinctions by entry visa', *Journal of Labor Economics*, 29(3), pp. 417–57.

28 Mark Hart et al., 2017, *Global Entrepreneurship Monitor: United Kingdom 2017 Monitoring Report*, NatWest, https://gemconsortium.org/report/gem-united-kingdom-2017-report

29 See A. Alesina et al., 2016, 'Birthplace diversity and economic prosperity', *Journal of Economic Growth*, 21, pp. 101–38.

30 M. Piore, 1979, *Birds of Passage: Migrant Labor and Industrial Societies*, Cambridge, Cambridge University Press.
31 'UK farms migrant workers picking fruit and vegetables', YouTube video, https://www.youtube.com/watch?v=TFInOucNZsQ
32 'UK farmers need "thousands of foreign workers" next summer', BBC News, 7 October 2020, https://www.bbc.com/news/business-54712374
33 Kieran Guilbert, 'Brexit farm workers scheme found fueling risk of slavery in UK', Reuters, 16 March 2021, https://www.reuters.com/article/us-britain-farming-slavery-idUSKBN2B828O
34 Adam McCullock, 'Pick for Britain campaign fails to bear fruit', *Personnel Today*, 19 April 2021, https://www.personneltoday.com/hr/pick-for-britain-campaign-fails-to-bear-fruit/
35 Home Office, 'Why do people come to the UK?', 23 February 2023, https://www.gov.uk/government/statistics/immigration-system-statistics-year-ending-december-2022/why-do-people-come-to-the-uk-to-work
36 David Card in Roger Lowenstein, 'The Immigration Equation', *New York Times*, 9 July 2006, https://www.nytimes.com/2006/07/09/magazine/the-immigration-equation.html

Myth 9: Immigration undermines the welfare state

1 See Arlie Hochschild, 2016, *Strangers in Their Own Land: Anger and Mourning on the American Right*, The New Press, 2016.
2 'Reid targets illegal immigrants', BBC News, 7 March 2007, http://news.bbc.co.uk/2/hi/uk_news/politics/6424377.stm
3 Jan Strupczewski and Robin Emmott, 'Migrant job-seekers can be denied benefits, EU lawyer says', Reuters, 26 March 2015, https://www.reuters.com/article/uk-eu-migration-benefits-idUKKBN0MM1T920150326
4 'Seehofer und Merkel befeuern Leitkultur-Debatte', *Der Spiegel*, 15 October 2010, https://www.spiegel.de/politik/deutschland/integration-seehofer-und-merkel-befeuern-leitkultur-debatte-a-723466.html
5 'Transcript of Donald Trump's Immigration Speech', *New York Times*, 1 September 2016, https://www.nytimes.com/2016/09/02/us/politics/transcript-trump-immigration-speech.html
6 See C. Vargas-Silva, 2014, *The Fiscal Impact of Immigration in the UK*, Migration Observatory, University of Oxford.

7 See P. M. Orrenius, 2017, *New Findings on the Fiscal Impact of Immigration in the United States*, Federal Reserve Bank of Dallas Research Department; J. P. Smith, 2018, 'Taxpayer effects of immigration', IZA World of Labor.

8 R. Rowthorn, 2008, 'The fiscal impact of immigration on the advanced economies', *Oxford Review of Economic Policy*, 24(3), pp. 560–80.

9 Ibid.

10 D. Sriskandarajah et al., 2005, *Paying their Way: The Fiscal Contribution of Immigrants in the UK*, London, IPPR; see also Vargas-Silva et al., 2022.

11 Rowthorn, 2008, p. 577.

12 Ana Damas de Matos, 2021, 'The fiscal impact of immigration in OECD countries since the mid-2000s', in OECD, *International Migration Outlook 2021*, OECD Publishing, pp. 111–62.

13 Ibid.

14 Ibid.

15 Ibid.

16 See for instance National Academies of Sciences (NAS), Engineering, and Medicine, 2017, *The Economic and Fiscal Consequences of Immigration*, Washington, DC, The National Academies Press.

17 C. Dustmann and T. Frattini, 2014, 'The fiscal effects of immigration to the UK', *The Economic Journal*, 124(580), F593–F643.

18 NAS, 2017; Smith, 2018.

19 Ibid.

20 G. J. Borjas, 1996, 'The Welfare Magnet', *National Review*; Borjas, 1999, 'Immigration and Welfare Magnets', *Journal of Labor Economics*, 17(4), pp. 607–37.

21 Borjas, 1999; P. B. Levine and D. J. Zimmerman, 1999, 'An empirical analysis of the welfare magnet debate using the NLSY', *Journal of Population Economics*, 12(3), pp. 391–409.

22 C. Giulietti and J. Wahba, 2013, 'Welfare migration', in *International Handbook on the Economics of Migration*, Edward Elgar Publishing, pp. 489–504.

23 L. C. Gee et al., 2016, *Undocumented Immigrants' State & Local Tax Contributions*, The Institute on Taxation and Economic Policy.

24 D. T. Grisworld, 2012, 'Immigration and the welfare state', *Cato Journal*, 32 (1), pp. 159–74.

25 Ismael Gálvez Iniesta, 2002, 'The size, socio-economic composition and fiscal implications of the irregular immigration in Spain', Universidad Carlos III de Madrid, Departamento de Economía.

26 Mariña Fernández Reino and Carlos Vargas-Silva, 2022, *Migrants and Housing in the UK*, Migration Observatory, University of Oxford.

27 P. Boelhouwer and H. Priemus, 2014, 'Demise of the Dutch social housing tradition: impact of budget cuts and political changes', *Journal of Housing and the Built Environment*, 29(2), pp. 221–35.

28 C. Hochstenbach, 2022, *Uitgewoond: Waarom het hoog tijd is voor een nieuwe woonpolitiek*, Amsterdam, Das Mag.

29 Ibid.; personal communication with Cody Hochstenbach.

30 Ibid.

31 See Liam Halligan, 2021, *Why aren't we building more council houses?*, GBNews, 1 December 2021, https://www.gbnews.com/opinion/liam-halligan-why-arent-we-building-more-council-houses/169343

32 Lydia McMullan et al., 'UK housing crisis: How did owning a home become unaffordable?', *Guardian*, 31 March 2021; H. Carr, 2011, 'The Right to Buy, the Leaseholder, and the Impoverishment of Ownership', *Journal of Law and Society*, 38, pp. 519–41; P. Malpass and C. Victory, 2010, 'The modernisation of social housing in England', *International Journal of Housing Policy*, 10(1), pp. 3–18.

33 D. Bailey and C. Kirkland, 'The rise of Housing Support', 10 June 2015, https://blogs.lse.ac.uk/politicsandpolicy/the-rise-of-housing-support-and-the-free-market-principles-holding-back-deficit-reduction/

34 McMullan et al., 'UK housing crisis'.

35 'Social housing deficit', Shelter [website], https://england.shelter.org.uk/support_us/campaigns/social_housing_deficit

36 Shashaty, Andre, 'U.S Cuts Back and Shifts Course on Housing Aid', *New York Times*, 18 October 1981.

37 Peter Dreier, 2004, 'Reagan's Legacy: Homelessness in America', Shelterforce, 1 May 2004, https://shelterforce.org/2004/05/01/reagans-legacy-homelessness-in-america/

38 Jenny Schuetz and Cecile Murray, 'Unpacking the housing shortage puzzle', Brookings, 25 April 2018, https://www.brookings.edu/research/unpacking-the-housing-shortage-puzzle/; James Rodriguez, 'Bad news for millennials', *Business Insider*, 22 January 2023, https://www.businessinsider.nl/bad-news-for-millennials-things-have-never-looked-bleaker-for-first-time-homebuyers/

39 M. B. Aalbers and A. Holm, 2008, 'Privatising Social Housing in Europe: The Cases of Amsterdam and Berlin', in K. Adelhof et al. (eds.), *Urban*

trends in Berlin and Amsterdam, Geographisches Institut der Humboldt-Universität zu Berlin, pp. 12–23.

40 See also A. J. Auerbach and P. Oreopoulos, 1999, 'Analyzing the fiscal impact of US immigration', *American Economic Review*, 89(2), pp. 176–80.

41 Carl Baker, 2022, *NHS Staff from Overseas: Statistics*, London, House of Commons Library, https://researchbriefings.files.parliament.uk/documents/CBP-7783/CBP-7783.pdf

Myth 10: Immigrant integration has failed

1 Youth conference, Christian Democratic Union (CDU), 16 October 2010.

2 J. Duyvendak and J. Kesic, 2022, *The Return of the Native: Can Liberalism Safeguard Us Against Nativism?*, Oxford University Press.

3 See J. Duyvendak et al. (eds.), 2016, *The Culturalization of Citizenship: Belonging and Polarization in a Globalizing World*, London, Palgrave.

4 Samuel P. Huntington, 2004, 'The Hispanic Challenge', *Foreign Policy*, 28 October 2009.

5 There is a huge amount of literature on immigrant integration. For major overview studies see NAS, 2015, *The Integration of Immigrants into American Society*, Washington, DC, The National Academies Press; OECD/EU, 2018, *Settling In 2018: Indicators of Immigrant Integration*, Brussels, OECD Publishing, Paris/European Union; Richard Alba and Victor Nee, 2003, *Remaking the American Mainstream: Assimilation and Contemporary Immigration*, Harvard University Press.

6 NAS, 2015.

7 Ibid.

8 T. Gries et al., 2021, 'Educational assimilation of first-generation and second-generation immigrants in Germany', *Journal of International Migration and Integration*, pp. 1–31; OECD/EU, 2018.

9 L. Lessard-Phillips and Y. Li, 2017, 'Social stratification of education by ethnic minority groups over generations in the UK', *Social Inclusion*, 5(1), pp. 45–54.

10 See also Y. Li and A. Heath, 2016, 'Class matters: A study of minority and majority social mobility in Britain, 1982–2011', *American Journal of Sociology*, 122(1), pp. 162–200.

11 Peach, 2006.

12 T. Frattini et al., 2011, *Ethnicity and second generation immigrants in Britain*, CReAM Discussion Paper No. 04/10.

13 See for instance CPB, 2018, Jaarraport Integratie, Den Haag, Centraal Bureau voor de Statistiek, p. 61; OECD, 2018, *Catching Up? Country Studies on Intergenerational Mobility and Children of Immigrants*, Paris, OECD Publishing.

14 E. Zschirnt and D. Ruedin, 2016, 'Ethnic discrimination in hiring decisions: a meta-analysis of correspondence tests 1990–2015', *Journal of Ethnic and Migration Studies*, 42(7), pp. 1115–34.

15 B. Lancee, 2021, 'Ethnic discrimination in hiring: Comparing groups across contexts. Results from a cross-national field experiment', *Journal of Ethnic and Migration Studies*, 47(6), pp. 1181–200.

16 M. Ramos et al., 2019, 'Labour Market Discrimination Against Moroccan Minorities in the Netherlands and Spain: A Cross-National and Cross-Regional Comparison', *Journal of Ethnic and Migration Studies*; L. Thijssen et al., 2019, 'Discrimination Against Turkish Minorities in Germany and the Netherlands', *Journal of Ethnic and Migration Studies*; V. Di Stasio et al., 2021, 'Muslim by default or religious discrimination?', *Journal of Ethnic and Migration Studies*, 47(6), pp. 1305–26.

17 R. Yemane and M. Fernández-Reino, 2021, 'Latinos in the United States and in Spain: The impact of ethnic group stereotypes on labour market outcomes', *Journal of Ethnic and Migration Studies*, 47(6), pp. 1240–60.

18 L. Quillian et al., 2019, 'Do some countries discriminate more than others? Evidence from 97 field experiments of racial discrimination in hiring', *Sociological Science*, 6, pp. 467–96.

19 NAS, 2015.

20 Ibid.

21 Dowell Myers and John Pitkin, 2010, *Assimilation Today: New Evidence Shows the Latest Immigrants to America Are Following in Our History's Footsteps*, Washington, DC, Center for American Progress.

22 R. Alba et al., 2011, 'Downward Assimilation and Mexican Americans', in *The Next Generation: Immigrant Youth in a Comparative Perspective*, p. 108.

23 C. Dustmann and F. Fabbri, 2005, 'Immigrants in the British labour market', *Fiscal Studies*, 26(4), pp. 423–70.

24 Frattini et al., 2011.

25 Office for National Statistics, 'Ethnicity pay gaps: 2019'.

26 OECD, 2018.

27 OECD/EU, 2018.

28 De Haas et al., 2020.

29 I. Kogan, 2011, 'New immigrants – old disadvantage patterns? Labour market integration of recent immigrants into Germany', *International Migration*, 49(1), pp. 91–117; OECD, 2008, *International Migration Outlook*, Paris, OECD Publishing, pp. 68–78; OECD, 2018.

30 OECD/EU, 2018.

31 B. Coulmont and Patrick Simon, 2019, 'Quels prénoms les immigrés donnent-ils à leurs enfants en France?', *Population & Société* 565, pp. 1–4.

32 See for instance E. F. Ersanilli, 2010, *Comparing Integration: Host culture adaption and ethnic retention among Turkish immigrants and their descendants in France, Germany and the Netherlands*, PhD thesis, Amsterdam, Vrije Universiteit.

33 L. Platt et al., 2022, 'Which integration policies work?', *International Migration Review*, 56(2), pp. 344–75. For a review of 22 studies, see O. Bilgili et al., 2015, 'The dynamics between integration policies and outcomes: A synthesis of the literature', Migration Policy Group.

34 J. Clausen et al., 2009, 'The effect of integration policies on the time until regular employment of newly arrived immigrants: Evidence from Denmark', *Labour Economics*, 16(4), pp. 409–17; H. Qi et al, 2019, *Does Integration Policy Integrate? The Employment Effects of Sweden's 2010 Reform of the Introduction Program*, DP No. 12594, Bonn, IZA.

35 R. Euwals et al., 2007, *Immigration, integration and the Labour market: Turkish Immigrants in Germany and the Netherlands*, IZA Discussion Paper No. 2677.

36 I. Van Liempt, 2011, 'From Dutch dispersal to ethnic enclaves in the UK: The relationship between segregation and integration examined through the eyes of Somalis', *Urban Studies*, 48(16), pp. 3385–98.

37 R. Kloosterman et al., 1999, 'Mixed embeddedness: (in)formal economic activities and immigrant businesses in the Netherlands', *International Journal of Urban and Regional Research*, 23(2), pp. 252–66; R. Kloosterman, 2003, 'Creating opportunities: Policies aimed at increasing openings for immigrant entrepreneurs in the Netherlands', *Entrepreneurship & Regional Development*, 15(2), pp. 167–81.

38 H. Ghorashi, 2003, *Ways to Survive, Battles to Win: Iranian Women Exiles in the Netherlands and United States*, Nova Publishers.

39 M. Vink, 2017, 'Citizenship and Legal Statuses in Relation to the Integration of Migrants and Refugees', in R. Bauböck and M. Tripkovic (eds.), *The Integration of Migrants and Refugees*, European University Institute, pp. 24–46.

40 F. Peters et al., 2020, 'Naturalisation and immigrant earnings: why and to whom citizenship matters', *European Journal of Population*, 36(3), pp. 511–45.

41 M. Vink et al., 'Long-Term Heterogeneity in Immigrant Naturalization', *European Sociological Review*, 37(5), pp. 751–65.

42 In fact, sociologists Jan Willem Duyvendak and Peter Scholten argued that 'multiculturalism' was always more an ideology than an actual set of policies. See Duyvendak and Scholten, 2012, 'Deconstructing the Dutch multicultural model', *Comparative European Politics*, 10, pp. 266–82.

43 H. de Haas, 1997, *The Role of Self-Organisations of Migrants and Ethnic Minorities in the Local Authority*, Maastricht, European Centre for Work and Society.

44 H. de Haas, 1997, *Political Participation of Migrants and Ethnic Minorities in the Local Authority*, Maastricht, European Centre for Work and Society.

45 See S. Castles, 1985, 'The guests who stayed – the debate on foreigners policy in the German Federal Republic', *International Migration Review*, 19(3), pp. 517–34.

46 De Haas et al., 2020, p. 295.

47 A. Portes, 2010, 'Migration and social change: Some conceptual reflections', *Journal of Ethnic and Migration Studies*, 36(10), pp. 1537–63.

Myth 11: Mass migration has produced mass segregation

1 *Daily Mail*, 3 November 2016; *Guardian*, 23 September 2005; the two last headlines are from French newspapers cited in Loïc J. D. Wacquant, 1992, 'Banlieues françaises et ghetto noir américain: De l'amalgame à la comparaison', *French Politics and Society* 10(4), pp. 81–90.

2 Fergus O'Sullivan, 'How Denmark's ghetto is ripping apart migrant communities', *Guardian*, 11 March 2020, https://www.theguardian.com/world/2020/mar/11/how-denmarks-ghetto-list-is-ripping-apart-migrant-communities

3 Suzan Quitaz, 'Denmark's Ghetto Laws Replicated in other Scandinavian Countries', *Mjalla*, 12 August 2012, https://eng.majalla.com/node/246696/politicsdenmark%E2%80%99s-ghetto-laws-replicated-other-scandinavian-countries

4 Trevor Phillips, 2015, 'After 7/7: Sleepwalking to Segregation', Speech to the Manchester Council for Community Relations, 22 September 2005.

5 C. Peach, 1996, 'Good segregation, bad segregation', *Planning Perspectives*, 11(4), pp. 379–98.

6 D. S. Massey et al., 1987, 'The effect of residential segregation on black social and economic well-being', *Social Forces*, 66(1), pp. 29–56; D. S.

Massey, 2020, 'Still the Linchpin: Segregation and Stratification in the USA', *Race and Social Problems*, 12(1), pp. 1–12.

7 R. Johnston et al., 2007, 'The geography of ethnic residential segregation: A comparative study of five countries', *Annals of the Association of American Geographers*, 97(4), pp. 713–38; S. Musterd, 2005, 'Social and ethnic segregation in Europe: Levels, causes, and effects', *Journal of Urban Affairs*, 27(3), pp. 331–48.

8 Massey, 2020.

9 Musterd, 2005; see also Benassi et al., 2020.

10 Ibid.

11 See also Johnston et al., 2007.

12 Musterd, 2005.

13 Peach, 2006.

14 S. Musterd (ed.), 2022, *Handbook of Urban Segregation*, Cheltenham, UK, Edward Elgar Publishing.

15 G. Catney, 2018, 'The complex geographies of ethnic residential segregation', *Transactions of the Institute of British Geographers*, 43(1), pp. 137–52; Tian Lan et al., 2020, 'Geographic scales of residential segregation in English cities', *Urban Geography*, 41(1), pp. 103–23; R. Johnston et al., 2016, 'Macro-scale stability with micro-scale diversity: Modelling changing ethnic minority residential segregation – London 2001–2011', *Transactions of the Institute of British Geographers*, 41(4), pp. 389–402.

16 Massey, 2020.

17 Peach, 1996, 'Does Britain have ghettos?', *Transactions of the Institute of British Geographers*, pp. 216–235. See also T. L. Philpott, 1978, *The Slum and the Ghetto: Neighborhood Deterioration and Middle Class Reform, Chicago, 1880–1930*, New York, Oxford University Press.

18 Wacquant, 1992.

19 See also H. E. Aldrich and R. Waldinger, 1990, 'Ethnicity and entrepreneurship', *Annual Review of Sociology*, pp. 111–35; J. Rath and A. Swagerman, 2016, 'Promoting ethnic entrepreneurship in European cities', *International Migration*, 54(1), pp. 152–66.

20 De Haas et al., 2020.

21 Ibid.

22 Ibid.

23 S. Musterd and S. D. Vos, 2007, 'Residential dynamics in ethnic concentrations', *Housing Studies*, 22, pp. 333–53; S. Musterd and R. Van Kempen, 2009, 'Segregation and housing of minority ethnic groups in Western European cities', *Tijdschrift voor economische en sociale geografie*, 100, pp. 559–66.

24 D. S. Massey and Nancy A. Denton, 1993, *American Apartheid: Segregation and the Making of the Underclass*, Cambridge, MA: Harvard University Press.
25 De Haas et al., 2020.
26 Massey, 2020.
27 Massey and Denton, 1993.
28 I. Katznelson, 2005, *When Affirmative Action Was White: An Untold History of Racial Inequality in Twentieth-Century America*, New York, W. W. Norton.
29 W. J. Wilson, 1987, *The Truly Disadvantaged: The Inner City, The Underclass, and Public Policy*, Chicago University Press.
30 Loïc Wacquant, 2007, 'French working-class banlieues and the black American ghetto: From conflation to comparison', *Qui Parle*, 16(2).
31 Ibid.
32 For instance, Pat Buchanan's remarks that '[T]hey are not assimilated into America. Many Hispanics, as a matter of fact, you know what culture they are assimilating to? The rap culture, the crime culture, anti-cops, all the rest of it', 23 August 2006. See https://archive.thinkprogress.org/buchanan-hispanic-immigrants-not-assimilating-into-america-because-they-embrace-rap-culture-f7e9013b749/
33 J. A. Agnew, 2010, 'Slums, ghettos, and urban marginality', *Urban Geography*, 31(2), pp. 144–7.
34 Daniel Schwartz, 'How America's Ugly History of Segregation Changed the Meaning of the Word "Ghetto"', *Time*, 24 September 2019, https://time.com/5684505/ghetto-word-history/
35 Kieran Yates, 'The twinned injustices of race', *Guardian*, 1 August 2020, https://www.theguardian.com/commentisfree/2020/aug/01/the-twinned-injustices-of-race-and-class-lie-at-the-heart-of-the-grenfell-tragedy; Dan Bulley et al. (eds.), 2019, *After Grenfell: Violence, Resistance and Response*, London, Pluto Press.
36 Victoria Pinoncely, 'Sink estates are not sunk', *Guardian*, 11 May 2016, https://www.theguardian.com/housing-network/2016/may/11/sink-estates-starved-funding-poverty-housing
37 Patrick Mulrenan, 'The long history of social housing segregation in Britain', LSE, 3 May 2019, https://blogs.lse.ac.uk/politicsandpolicy/social-housing-segregation/
38 A. Murie, 2018, 'Decline and response? Lifecycle change and housing estates in Birmingham, England', *Housing Estates in Europe: Poverty, Ethnic Segregation and Policy Challenges*, pp. 121–44.

39 Moa Tunström and Shinan Wang, 2019, *The Segregated City: A Nordic Overview*, Copenhagen, Nordic Council of Ministers. See also J. Östh et al., 2015, 'Measuring the scale of segregation using k-nearest neighbor aggregates', *Geographical Analysis*, 47(1), pp. 34–49.

40 C. Caldwell, 'Islam on the Outskirts of the Welfare State', *New York Times Magazine*, 5 February 2006, https://www.nytimes.com/2006/02/05/magazine/islam-on-the-outskirts-of-the-welfare-state.html

41 Owen Hatherley, 'How Sweden's innovative housing programme fell foul of privatization', *Guardian*, 16 June 2013, https://www.theguardian.com/commentisfree/2013/jun/16/sweden-housing-programme-privatisation

42 Jane Jacobs, 1961, *The Death and Life of Great American Cities*, New York, Random House.

43 W. R. Boterman et al., 2021, 'Multiple dimensions of residential segregation. The case of the Metropolitan Area of Amsterdam', *Urban Geography*, 42(4), pp. 481–506; S. Musterd, 2020, 'Een ontspannen perspectief op residentiële segregatie', *Beleid en Maatschappij*, 47(4), pp. 339–58; S. Musterd et al., 2017, 'Socioeconomic segregation in European capital cities: Increasing separation between poor and rich', *Urban Geography*, 38(7), pp. 1062–83; T. Tammaru et al., 2016, *Socio-Economic Segregation in European Capital Cities*, London/New York, Routledge.

44 Massey, 2020.

Myth 12: Immigration sends crime rates soaring

1 Presidential campaign announcement speech, 16 June 2015, cited by *Washington Post*, 2 October 2019; 27 June 2017 rally in Youngstown, OH, quoted in C. R. Kelly, 2020, 'Donald J. Trump and the rhetoric of ressentiment', *Quarterly Journal of Speech*, 106(1), p. 2.

2 'Britain and the EU are better together', Debate, Oxford Union, 23 November 2015.

3 Brian Bell, Crime and Immigration, IZA World of Labor, https://wol.iza.org/uploads/articles/469/pdfs/crime-and-immigration.pdf?v=1

4 M. T. Light et al., 2020, 'Comparing crime rates between undocumented immigrants, legal immigrants, and native-born US citizens in Texas', *Proceedings of the National Academy of Sciences*, 117(51), pp. 32340–7.

5 L. H. Laub and R. J. Sampson, 1988, 'Unraveling families and delinquency: A reanalysis of the Gluecks' data', *Criminology*, 26(3), pp. 355–80.

6 See pp. 326–30 of NAS, 2015; G. C. Ousey and C. E. Kubrin, 2014, 'Immigration and the changing nature of homicide in US cities, 1980–2010', *Journal of Quantitative Criminology*, 30(3), pp. 453–83.

7 See also A. Chalfin, 2014, 'What is the contribution of Mexican immigration to US crime rates? Evidence from rainfall shocks in Mexico', *American Law and Economics Review*, 16(1), pp. 220–68; J. L. Spenkuch, 2014, 'Understanding the impact of immigration on crime', *American Law and Economics Review*, 16(1), pp. 177–219.

8 R. G. Rumbaut et al., 2006, 'Immigration and incarceration: Patterns and predictors of imprisonment among first- and second-generation young adults', in R. Martinez and A. Valenzuela (eds.), *Immigration and Crime*, New York, New York University Press, pp. 64–89.

9 R. Martinez Jr and M. T. Lee, 2000, 'Comparing the context of immigrant homicides in Miami: Haitians, Jamaicans and Mariels', *International Migration Review*, 34(3), pp. 794–812 ; Lee et al., 2001, 'Does immigration increase homicide? Negative evidence from three border cities', *The Sociological Quarterly*, 42(4), pp. 559–80.

10 R. J. Sampson, 2008, 'Rethinking crime and immigration', *Contexts*, 7(1), p. 30; R. J. Sampson et al., 2005, 'Social anatomy of racial and ethnic disparities in violence', *American Journal of Public Health*, 95(2), pp. 224–32.

11 F. D. Boateng et al., 2021, 'I may be an immigrant, but I am not a criminal: Examining the association between the presence of immigrants and crime rates in Europe', *Journal of International Migration and Integration*, 22(3), pp. 1105–124.

12 B. Bell and S. Machin, 2013, 'Immigrant enclaves and crime', *Journal of Regional Science*, 53(1), pp. 118–41.

13 I. Goldin et al., 2011, *Exceptional People: How Migration Shaped Our World and Will Define Our Future*, Princeton and Oxford, Princeton University Press.

14 C. Moehling and A. M. Piehl, 2009, 'Immigration, crime, and incarceration in early twentieth-century America', *Demography*, 46(4), pp. 739–63.

15 Annie Laurie Hines and Giovanni Peri, 2019, *Immigrants' Deportations, Local Crime and Police Effectiveness*, IZA Discussion Papers, No. 12413; T. J. Miles and A. B. Cox, 2014, 'Does immigration enforcement reduce crime? Evidence from secure communities', *The Journal of Law and Economics*, 57(4), pp. 937–73.

16 M. T. Light and T. Miller, 2018, 'Does undocumented immigration increase violent crime?', *Criminology*, 56(2), pp. 370–401.

17 M. T. Light et al., 2020, 'Comparing crime rates between undocumented immigrants, legal immigrants, and native-born US citizens in Texas', *Proceedings of the National Academy of Sciences*, 117(51), pp. 32340–7.
18 Alex Nowrasteh, 2018, 'Criminal Immigrants in Texas: Illegal Immigrant Conviction and Arrest Rates for Homicide, Sex Crimes, Larceny, and Other Crimes', Cato Institute.
19 A. Portes and M. Zhou, 1993, 'The new second generation: Segmented assimilation and its variants', *The Annals of the American Academy of Political and Social Science*, 530(1), pp. 74–96; M. Zhou, 1997, 'Segmented assimilation: Issues, controversies, and recent research on the new second generation', *International Migration Review*, 31(4), pp. 975–1008.
20 Ibid.
21 Or 20.7 per cent among those aged 18–30 in 2000. *Bureau of Justice Statistics Bulletin*, 2004.
22 See R. J. Sampson et al., 1997, 'Neighborhoods and violent crime: A multilevel study of collective efficacy', *Science*, 277(5328), pp. 918–24; L. H. Laub and R. J. Sampson, 1988, 'Unraveling families and delinquency: A reanalysis of the Gluecks' data', *Criminology*, 26(3), pp. 355–80; D. S. Elliott et al., 1996, 'The effects of neighborhood disadvantage on adolescent development', *Journal of Research in Crime and Delinquency*, 33(4), pp. 389–426.
23 L. Jong and A. M'charek, 2018, 'The high-profile case as "fire object": Following the Marianne Vaatstra murder case through the media', *Crime, Media, Culture*, 14(3), pp. 347–63.
24 P. Fortuin, 1999, *Kollumer Stront*, Elsevier, 16 October 1999.
25 Jong and M'charek, 2018.
26 M. T. Light, 2022, 'The declining significance of race in criminal sentencing: Evidence from US federal courts', *Social Forces*, 100(3), pp. 1110–41.
27 E. Bonilla-Silva, 2006, *Racism without Racists: Color-Blind Racism and the Persistence of Racial Inequality in the United States*, Rowman & Littlefield Publishers; P. Essed, 1991, *Understanding Everyday Racism: An Interdisciplinary Theory*, vol. 2, Sage.
28 W. E. Bezemer and A. S. Leerkes, 2021, *Oververtegenwoordiging verder ontcijferd: een kwantitatief onderzoek naar sociale verschillen in verdenkingskans en zelfgerapporteerd crimineel gedrag onder jongeren in Nederland*, Sdu Uitgevers, Den Haag; Politie & Wetenschap, Den Haag; Erasmus Universiteit, Rotterdam.
29 P. L. Martens, 2001, 'Immigrants as victims of crime', *International Review of Victimology*, 8(2), pp. 199–216.

30 See M. Kagan, 2014, 'Immigrant victims, immigrant accusers', *U. Mich. JL Reform*, 48, p. 915.

31 A. Tseloni et al., 2010, 'Exploring the international decline in crime rates', *European Journal of Criminology*, 7(5), pp. 375–94.

32 Oliver K. Roeder et al., 2015, *What Caused the Crime Decline?*, Columbia Business School Research Paper No. 155.

33 Source: IHME, Global Burden of Disease (2019), from OurWorldInData.org/homicides [accessed 16 April 2023].

34 In the US, increased incarceration has been declining in its effectiveness as a crime control tactic for more than thirty years. Its effect on crime rates after 1990 was limited, and it has been non-existent since 2000. See Roeder et al., 2015. For European crime trends, see D. Ignatans and R. Matthews, 2017, 'Immigration and the crime drop', *European Journal of Crime, Criminal Law and Criminal Justice*, 25(3), pp. 205–29.

Myth 13: Emigration leads to a brain drain

1 A. Sayad, 1977, 'Les trois « âges » de l'émigration algérienne en France', *Actes de la recherche en sciences sociales*, 15(1), pp. 59–79.

2 Rufaro Samanga, GCIM, 2005, 'Migration in an Interconnected World: New Directions for Action', Geneva: Global Commission on International Migration, p. 24.

3 Paul Collier, 2013, *Exodus: How Migration Is Changing Our World*, Oxford, Oxford University Press.

4 R. H. Adams, 2003, *International Migration, Remittances, and the Brain Drain: A Study of 24 Labor-Exporting Countries*, Washington, DC, World Bank.

5 F. Docquier et al., 2007, 'Brain drain in developing countries', *The World Bank Economic Review*, 21(2), pp. 193–218. For lower-middle and upper-middle income countries these percentages were 7.6 and 7.9 per cent, respectively. This was based on estimates on migration to member states of the Organisation for Economic Co-operation and Development (OECD).

6 Author's analyses based on data downloaded from the World Development Indicators database of the World Bank [accessed 5 December 2022].

7 See A. Hutch et al., 2017, 'The brain drain myth: Retention of specialist surgical graduates in East, Central and Southern Africa, 1974–2013', *World Journal of Surgery*, 41(12), pp. 3046–53.

8 E. Lizi et al., 2013, 'Point of view: Modern medical myth: "more doctors in Manchester than in Malawi",: a preliminary communication', *Malawi Medical Journal: The Journal of Medical Association of Malawi*, 25(1), pp. 20–21.

9 Charlotte McDonald, 'Malawian doctors – are there more in Manchester than Malawi?', BBC News, 15 January 2012, https://www.bbc.com/news/magazine-16545526

10 See Hutch et al., 2017.

11 E. Adovor et al., 2021, 'Medical brain drain: how many, where and why?', *Journal of Health Economics*, 76, p. 102409. According to this study, the Caribbean region has the highest rate of medical migration, with 28.4 per cent of all physicians living abroad in 2014. In sub-Saharan Africa, between 2004 and 2014 the physicians expatriate rate decreased from 18.2 to 14.5 per cent.

12 S. Elder et al., 2015, *Youth and Rural Development: Evidence from 25 School-to-Work Transition Surveys*, Geneva: ILO.

13 Source: World development Indicators database. Indicator: Unemployment, youth total (% of the labour force ages 15–25). Modelled ILO estimate. Between 2020 and 2021, youth employment in Nepal rose from 3.2 to 9.5 per cent; in Bangladesh from 6.4 to 14.7 per cent; in Honduras from 6.0 to 14.7 per cent.

14 Michael A. Clemens, 2007, *Do Visas Kill? Health Effects of African Health Professional Emigration*, Washington, DC, Center for Global Development.

15 Ibid.; Dr Khumbo Kalua, 'Reversing doctors brain drain from Malawi' [blog post], 17 May 2009, http://khumbokalua.blogspot.com/2009/05/reversing-doctors-brain-drain-from.html

16 B. Balmer et al., 2009, 'The Royal Society and the "brain drain": Natural scientists meet social science', *Notes and Records of the Royal Society*, 63(4), pp. 339–53.

17 M. Gove, 2018, 'Migration as development: Household survey evidence on migrants' wage gains', *Social Indicators Research*, 137(3), pp. 1033–60.

18 O. Stark et al., 1997, 'A brain gain with a brain drain', *ECOLET*, 55, pp. 227–34; O. Stark, 2004, 'Rethinking the brain drain', *World Development*, 32(1), pp. 15–22.

19 F. Docquier and H. Rapoport, 2012, 'Globalization, brain drain, and development', *Journal of Economic Literature*, 50(3), pp. 681–730.

20 P. Abarcar and C. Theoharides, 2021, 'Medical worker migration and origin-country human capital: Evidence from US visa policy', *Review of Economics and Statistics*, pp. 1–46.

21 S. A. Shrestha, 2017, 'No man left behind: Effects of emigration prospects on educational and labour outcomes of non-migrants', *The Economic Journal*, 127(600), pp. 495–521.

22 H. de Haas, 2007, *Remittances, Migration and Social Development: A Conceptual Review of the Literature*, Geneva, United Nations Research Institute for Social Development; see also M. C. Zhunio et al., 2012, 'The influence of remittances on education and health outcomes: A cross country study', *Applied Economics*, 44(35), pp. 4605–16.

23 A. C. Edwards and M. Ureta, 2003, 'International migration, remittances, and schooling: evidence from El Salvador', *Journal of Development Economics*, 72(2), pp. 429–61.

24 De Haas, 2003; H. de Haas and A. Van Rooij, 2010, 'Migration as emancipation? The impact of internal and international migration on the position of women left behind in rural Morocco', *Oxford Development Studies*, 38(1), pp. 43–62.

25 This positive effect is not universal, however. Particularly in the case of lower-skilled and often illegal migration, where few positive returns from education can be expected, the prospect of emigrating may discourage families from investing in education. One study found that emigration from Mexico to the United States had a negative effect on school attendance and the educational attainment of children. After all, a college-educated Mexican working as a farmworker in the US is unlikely to earn more than their colleague with only primary education. See D. McKenzie and H. Rapoport, 2011, 'Can migration reduce educational attainment? Evidence from Mexico', *Journal of Population Economics*, 24(4), pp. 1331–58.

26 D. Bahar et al., 2022, 'Migration and Knowledge Diffusion: The Effect of Returning Refugees on Export Performance in the Former Yugoslavia', *Review of Economics and Statistics*, forthcoming; H. Rapoport, 2018, 'Migration and Trade', in A. Triandafyllidou (ed.), *Handbook of Migration and Globalization*, Edward Elgar Publishing; D. Bahar and H. Rapoport, 2018, 'Migration, knowledge diffusion and the comparative advantage of nations', *The Economic Journal*, 128(612), F273–F305; Özden and Rapoport, 2018, 'Cross-country perspectives on migration and development: Introduction', *The Economic Journal*, 128(612), F174–F178.

27 K. Newland, 2007, *A New Surge of Interest in Migration and Development*, Washington, DC, Migration Policy Institute.

28 B. Khadria, 'India: Skilled migration to developed countries, labour migration to the Gulf', in S. Castles and R. Delgado Wise (eds.), *Migration and*

Development: Perspectives from the South, Geneva, International Organization for Migration; P. M. Rao and M. Balasubrahmanya, 2017, 'The rise of IT services clusters in India: A case of growth by replication', *Telecommunications Policy*, 41, pp. 90–95.

29 P. Levitt, 1998, 'Social remittances: Migration driven local-level forms of cultural diffusion', *International Migration Review*, 32, pp. 926–48.

30 A. Spilimbergo, 2009, 'Democracy and foreign education', *American Economic Review*, 99(1), pp. 528–43; T. Barsbai et al., 2017, 'The effect of labor migration on the diffusion of democracy: Evidence from a former Soviet Republic', *Mimeo*, The Kiel Institute for the World Economy; F. Docquier et al., 2015, 'Emigration and Democracy', *Journal of Development Economics*, 120, pp. 209–23.

31 Hein de Haas, 2007, *Between Courting and Controlling: The Moroccan State and 'Its' Emigrants*, Working paper No. 54, Oxford, Centre on Migration, Policy and Society, University of Oxford, 2007.

32 De Haas et al., 2020.

33 P. Fargues, 2011, 'International migration and the demographic transition: A two-way interaction', *International Migration Review*, 45(3), pp. 588–614. See also M. Beine et al., 2013, 'International migration, transfer of norms and home country fertility', *Canadian Journal of Economics/Revue canadienne d'économique*, 46(4), pp. 1406–30.

34 Mark Hosenball, 'Dealings with Gaddafi son embarrass London college', Reuters, 28 October 2011, https://www.reuters.com/article/us-libya-britain-college-idUSTRE79R49R20111028

35 A. Barajas et al., 2009, *Do workers' remittances promote economic growth?*, IMF Working Paper; M. A. Clemens and D. McKenzie, 2018, 'Why don't remittances appear to affect growth?', *The Economic Journal*, 128(612), pp. F179–F209.

36 H. de Haas, 2010, 'Migration and Development: A theoretical perspective', *International Migration Review*, 44, pp. 227–64; H. de Haas, 2020, 'Paradoxes of Migration and Development', in T. Bastia and R. Skeldon (eds.), *Routledge Handbook of Migration and Development*.

Myth 14: Immigration lifts all boats

1 Ronald Reagan, 'Remarks at the Presentation Ceremony for the Presidential Medal of Freedom', 19 January 1989, https://www.reaganlibrary.gov/archives/speech/remarks-presentation-ceremony-presidential-medal-freedom-5

2 World Bank, 'Moving for Prosperity: Global Migration and Labor Markets', 15 June 2018, https://www.worldbank.org/en/research/publication/moving-for-prosperity
3 M. A. Clemens, 2011, 'Economics and emigration: Trillion-dollar bills on the sidewalk?', *Journal of Economic Perspectives*, 25(3), pp. 83–106. The studies reviewed by Clemens reported efficiency gains of between 67 and 147 per cent of world GDP if all barriers to labor mobility were removed, against efficiency gains ranging between 0.3 and 4.1 per cent for the removal of all trade barriers, and 0.1 and 1.7 per cent for the removal of all barriers to capital flows. This implies that even a modest liberalization of migration policies would yield much higher gains than a full global liberalization of trade and capital flows.
4 See also A. Barajas et al., 2009, *Do Workers' Remittances Promote Economic Growth?*, IMF Working Paper; Clemens and McKenzie, 2018.
5 Author's calculation based on data from the World Development Indicators (WDI) database, World Bank [accessed on 6 December 2022].
6 Ibid.
7 *This American Life* is produced in collaboration with WBEZ Chicago and delivered to stations by PRX The Public Radio Exchange. See https://www.thisamericanlife.org/
8 Giovanni Peri with Justin Wiltshire, 'Analysis of Marshall-DeKalb area, relative to similar labor markets in Alabama, 1980–2010', *Our Town: The Economist's Report*, 8 December 2017, https://www.thisamericanlife.org/extras/our-town-the-economists-report
9 'Wage stagnation in nine charts', EPI, 6 January 2015, https://www.epi.org/publication/charting-wage-stagnation/
10 See J. Gabriel, 2006, 'Organizing the jungle: Industrial restructuring and immigrant unionization in the American meatpacking industry', *WorkingUSA*, 9(3), pp. 337–59.
11 Ira Glass and Miki Meek, *Our Town*, Part 2, https://www.thisamericanlife.org/633/transcript

Myth 15: We need immigrants to fix the problems of ageing societies

1 Cook et al., 2023, 'Trying to reverse demographic decline: Pro-natalist and family policies in Russia, Poland and Hungary', *Social Policy and Society*, 22(2), pp. 355–75.

2 United Nations, 2000, *Replacement Migration: Is It a Solution to Declining and Ageing Population?*, New York, Population Division, UNDESA, United Nations. The reported estimates are based on the 'medium variant' of the UN's population projections.

3 Ronald Lee, 2017, 'The economic and fiscal consequences of immigration', *Population and Development Review*, 43(8), p. 169.

4 See K. Ford, 1990, 'Duration of residence in the United States and the fertility of US immigrants', *International Migration Review*, 24(1), pp. 34–68.

5 H. Kulu et al., 2017, 'Fertility by birth order among the descendants of immigrants in selected European countries', *Population and Development Review*, pp. 31–60.

6 S. Dubuc, 2012, 'Immigration to the UK from High-Fertility Countries: Intergenerational Adaptation and Fertility Convergence', *Population and Development Review*, 38(2), pp. 353–68.

7 Hill Kulu and Tina Hannemann, 'Why does fertility remain high among certain UK-born ethnic minority women?', *Demographic Research*, 35(49), pp. 1441–8.

8 Gretchen Livingstone, 'Hispanic women no longer account for the majority of immigrant births in the US', Pew Research Center, 8 August 2019, https://www.pewresearch.org/fact-tank/2019/08/08/hispanic-women-no-longer-account-for-the-majority-of-immigrant-births-in-the-u-s/

9 Ibid.

10 Flahaux and de Haas, 2016.

11 Jonathan Watts, 'World population bomb may never go off', *Guardian*, 27 March 2023, https://www.theguardian.com/world/2023/mar/27/world-population-bomb-may-never-go-off-as-feared-finds-study

12 B. Callegari and P. E. Stoknes, 'People and Planet: 21st century sustainable population scenarios and possible living standards within planetary boundaries', Earth4All, March 2023, version 1.0.

13 De Haas et al, 2020.

14 See Marois et al., 2020, 'Population aging, migration, and productivity in Europe', *Proceedings of the National Academy of Sciences*, 117(14), pp. 7690–5.

Myth 16: Borders are closing down

1 Michael Finnegan, '"It's going to be a big, fat, beautiful wall!": Trump's words make his California climb an even steeper trek', *LA Times*, 2 June 2016.

2 'Transcript: Obama's immigration speech', *Washington Post*, 20 November 2014.

3 De Haas et al., 2015, 'Conceptualizing and measuring migration policy change', *Comparative Migration Studies*, 3(1), pp. 1–21.

4 For a more extensive analysis of migration policy trends on the basis of DEMIG POLICY data, see de Haas et al., 2018, 'Growing restrictiveness or changing selection? The nature and evolution of migration policies', *International Migration Review* 52(2), pp. 324–67. An update of DEMIG POLICY showed that this trend continued over recent years. See M. Czaika et al., 2022, 'European migration governance in the context of uncertainty', QuantMig Project Deliverable 1.5.

5 See J. C. Torpey, 2018. *The Invention of the Passport: Surveillance, Citizenship and the State*, Cambridge University Press; de Haas and Vezzoli, 2011.

6 Source: Data compiled by the author from various Annual Reports of the Immigration and Naturalization Service (INS) (1975–1977); Statistical Yearbooks of the Immigration and Naturalization Service (1978–2001), and Yearbooks of Immigration Statistics of the Department of Homeland Security (DHS) (2002–2021). Data on temporary immigration for 1980 and 1997 was not available from US sources.

7 Ibid; author's calculations.

8 House of Commons, 'Research briefing: Migration statistics', 24 November 2022, https://commonslibrary.parliament.uk/research-briefings/sn06077/

9 G. P. Freeman, 1995, 'Modes of Immigration Politics in Liberal Democratic States', *International Migration Review*, 24, pp. 881–902.

10 This argument is corroborated by evidence, reviewed in chapter 14, that the economic benefits of immigration primarily go to the already affluent.

11 I am grateful to Lena Gloeckler for providing invaluable assistance in compiling labour enforcement data for this section.

12 P. Martin and M. Miller, 2000, *Employer Sanctions: French, German and US Experiences*, Geneva, ILO.

13 Department of Homeland Security, Budget Overview 2023, https://www.dhs.gov/sites/default/files/2022-03/U.S.%20Immigration%20and%20Customs%20Enforcement_Remediated.pdf

14 US Immigration and Customs Enforcement, 'Working for Ice: Criminal Investigator', https://www.ice.gov/careers/criminal-investigator

15 US Customs and Border Protection, 'About CBP', https://www.cbp.gov/about/

16 US Immigration and Customs Enforcement, Budget 2010, https://www.ice.gov/factsheets/budget2010

17 'Few prosecuted for illegal employment of immigrants', TRAC Immigration, https://trac.syr.edu/immigration/reports/559/ (according to an analysis of government data obtained under the Freedom of Information Act by the Transactional Records Access Clearinghouse at Syracuse University).

18 Lorraine Schmall, *Federal Worksite Enforcement of US Immigration Laws*, 1 June 2009, https://www.ilo.org/legacy/english/protection/travail/pdf/rdwpaper36a.pdf, p. 7.

19 'Civil Monetary Penalty Adjustments for Inflation', *Federal Register*, 18 October 2021, https://www.federalregister.gov/documents/2021/10/18/2021-22564/civil-monetary-penalty-adjustments-for-inflation

20 Wendy Fry, 'ICE says it's targeting employers but workplace raids impacting more workers', *Baltimore Sun*, 15 April 2019.

21 Yearly worksite arrests ranging from 120 to 779, while, on average, 270 people in the US get struck by lightning each year. See https://www.britannica.com/question/What-are-the-chances-of-being-struck-by-lightning

22 UK Parliament, 'Undocumented Workers: Convictions', Question for Ministry of Justice, https://questions-statements.parliament.uk/written-questions/detail/2018-06-25/157125

23 Colin Yeo, 'Home Office stats show immigration enforcement activity declining across the board', Free Movement, 1 October 2018, https://freemovement.org.uk/home-office-enforcement/

24 National Audit Office, *Immigration Enforcement*, 17 June 2020, https://www.nao.org.uk/wp-content/uploads/2020/06/Immigration-enforcement.pdf, p. 20.

25 Hayley Kirton, 'Number of employers suspended from hiring overseas staff drops by a third', 1 June 2018, People Management, https://www.peoplemanagement.co.uk/article/1744552/employers-suspended-hiring-overseas-staff

26 Independent Chief Inspector for Borders and Immigration, 2019, *An Inspection of the Home Office's Approach to Illegal Working, August–December 2018*, Her Majesty's Stationery Office.

27 Ibid; Independent Chief Inspector of Borders and Immigration, 2015, *An Inspection of How the Home Office Tackles Illegal Working*, October 2014–March 2015, Her Majesty's Stationery Office.

28 Julia Pascual, 'JO de Paris 2024: des travailleurs sans papiers sur les chantiers', *Le Monde*, 5 December 2022.

29 See J. Hollifield, 1992, *Immigrants, Markets and States: The Political Economy of Postwar Europe*, Cambridge, MA, Harvard University Press.
30 G. J. Borjas, 1990, *Friends or Strangers: The Impact of Immigration on the US Economy*, New York, Basic Books.
31 D. S. Massey, and K. A. Pren, 2012, 'Unintended consequences of US immigration policy: Explaining the post-1965 surge from Latin America', *Population and Development Review*, 38(1), pp.1–29.
32 See C. Joppke, 2001, 'The legal-domestic sources of immigrant rights: The United States, Germany, and the European Union', *Comparative Political Studies*, 34, pp. 339–66.
33 De Haas et al., 2020.
34 P. Plewa, 2006, 'How have regularization programs affected Spanish governmental efforts to integrate migrant populations', in O. Majtczak (ed.), *The Fifth International Migration Conference*, Warsaw, Independent University of Business and Government; A. Sabater and A. Domingo, 2012, 'A new immigration regularization policy: The settlement program in Spain', *International Migration Review*, 46, pp. 191–220.
35 J. Hollifield, 1992, *Immigrants, Markets and States: The Political Economy of Postwar Europe,* Cambridge, MA, Harvard University Press.
36 D. S. Massey, 1999, 'International migration at the dawn of the twenty-first century: The role of the state', *Population and Development Review*, 25(2), pp. 303–22.

Myth 17: Conservatives are tougher on immigration

1 'Full text: Tony Blair's speech on asylum and immigration', *Guardian*, 22 April 2005.
2 Steve Bloomfield, 'Hillary Clinton thinks you can beat the right on immigration', *Prospect*, 27 November 2018, https://www.prospectmagazine.co.uk/politics/hillary-clinton-thinks-you-can-beat-the-right-on-immigration-clearly-shes-never-heard-of-new-labour
3 The DEMIG POLICY database containing detailed information on 6,500 immigration policy changes in thirty-four countries across the Western world between 1900 and 2014. For more details, see chapter 16 and H de Haas et al., 2015, 'Conceptualizing and measuring migration policy change', *Comparative Migration Studies*, 3(1), pp. 1–21; H. de Haas et al., 2018.

4 See K. Natter et al., 2020, 'Political party ideology and immigration policy reform: An empirical enquiry', *Political Research Exchange*, 2(1), p. 1735255.

5 Source: DEMIG POLICY database, www.migrationinstitute.org

6 See T. Perlmutter, 1996, 'Bringing Parties Back In: Comments on "Modes of Immigration Politics in Liberal Democratic Societies"', *International Migration Review* 30(1), pp. 375–88.

7 *Federal Register*, 73(59), 2008, https://www.govinfo.gov/content/pkg/FR-2008-03-26/html/E8-6168.htm

8 Ibid.

9 As reported in *Our Town* (see chapter 14, n. 11).

10 Ibid.

11 De Haas et al., 2020.

12 T. Lacroix, 2005, *Les réseaux marocains du développement*, PhD thesis, Paris, Presses de Sciences Po.

13 De Haas et al., 2020.

14 See 'The Bible says to welcome refugees', The Conversation, 17 July 2019, https://theconversation.com/the-bible-says-to-welcome-refugees-120477

15 Muhammad Nur Manuty, 2008, 'The protection of refugees in Islam: pluralism and inclusivity', *Refugee Survey Quarterly*, 27(2), pp. 24–9; Anashwara Ashok, 'Religion's Response to Refugees', *The Interfaith Observer*, 28 January 2018, http://www.theinterfaithobserver.org/journal-articles/2018/5/12/religions-response-to-refugees

16 M. Lubbers et al., 2006, 'Objections to asylum seeker centres', *European Sociological Review*, 22(3), pp. 243–57; A. Bohman and M. Hjerm, 2014, 'How the religious context affects the relationship between religiosity and attitudes towards immigration', *Ethnic and Racial Studies*, 37(6), pp. 937–57; I. Storm, 2017, '"Christian Nations": Ethnic Christianity And Anti-Immigration Attitudes In Four Western European Countries', *Nordic Journal of Religion and Society*, 24(1), pp. 75–96.

17 'Pope Francis visits Italy's migrant island of Lampedusa', BBC News, 8 July 2013, https://www.bbc.com/news/world-europe-23224010

18 J. A. Olayo-Méndez, 2018, *Migration, Poverty, and Violence in Mexico: The Role of Casas de Migrantes*, DPhil thesis, University of Oxford.

19 See J. Berriane, 2020, 'Religion in spaces of transit: African Christian migrant churches and transnational mobility in Morocco', *Journal of Intercultural Studies*, 41(4), pp. 424–41.

20 Office of Refugee Resettlement, 'Resettlement Agencies', updated 23 February 2023, https://www.acf.hhs.gov/orr/grant-funding/resettlement-agencies.

21 Elizabeth Dias, 'Evangelical Leaders Lament Border Separations, but Stand Behind Trump', *New York Times*, 30 June 2018, https://www.nytimes.com/2018/06/20/us/politics/evangelicals-immigration-trump.html

22 Stephanie Nawyn, 2021, 'Resettling refugees: Why white communities object to religious groups for helping people displaced by war', *Milwaukee Independent*, 5 September 2021, https://www.milwaukeeindependent.com/syndicated/resettling-refugees-white-communities-object-religious-groups-helping-people-displace-war/

Myth 18: Public opinion has turned against immigration

1 The first two headlines were run by the *Daily Express*, the third by the *Daily Mail*, all in 2013; 'Poll finds xenophobia on the rise in France', France 24, 22 January 2014, https://www.france24.com/en/20140121-france-poll-finds-xenophobia-rise-racism-muslims-islam-hollande-death-penalty

2 Patrick Wintour, 'Hillary Clinton: Europe must curb immigration to stop rightwing populists', *Guardian*, 22 November 2018, https://www.theguardian.com/world/2018/nov/22/hillary-clinton-europe-must-curb-immigration-stop-populists-trump-brexit

3 Gallup poll: Immigration, https://news.gallup.com/poll/1660/immigration.aspx

4 'Shifting Public Views on Legal Immigration into the U.S.', Pew Research Center, 28 June 2018, https://www.pewresearch.org/politics/2018/06/28/shifting-public-views-on-legal-immigration-into-the-u-s/

5 *UK Public Opinion toward Immigration: Overall Attitudes and Level of Concern*, Migration Observatory, University of Oxford, 20 January 2020, https://migrationobservatory.ox.ac.uk/resources/briefings/uk-public-opinion-toward-immigration-overall-attitudes-and-level-of-concern/

6 Heather Rolfe et al., 'Immigration policy from post-war to post-Brexit: How new immigration policy can reconcile public attitudes and employer preferences', *National Institute Economic Review*, 248(2019), R5–R16.

7 S. Goubin et al., 2022, *Trends in attitudes towards migration in Europe: A comparative analysis*, HIVA – Research Institute for Work and Society.

8 Ibid.

9 W. Lutz et al., 2006, 'The demography of growing European identity', *Science*, 314(5798), p. 425.

10 S. Goubin et al., 2022.

11 A. Igarashi and J. Laurence, 2021, 'How does immigration affect anti-immigrant sentiment, and who is affected most?', *Comparative Migration Studies*, 9, a24.

12 R. Ford and M. Goodwin, 2017, 'Britain after Brexit: A nation divided', *Journal of Democracy*, 28(1), pp. 17–30.

13 R. Ford and K. Lymperopoulou, 2017, 'Immigration: How attitudes in the UK compare with Europe', in *British Social Attitudes*, p. 34.

14 S. Blinder et al., 2011, *Thinking Behind the Numbers: Understanding Public Opinion on Immigration in Britain*, Migration Observatory, University of Oxford.

15 R. Ford, 2011, 'Acceptable and unacceptable immigrants: How opposition to immigration in Britain is affected by migrants' region of origin', *Journal of Ethnic and Migration Studies*, 37, pp. 1017–37; R. Ford and J. Mellon, 2019, 'The skills premium and the ethnic premium: A cross-national experiment on European attitudes to immigrants', *Journal of Ethnic and Migration Studies*.

16 Various studies reviewed in Rolfe et al., 2019; H. Newman et al., 2017, 'Beyond the Westminster bubble: What people really think about immigration', *Open Europe*; S. Gaston, 2018, Citizens' Voices Insights from focus groups conducted in England for the project 'At Home in One's Past', DEMOS.

17 J. Rutter and R. Carter, 2018, 'National conversation on immigration: final report', British Future and HOPE not hate.

18 Helen Dempster et al., 2020, *Public Attitudes towards Immigration and Immigrants*, London, Overseas Development Institute (ODI).

19 European Commission, 2018, 'Integration of immigrants in the European Union', Special Eurobarometer 469, Wave EB88.2.

20 G. W. Allport, 1954, *The Nature of Prejudice*, Cambridge, MA, Perseus Books; T. F. Pettigrew and L. R. Tropp, 2006, 'A meta-analytic test of intergroup contact theory', *Journal of Personality and Social Psychology*, 90(5), pp. 751–83.

21 P. English, 'Thermostatic public opinion: Why anti-immigrant sentiments rise then fall', LSE [blog], 29 October 2018, https://blogs.lse.ac.uk/politicsandpolicy/pro-and-anti-immigrant-sentiments/

22 Bonilla-Silva, 2006; Essed, 1991.

23 I. Grosvenor, 2018, '"What do they know of England who only England know": A case for an alternative narrative of the ordinary in twenty-first-century Britain', *History of Education*, 47(2), pp. 148–68.

24 Ten years later, in 1978, Margaret Thatcher famously remarked that 'people are really rather afraid that this country might be rather swamped by people with a different culture'.

Myth 19: Smuggling is the cause of illegal migration

1 UNODC, 2006, *Organized Crime and Irregular Migration from Africa to Europe*, Vienna, United Nations Office on Drugs and Crime, p. 20
2 https://www.iom.int/counter-migrant-smuggling [accessed 2 May 2023].
3 Oral Statement to Parliament: Home Secretary's opening speech for Nationality and Borders Bill, House of Commons, 19 July 2021, https://www.gov.uk/government/speeches/home-secretary-opening-speech-for-nationality-borders-bill
4 Priscilla Alvarez, 2022, 'Biden administration launches "unprecedented" operation to disrupt human smuggling as caravan moves north', CNN, 10 June 2022.
5 DEMIG VISA database.
6 J. Zaragoza, Cristiani, 2016, *Empowerment through migration control cooperation: the Spanish–Moroccan case*, Doctoral dissertation, Florence, European University Institute (EUI).
7 M. Berriane et al., 2013, 'Immigration to Fes: The meaning of the new dynamics of the Euro-African migratory system', *Journal of Intercultural Studies*, 34(5), pp. 486–502.
8 De Haas, 2008a; de Haas, 2008b.
9 Ibid.
10 Ibid.
11 D. S. Massey at al., 2016, 'Why border enforcement backfired', *American Journal of Sociology*, 121(5), pp. 1557–1600.
12 Olayo-Méndez, 2018.
13 De Hass, 2008a; de Haas, 2008b.
14 James Verini, 'How US Policy Turned the Sonoran Desert into a Graveyard for Migrants, *New York Times*, 18 August 2020, https://www.nytimes.com/2020/08/18/magazine/border-crossing.html
15 Olayo-Méndez, 2018.
16 F. Pastore et al., 2006, 'Schengen's soft underbelly? Irregular migration and human smuggling across land and sea borders to Italy', *International Migration*, 44(4), pp. 95–119; J. Brachet, 2018, 'Manufacturing smugglers: From irregular

to clandestine mobility in the Sahara', *The Annals of the American Academy of Political and Social Science*, 676, pp. 16–35; S. X. Zhang et al., 2018, 'Crimes of solidarity in mobility'. *The Annals of the American Academy of Political and Social Science*, 676(1), pp. 6–15.

17 G. Sanchez, 2018, 'Five misconceptions about migrant smuggling', *Policy Brief* 2018/07, Florence, European University Institute; G. Sanchez and S. X. Zhang, 2020, 'In their own words: Children and the facilitation of migrant journeys on the US–Mexico border', *Victims & Offenders*, 15(3), pp. 370–89; G. Sanchez, 2021, *Latinas in the Criminal Justice System: Victims, Targets, and Offenders*, pp. 237–56.

18 G. Sanchez, 2016, 'Women's participation in the facilitation of human smuggling: The case of the US southwest', *Geopolitics*, 21(2), pp. 387–406; L. Achilli, 2018, 'The "good" smuggler: The ethics and morals of human smuggling among Syrians', *The Annals of the American Academy of Political and Social Science*, 676(1), pp. 77–96.

19 J. Brachet, 2009, *Migrations transsahariennes. Vers un désert cosmopolite et morcelé (Niger)*, Paris, Éditions du Croquant; Brachet, 2017, 'Entre saline et masure. Note sur la vie quotidienne des migrants étrangers dans l'oasis de Bilma (Niger)', *Outre-Terre*, 53(4), pp. 114–27 ; Brachet, 2018; Brachet, 2005, 'Migrants, transporteurs et agents de l'État: rencontre sur l'axe Agadez-Sebha', *Autrepart*, 36, pp. 43–62.

20 Ibid.

21 De Haas, 2008a; de Haas, 2008b; Brachet, 2018.

22 Luc Leroux, 2017, 'Coupable d'avoir aidé des migrants, Cédric Herrou «continuera à se battre» ' *Le Monde*, 8 August 2017.

23 L. M. Mbaye, 2014, ' "Barcelona or die": Understanding illegal migration from Senegal', *IZA Journal of Migration*, 3(1), pp. 1–19.

24 The Migrants' Files, 2015, 'The Human and Financial Cost of 15 Years of Fortress Europe', 18 June 2015, http://www.themigrantsfiles.com/ [accessed 6 January 2023].

25 Data extracted from the Frontex website, https://frontex.europa.eu/about-frontex/faq/key-facts/ [accessed 7 January 2023].

26 Alessandro D'Alfonso, 2021, 'Migration and border management, Heading 4 of the 2021–2027 MFF', European Parliament Briefing, April 2021, https://www.europarl.europa.eu/RegData/etudes/BRIE/2021/690544/EPRS_BRI(2021)690544_EN.pdf

27 D. Meissner et al., 2013, *Immigration Enforcement in the United States: The Rise of a Formidable Machinery*, Washington, DC, Migration Policy Institute.

28 D. Meissner and J. Gelatt, 2019, *Eight Key U.S. Immigration Policy Issues: State of Play and Unanswered Questions*, Washington, DC, Migration Policy Institute.

Myth 20: Trafficking is a form of modern slavery

1 UNODC, 2012, 'Human trafficking: Organized crime and the multibillion dollar sale of people', https://www.unodc.org/unodc/en/frontpage/2012/July/human-trafficking-organized-crime-and-the-multibillion-dollar-sale-of-people.html

2 Reported in Michael Hobbes and Sarah Marshall, 2019, 'Human Trafficking', *You're Wrong About* [podcast], 25 November 2019, www.yourewrongabout.com. See https://usiaht.org/the-problem/ [accessed 27 April 2021].

3 ILO and WFF, 2017, *Global Estimates of Modern Slavery: Forced Labour and Forced Marriage,* Geneva, International Labour Organization and Walk Free Foundation.

4 Ann Simmons, 2017, 'Slavery is alive and well: 89 million have been in some form of bondage in the last five years, report says', *Los Angeles Times*, 19 September 2017.

5 Kate Hodal, 2019, 'One in 200 people is a slave. Why?' *Guardian*, 25 February 2019.

6 P. E. Lovejoy, 1989, 'The Impact of the Atlantic Slave Trade on Africa: A Review of the Literature', *The Journal of African History*, 30, pp. 365–94.

7 De Haas, 2007, 'International migration, national development and the role of governments: The case of Nigeria', in A. Adepoju, T. van Naerssen and A. Zoomers (eds.), *International Migration and National Development in Sub-Saharan Africa*, Leiden, Brill Publishers.

8 Michael Hobbes, 2020, 'The Futile Quest for Hard Numbers on Child Sex Trafficking', *Huffington Post*, 23 September 2020. Hobbes reported that surveys of every human trafficking case prosecuted from 2000 to 2015 in the US found no single cases were linked to international cartels or organized crime. See also M. Sobel, 2018, *Sex Trafficking and the Media: Perspectives from Thailand and the United States*, Routledge.

9 Jo Boyden and Neil Howard, 2013, 'Why does child trafficking policy need to be reformed?', *Children's Geographies*, 11(3), pp. 354–68; Abdou Ndao, *Anthropological Approaches to Studying the Mobility of Children in West Africa*, in *African Migrations Research*, Africa World Press, pp. 235–54.

10 Helen Carter, 2010, 'Rochdale child sex ring case: respected men who preyed on the vulnerable', *Guardian*, 8 May 2010; 'Rochdale grooming trial: Nine found guilty of child sex charges', BBC News.
11 B. Anderson and B. Rogaly, 2005, *Free Market, Forced Labour*. London, TUC.
12 J. A. Chuang, 2014, 'Exploitation creep and the unmaking of human trafficking law', *American Journal of International Law*, 108(4), pp. 609–49.
13 Ibid.
14 The full definition is 'the recruitment, transportation, transfer, harbouring or receipt of persons, by means of the threat or use of force or other forms of coercion, of abduction, of fraud, of deception, of the abuse of power or of a position of vulnerability or of the giving or receiving of payments or benefits to achieve the consent of a person having control over another person, for the purpose of exploitation. Exploitation shall include, at a minimum, the exploitation on the prostitution of others or other forms of sexual exploitation, forced labour or services, slavery or practices similar to slavery, servitude or the removal of organs'. General Assembly resolution 55/25, 15 November 2000.
15 Karen E. Bravo, 2007, 'Exploring the Analogy Between Modern Trafficking in Humans and the Trans-Atlantic Slave Trade', *Boston University International Law Journal* 25(2), pp. 207–96.
16 R. Weitzer, 2007, 'The social construction of sex trafficking: Ideology and institutionalization of a moral crusade', *Politics & Society*, 35(3), pp. 447–75.
17 Hobbes, 2020.
18 Ibid.
19 J. O'C. Davidson, 2006, 'Will the real sex slave please stand up?', *Feminist Review*, 83(1), pp. 4–22.
20 Ibid.
21 Mendoza, 2009; Mendoza, 2020.
22 De Haas, 2007; E. Ratia and C. Notermans, 2012, '"I was crying, I did not come back with anything": Experiences of Deportation from Europe to Nigeria', *African Diaspora*, 5(2), pp. 143–64.
23 Jørgen Carling, 2006, *Migration, Human Smuggling and Trafficking from Nigeria to Europe*, Geneva, IOM.
24 Carling, 2007; de Haas, 2007.
25 De Haas, ibid.
26 Ibid.
27 Davidson, 2006, pp. 15–16.

28 Nick Mai, 2009, 'Migrant workers in the UK sex industry. ESRC final project report'; Mai, 2013, 'Embodied cosmopolitanisms: The subjective mobility of migrants working in the global sex industry', *Gender, Place & Culture*, 20 (1), pp. 107–124.

29 'Sex workers anger as riot police raid 40 premises in Soho', *West End Extra*, December 2013, http://www.westendextra.com/news/2013/dec/sex-workers-anger-riot-police-raid-40-premises-soho-stolen-goods-clampdown, cited on English Collective of Prostitutes website, www.prostitutescollective.net [accessed 7 January 2023].

30 Frankie Miren, 2016, 'Are London's Brothel Raids Really About Saving Sex Workers?', VICE, 27 October 2016, https://www.vice.com/en/article/5gqdbb/operation-lanhydrock-soho-chinatown-sex-worker-raids

31 Patricia Mazzei, 2019, '"The Monsters Are the Men": Inside a Thriving Sex Trafficking Trade in Florida', *New York Times*, 23 February 2019.

32 May Jeong, 2019, 'The Disturbing Saga of Robert Kraft', *Vanity Fair*, October 2019, https://www.vanityfair.com/news/2019/10/the-disturbing-saga-of-robert-kraft

33 ILO and WFF, 2017, *Global Estimates of Modern Slavery: Forced Labour and Forced Marriage*, Geneva, International Labour Organization and Walk Free Foundation.

34 See Anne T. Gallagher, 2017, 'What's Wrong with the Global Slavery Index?' *Anti-Trafficking Review*, 8, pp. 90–112.

35 Ibid., p. 29.

36 Rhacel Parreñas, 2011, *Illicit Flirtations: Labor, Migration, and Sex Trafficking in Tokyo*, Stanford University Press.

37 Ibid.

38 Cathryn Costello, 'Migrants and forced labour: A labor law response', in A. Bogg et al. (eds.), 2015, *The Autonomy of Labour Law*, Bloomsbury Publishing.

Myth 21: Border restrictions reduce immigration

1 This chapter is largely based on the findings of the DEMIG (Determinants of International Migration) project. For a summary of the project findings, see De Haas et al., 2019.

2 D. S. Massey et al., 2016, 'Why border enforcement backfired', *American Journal of Sociology*, 121(5), pp. 1557–600.

3 Dominic Casciani, 'UK net migration hits all-time record at 504,000', BBC News, 24 November 2022, https://www.bbc.com/news/uk-63743259, as reported by Office for National Statistics (ONS) estimates.

4 *Net Migration to the UK*, Migration Observatory, University of Oxford, 20 December 2022, https://migrationobservatory.ox.ac.uk/resources/briefings/long-term-international-migration-flows-to-and-from-the-uk/

5 This record high immigration was partly driven by the immigration of Ukrainian refugees and Hong Kong British nationals.

6 Mendoza, 2020; A. Andrikopoulos, 2017, *Argonauts of West Africa*, PhD thesis, University of Amsterdam.

7 De Haas et al., 2020.

8 Taking inflation into account, $550 in 1989 equals about $986 in 2010.

9 Massey et al., 2016.

10 Ibid.

11 *Modes of Entry for the Unauthorized Migrant Population*, Factsheet, 22 May 2006, Pew Research Center.

12 OECD, 2008, International Migration Outlook, Sopemi, Paris, OECD, p. 39; Bastian Vollmer, 2011, *Irregular Migration in the UK: Definitions, Pathways and Scale*, briefing, Migration Observatory, University of Oxford.

13 'Number of those here on visas not recorded as leaving on time nearly doubled in five years', press release, Migration Watch, 24 February 2011, https://www.migrationwatchuk.org/press-release/633/number-of-those-here-on-visas-not-recorded-as-leaving-on-time-nearly-doubled-in-five-years

14 A. Kubal et al., 2011, *The Evolution of Brazilian Migration to the UK*, University of Oxford, International Migration Institute; G. Maher and M. Cawley, 2016, 'Short-term labour migration: Brazilian migrants in Ireland', *Population, Space and Place*, 22(1), pp. 23–35.

15 H. van Amersfoort, 2011, *How the Dutch Government Stimulated the Unwanted Migration from Suriname*, IMI working paper no. 47, International Migration Institute, University of Oxford.

16 Ibid.

17 C. Peach, 1965, 'West Indian migration to Britain: The economic factors', *Race*, 7(1), pp. 31–46; 1994, 'Three phases of South Asian emigration', in *Migration: The Asian Experience*, London, Palgrave Macmillan, pp. 38–55; 2018, 'Patterns of Afro-Caribbean migration and settlement in Great Britain: 1945–1981', in *The Caribbean in Europe*, Routledge, pp. 62–84.

18 S. M. Otterstrom and B. F. Tillman, 2013, 'Income change and circular migration: The curious case of mobile Puerto Ricans, 1995–2010', *Journal of Latin American Geography*, pp. 33–57.

19 Czaika and de Haas, 2017.

20 De Haas et al., 2020.

21 Mexican Migrant Project, Princeton University, mmp.opr.princeton.edu. See also J. Durand and D. S. Massey, 2019, 'Evolution of the Mexico-US migration system: Insights from the Mexican migration project', *The Annals of the American Academy of Political and Social Science*, 684(1), pp. 21–42; Massey et al., 2016; Massey and K. A. Pren, 2012, 'Unintended consequences of US immigration policy: Explaining the post-1965 surge from Latin America', *Population and Development Review*, 38(1), pp. 1–29.

22 S. Vezzoli, 2015, *Borders, Independence and Post-Colonial Ties: The Role of the State in Caribbean Migration*, PhD thesis, Maastricht, University of Maastricht; Vezzoli, 2021, 'How do borders influence migration? Insights from open and closed border regimes in the three Guianas', *Comparative Migration Studies*, 9(1), pp. 1–23.

23 Hein de Haas et al., 2019, *Opening the Floodgates? European Migration under Restrictive and Liberal Border Regimes 1950–2010*, MADE/IMI working paper no. 150, International Migration Institute.

24 It shows cross-border movement between the EU25 countries (the EU27 minus Romania and Bulgaria, but including the UK) as well as movement from outside the EU25 area towards the EU25 area, and movements from inside the EU25 area to non-EU25 countries. Source: DEMIG C2C database (www.migrationinstitute.org).

25 Over the 2010s, intra-EU migration would remain relatively stable at levels of around 1 million for the EU28, including Bulgaria and Romania. Source: Elena Fries-Tersch et al., 2021, *Annual Report on Intra-EU Labour Mobility 2020*, Luxembourg, Publications Office of the European Union.

26 According to Eurostat data, in the 2010s, total non-EU28 immigration would continue to hover around 2 million per year, with fluctuations strongly depending on business cycles and labour demand in Europe.

27 This is also confirmed by micro-level survey research. For instance, an analysis of survey data by Marie-Laurence Flahaux showed that Senegalese migrants in France, Italy and Spain are less likely to return over time because of increasing entry restrictions. See M. L. Flahaux, 2017, 'The role

of migration policy changes in Europe for return migration to Senegal', *International Migration Review*, 51(4), pp. 868–92.

Myth 22: Climate change will lead to mass migration

1 *New York Times*, 23 July 2020; *Guardian*, 9 September 2020; *Financial Times*, 3 October 2021.

2 N. Myers, 1995, *Environmental Exodus: An Emergent Crisis in the Global Arena*, Washington, DC, Climate Institute.

3 Axel Bojanowski, 2011, 'Feared Migration Hasn't Happened. UN Embarrassed by Forecast on Climate Refugees', *Der Spiegel*, 18 April 2011.

4 Christian Aid, 2007, *Human Tide: The Real Migration Crisis*.

5 Jon Henley, 'Climate crisis could displace 1.2bn people by 2050, report warns', *Guardian*, 9 September 2020, https://www.theguardian.com/environment/2020/sep/09/climate-crisis-could-displace-12bn-people-by-2050-report-warns

6 The White House, 2021, Report on the Impact of Climate Change on Migration, October 2021, Washington, DC.

7 IPCC, 2023, Synthesis report of the IPCC sixth assessment report (AR6), Geneva, Intergovernmental Panel on Climate Change.

8 Ibid.

9 NASA, Sea Level Change, https://sealevel.nasa.gov/faq/9/are-sea-levels-rising-the-same-all-over-the-world-as-if-were-filling-a-giant-bathtub/

10 For an excellent overview of the methodological problems underlying such estimates, see F. Gemenne, 2011, 'Why the numbers don't add up: A review of estimates and predictions of people displaced by environmental changes', *Global Environmental Change*, 21, S41–S49.

11 *Foresight*: *Migration and Global Environmental Change*, 2011, Government Office for Science, London; H. de Haas, 2011, 'Mediterranean migration futures: Patterns, drivers and scenarios', *Global Environmental Change*, 21, S59–S69.

12 A. Findlay and A. Geddes, 2011, 'Critical views on the relationship between climate change and migration: Some insights from the experience of Bangladesh', in E. Piguet et al. (eds.), *Migration and Climate Change*, UNESCO/Cambridge University Press, pp. 138–59.

13 Fenna Imara Hoefsloot, 2017, '"The good land is there where the flood is": The role of structures and imaginaries in shaping migration decisions in a context of environmental risks in Chokwe, Mozambique', MSc thesis, International Development Studies, University of Amsterdam.

14 J. H. Nienhuis et al., 2020, 'Global-scale human impact on delta morphology has led to net land area gain', *Nature*, 577(7791), pp. 514–18.

15 A. Ahmed et al., 2018, 'Where is the coast? Monitoring coastal land dynamics in Bangladesh: An integrated management approach using GIS and remote sensing techniques', *Ocean & Coastal Management*, 151, pp. 10–24.

16 I. Boas, 2020, 'Social networking in a digital and mobile world: the case of environmentally-related migration in Bangladesh', *Journal of Ethnic and Migration Studies*, 46(7), pp. 1330–47.

17 V. K. Duvat, 2019, 'A global assessment of atoll island platform changes over the past decades', *Wiley Interdisciplinary Reviews: Climate Change*, 10(1), e557.

18 P. S. Kench et al., 2018, 'Patterns of island change and persistence offer alternate adaptation pathways for atoll nations', *Nature Communications*, 9(1), pp. 1–7.

19 *Foresight 2011* ; Susan Fratzke and Brian Salant, 2017, *Understanding the Impact of Livelihood Opportunities and Interventions on Migration Patterns*, report commissioned by the Research and Evidence Division in the UK Department for International Development.

20 F. Gemenne, 2010, 'What's in a name: Social vulnerabilities and the refugee controversy in the wake of Hurricane Katrina', in *Environment, Forced Migration and Social Vulnerability*, Berlin, Heidelberg, Springer, pp. 29–40.

21 G. Jónsson, 2010, 'The environmental factor in migration dynamics – a review of African case studies', IMI working paper no. 21, International Migration Institute, University of Oxford.

22 S. E. Findley, 1994, 'Does drought increase migration? A study of migration from rural Mali during the 1983–1985 drought', *International Migration Review*, 28(3), pp. 539–53.

23 P. A. Lewin et al., 2012, 'Do rainfall conditions push or pull rural migrants: Evidence from Malawi', *Agricultural Economics*, 43(2), pp. 191–204.

24 S. Henry et al., 2004, 'The impact of rainfall on the first out-migration: A multi-level event-history analysis in Burkina Faso', *Population and Environment*, 25(5), pp. 423–60.

25 Hein de Haas, 2014, 'Un siècle de migrations marocaines: Transformations, transitions et perspectives d'avenir', in M. Berriane (ed.), *Marocains de*

l'Extérieur, Rabat, Fondation Hassan II pour les Marocains Résident à l'Etranger, pp. 61–92.

26 See M. Beine, and C. R. Parsons, 2017, 'Climatic factors as determinants of international migration: Redux', *CESifo Economic Studies*, 63(4), pp. 386–402.

27 M. Brandt et al., 2015, 'Ground- and satellite-based evidence of the biophysical mechanisms behind the greening Sahel', *Global Change Biology*, 21(4), pp. 1610–20; C. Dardel et al., 2014, 'Re-greening Sahel: 30 years of remote sensing data and field observations (Mali, Niger)', *Remote Sensing of Environment*, 140, pp. 350–64.

28 G. Sterk and J. J. Stoorvogel, 2020, 'Desertification: Scientific Versus Political Realities', *Land*, 9(5), p. 156; D. S. Thomas, 1994, *Desertification: Exploding the Myth*, Middleton, NJ, Wiley.

29 H. de Haas (ed.), 2001, *Migration, Agricultural Transformations and Natural Resource Exploitation in the Oases of Morocco and Tunisia*, Amsterdam, University of Amsterdam; De Haas, 2007, 'Gestion d'eau dans les oasis marocaines et le rôle de l'état: crise ou transformation?', in *L'eau entre moulin et noria*, Rabat/ Mohammedia/ Marrakech, NIMAR/ Université Hassan II/ Université Cadi Ayyad; de Haas, 2003, 'De Oprukkende Woestijn versus de Terugtrekkende Mens', in M. Wolinsk and M. Baumeister (eds.), *Van Nijlpaard tot Maasbedding*, Van Arkel, pp. 239–61.

30 See J. P. Syvitski et al., 2009, 'Sinking deltas due to human activities', *Nature Geoscience*, 2(10), pp. 681–6.

31 A. Jeuken et al., 2015, 'Lessons learnt from adaptation planning in four deltas and coastal cities', *Journal of Water and Climate Change*, 6(4), pp. 711–28; Syvitski et al., 2009.

32 Deltares, 2015, *Sinking Cities: An Integrated Approach Towards Solutions*, Delft, Utrecht, Deltares, https://publications.deltares.nl/Deltares142.pdf

33 Axel Bojanowski, 2011, 'Feared Migration Hasn't Happened. UN Embarrassed by Forecast on Climate Refugees', *Der Spiegel*, 18 April 2011.

34 Viviane Clement et al., 2021, *Groundswell: Acting on Internal Climate Migration, Part II*, Washington, DC, World Bank Publications.

35 U. Kothari, 2014, 'Political discourses of climate change and migration: Resettlement policies in the Maldives', *Geographical Journal*, 180, pp. 130–40.

36 John Vidal, 2017, '"We need development": Maldives switches focus from climate threat to mass tourism', *Guardian*, 3 March 2017.

37 M. M. Cernea and C. McDowell (eds.), 2000, *Risks and Reconstruction: Experiences of Resettlers and Refugees*, World Bank Publications.

The Road Ahead

1 Thomas Spijkerboer, 'Fact Check: Did the EU-Turkey Deal Bring Down the Number of Migrants and of Border Deaths?', University of Oxford, Faculty of Law blog, 28 September 2016.

2 It is a myth, however, that Angela Merkel's statement '*Wir Schaffen Das*' ('We will manage it') on 31 August 2015 was a cause of increased refugee migration to Germany and Europe, if only because the increase took place *before* Merkel's statement. See L. Pries, 2020, '"We Will Manage It"– Did Chancellor Merkel's Dictum Increase or Even Cause the Refugee Movement in 2015?', *International Migration*, 58(5), pp. 18–28; Thomas Spijkerboer, 2016. 'Did "Wir Schaffen Das" Lead to Uncontrolled Mass Migration?', University of Oxford, Faculty of Law blog, 28 September 2016.

Acknowledgements

They say it takes a village to raise a child. Almost the same can be said about writing a book. So many people helped me in many different ways while writing this book that I will never be able to appropriately express the deep gratitude and appreciation I feel. I would like to thank in particular the following people for providing criticism, feedback and encouragement: Geraldine Adiku, Anar Ahmadov, Yacine Ait Larbi, Jeanne Batalova, Irene Bloemraad, Julien Brachet, Jan Willem Duyvendak, David Scott FitzGerald, Fenella Fleischmann, Filiz Garip, Halleh Ghorashi, Romy Hanoeman, Cody Hochstenbach, Bas Jacobs, Karin Jongsma, Leander Kandilige, Bram Lancee, Arjen Leerkes, Peggy Levitt, Leo Lucassen, Amade M'charek, Douglas Massey, Ludger Pries, Sako Musterd, Alejandro Olayo-Méndez, Rhacel Parreñas, Alejandro Portes, Ladan Rahbari, Hillel Rapoport, Gabriella Sanchez, Thomas Spijkerboer, Hélène Thiollet, Helga de Valk, Carlos Vargas-Silva, Nanke Verloo, Maarten Vink, Jack Vromen and Myungji Yang.

Without the generous financial support of several organizations and people, I could never have carried out the kind of fundamental, independent research needed to generate the insights that form the scientific backbone of this book. The European Commission's INCO-DC programme and the Netherlands Organisation for Scientific Research (NWO) provided essential support for my doctoral and postdoctoral research in Morocco, Tunisia, Egypt and Turkey. I am particularly grateful to Dr James Martin (1933–2013), founder of the Oxford Martin School (OMS), for providing generous funding, allowing the establishment of the International Migration Institute (IMI) at the University of Oxford in 2006. I am also grateful to the John D. and Catherine T. MacArthur Foundation, the Alfred P. Sloan Foundation and the European Research Council (ERC) for their generous funding for a range of research projects at IMI at the University of Oxford and, since 2015, at the University of Amsterdam.

I am also thankful to the Royal Netherlands Academy of Arts and Sciences (KNAW) for funding a one-year fellowship during the

2020–21 academic year at the Netherlands Institute for Advanced Study (NIAS), which gave me the essential time and headspace to write the first draft of this book.

To me, research has always been about teamwork. I could have never conducted my research without the help of a great number of wonderful colleagues, collaborators and friends. I would like to thank in particular Oliver Bakewell, Ayla Bonfiglio, Mathias Czaika, Ibylou Bandala-Golla, Raúl Delgado Wise, Mehmet Demiray, Franck Düvell, Evelyn Ersanilli, Brahim Essaady, Mohammed Fatihi, Hassan El Ghanjou, Tineke Fokkema, Sonja Fransen, Marie-Laurence Flahaux, Mohamed 'Clay' Jalili, Dominique Jolivet, Thomas Lacroix, Edo Mahendra, Lea Müller-Funk, Katharina Natter, Naiara Rodríguez Peña, Kerilyn Schewel, Mohamed Temraoui, Ellie Vasta, Simona Vezzoli, María Villares-Varela and Siebert Wielstra. In teaching I am grateful for the fruitful collaborations with Debby Gerritsen, Anja van Heelsum, Maryam Babur and Melissa Siegel. I also thank Gaby Evers, Zoe Falk, Sally Kingsborough, Ingrid Locatelli, Flor Macías Delgado, Erik van Loon, Julia Knight, Briony Truscott and Jeske de Vries for their invaluable adminstrative support.

I am also grateful to my academic mentors, who have encouraged my growth as a researcher. Paolo De Mas has been an enthusiastic supporter of my research from my first fieldwork in Morocco in 1993 to the present day. Leo de Haan, my main PhD adviser, made me believe in myself again when I thought that my academic career was in the gutter. Ton Dietz, my second PhD supervisor, has kept me sharp with his unremitting supply of energy and ideas. Ronald Skeldon's seminal work not only revolutionalized my views on migration but, later, when he was a colleague, his enthusiasm and feedback encouraged me to discover new research avenues. Since my Oxford years, I have enjoyed Robin Cohen's wise counsel, always wrapped up in an infectious sense of humour. In Morocco, I am deeply thankful to Mohamed Berriane for the trust, support and opportunities he has given me.

I owe a huge debt of gratitude to Stephen Castles. Since joining IMI in Oxford in 2006, I was incredibly lucky to have Stephen as a director, mentor and friend. Stephen was not only one of the most influential thinkers on migration of his generation, but also a great example of academic leadership. Sadly, Stephen passed away in 2022, but his vision and humility will continue to be an inspiration.

I really don't know how to thank the countless migrants, refugees and other people I met while doing fieldwork over the past thirty years, who put their trust in me and took the time to share their experiences with me. I have tried to represent your voices and stories in this book to the best of my abilities.

Many years of teaching have perhaps been the biggest motivation to write this book. I am very thankful to my students for asking critical questions, for coming up with valuable examples and for showing their surprise – and often outrage – at the fact that all this knowledge about migration hasn't found its way to the general public. I hope this book lives up to your expectations.

Tom Killingbeck, my agent at AM Heath, has been of great support, patiently encouraging me and coming up with excellent suggestions when I felt stuck. Most importantly, we shared the same vision about this book from the very beginning. At Penguin, I was very lucky to have Alpana Sajip as my editor, playing an essential role in guiding me, providing valuable feedback – and constraining me when it was needed. I am also grateful to Gemma Wain for her efficient and thoughtful copy-editing. At Penguin, I thank Natalie Wall, Chloe Davies and Charlotte Daniels for their essential contributions to this book; at Basic Books, I thank Michael Kaler for important feedback on later drafts of the book.

More practically, while I was writing this book, Yosra Daki Azad, Julius Illeris, Sarah Salehi and Zuzanna Ściborska provided essential research assistance in stressful times. I am particularly grateful to Lena Gloeckler for doing essential background research and providing feedback on the structure of the book.

I dedicate this book to my parents, Stef de Haas and Annie de Jonge. So much of what you showed and taught me is in here, in ways both noticeable and more mysterious. I feel incredibly privileged to have grown up in a home without a shred of prejudice, where (nearly) everything was debatable. Hanna, my dear sister, I miss you every step of the way, but I am so grateful that you live on in Sacha and Kaspar.

I am also immensely grateful to my family and friends, for having had the patience to put up with my constant preoccupation with this book for three years, and for tolerating me when I was irritable, distracted – or, worse, unreachable. At home, Selma, Dalila, Edgar and Stefano have been loyal fans and cheerleaders – thanks for never getting tired of asking 'When is the book finished?', for the countless dinner table discussions and for your radiant presence.

Last, but certainly not least, the greatest debt of gratitude I owe is to Dovelyn Rannveig Mendoza. This book would not have seen the light of day without your emotional, practical and intellectual support. You not only encouraged me to write it, but also scrutinized several drafts of the manuscript, word by word. Your insights and vision have sharpened my mind and lifted this book to an entirely new level. By this time, I have lost sight of where my ideas end and where yours begin.

Amsterdam
July 2023

Index

Page references in *italics* indicate images.

Afghanistan 15, 23, 48, 50, 54, *55*, 91, 203, 243, 244, 306
Africa
African Americans *see* African Americans
Agricultural Revolution and 28
'brain drain' and emigration from 210, 211, 212–13, 214, 219
climate change and 344, 345, 350, 351–2, 355
deaths of migrants crossing borders in 305
demographic factors and emigration from 240, 242
development in, emigration and 78–9, 80*n*, 82, 86–7, 88, 90, 91, 92
European colonialism and 17, 18, 19–20, 21, 22
future of migration and 92, 243, 244
guest workers from 7, 105–6
integration of African immigrants in Europe 164, 166, 168, 176, 177, 179
'invasion' myths and emigration from 32, 34–5, 36
labour recruitment and emigration from 37, 41, 158, 210
major long-distance migrations (1950–2020) and *24–5*
'Marshall Plan for Africa' 79
Mediterranean boat migration and 1, 6, 7, 32, 34–5, 296–7, *300–301*, 329
overland and maritime migration routes to North Africa, the Middle East and western Europe and *300–301*
'refugee crisis' and 45, 48
regional migration and 27, 90, 106
slave trade and *see* slavery
smuggling of migrants and 297, 298, *300–301*, 304, 305
trafficking of migrants and 310, 312
urbanization 29, 88
visa restrictions/border enforcement and emigration from 295, 297, 298, 326, 328, 329, 330, 334–5, 367
warfare in, asylum seekers flee 6, 54, 56
See also North Africa *and individual country name*
African Americans 40, 64–5, 72, 173, 182, 184, 187, 189, 196, 206, 272, 350
ageing populations 1, 121, 125, 140, 158, 207, 234–45, 366, 370, 371
Agnew, John 189
agriculture 28, 37, 39, 40, 41, 80*n*, 88, 89, 97, 107, 109, 120–21, 124, 140–43, 235, 243, 253, 254, 260, 293, 298, 312, 318, 322, 341, 347, 350, 351, 352, 353, 361, 366
Albania 196, 205, 295, 309, 315
Albertville, Alabama, US 227–32
Alesina, Alberto 76
Algeria 20, 21, 38, 41, 57, 71, 134, 164, 168, 169, 176, 183, 209, 296, 298
Ambrosini, Maurizio 122
American Federation of Labor (AFL) 187, 272, 273
American Federation of Labor and Congress of Industrial Organizations (AFL–CIO) 273
Amin, Idi 58, 164
amnesties, immigration 6, 36, 228, 257, 262, 263, 326, 368
Anderson, Benedict: *Imagined Communities* 69
Anderson, Bridget 314
anti-Semitism 57, 62, 63, 66, 67, 68, 75, 138, 139, 161, 179, 184, 186, 288, 289, 305

Arab Gulf 21, 22, 27, 103, 104, 105, 106, 107, 158, 219, 244, 309, 310, 314, 317, 350, 361
Arab Spring (2010–12) 48–9
Arendt, Hannah 138
Argentina 17, 20, 27
Asia 6, 22
  chain migration from 330
  displacement levels within 37, 91, 92
  diversity in 71
  European colonies in 17, 18, 19, 20, 21, 22
  female domestic and care workers within, demand for 122
  fertility levels in 234, 239, 242
  long-distance migrations, major (1950–2020) and *24–5*
  NHS and migration from 158
  racism directed against Asian immigrants 161, 261, 262
  regional migration and 27, 86, 106, 244
  segregation index and 182
  urbanization within 29
  See also individual country name
asylum seekers
  apprehension statistics 33–5, *34*
  Australian government and 47, 50–51
  'bogus' 6, 9, 46, 47, 48, 51–2, 53, 249, 266, 365
  border restrictions/efforts to limit arrival of 7, 33–5, *34*, 47, 50–51, 249, 253, 254, 257, 261, 262, 264, 326, 327, 329, 337
  centres 3–4, 58–9, 203, 275
  conservatives and 266, 268, 269, 274, 275–6, 286, 289
  definition of x, 10–11, 46
  development in poor countries and 78
  future of migration 364–5, 367
  illegal migration and x, 10–11, 33, 46
  Islam and 274
  numbers 33–5, *34*, 47–9, *48*
  racism and 58, 203
  refugees and, legal distinction between x
  'refugee crisis' narrative and 44–59
  'Remain in Mexico' policy and 47
  Rwanda, attempts to send to 47
  smuggling of migrants and 292, 293, 295, 298, 299–300, 302, 305
  social housing and 192
  subsidiary protection status 51
  trafficking of migrants and 321–2
  United Nations Convention relating to the Status of Refugees (1951) and x, 46
  unsolicited border arrivals x, 6, 10–11, 33, 34–5, *34*, 119
  warfare, fleeing 6, 16, 45, 49, 50, 54, 54–8, *55*, 298, 308
  War on Immigration and 6
  welfare states and 145, 151
au pairs 42, 123, 254, 359
austerity policies 154–7
Australia 17, 20, 21, 22, *25*, 42, 47, 50–51, 60, 76, 109, 117, 138, *148*, 169, 173, 184, 244, 253, 254, 261, 262, 345, 364
Austria 21, 62, 138, 149, 169, 174, 232
authoritarianism 219, 221, 251, 306
'Aztlan plot' 68

Balarajan, Meera: *Exceptional People* 138
Ballard, Roger 101
Bangkok, Thailand 353, 354
Bangladesh 38, 50, 60, 71, 91, 100, 164, 165, 168, 176, 183, 184, 186, 213, 238, 256, 333, 346, 347, 348, 349
Barroso, José Manuel 78
Bataclan attack, Paris (2015) 181
Belgium 21, 37–8, 39, 62, 73, 75, 80, 149, 163, 167, 169, 173, 174, 232, 261, 279, 282, 302, 328, 329, 330
Berlin Wall, fall of (1989) 35, 40, 53, *115*, *118*, 134, 339
Berriane, Mohamed 296
Bezemer, Willemijn 205
Biden, Joe 79, 94, 292, 344
birth rates 20, 120, 121, 137, 141, 234, 237, 238–9, 240, 241
Black Lives Matter 206, 287
Blair, Tony 6, 46, 119, 155, 266
boat migration 1, 6, 31, 32, *34*, 50–51, 78, 132–3, 275, 291, 292, 295, 296, 297, 298, 302, 304, 305, 326, 329, 330, 344, 358
border enforcement 1, 2, 5, 6, 7, 40, 41, 46, 58, 78, 110, 307
  border restrictions produce more migration 326–7, 333–5
  'border restrictions reduce immigration' myth 326–42
  border walls 257, 264, 330–31
  'borders are beyond control' myth 31–43, *34*, *43*
  'borders are closing down' myth 247–65

Brexit and acceleration of immigration 335–6
closed borders lead to migration obsession 338
corporate push to open borders and 254, *255*, 256–7
human rights and 260–63
immigration trilemma 263–5
liberalization of immigration policies and 250–51, *252*, 253–4
migration paradox 341–2
migration policy restrictiveness, yearly average of changes in (1900–2014) *252*
'now or never' migration and 331–2, *332*, 333
opening borders 338–41, *340*
smuggling of migrants and 291–308
underground migration, drives 330–31
US border enforcement backfires 337–8
waterbed effect 327–30
worksite enforcement and 257–60
See also individual country name
Borjas, George 133, 150–51
Bosnia 54, 75
Boston College School of Social Work 113, 275
Brachet, Julien 304
Bracero Program (1942–64) 40, 106, 272, 326
brain drain 139, 209–21
Braun, Wernher von 139
Braverman, Suella 31
Brazil 17, 18, 20, 26, 27, 29, 121–2, 158, 241, 243, 331
Bretton Woods Institutions 261
Brexit referendum (2016) 6, 7, 72, 109, *118*, 142, 143, 146, 196, 254, 264, 271–2, 280, 282, 302, 326, 328, 330, 331, 335–6, 363
Brick Lane Mosque, London 186
Britain *see* UK
brothels 309, 312, 320–21
Buchanan, Pat: *State of Emergency: The Third World Invasion and Conquest of America* 67–8
Bulgaria 7, *118*, 196, 283, 284, 336, 339
Burkina Faso 351
Burundi 48, 54
Bush, George H. W. 6
Bush, George W. 6, 231, 258, 271
business
cycles, immigration/emigration levels correlation with 114–17, *115*, 131–2, 269–70, 333, 336
lobbies 9, 222, 226, 256, 260–61, 263, 270–71, 368
migrant 185–6, 217–18, 341–2

Cameron, David 31, 146, 160
Cameron, Geoffrey: *Exceptional People* 138
Canada 17, 20, 21, 22, 50, 73, 76, 81, 102, 111, 117, *148*, 149, 167, 169, 173, 192, 222, 234, 261, 262, 286, 364
Canary Islands 298, 305, 329
capabilities-aspirations model 85–7, *86*, 90, 91, 92, 216, 240, 242
caravans, migrant 1, 32, 292
Card, David 133, 143
care workers 30, 41, 42, 114, 121, 122, 123, 124, 125, 141, 149, 158–9, 165, 186, 201, 210, 226–7, 232–3, 234, 235, 238, 243, 245, 259, 260, 366, 369, 370, 371, 372
Caribbean 7, 18, 19, 20, 21, *24*, 37, 38, 60, 123, 151, 161, 168, 173, 177, 179, 183, 184, 202, 205, 213, 256, 262, 289, 326, 327, 333, 336, 366
Carter, Jimmy 133
Castles, Stephen 368
Castro, Fidel 132–3
category jumping 330
Catholicism 62–3, 66, 67, 68, 68–9, 173, 200, 273, 275–6
Center for American Progress 167
Central America 1, 6, *24*, 32, 36, 45, 52, 79, 86, 91, 94, 113, 167, 211, 213, 275, 292, 299, 303, 330, 344, 355, 367 *see also individual country name*
Ceuta 297, *300*
chain migration 161, 330, 335
Charles, Prince 142
Charlie Hebdo attack, Paris (2015) 181
Chicago, US 180, 188
chicken tikka masala 178
childcare 41, 42, 121, 122, 123, 141, 158, 226–7, 254, 260, 359
Chile 50, 56
China 18, 19, 20, 21, 22, 23, 26, 27, 29, 40, 41, 57, 66, 67, 72, 92, 120, 130, 161, 163, 164, 165, 168, 235, 241, 243, 244, 302, 321, 356
Christian Aid 343–4
Christianity 62–3, 64, 274, 276
Chuang, Janie 314
Church of England 275

circular migration 7, 254, 256, 262, 296–7, 306, 333–8, 340, 341, 342, 362, 363, 366
Clemens, Michael 90–91, 133, 214
client politics 256–7, 260
climate change 1, 9, 10, 15, 16, 45, 343–57, 358
Clinton, Bill 6, 78
Clinton, Hillary 279–80
Club of Rome 242
colonialism 18, 19–21, 37–40, 42, 57–8, 63, 71, 91, 210, 261, 267, 288, 332
Colombia 50, 56, 121, 158, 264
Columbus, Christopher 19
Commission on Immigration Reform, US 270–71
Commission for Racial Equality, UK 181
Commonwealth 7, 327, 333, 336
Commonwealth Immigrants Act (1962) 327, 333, 336
communication technology 28, 29
concentrated benefits 256
Conference of Catholic Bishops, US 273
conformity bias 321–2
Congress, US 40, 78, 156, 258, 270–71, 326
Conservative Party, British 146, 266–7, 268, 271, 275, 289
conservatives, immigration and 266–78, *269*
contract substitution 104–5
Corbyn, Jeremy 266, 271
Costello, Cathryn 324–5
Côte d'Ivoire 27, 106, 351
Covid-19 pandemic 30, 79, 114, 124–5, 142, 161, 254
crime 1, 68, 161, 180, 181, 188, 189, 192, 193, 196–208, 224, 230, 231, 258, 259, 275, 291, 292, 299, 302, 303, 304, 304–5, 307, 309, 310, 311, 312, 314, 316, 320, 323, 324, 325, 359
culture of migration 101
Customs and Border Protection, US 257
Czaika, Mathias 112, 268, 335

Dakar, Senegal *300*, 305
Damas de Matos, Ana 149
Davidson, Julia O'Connell 316, 319
debt 94, 103–5, 112, 143, 145, 315, 316–17, 318, 322–4
DEMIG POLICY database 250–51, 268
Democratic Party, US 7, 270, 271
Democratic Republic of Congo 48, 50, 54, 298
demographics 3, 10, 15, 16, 84, 219, 234–45, 283, 370
Denmark 21, 47, 52, 78, 149, 169, 235, 282–3, 329
Denton, Nancy: *American Apartheid: Segregation and the Making of the Underclass* 187
desertification 345–6, 351–3
Determinants of International Migration (DEMIG) project, Oxford University International Migration Institute (IMI) xi, 250–51, 267–8, 293, 335, 339, 340
development, reductions in immigration due to origin nation 1, 78–92, *81*, *83*, *86*, 94, 98–100, *99*, 110, 111, 209–21, 224
Dewinter, Filip 279
discursive gap 256, 260, 267, 359, 366
displaced people x, 16, 49, 53–8, *55*, 113, 181, 272, 289, 303, 343–4, 346, 347, 349, 350, 355, 356–7
diversity 1, 6, 15, 60–77, *74*, 130, 139, 161, 165, 185, 195, 210, 218, 266, 267, 280, 283, 284, 290
domestic abuse 206, 313
domestic workers 37, 40, 41, 42, 93, 103, 105, 106, 107, 114, 120–22, 124, 132, 137, 141, 158, 235, 260, 272, 310, 314, 322, 366, 369
downward assimilation 168, 201–2, 207, 366
drugs 161, 188, 189, 196, 201, 203–5, 230, 291, 303, 307, 309, 312, 313, 315, 323
dual-income family 121–2
Dustmann, Christian 135, 150
Dutch East Indies 57

East End, London 186
Eastern Europe 6, 7, 41, 57, 63, 67, 123, 142–3, 152, 186, 205, 284, 286, 289, 321, 328, 335, 336, 339, 340 *see also individual country name*
education
ageing societies and 234, 235, 236, 238, 239, 240, 241, 242, 243–4
brain drain and 209, 210, 211, 212, 213–17, 220
crime rates and 197, 198, 201, 202, 205–6, 207, 208

education systems, pressure on 145, 146, 149–50, 153, 157
integration of immigrants and 161, 162–5, 169, 170, 172, 178, 179
labour shortages and 111–12, 114, 120, 121, 125
migration rates and 81, 82, 85–92, 94, 100
segregation and 185, 186, 187, 195
Egypt 21, 158, 164, 213, 219, 220, 221, 274, 346
Einstein, Albert 138
elder care 41, 121–2, 141, 149, 158–9, 210, 226–7, 234, 235, 366, 369, 370, 372
El Paso, Texas 113, 199, 275–6
El Salvador 216
emigration
ageing societies/demographic factors and 240–41, 242, 243
border restrictions and 328–9, 332, 334, 336, 338, 340, *340*, 341
brain drain and 209–21
climate change and 351
debt and 103–5
definition ix
'as desperate flight from misery' myth 93–108, *99*
development in origin countries and 79, 80–66, *81*, 90–92, 98–100, *99*, 111, 209–21, 224
diversity and 71–2
European, large-scale historical 17–21, 23, 33, 39
investment in better future 94–6
labour demand and 111, 112, 116, 117, *118*
migrants thinking for themselves and 108
migration prevention campaigns and 93–5
origin regions, impact on 100–103
overland and maritime migration routes to North Africa, the Middle East and western Europe *300–301*
policy changes 250, 251
rates of, present-day 18–19
rational decision 96–8
skilled emigration levels 211–13
smuggling and 305
social remittances and 218–19
South–South migration as road out of poverty 105–7
English Channel 1, 31, 293, 295, *300–301*, 302, 330
entrepreneurs 2, 17, 138, 139, 164, 167, 169–71, 177, 185, 186, 191, 193, 199, 201, 209, 217–18, 367
Eritrea 49, 52, 298
Ethiopia 15, 20, 23, 29, 50, 54, 55, 107, 212, 241, 244
eugenics 67, 289
Euro 2020 177
Eurobarometer 282–3, 284
Europe
apprehension statistics 34–5
border restrictions 326–31, 334–5, 336, 337, 339–40, *340*, 341
climate change and 344, 351
conservatives in 266, 272, 273
crime in 196, 197, 199, 202, 205
destination for migrants, transformation into 19–23
development in poor countries and 78, 79, 80, 80*n*, 81–2, 84
diversity in 60, 62, 64, 67–8, 69, 70–72, 75
emigration from, large-scale historical 17–21, 23, 33, 39
fertility rates 234, 238, 239, 240, 242
fiscal impact of lower-skilled immigration in 153–4
future of immigration in 364–5, 366, 371
illegal immigration in 34–6, *34*, 40–41, 42, *43*, 44, 257, 260, 262
integration of immigrants in 60, 160–79
labour recruitment and immigrants in 37–9, 40–41, 42, 102, 106, 117, 119, 123, 134, 135, 139, 142–3, 146, 151
major long-distance migrations (1950–2020) and *24–5*
overland and maritime migration routes to western *300–301*, 302
public opinion on immigration in 280, 282–3, 284, *285*, 286, 287, 288, 289
refugees in 3, 6, 31, 32, 33, 34, *34*, 35, 45, 46, 48, 50, 52, 57–8, 59, 253
segregation in 180–92, 194
smuggling of migrants and 291, 293, 295, 296, 297, 298, *300–301*, 305, 307
trafficking of migrants and 309, 311, 317–18, 319–20, 321
War on Immigration and 6–8
European Commission 78, 344

European Research Council (ERC) 250
European Social Survey (ESS) 282
European Union (EU) 35, 41
  assimilation of migrants in 169
  asylum seekers in 51, 52
  Berlin Wall, effect of fall in 35–6, 40–41, 53, *115*, *118*, 134, 339–40
  border enforcement in 253, 256, 264, 307, 326, 328, 330, 336, 338, 339–41, *340*
  Brexit referendum and *see* Brexit referendum
  Emergency Trust Fund 78, 80*n*
  enlargement of (2004/2007) 35, 40, *118*, 119, 152, 253, 339–40
  fiscal impacts of recent migrations from and to 152
  free movement within 35, 139, 142, 152, 196, 253, 256, 264, 271, 273, 328, 330, 331, 339–40, 362, 363
  French Guianese citizens and 338
  intra-European migration 339–40
  legalization ('amnesty') campaigns in 36
  Maastricht Treaty 152
  Mediterranean boat migration and 32, 34–5, 78, 80*n*, 296
  migration awareness campaigns 94
  non-EU immigration 32, 34–5, 51, 78, 80*n*, 119, 296, 336, 340–41, *340*, 359
  public opinion on immigration in 282–3, 284, *285*
  removal of migration barriers (1989–2007) 339–40, *340*
  Schengen agreement 152, 296, 297
  seasonal agricultural workers in Britain and 142, 146
  Settlement Scheme 336
  Turkey, 'deal' with (2016) on Syrian refugee migration 359
  War on Immigration and 32, 367
  yearly immigration within and towards (1953–2010) *340*
E-Verify 270–71
exceptional people, immigrants as 138–9, 199
'exodus' 23, 27, 31, 32, 41, 44, 88, 89, 291, 364
expatriates, role of 1–2
exploitation
  labour x, 2, 7, 41, 79, 93, 94, 97, 104–5, 123, 273, 302, 310, 311, 312, 313–17, 319, 320, 321, 322–5, 363, 368, 372
  smuggling and 291, 292, 299, 302
  trafficking and x, 8, 309, 310, 311, 312, 313–17, 319, 320, 321, 322–5, 368, 371

Fair Housing Act (1968) 156
family reunification 41, 102, 108, 119, 249, 253, 262, 268, 299, 330, 335, 361
Farage, Nigel 196, 279
Fargues, Philippe 219
fertility levels 219, 234–43, 245
First World War (1914–18) 57, 66
fiscal impact, immigration and 146–50, *148*, 151, 152–4, 157, 232
flexible work 123, 130, 141
flooding 16, 27, 95, 345, 346–50, 351, 353–4, 355
Floyd, George 206
forced labour 57, 64, 103, 104, 309, 312–16, 317, 320, 321, 322–5, 367
forced migration ix, x, 20, 38, 54, 57–8, 103, 302, 356
Forrest, Andrew 310
Fortuyn, Pim 203
France
  ageing society 235, 237
  Algerian independence and 57, 71, 134
  asylum seekers in 46, 50, 52
  banlieues 180, 183, 188, 191, 202, 232
  boat crossings originating in cross English Channel 31, 299–300, 330
  border camps in northern 299
  border restrictions and 326–7, 328, 330, 338
  colonial possessions, migration and 18, 19–20, 37–8, 38, 39, 57
  colons (Algerian descendants of French and other European settlers) in 20, 38, 57, 134
  dependence on migrant workers 371
  diversity/racist discrimination in 63, 69
  fertility rates 235
  fiscal contribution of immigration in *148*, 149
  French Revolution (1789) 69
  harkis (Algerians who served with the French Army) in 57, 134
  housing 191
  Huguenots in 63, 186
  immigration choisie ('chosen immigration') 31

immigration subie ('immigration undergone/suffered') 31
indentured workers and 18
integration of immigrants in 163, 166–7, 168, 169
job market discrimination 166–7
Moroccan migrants in 80, 81, 97, 101–2, 169, 328
murder rates in 207
post-war labour migrations to 38, 39
public opinion on immigration in 279, 283, 286
riots (2005 and 2007) among migrant youth 180
segregation in 180, 183, 186, 188, 191
smuggling of migrants and 299–300, 302, 305, 308
transport technology 29
wages in 97
worksite enforcement in 260
Francis, Pope 275
Fransen, Sonja 53, 56, 58
Frattini, Franco 32
Frattini, Tommaso 150
Freeman, Gary 256
French Guiana 338
Freud, Sigmund 138
Frisch, Max 175
Frontex *43*, 44, 307

Gabon 27, 106
Gaddafi, Muammar 32, 219
Gaddafi, Saif al-Islam 219
Garcia, Ruben 275–6
gross domestic product (GDP) 80*n*, *81*, 82, 83, 90–91, 106, 113, *115*, 116, 138, 147, 149, 166, 225, 231–3
General Social Survey (2006–14), US 75
gentrification 157, 192, 227
Germany
ageing society 234, 235, 236–7, 239
asylum seekers/refugee numbers 50, 52, 56, 68, 364–5
Aussiedler ethnic Germans living in eastern Europe 71
Berlin Wall, fall of (1989) 35, 40, 53, *115*, *118*, 134, 339
child and elder care in 158, 369
Covid-19 pandemic and 142
crime rates in 207
economic growth and net migration (1970–2021) 114, *115*, 116
education levels of immigrants in 163
emigration from 66–7, 111
federalist, decentralized structure 73
fertility levels in 234, 235
fiscal contribution of immigration in *148*, 149
guest worker agreements 39
integration of immigrants in 160, 161, 163, 166, 167, 169, 170, 172–3, 174, 178, 179
internal/domestic migration in 29
job market discrimination in 166, 167
Muslim migration in 68
origins of modern state 70
anti-Polish sentiment in nineteenth-century 63
post-colonial migrations and 21
public housing in 156
public opinion on immigration in 282, 283, 286, 364
Second World War and 57, 75, 138
segregation in 183, 186
social trust in 75
turnaround in immigration policy 364–5
welfare state 122, 142, 146, *148*, 149, 152, 369
worksite enforcement 260, 262
ghetto 180, 184, 186, 188, 189, 193, 194, 196, 199
Ghorashi, Halleh 171
Giammattei, Alejandro 32
gig economy 129, 143, 371
Glass, Ira 227
Global Commission on International Migration (GCIM) 210
global financial crisis (2007–2008) 102, 116, 129–30
globalization 15, 72
Global North 16, 44, 79, 87
Global South 16, 44, 62, 79, 312
Goldin, Ian: *Exceptional People* 138
Gören, Erkan 73
Government Office for Science, UK 346
Grandi, Filippo 45
Grant, Edwin 67
'great replacement' conspiracy theory 67, 68, 181, 238
Greco-Turkish War (1919–22) 71
Greece 21, *34*, 35, 39, 47, 52, 57, 71, 149, 235, 243, 260, 283, 286, 298, 328, 329, 339, 359

Grenfell Tower block fire (2017) 190
gross national income (GNI) 82
Groundswell report (2021) 354
Guardian 310
guest workers 7, 21, 39, 106, 130, 160, 163, 174, 175, 176, 271, 272, 273, 326–7, 334–5, 339, 360, 361, 366
Gulf War (1991) 54, 55
Guyana 264, 338

Haiti 52, 90, 91, 198, 213, 243, 275, 355
Haratin 102
Harvard University 75, 198
Hatton, Timothy 52; *The Age of Mass Migration* 84
Herrou, Cédric 305
higher-skilled workers ix–x, 30, 41, 102, 110, 114, 124–5, 135, 137, 150, 152–3, 158, 164, 211–18, 219, 220, 227, 239, 253, 283
Hitler, Adolf 138, 139
Hobbes, Michael 316
Ho Chi Minh City, Vietnam 354
Hochstenbach, Cody: *Uitgewoond (Worn Out)* 154–5
holiday worker programmes 42
Hollifield, James 263
Holocaust 57, 63
Homeland Security Investigations (HSI), US 257–8
Home Office, UK 259, 320–21, 331
Hong Kong 106, 244, 264
Huguenots 63, 186
Human Development Index (HDI) 82, 83, *83*
Hungary 45, 52, 186, 283, 284, 287, 339
Hunt, Jennifer 133
Huntington, Samuel P. 161
Hurricane Katrina (2005) 350, 355

illegal migration
  apprehension statistics 33–4, *34*
  asylum seekers and x, 46
  border enforcement and 6, 7, 249, 253, 254, 257, 258–63, 264, 308, 326, 327, 329–31, 337, 341, 343
  'borders beyond control' myth and 31–7, 39, 40–42, *43*, 44
  conservatives and 266, 271, 277
  crime and 196, 197, 200–201
  debt and 104
  definition of x–xi
  development in poor countries and 78–9, 86, 94, 95, 96, 97–8
  European colonialism as biggest illegal migration in human history 20
  future of immigration and 359, 361, 362, 366, 367–8, 369
  'great replacement' conspiracy theory and 68
  'hostile environment' for illegal migrants, UK 31, 249, 259
  'illegal asylum seeker' 46
  illegal entry x–xi
  illegal stay x–xi, 35, 330–31 *see also* overstaying
  labour recruitment as origin of 37, 39, 40–42, 102, 116, 117, 119, 122, 123, 124, 125, 228, 231, 308
  levels of 31–7
  overstaying xi, 35, 36, 41, 102, 125, 293, *294*, 305, 330–31, 337, 341
  public opinion and 283, 286, 289
  smuggling as main cause of 2, 8, 10, 291–308, *294*, *300–301*
  term, use of x, xi
  trafficking and 309, 311, 314, 315, 317, 318–19, 324
  undocumented migrants *see* undocumented migrants
  unsolicited border arrivals x, 6, 10–11, 33, 34–5, *34*, 119
  welfare state and 146, 152–4
immigration, definition ix *see also individual area and type of immigration*
Immigration Act
  (1971), UK *118*, 327
  (1976), US 330
Immigration and Customs Enforcement (ICE), US 231, 257–8
Immigration and Nationality Act (1952), US 261–2
Immigration Reform and Control Act (IRCA) (1986), US 6, 228, 257, 271, 326, 337
Immigration Restrictiveness Index (IRI) 250–51, 268
immigration shocks 132–4
indentured workers 18, 20, 164, 324

India 18, 20, 21, 22, 23, 26, 38–9, 57, 58, 71, 73, 92, 98, 106, 120, 158, 161, 163, 164, 168, 183, 184, 218, 238, 239, 241, 244, 333
Indonesia 18, 20, 21, 22, 23, 26, 38, 57, 61, 71, 73, 106, 121, 123, 170, 241, 244, 353–4
industrialization 18, 20, 23, 28, 241, 344, 347
Industrial Revolution 28, 344
inequality 27, 75–6, 110–14, 129–30, 143, 144, 161–2, 163–4, 177, 181, 183, 185–95, 201–4, 272, 273, 367, 369–70
innovation 1, 60, 61, 129, 138–9, 209, 222, 224
Institute Against Human Trafficking, US 309
Institute for Economics and Peace 344
integration 1, 6, 7–8, 9, 10, 11, 60, 68, 76, 109–10, 149, 160–79, 180, 181, 182, 183, 185, 186, 192, 194, 201, 231, 266, 268, *269*, 284, 362, 363, 365
intelligence ix, x, 67, 68
Intergovernmental Panel on Climate Change (IPCC) 344, 345
internal/domestic migration ix, 23, *24–5*, 26, 27, *27*, 28, 29, 70, 84, 89–90, 102, 272, 334, 350
  see also displaced people
internally displaced persons (IDPs) x, 49, 54, 113, 303, 356
Internal Revenue Service (IRS) 153
International Organization for Migration (IOM) 9, 16, 46, 53, 93, 94, 292, 305, 311, 316
internet 15, 30, 56, 70, 72, 87, 88, 217, 316
'invasion' narrative 31–2, 36–7, 41, 42, *43*, 44, 56, 68, 279, 289, 306–7, 364, 365
Iran 50, 54, 163, 171, 241
Iraq 48, 54, 191, 203
Ireland 63, 66, 67, 68, 70, 75, 91, 149, 161, 168, 170, 179, 186, 200, 202, 243, 282
Islam 60, 161, 165, 219, 274–5
Israel 102, 106, 134, 274
Italy
  anti-Italian sentiment and migrants from 67, 161, 179, 200, 202
  badante (migrant domestic worker) 122
  cuisine transforms eating worldwide 72
  emigration from 18, 21, 39, 63, 66, 67, 111, 161, 179, 186, 200, 202, 339
  fertility levels 234, 235
  fiscal ratio of foreign- versus native-born people in, total (2006–2018) *148*, 149
  labour shortages in 41, 141, 152, 341–2, 260
  legalization programmes for migrants in 262, 341
  Mediterranean boat migration and 32, *34*, 78, 275, 296, 297, 329
  migration transition in 91, 243
  Morocco, migrants from within 81, 102, 296, 297–8, 328–9, 334, 341–2
  nation building in 70
  public opinion of migration in 279, 283, 286–7
  Schengen agreement and 296, 297–8, 328–9, 334
  Second World War and 38
  sex trafficking in 311, 317–19
  visa overstayers in 331
  waterbed effect in 328–9
  welfare state in 159, 369
  worksite enforcement in 260

Jacobs, Jane: *The Death and Life of Great American Cities* 192–3
Jakarta, Indonesia 353–4
Japan 18, 20, 22, 23, *24–5*, 29, 42, 57, 66, 123–4, 161, 234, 235, 237, 240, 244, 283, 323–5, 331, 362, 370
Jews 57, 62, 63, 66, 67, 68, 75, 102, 138–9, 161, 173, 179, 184, 186, 189, 276, 288, 289, 305, 321
jobs *see* labour
Johnson, Boris 109, 177, 254
Jordan 105, 106
Juncker, Jean-Claude 78, 344

kafala system 105
Kazakhstan 18, 22
Kennedy, John F. 68
Kenya 18, 20, 29, 38, 50, 58, 164, 212
knowledge economy 110
Kosovo 54, *55*, 56
Kuwait 21, 106, *301*

labour
  blue-collar workers ix, 110
  continuation of labour migration, reasons behind 119–21

labour – *cont'd.*
demand/shortages 1, 2, 7, 18, 20, 21, 28, 29, 30, 35–44, 83, 102, 109–25, *118*, 131–2, 140, 141, 142, 143, 151, 210, 222–3, 228, 229, 234, 235, 236, 237, 242, 243, 245, 260, 269, 293, 298, 306, 330, 331, 333–4, 337–8, 340, 341, 347, 352, 361, 366, 368–9, 370, 371
domestic workers *see* domestic workers
essential jobs 11, 124–5, 143, 158, 366
exceptional people, immigrants as 138–9
exploitation 105, 123, 312, 314, 315–18, 322, 324, 325, 363
female migrant workers 103, 120–22, 124, 140, 141, 158, 213, 218, 239, 244, 309, 310, 311, 312, 314, 315, 317–19, 321, 322, 323, 324
forced 57, 64, 103, 104, 309, 312–16, 317, 320, 321, 322–5, 367
higher-skilled *see* higher-skilled workers
illegal migrants as wanted workers 41–2
job creation 136–8
job insecurity ix–x, 9, 29, 37, 38, 40, 129–44, 359, 371
labour market effects of immigration, negligible 134–6
liberalization of labour market policies 253–4
lower-skilled workers *see* lower-skilled workers
low-wage economy, governments and 123, 143–4
lump of labour fallacy 136
manual ix, 97, 109, 114, 121, 125, 132, 137, 167, 217, 239, 244, 366, 372
Mariel boatlift and 132–4
market effects of immigration, negligible 134–6
market integration 165–9
mid-skilled workers ix–x, 114, 364, 372
native workers as unfit for migrant jobs 140–43
need of migrant workers 109–25
overqualified workers x, 210
'pick for Britain', British workers refuse to 141–3
post-colonial labour recruitment 37–40
recruitment 18, 20, 21, 37–42, 85, 93, 96, 100, 101, 102, 103, 104, 105–6, 109, 110, 114, 116, 122–4, 125, 130–31, 142, 143, 158, 163, 164, 176, 210, 214, 257, 267, 269, 272–3, 314–15, 317, 318, 368
sex workers 124, 311, 317–21
standards 131, 152, 229, 230, 232, 363, 372
supply, myth of unlimited 241–3
supply shocks 132–4
unions 9, 130–31, 144, 163, 185, 187, 228, 229, 230, 267, 269, 270, 271, 272–3, 274, 277
'unwanted' workers, recruitment of officially 122–4
white-collar workers ix, 124–5, 186
worksite enforcement 35, 153, 257–60, 270, 337–8
Labour Party, British 145–6, 266–7, 268–9, 271–2, 275
La Ferrara, Eliana 76
Lampedusa 32, 275
Lancee, Bram 165–6
land subsidence 353–4
languages 26, 32, 49, 60, 62, 66, 69, 70, 71, 72, 73, 161, 162–3, 165, 166, 170, 174, 177, 179, 181, 184–5, 194, 231, 249, 289, 326, 332, 362
Latino immigrants 32, 37, 60, 62, 64, 66, 67, 98, 135, 150, 151, 153, 161, 163, 164, 166–8, 172, 173, 181, 182, 184, 194, 204, 227–31, 238, 241, 263, 270, 337, 366
Lebanon 49–50, 106, 107
Le Pen, Jean-Marie 279
Le Pen, Marine 279
Leerkes, Arjen 205
left-wing parties 79, 130–31, 210, 266, 268–9, 276–7, 279, 283, 355
Lesbos 46
Levitt, Peggy 218
liberal paradox 263
Libya 32, 49, 78, 106, 219–20, 298, 304, 329, 367
Light, Michael 200
Lower East Side, New York City 186
lower-skilled workers ix, 68, 109–10, 119, 120, 124–5, 132, 133, 135, 140, 143, 145, 146, 150, 152–3, 157, 161, 163, 164, 167, 176, 201–2, 211, 214, 222, 223, 227, 232, 243–4, 249, 253, 256, 272, 283, 308, 321, 364, 365–8 *see also* labour

low-income economies 23, 86, 90, 91, 96, 111, 150, 156, 172, 183, 190, 204, 211, 213, 224, 229, 241, 243, 283
low-wage economies 106, 109, 120, 130, 143–4
lump of labour fallacy 136
Lutz, Helma 122

Mabogunje, Akin 88
Mai, Nicola 319–20
Malaysia 22, 27, 106, 120, 243, 244
Maldives 344, 356
Mali 21, 38, 168, 260, 298, 351
Malta 34, *34*, 286, 298, 339
Manchester University 212
Manila, Philippines 29, 96, 353, 354
Mariel boatlift (1980) 132–4
Maroni, Roberto 32
Martinez, Ramiro 198
Massey, Douglas 337; *American Apartheid: Segregation and the Making of the Underclass* 187, 194, 264
mass immigration 31, 78, 131, 279, 339
May, Theresa 61
Mbaye, Linguère Mously 305–6
McCluskey, Len 130
media 2, 16, 23, 27
  'borders beyond control' myth and 31, 32, 33, 36, 44
  border restrictions and 264, 334, 335–6
  climate change and 344, 349, 352, 353, 355
  crime rates and 196, 203, 204, 207
  development in poor countries, exposure to and 85, 87
  diversity and 65–6, 70
  future of immigration and 358–9, 363, 364
  'illegal migration' definition and xi
  pro- and anti- immigration camp framing 5, 267, 277
  public opinion and 282, 287
  'refugee crisis' myth and 19, 45–6, 47, 53, 56
  segregation and 180, 181, 186, 189
  smuggling of migrants and x, 291, 302, 303, 304
  South–North migration as 'desperate flight from misery' myth and 93, 95, 96, 103, 107, 108
  trafficking of migrants and x, 311, 312, 315, 316, 322, 324
  'welfare scroungers' or 'welfare tourists' and 145
Mediterranean 1, 7, 31, 34, 35, 78, 291, 296–302, *300–301*, 305, 308, 326, 329, 334, 343, 345
Meek, Miki 227
Melilla 297, *300*
Meloni, Giorgia 279
Mendoza, Dovelyn Rannveig 104, 105, 106
Merkel, Angela 160, 176
Mexico
  'Aztlan plot' 68
  Bracero Program and 40, 106, 272, 326
  brain drain in 211, 215, 220
  climate migration and 343
  crime and migrants from 196, 198–9, 202, 303
  Deferred Action for Childhood Arrivals (DACA) and 263, 271
  diversity in US and migration from 60, 68
  emigration heartland areas 100, 103
  emigration rates 17–19
  export processing zones (*maquiladoras*) 29
  fertility levels and 239, 241, 243, 244
  Immigration Reform and Control Act (IRCA), US and 6, 228, 257, 271, 326, 337
  integration of migrants from 161, 163, 164, 167, 168, 176
  internal migration 26, 29
  internally displaced people (IDPs) from 113
  labour demand in US and 7, 40, 41, 106, 113–14, 116, 119, 272
  Mexican Migration Project (MMP), Princeton University 337
  migration transition in 91
  North American Free Trade Agreement (NAFTA) and 78
  Our Town documentary and migrants from 227–9
  Piénsalo 2 Veces (*Think Twice*) campaign 94
  'Remain in Mexico' policy, US and 47
  remittances and 98
  smuggling of migrants and 295, 299, 303–4, 307, 308

Mexico – *cont'd.*
transit country for Central American refugees 45, 275, 367
US car industry relocates to 120
wages in 97
Mexico–US border
border enforcement 7, 295, 299, 303–4, 307, 308, 326, 329, 330, 331, 334, 337–8, 341
'caravans' of Central Americans attempt to reach 1, 292
'climate migration' and 343
export processing zones (*maquiladoras*) 29
illegal immigration levels 34, 35–6, 37, 39–40, 41
internally displaced people (IDPs) at 113
labour demand in US and crossings of 113–14
migration industry and 307–8
religious organizations at 275–6
separation of children from their parents at 276
smuggling of migrants over 295, 299, 303, 307, 308
waterbed effect and 329
Miami South Beach 321
middle-class 26, 72, 122, 158, 164, 185–6, 189, 190, 202, 203–4, 206, 219, 226, 227, 271, 356
Middle East 6, 21, 28, 29, 36, 45, 72, 91, 106–7, 122, 165, 166, 203, 213, 219, 242, 244, 295, *300–301*, 355 *see also individual country name*
mid-skilled workers ix–x, 114, 364, 372
migrant
definition/term ix–xi, 17
types ix–xi *see also individual type name*
Migrants' Files 307
migration
'crisis' 1, 15, 16, 28, 31, 45–59, *48*, 55, 359
definition/term ix–xi
'jackpot' 100–101
levels of 15–30, *17*, *24–5*, *27*
myths of 13–245
paradox 90–92, 341–2
propaganda 247–357
trilemma 263–5
types ix–xi, 23 *see also individual type name*
Migration Policy Institute (MPI) 308
mixed flows 52
mobility transition/migration transition 84, 91, 242–3
Moldova 45
Morocco 21, 26, 276, 336
brain drain, emigration from and 211, 213, 216, 219, 220, 221
circular migration and 296–300, *300–301*, 302, 362
criminal activity and migrants from 196, 205
discrimination and migrants from 166
education levels of migrants from 163, 164
emigration seen as investment in better future within 94–5, 97
fertility levels 241
French army recruitment in 38
global recession (2007–2008) and migrants from 336
illegal migration from as response to labour shortages 116, 260
income levels and emigration from (1965–2019) 80–82, *81*, 84, 351
integration of emigrants within Europe 60, 163, 164, 166, 168, 169, 171, 174
labour shortages within Europe and emigration from 39, 41, 116, 260
'migration jackpot' and 100, 101–3
migration paradox and 341–2
migration transition and 91, 243, 244
oasis agriculture, crisis of traditional 352–3
Olympics 2024 and emigration from 260
re-admission agreements and workers from 298
salary of unskilled worker in 97
segregation and immigrants from 183
smuggling and immigrants from 305
Todgha valley 80–81, 87, 101–2, 216
visa requirements and emigration from 296–300, *300–301*, 302, 328, 329, 331, 334
Mozambique 54, 347
multiculturalism 6, 71, 160, 162, 170, 172–6, 264, 266, 364
multiple identities 73–4
multiplier effect 137
murder rates 198, 206, 207
Muslim immigrants 6, 49, 57, 60, 62, 66, 67, 68, 71, 161, 164, 165, 166, 169, 179, 180–81, 197, 204, 205, 241, 274
Myanmar 22, 23, 49, 50, 56, 91, 106, 120, 243, 244
Myers, Norman 343

names, migrant 169
nation building 69–70, 75
National Academy of Sciences (NAS), US 135, 167
National Agency for the Prohibition of Traffic in Persons (NAPTIP) 318
National Health Service (NHS) 38, 146, 158, 210, 212, 369
national security 6, 292
Native Americans 64, 65, 173, 288
native workers 120, 124, 131, 132, 133, 134, 135, 136, 137, 140–41, 145, 146, 149, 192, 229, 235, 273, 370, 371
nativism 16, 63, 66, 67, 68, 75, 181, 277, 287, 289–90
NATO 54, *55*
Natter, Katharina 268
natural growth 137, 234–5
Nazi regime 57, 63, 75, 138–9, 261, 305
Nepal 22, 90, 91, 106, 123, 213, 216, 243, 244, 328
Netherlands 3–4, 18, 20, 21, 29, 31, 37–8, 39, 50, 57–8, 62, 75, 80, 81, 97, 101–2, 107, 123, 141, 142, 149, 154–5, 161, 163, 166, 167, 169, 170, 171, 172–3, 174, 175, 183, 203, 205, 254, 260, 279, 282–3, 286, 326–7, 328, 329, 332–3, *332*, 338, 369
New Deal 187–8, 190
New Zealand 17, 20, 21, 22, *25*, 60, 76, 111, 117, 138, 169, 173, 184, 222, 244, 253, 261, 262
Niger 304, 346
Nigeria 26, 27, 41, 88, 106, 158, 164, 239, 244, 298, 311, 317–19, 346
Nigerian Women Trafficking and Child Labour Eradication Foundation (WOTCLEF) 318 9/11 6, 60, 161, 181
non-migrant 27, *27*, 28, 62, 137, 157, 163, 175, 197, 201, 205, 287
North Africa 7, 34, 38, 41, 105, 176, 183, 213, 242, 272, 296, 297, 298, *300*, 304, 326, 329, 330, 334–5, 352 *see also individual country name*
North American Free Trade Agreement (NAFTA) 78, 232
Norway 52, 166, 167, 169
Nusantara 353

Obama, Barack 6, 249, 258, 263, 266, 271
Office for National Statistics, UK 168
Ogaden War (1977–8) 54, *55*
oil crisis (1973) *115*, 326–7, 335, 339
Olayo-Méndez, Alejandro 113, 275
open borders 119, 254–7, *255*, 276, 297, 327, 331, 334, 339, 362–3
Organization for Economic Cooperation and Development (OECD) 149, 169
organized crime 196, 291, 303, 304, 309, 312, 323
'other'/othering 62, 68, 69, 75, 173–4, 286, 290
Our Town (documentary) 227–9, 230
outsourcing 29–30, 47, 109, 120, 122, 226, 256, 369–70, 372
overstaying xi, 35, 36, 41, 102, 125, 293, *294*, 305, 330–31, 337, 341
Oxford University 2, 3, 110, 112, 257, 275, 325, 338, 339
  DEMIG POLICY 250–51, 268
  Determinants of International Migration (DEMIG) project xi, 250–51, 267–8, 293, 335, 339, 340
  International Migration Institute (IMI) xi, 250–51, 267–8, 293, 335, 339, 340
  Migration Observatory 51, 282

Pakistan 21, 22, 26, 38, 50, 54, 57, 60, 71, 75, 100, 101, 105, 158, 164, 165, 168, 175, 176, 183, 184, 186, 213, 238, 243, 244, 256, 328, 333, 346
Palenga-Möllenbeck, Ewa 122
Palme, Olaf 191–2
parallel lives, migrant communities living in 1, 61, 181, 193
Parreñas, Rhacel 323; *Illicit Flirtations* 323
Patel, Priti 292
patent holders 138, 139
pateras (small fishing boats) 297, 304, 329
pay gap, ethnicity 168
Peach, Ceri 333
Pearl Harbor, attack on (1941) 66
pensions 226, 234, 235, 238, 371
Peri, Giovanni 229
Peru 18, 50, 56, 264
Pew Research Center 281
Philippines 20, 21, 22, 29, 39–40, 82, 91, 92, 98, 99, 103, 105, 106, 120, 121, 158, 202, 211, 216, 219, 220, 221, 244, 314, 323–4
Phillips, Trevor 181

Pickett, Kate: *The Spirit Level* 76
Piketty, Thomas: *Capital in the Twenty-First Century* 130
Piore, Michael: *Birds of Passage: Migrant Labor and Industrial Societies* 140–41
Poland 7, 45, 50, 56, 63, 66, 67, 119, 161, 170, 243, 289, 328, 339, 340
political discourse/rhetoric
  ageing societies and 234, 235, 236, 237, 240, 241, 243, 244, 245
  border enforcement and 2, 31–3, 36, 37, 38, 42, 44, 249, 250, 251, 253–4, 256–7, 258, 259–60, 262–5, 266, 327, 332, 333, 334, 337, 339, 342
  'borders as beyond control' myth and 31–3, 36, 37, 38, 42, 44
  brain drain myth and 209, 212, 218–19, 221
  climate change and 343, 344, 347, 352, 353, 354, 355–6
  conservative reputation on immigration and 266–78
  crime and 196, 200, 206, 207
  development in poor countries and 78, 79, 83, 91
  diversity and 60–61, 65, 66, 67–8, 69, 72, 75–6, 77
  future of immigration and 358, 359, 360–61, 363, 364–8, 371, 372
  illegal migration and xi, 2
  integration of immigrants and 160, 161, 162, 171, 172–3, 174, 175, 178
  internal migration and 23, 27
  labour migration and 113, 114, 117, 122, 123, 124–5, 129, 131, 132, 133, 139, 140, 141, 143, 144
  public opinion on immigration and 279–90
  'refugee crises'/'migration crisis' narrative and 16, 19, 28, 45, 46–7, 48, 49, 50–51, 52, 53, 56–7, 58–9
  segregation and 180, 181, 186, 189, 190
  smuggling and x, 2, 53, 291–3, 302, 306, 308
  South–North migration as 'desperate flight from misery' narrative and 93, 95, 96, 99–100, 103, 108
  trafficking and x, 53, 302, 310, 312, 319, 322
  War on Immigration 6–8
  welfare state, migrant use of and 145–6, 147, 154, 157, 159
population growth 1, 15, 17, *17*, 18, 81, 83, 88, 182, 237, 239–42, 277
populism 131, 145, 279, 280
Portes, Alejandro 178, 201, 202
Portugal 19, 20, 21, 37, 39, 63, 81, 102, 138, 149, 183, 243, 260, 261, 282, *300*, 326, 328, 339
poverty 1, 15, 32, 33, 45, 95, 96, 105, 106, 108
  as a presumed cause of migration 78, 79, 80–81, 82, 85, 86, 88, 90, 111, 113
  climate change and 350, 351, 355, 357
  development in poor countries and 78, 79, 80–81, 82, 85, 86, 88, 90, 111
  future migration and 243, 244
  immigrant integration and 162, 167–8, 170
  prevents people from migrating 78, 79, 80–81, 82, 85, 86, 88, 90, 111
  reducing, immigration as most effective way of 222–7
  segregation and 180, 182, 184, 188, 189, 192, 193–4
  smuggling and 291
  South–South migration and 105–7
  trafficking of migrants and 313, 320, 324
Powell, Enoch: 'Rivers of Blood' speech 289
privatization 154, 155, 156, 157, 189, 192, 194
pro- and anti- immigration camp framing 2, 4, 5, 6, 143, 228, 267, 277, 358
productivity 129, 137, 138, 150, 222, 223, 224, 225, 226, 350, 354–5
protectionism, economic 251, 261
Protestantism 62–3, 64, 65, 67, 161, 173, 186, 276
public opinion, immigration and 10, 11, 279–90, *281*, *285*
Puerto Rico 21, 39, 40, 60, 334
push-pull models 85, 239–40, 350
Putnam, Robert: *Bowling Alone* 75–6

Qatar 21, 105, 106, 240, 310

racism 6, 8, 40, 61, 76, 187, 202, 208, 261, 279, 283, 284, 286, 361, 367
  African Americans and 40, 64–5, 173, 181, 182, 184, 187–90, 206, 272, 288, 315, 350
  American indigenous peoples and 64
  anti-Semitism 57, 62, 63, 66, 67, 68, 75, 138, 139, 161, 179, 184, 186, 288, 289, 305

Asians and 66, 161, 164
discrimination in job hiring and 165
diversity and 61, 62
German Americans and 66–7
Italy, domestic racism in 67
Muslims and 67, 68, 161, 164, 165, 166, 197, 204, 205, 241
persistence as major problem 287
racial redlining 65, 187–8, 194
racial segregation 182, 183, 187–90
reductions in linked to increase in immigration 288–90
southern Europeans and 63
US anti-immigrant 66–8
'whites only' immigration policies 261–2
Rapoport, Hillel 217
Rasmussen, Poul Nyrup 78
Reagan, Ronald 6, 156, 222, 228, 257, 263, 271, 326
receiving-country bias 9, 209
recruitment, labour *see* labour
refugees 7–8
ageing societies and 235
asylum seekers *see* asylum seekers
border enforcement and 251–3, 261, 263, 264, 326, 367
changing attitudes towards 364–5
climate change and 9, 343–4, 346, 353, 354, 358
crime rates and 203
definition of ix, x–xi
global refugee displacements (1977–2022) *55*
innovation and 138–9
integration and 163, 164, 169, 170, 171–2, 177
labour demand and 117, 132–4, 135, 138–9, 140, 143
major long-distance migrations (1950–2020) and *24–5*
Mariel boatlift 132–4
numbers, relatively small and not accelerating 47–9, *48*
numbers, UN agencies exaggerate or misrepresent 9, 16, *43*, 44, 53–4, 58–9
origin regions, real refugee crisis in 49–51
as percentage of world population (2020) *27*, 28
political crisis, refugee crisis as a 58–9
political rhetoric and 16, 19, 28, 45, 46–7, 48, 49, 50–51, 52, 53, 56–7, 58–9
public opinion on 280, 282, 283, 286
'refugee crisis' myth 9, 15, 16, 19, 31, 35, 42, *43*, 44–59, 282, 359
resettlement schemes 1, 50
right-wing/left-wing politics and 266, 274–7
segregation and 186, 192
smuggling of migrants and 291, 292–3, 295, 298, 299, 302, 303, 304, 305, 306, 308
Syrian 3, 6, 31, 35, 45, 49–50, 52, *55*, 56, *115*, 134, 298, 359, 360, 364–5
Ukrainian 45, 49, 50, *55*, 56, 142, 364
warfare and flows of 54–8, *55*, 70
welfare and 145, 146, 152, 154, 155, 157
worldwide refugee numbers as percentage of global population, total (1985–2021) *48*
Reid, John 145–6
religion
conservatives and 274–5, 277
diversity and 60, 61, 62–3, 68, 69, 71–2, 73, 76
fertility rates and 241
fundamentalism 180–81, 202, 204, 205
integration and 162–6, 174–5, 176, 179
segregation and 181, 184, 189, 193, 194
remittances 80, 98–100, *99*, 102, 108, 215–21, 223, 224, 225
Replacement Migration: Is It a Solution to Declining and Ageing Populations? (UN Population Division study) 236
Republican Party, US 7, 270, 271, 281
Right to Buy initiative 155
Rocard, Michel 46
Rogaly, Ben 314
Rohingya 49, *55*, 56
role models, migrant 87, 218
Romania 7, *118*, 152, 186, 336, 339
Romani people 62, 184, 288
Ross, Edward 67, 68, 289
Rowthorn, Robert 147, 149
Royal Society 215
Rudd, Kevin 47
Ruedin, Didier 165
Russia 18, 22, 26, 41, 45, 57, 71, 134, 186, 239
Ukraine, invasion of (2022–) 45, 49, 50, *55*, 364

Rutte, Mark 31
Rwanda 47, 48, 54, *55*, 75, 212

Sahara Desert 102, 304
Sahel zone 351–2
Sall, Macky 79
Sampson, Robert 198–9
San Antonio, Texas trailer deaths (2022) 303
Sanchez, Gabriella 303–4
Sanders, Bernie 130
Sarrazin, Thilo: *Deutschland schafft sich ab* (*Germany Abolishes Itself*) 68
Saudi Arabia 21, 105, 106, 107, 219, 240, 241, 356
Sayad, Abdelmalek 209
Schewel, Kerilyn 107
sea level rise 343, 344, 345–6, 347, 348–9, 353–4, 356
Second World War (1939–45) 19, 20, 37, 38, 46, 53, 57, 60, 61, 66, 71, 123, 155, 163, 177, 189, 191, 251, 261, 305
second-generation migrants 150, 164, 167, 200–202, 330
Seehofer, Horst 146
segmented assimilation 168, 201
segregation 1, 6, 7–8, 9, 10, 11, 64–5, 109, 160, 168, 170, 174, 175–6, 177, 180–95, 201, 202, 207, 272, 286, 287, 288, 360, 362, 366
Senegal 21, 38, 41, 79, 168, 296, 297, 298, 305–6
Serbia 54, *55*, 56
7/7 bombings, London (2005) 181
sex
  assault 105, 197, 199, 201
  harassment 161
  predators 205, 315
  trafficking 309–25
  workers 124, 309–11, 317–22
Sicily 67
Sikhs 38–9, 71, 164
Singapore 22, 27, 106, 244
Skeldon, Ronald 358; *Migration and Development* 84
slavery 1, 10, 20, 63, 64, 65, 93, 95, 102, 103, 138, 181, 274, 287, 288, 291, 309–25
Slovakia 45, 284
smuggling x, 1, 2, 7, 8, 9, 10, 31, 33, 42, 44, 79, 86, 93, 104, 108, 249, 264, 291–308, *294*, *300–301*, 309, 312, 315, 316, 317, 329, 330, 334, 359, 366
social dumping 190
social housing 145, 154–7, 180, 189–92, 194, 202
social trust 75–6
Somalia 48, 50, 54, *55*, 191, 298
Sonoran Desert 299
South Africa 20, 27, 90, 106
South Korea 22, 42, 91, 92, 123, 161, 218, 221, 234, 240, 243, 244, 362
South Sudan 49, 50
Soviet Union 18, 22, 54, *55*, 56, 71
Spain 19, 20, 21, 34, *34*, 39, 41, 52, 63, 72, 73, 80, 81, 91, 97–8, 101–2, 103, 116, 122, 141, *148*, 149, 152, 158, 159, 166, 243, 260, 262, 282, 286, 296, 297, 298, 299, *300*, 306, 326–7, 328, 329, 331, 334, 339, 362, 369
Stark, Oded 215
Strait of Gibraltar 102, 116, 296, 297, 298, *300*, 329
strange bedfellow coalitions 270
student
  debt 143, 145
  migrants ix, 116, 117, 119, 153, 212, 217, 218, 219, 223, 239, *254*, 255, 364, 369
Sunak, Rishi 177
surges, immigration 36–7, 46, 78, 79, 330, 332–3
Suriname 21, 205, 332–3, *332*, 338
Sweden 21, 39, 147, *148*, 150, 167, 169, 180, 191–2, 235, 282, 283, 286, 329
Switzerland 21, 39, 52, 73, 232, 282–3
Syria 3–4, 6, 31, 35, 45, 49–50, 52, *55*, 56, *115*, 134, 191, 298, 359, 360, 364–5

Taken (film) 309, 315
Tanzania 54, 164, 212
tax xi, 110, 147, 150, 153, 154, 234, 235, 283
technology, impact on migration of 28, 29–30, 249, 307
temporary migration 21, 351, 361–2
Texas Department of Public Safety 200–201
Thailand 20, 22, 27, 91, 106, 120, 243, 244
Thatcher, Margaret 155
third-generation migrants ix, 167, 168, 198
Third World 89, 95, 108, 215, 312
This American Life 227
3D (dirty, dangerous and demeaning) jobs 120, 124
Tilly, Charles 71

tolerance 61, 153, 175, 176, 276, 361
Torah 274
trade 2, 78, 79, 119, 217, 223, 262, 263, 304, 315, 316, 319, 320
trade unions 9, 130–31, 144, 163, 185, 187, 228, 229, 230, 267, 269, 270–73, 274, 277, 363
trafficking 1, 7, 8, 9, 10, 31, 44, 79, 96, 103, 108, 196, 205, 249, 264, 296, 302, 309–25, 359, 368, 371
trailer deaths 302, 303
trainee or intern programmes 42, 123–4, 254, *255*, 370
transport technology 28, 29, 30, 84
Trends in International Migrant Stock: The 2017 Revision database xi
Trump, Donald 6, 31, 47, 95, 146, 196, 249, 254, 258, 270, 276, 279–80
Truss, Liz 177
Tunisia 21, 32, 38, 39, 41, 103, 164, 168, 169, 213, 220, 296, 298, 329, 334
Turkey 7, 18, 21, 35, 37, 39, 41, 49, 57, 60, 71, 91, 99, 106, 134, 163, 164, 166, 168, 170, 171, 174, 176, 183, 205, 211, 213, 220, 241, 243, 272, 298, 326, 329, 330, 334, 359, 362, 364
Tuvalu 344, 349

Uganda 18, 38, 50, 58, 164, 212
UK
ageing society/fertility levels 234, 237, 238, 239
anti-Catholicism in 63
asylum seekers in 6, 46, 47, 50, 51, 52
border restrictions and immigrant population of 326–8, 330, 331, 333, 336, 338, 340
brain drain and 210, 212, 215, 219
Brexit referendum *see* Brexit referendum
British Nationality Act (1981) *118*, 327
'Britishness' 73, 75
call centres, relocation of 120
Channel crossings of migrants into 1, 31, 293, 295, 299, *300–301*, 302, 330
child sex abuse rings in 312
colonies 7, 18, 19, 20, 21, 38–9, 117, 327, 333, 336, 338
Commonwealth countries and 7, 327, 333, 336
Commonwealth Immigrants Act (1962) 327, 333, 336
crime rates and immigration in 196, 207
customer services in 29
East End of London, immigration into 186
East European workers, arrival of 6, 7, 142–3, 286, 289, 321, 335, 336, 339–40
economic consequences of immigration to 135–6, 147, *148*, 149, 150
education levels of immigrants in 163, 164–5
emigration from 111
employment placement agencies 123
entrepreneurs in 139
fiscal contribution of immigration 147, *148*, 149, 150, 152, 153
general election (2020) 109
Grenfell Tower block fire (2017) 190
'hostile environment' for illegal migrants 31, 249, 259
Immigration Act (1971) *118*, 327
immigration trilemma and 264
Industrial Revolution and 28
integration of migrants in 160, 161, 163–7, 168, 169, 170, 171, 172–3, 175, 176, 177, 178
internal migration 28, 29
job market discrimination 167
labour shortages 38–9, 117, *118*, 119, 130, 141–3
migration to and from (1964–2022) *118*
Mirpur, migration from 100–101
nation building 70
net migration levels *118*, 237, 254, 328
NHS *see* National Health Service (NHS)
'now or never' migration spike in 333
'Pick for Britain' campaign 142–3
political parties divided internally on immigration issue 266–7, 271–2, 275
positive contribution of immigration to 139, 140
post-colonial emigrations 38–9
public opinion on immigration in 279, 282, 283, 284, *285*, 286, 287, 289
racism in 289
refugee numbers in 6, 46, 47, 50, 51, 52
riots (2001) 180
Rwanda, sends asylum seekers to 47
Seasonal Agricultural Workers Scheme (SAWS) 142

UK – *cont'd.*
  Seasonal Workers Pilot 142
  segregation in 180, 181, 183, 184, 186, 190, 191
  7/7 bombings 181
  smuggling of migrants and 292, 293, 295, 299, 302
  social housing 154, 155, 190, 191
  social mobility in immigrants 168, 186
  social trust in 75
  supply chain crisis and 143
  trafficking of migrants and 314, 316, 318, 319–21
  net emigration country to net immigration country transformation 117, *118*, 119
  undocumented migrant numbers 35
  visa overstayers in 331
  wages 130, 135
  waterbed effect in 330
  welfare impacts of migrants in 145–6, 147, 149, 150, 151, 152, 153, 154, 155, 158, 159
  Windrush generation 38
  worksite enforcement in 258–9
Ukraine 18, 22, 41, 45, 49, 50, 55, 56, 71, 142, 186, 256, 364
undocumented migrants
  'conformity bias' and 321–2
  conservatives and 271, 273, 275
  crime and 200–201, 206
  employers exploit 105
  EU and 35–6
  fiscal contribution of 153–4
  government toleration of 41, 122, 228–9, 231, 249, 256, 257–60, 262–3, 271, 273, 326, 337–8, 361, 366, 368
  numbers of 35–6
  pathways to legal status for 8, 172
  rationality of decision to migrate as 97–8
  religious groups and 275
  term xi
  United States and 7, 35, 97–8, 114, 153–4, 200–201, 228–9, 231, 257–60, 271, 273, 275, 326, 337, 366, 368
  visa overstaying xi, 35, 36, 41, 102, 125, 293, *294*, 305, 330–31, 337, 341
  wages 97
Ukraine 18, 22, 41, 45, 49, 50, 55, 56, 71, 142, 186, 256, 364
undocumented migrants
  'conformity bias' and 321–2
  conservatives and 271, 273, 275
  crime and 200–201, 206
  employers exploit 105
  EU and 35–6
  fiscal contribution of 153–4
  government toleration of 41, 122, 228–9, 231, 249, 256, 257–60, 262–3, 271, 273, 326, 337–8, 361, 366, 368
  numbers of 35–6
  pathways to legal status for 8, 172
  rationality of decision to migrate as 97–8
  religious groups and 275
  term xi
  United States and 7, 35, 97–8, 114, 153–4, 200–201, 228–9, 231, 257–60, 271, 273, 275, 326, 337, 366, 368
  visa overstaying xi, 35, 36, 41, 102, 125, 293, *294*, 305, 330–31, 337, 341
  wages 97
unemployment 75, 81, 109, 114, 116, 117, 131, 132, 133, 134, 136, 138, 140, 141–2, 143, 145, 149–50, 151, 269, 334, 359
UNESCO 72
Unite 130
United Arab Emirates (UAE) 21, 105, 106, 240
United Nations (UN)
  Convention relating to the Status of Refugees (1951) x, 46
  Development Programme (UNDP) 209
  Environmental Programme (UNEP) 343, 354
  Food and Agriculture Organization (FAO) 89
  High Commissioner for Refugees (UNHCR) 9, 16, 45, 46, 48, 49, 53–4, 57, 58, 251
  International Labour Organization (ILO) 309–10, 311, 322
  International Organization for Migration (IOM) 9, 16, 46, 53, 93, 94, 292, 305, 311, 316
  Office on Drugs and Crime (UNODC) 291–2, 309
  origins of 261
  Population Division, Department of Economic and Social Affairs xi, 17, 236, 242

Protocol to Prevent, Suppress and Punish Trafficking in Persons (2000) 315
Refugee Convention x, 46, 251, 253
Revision of World Population Prospects (2022) 242
United States of America (USA)
African Americans *see* African Americans
apprehension statistics 34, 119
asylum seekers and 52
border enforcement 6–7, 31–2, 34, 35–6, 39–40, 251, 254, *255*, 257, 258, 259–63, 326, 327–8, 329, 330, 331, 334, 337–8, 341, 364
Bracero Program 40, 106, 272, 326
brain drain and 216, 218, 219
call centre relocation 120
car industry, relocation to Mexico 120
Catholic immigrants 67, 68–9
Chinese Exclusion Act (1882) 40, 66
climate change and 343, 344, 355–6
Comprehensive Immigration Reform Act (2007) 271
crime rates, immigration and 196, 197, 198, 199, 200–201, 204, 207
Deferred Action for Childhood Arrivals (DACA) policy 263, 271
diversity in 60, 62, 64, 65, 66, 67–8, 75, 76
downward assimilation in 168
education levels of immigrants in 163
E-Verify 270–71
export processing zones (*maquiladoras*), Mexican side of US–Mexico border 29
fertility rates 234, 237, 238, 239
fiscal contribution of immigration in 147, *148*, 150
German migration into 66–7
global migration reversal and 21, 22
Great Migration 40, 65, 187, 188, 368
green cards 98, 119, 254, *255*
H1B (skilled) visas 119, 254, 314
H2-category seasonal worker visas 119, 254
housing supply 156, 189, 190
illegal immigration in 6, 7, 32, 34, 35–6, 37, 39–40, 41, 116, 146, 153–4, 197, 200–201, 228–9, 231, 249, 254, 257, 271, 293, 299, 308, 329, 330, 337–8, 369
Immigration Act (1976) 330
Immigration and Nationality Act (1952) 261–2
Immigration Reform and Control Act (IRCA) (1986) 6, 228, 257, 271, 326, 337
increasing demand for migrant labour in 119
independence from Britain (1776) 20
integration of immigrants in 161, 163, 164, 166, 167–8, 169, 171, 172, 173, 176, 178, 179
internal migration 26, 29
Japanese internment in 66
Jim Crow laws 64–5, 287
labour demand 7, 37, 39–40, 41, 64–6, 78, 91, 94, 98, 100, 111, 113, 114, 116, 117, 119, 120, 121, 122, 123, 129–30, 133, 135, 138, 139, 141
labour unions and immigration in 187, 228, 229, 230, 270, 272–3
Latino populations in *see* Latino immigrants *and individual country name*
lynchings 65, 67, 315
Mexico border *see* Mexico–US border
migration industry 307–8
Native Americans 64, 65, 173, 288
9/11 and 6, 60, 161, 181
North American Free Trade Agreement (NAFTA) and 78, 232
political parties divided internally on immigration issue 270–71
Piénsalo 2 Veces (*Think Twice*) campaign 94
positive contribution of immigration to 138–9
presidential election (1960) 68
presidential election (2016) 6, 196, 279–80
public opinion on immigration in 279, 281–2, *281*, 287, 288, 289
racism and 40, 64–6, 67, 68, 181, 187–90, 206, 287, 288, 289, 315
'Remain in Mexico' policy 46
'Root Causes of Migration' policy 79
segregation in 180, 181, 182, 184, 186, 187–90, 192, 194
smuggling of migrants and 293, 295, 299, 303, 307, 308
social trust in 75, 76
staffing and recruitment agencies 123
State Department 94, 311, 323, 324

United States of America (USA) – *cont'd.*
trafficking of migrants and 309–10, 315, 316, 321, 323
undocumented migrant population 7, 8, 35, 36, 94, 97, 98, 153, 172, 200–201, 227–31, 257, 258, 263, 271, 273, 275, 326, 337–8, 368
views on immigration in (1966– 2020) *281*
visa category, levels of temporary and permanent immigration to, by *255*
visa overstayers 331
visa types 119, 254, 314
War on Immigration in 6
welfare impacts of migrants in 146, 147, 149, 150, 151, 153, 156, 159
worksite enforcement in 257–8
Universal Declaration of Human Rights (1948) 251
unsolicited border arrivals x, 6, 10–11, 33, 34–5, *34*, 119
unwanted migration 37, 78, 122–5, 253, 257, 364
urbanization 4, 20, 23, 28–9, 80, 84, 88–90, 92, 241, 347, 374
Uyl, Joop den 332

Vaatstra, Marianne 203
vasudhaiva kutumbakam (the world is one family), Hindu concept of 274
Venezuela 45, 49, 50, 52, 55, 56, 113, 275, 367
Vezzoli, Simona 338, 339
Vietnam 21, 123, 156, 302, 346
Villares-Varela, María 339
Vink, Maarten 171–2
visas 33, 39, 40, 85, 86, 87, 94, 106, 107, 116, 119, 215, 225, 249, 253, 254, 256, 268, 326, 334, 341, 362, 363
Convenant Aziatische Horeca and 123
overstayers xi, 35, 36, 41, 102, 125, 293, *294*, 305, 330–31, 337, 341
restrictions drive migration underground 293, *294*, 295, 296–302, *300–301*, 318, 328, 329
restrictions reduce responsiveness of migration 335, 336, 337, 341
Schengen agreement and 296–302, *300–301*, 318, 328, 329
seasonal worker 119, 143, 254, *255*, 364
spikes in migration and 332–3, *332*
travel visa restrictiveness – % of destination countries for which a visa is needed 293, *294*, 295
UK abolishes for citizens from Guyana, Colombia and Peru (2022) 264
UK introduces for most Commonwealth citizens (1986) 327
US H1B skilled worker 119, 254, *255*, 314, 364
US H2–category seasonal worker 119, 254, *255*, 364
visa runs 331

Wacquant, Loïc 188
wages 9, 97, 104–5, 106, 107, 109, 110, 111, 112, 113, 120, 129–44, 152, 157, 167, 168, 196, 198, 202, 222, 223–4, 225–6, 229–30, 233, 272, 306, 322, 359, 372
Walk Free 310, 322
warfare, refugees and 3–4, 6, 16, 31, 35, 45, 46, 49–50, 52, 54–8, *55*, 56, 70, *115*, 134, 142, 191, 298, 359, 360, 364–5 *see also individual conflict name*
WASP (White Anglo-Saxon Protestant) identity 65, 67
Weber, Max 63, 289
Weitzer, Ronald 316
welfare state 9, 20, 68, 109, 145–59, *148*, 160, 171, 175, 177, 181, 182, 192, 196, 224, 235, 359, 372
Wilders, Geert 279
Wilkinson, Richard: *The Spirit Level* 76
Williamson, Jeffrey: *The Age of Mass Migration* 84
Wilson, William Julius: *The Truly Disadvantaged: The Inner City, the Underclass, and Public Policy* 188
Wilson, Woodrow 66
women
African American 65
autonomy of, emigration and 218
birth rates and 120, 121, 141, 219, 234, 235, 236, 238, 239, 241, 242, 243
crime and 197, 205
discrimination and 166
education 120, 121, 141, 216, 235, 236, 241, 242, 243

emancipation 120–22, 140, 141, 158, 165, 235, 236, 241, 243, 244, 366
empowering experience of emigration 107, 218
integration and 166, 167, 171
intergenerational mobility and 167
smuggling of 303
trafficking of 309–24
workers, migrant 103, 120–22, 124, 140, 141, 158, 165, 213, 218, 239, 241, 244, 309, 310, 311, 312, 314, 315, 317–19, 321, 322, 323, 324
workers, migrant *see* labour
worksite enforcement 35, 257–60, 270, 337–8
World Bank xi, 82, 83, *83*, 98, 223, 261, 354
World Cup, Qatar (2022) 310
World Value Survey 284

xenophobia 32, 61, 75, 277, 279, 280, 282, 284–90

Yemen 49, 52, 91
Yugoslavia 6, 21, 39, 48, 50, 56, 71, 75

Zelinsky, Wilbur: 'The Hypothesis of the Mobility Transition' 84
zero immigration, European politicians declare state of 363
Zimbabwe 20, 90, 212
Zschirnt, Eva 165

Credit: Wilma Hoogendoorn

Hein de Haas is professor of sociology at the University of Amsterdam (UvA). He formerly taught at the University of Oxford, where he codirected the International Migration Institute (IMI). One of the world's top migration scholars, he continues to direct IMI from its current home at UvA. He lives in Amsterdam.

www.heindehaas.org